NATURAL LAW & THE SECULAR MYTHOS

T&T Clark Studies in Ressourcement Catholic Theology and Culture

Series editors
Matthew Levering
Tracey Rowland

NATURAL LAW & THE SECULAR MYTHOS

What Has Been Left 'Unsaid' in Current Debates in Natural Law

Gregory M. W. Morgan

t&tclark

LONDON • NEW YORK • OXFORD • NEW DELHI • SYDNEY

T&T CLARK
Bloomsbury Publishing Plc
50 Bedford Square, London, WC1B 3DP, UK
1385 Broadway, New York, NY 10018, USA
29 Earlsfort Terrace, Dublin 2, Ireland

BLOOMSBURY, T&T CLARK and the T&T Clark logo are trademarks
of Bloomsbury Publishing Plc

First published in Great Britain 2025

Cover image: The School of Athens by Raphael, Vatican Museums,
Rome © Getty Images Europe
Series design by Annabel Hewitson

A catalogue record for this book is available from the British Library.

Library of Congress Cataloging-in-Publication Data
Names: Morgan, Gregory M. W., author.
Title: Natural law & the secular mythos / Gregory M. W. Morgan.
Other titles: Natural law and the secular mythos
Description: London ; New York : T&T Clark, 2025. |
Series: T&t clark studies in ressourcement catholic theology and culture; vol 2 |
Includes bibliographical references and index.
Identifiers: LCCN 2024026859 (print) | LCCN 2024026860 (ebook) |
ISBN 9780567716972 (hardback) | ISBN 9780567716989 (paperback) |
ISBN 9780567716996 (pdf) | ISBN 9780567717009 (epub)
Subjects: LCSH: Natural law. | Secularism. |
Knowledge, Theory of. | Christian ethics.
Classification: LCC K420 .M67 2025 (print) | LCC K420 (ebook) |
DDC 171/.2–dc23/eng/20240617
LC record available at https://lccn.loc.gov/2024026859
LC ebook record available at https://lccn.loc.gov/2024026860

ISBN: HB: 978-0-5677-1697-2
ePDF: 978-0-5677-1699-6
ePub: 978-0-5677-1700-9

Series: T&T Clark Studies in Ressourcement Catholic Theology and Culture

Typeset by Newgen KnowledgeWorks Pvt. Ltd., Chennai, India

To find out more about our authors and books visit www.bloomsbury.com
and sign up for our newsletters.

I dedicate this book in honour of my two mothers;
both of whom are named Mary.

Totus Tuus.

Naturam expelles furca, tamen usque recurret…

(Horace, *The Epistles*)

CONTENTS

PREFACE

This book argues that natural law – when construed as an epistemological and trans-cultural *lingua franca*, adjudged capable of legitimating the rational intelligibility and universal applicability of specific Christian moral principles within contemporary 'secular' discourse – has failed. Through a detailed analysis of the contributions of three prominent natural law theorists who are located within a shared philosophical-theological tradition, namely, John Finnis, Jean Porter and John Milbank, the thesis illuminates the extent to which this failure is as much intramural as it is extramural. The contribution of this thesis is borne out of a twofold realization: (1) that despite renewed levels of interdisciplinary interest within the academy, the discourse has become increasingly fragmented and will continue to fragment in the absence of a critical analysis of the deeper theo-cultural assumptions and aporias that animate current debates in natural law; and (2) that by illuminating and attending to the theological and methodological 'unsaid(s)' that have heretofore been seldom acknowledged, one can begin to appreciate how the fragmentation of the discourse is inexorably linked to the fragmentation of the secular *mythos*. Once this twofold realization has been critically substantiated, the thesis develops its contribution to knowledge by exploring how new horizons open up for natural law if the theological 'unsaid(s)' are allowed to surface and the disremembering power of the secular *mythos* is overcome. The thesis addresses one such horizon as a gateway to further research – that the theoretical fulcrum of the natural law lies not in its perceptual self-evidence or its immanent secularity but rather in its subtle provision of an immanent eschatology. This insight not only provides an immanent critique of current debates in natural law but is also theologically generative and subversive. More specifically, I argue that natural law is a theory of dialogical *anamnesis* – a 'work of memory'.

ABBREVIATIONS

BSO	*Beyond Secular Order*
CofR	Critique of the Theology of Right
CUP	Cambridge University Press
DFG	Desire for God: Ground of the Moral Life in Aquinas
FoE	*Fundamentals of Ethics*
IAITT	Italics as in the original text
MA&CE	*Moral Action & Christian Ethics*
MOL	*Ministers of the Law*
N&D	*Natural & Divine Law*
NasR	*Nature as Reason*
NLNR	*Natural Law and Natural Rights*
NNLT	New/Neo-Classical Natural Law Theory
OUP	Oxford University Press
RD1	*The Religious Dimension in the Thought of Giambattista Vico (Part 1)*
RD2	*The Religious Dimension in the Thought of Giambattista Vico (Part II)*
ST	*Summa Theologica*[1]

1. Unless stated otherwise, all references to, and citations from, Aquinas's *Summa Theologiae* are taken from the following translation: Thomas Aquinas, *Summa Theologica*, trans. Fathers of the English Dominican Province (Notre Dame, IN: Ave Maria Press, 1948).

Part One

DECONSTRUCTION

INTRODUCTION

A jurisprudential incubus

Writing during the so-called Second Renaissance of natural law jurisprudence in the twentieth century, the Jewish rabbi Robert Gordis declared that 'natural law needs only to be saved from its friends in order to convert its enemies'.[1] This statement resonates strongly with today's intellectual climate, where the dichotomy between 'friends' and 'enemies' continues to remain paradigmatic of how current debates in natural law are often constructed. The most fervent 'friends' of natural law, predominantly Christian and usually Catholic, have long anchored the value of natural law to its purported apologetical and rhetorical power – specifically, the power to defend the universalizability of the moral law in a language uninflected by contentious metaphysico-theological assumptions. This discourse is then strategically employed as a vehicle of 'public reason', aimed at persuading the Church's intellectual 'enemies', often broadly labelled as 'the secular', of the rationality of Christian-Catholic moral principles and norms.[2]

1. Robert Gordis, 'Natural Law and Religion', in *Natural Law and Modern Society*, ed. John Cogley (New York: World Publishing Company, 1961), 250. The twentieth century witnessed the revival of natural law theory in response to what have been perceived as three moments of 'crisis' for legal positivism. The first renaissance took place in light of the First World War. The second took place in the aftermath of Nazi Germany. The third after the collapse of the Berlin Wall. cf. Stephan Kirste, 'Natural Law in Germany in the 20th Century', in *A Treatise of Leal Philosophy and General Jurisprudence, Volume 12*, ed. Enrico Pattaro and Corrado Roversi (Netherlands: Springer, 2016), 95.

2. The friends of natural law tend to speak a lot about the secular. In fact, it would be hard to think of another context, at least within Christian moral philosophy, where the notion features more prominently. During the course of this book, the extent to which the theories espoused by 'friends' of natural law are shaped by reactions to the secular will become apparent. At this point, it is worth citing the International Theological Commission's document, *In Search of a Universal Ethic: A New Look at the Natural Law*, which affirms the historical and epistemological link between natural law and the secular: 'When the Magisterium of the Church was led not only to resolve particular moral discussions, but

Yet, amidst the frequent invocation of the secular in contemporary natural law discourse, little attention has been given to assessing what exactly the secular is and, moreover, why contemporary natural law theory has become so wedded to this notion. Little attention has also been given in current jurisprudential scholarship to examining whether, or to what extent, the idea of the secular is itself a constructed *mythos*.[3] Moreover, minimal attention has been given to examining whether, or to what extent, this construction is inflecting and eschewing the way in which the tradition of natural law is being retrieved, read and recapitulated. This realization raises an interesting question: what transformative horizons might unfold in the realm of natural law theory if this attachment to the secular was not only questioned but also definitively disentangled?

This book endeavours to examine this question. In essence, it evaluates whether, or to what extent, the interpretive fragmentation that is taking place among those 'friends' who have sought to revive the tradition of natural law (particularly according to St Thomas Aquinas) is linked to the fragmenting way in which these same 'friends' interpret the 'enemies' or 'interlocutors' of the natural law, particularly under the category of the secular. During the course of this evaluation, it will become increasingly apparent that what natural law theorists mean by the secular is modulated, definitionally and discursively, by a host of distinct theo-cultural and metaphysical assumptions. This realization raises another significant question of equally significant import. Could the apparent dialogical failure of natural law – as evidenced, both intramurally and extramurally, by its theoretical and normative fragmentation – be a consequence of the discoursal failure and fragmentation of the secular *mythos*? Could the secular *mythos* be the unacknowledged incubus within current debates in natural law – an incubus that prevents the genuine

also to justify its own position before a secularized world, it appealed more explicitly to the notion of natural law.' The document asserts that this mindset was especially true in the nineteenth century but continued to influence central magisterial documents like the *Catechism of the Catholic Church* (1992) and *Veritatis Splendor* (1993). In more recent times,

> Facing an aggressive secularism that wants to exclude believers from public debate, the Church points out that the interventions of Christians in public life on subjects that regard natural law (the defence of the rights of the oppressed, justice in international relations, the defence of life and of the family, religious freedom and freedom of education), are not in themselves of a confessional nature, but derive from the care which every citizen must have for the common good of society. (International Theological Commission, 'In Search of a Universal Ethics', 2009, http://www.vatican.va/roman_curia/ congregations/ cfaith/cti_documents /rc_con_cfaith_doc_20090520_legge-naturale_en.html. Accessed on 1 May 2019).

3. Throughout the course of this book, I will refer to the secular as a '*mythos*'. This is to accentuate the pre-eminence of its narratological and incommensurable quality. It will become apparent that it is only by identifying how this *mythos* is constructed that the deeper rationale behind several influential contributions on natural law begins to surface.

ressourcement of, and a genuine renaissance in, contemporary natural law theory? In other words, does natural law theory need to be saved from the vision of its 'friends' in order to become more effective in converting its 'enemies'?

The 'three voices'

To investigate and answer such questions, Part One of this book successively analyses the literary contributions of three professed 'friends' of natural law from the twentieth and twenty-first centuries: John Finnis, Jean Porter and John Milbank – all of whom declare themselves to be faithful receptors and mediators of the Thomistic natural law tradition. I refer to them collectively as the 'three voices'. It is appropriate to give a brief word of introduction about each of them.

Australian-born legal philosopher, John Finnis is Emeritus Professor of Law and Legal Philosophy at the University of Oxford (1989–2010) and Biolchini Family Emeritus Professor of Law at the University of Notre Dame, Indiana. Finnis is arguably the most influential natural law theorist of the past century. This is particularly due to the widespread interest expressed in his seminal work, *Natural Law & Natural Rights* (*NLNR*). The late Sir Neil MacCormick testified to this seismic influence in his review of *NLNR*: 'It is scarcely easier … to make a radical impression by … bringing old themes back to new life by the vigour and vividness with which they are translated into a contemporary idiom. That has been the achievement of John Finnis' *Natural Law and Natural Rights*'.[4]

As the inaugurator of a new epoch in the history of natural law jurisprudence, it is appropriate that Finnis is the 'first voice' to be heard in this three-way conversation, not just because he has made a permanent impression upon the paradigm of natural law within the academy but, as will become apparent, his analytical-Thomistic contribution has defined, even if contentiously so, many of the archetypical themes that regulate contemporary debate about natural law, even among theologians. Chapter 2 will provide a comprehensive analysis and evaluation of this remarkable contribution.

Chapter 3 will introduce the equally voluminous contribution of the American theological scholar and self-described feminist, Jean Porter. Professor Porter is currently the John A. O'Brien Professor of Theology at the University of Notre Dame, Indiana, and is the author of two highly influential monographs on natural law, namely, *Natural Law & Divine Law* and *Nature as Reason*. Significant elements of her work are motivated by a desire to correct what she perceives as a series of

4. Neil MacCormick, 'Natural Law and the Separation of Law and Morals', in *The Autonomy of Law: Essays on Legal Positivism*, ed. Robert P. George (Oxford: Clarendon Press, 1996), 105. MacCormick (1941–2009) was another intellectual giant in twentieth-/twenty-first-century jurisprudence. He was the Regius of Public Law at the University of Edinburgh, as well as the president of the International Association for Philosophy of Law and Social Philosophy.

fatal interpretive flaws in Finnis's reading and retrieval of the Thomistic tradition. To counteract this trajectory, Porter draws broadly upon scholastic jurisprudential thought in order to explicate a 'desacralized' account of ethical naturalism, but one that is recalibrated by a tradition-constituted inspired theory of cultural pragmatism that, *contra* Finnis, allows for a plurality of legitimate natural law theories.

An analysis of John Milbank's diasporic contribution to current debates in natural law will be the subject of Chapter 4. Professor Milbank is an English philosopher-theologian and the Emeritus Professor in Religion, Politics and Ethics at the University of Nottingham. He has attracted global interest as the co-founder of an intellectual and political movement known as 'Radical Orthodoxy'. Its originating impetus was to illuminate, genealogically, how the secular is animated by a series of heretical theologies, guised by the seemingly philosophical language of 'pure nature' and 'pure reason'. This theo-cultural awakening emboldens Milbank and his colleagues to 'visit sites in which secularism has invested heavily' in order to try and restore their forgotten theological and metaphysical significance.[5] One such site is the law. In opposition to 'modern secular' theories of natural law, which he narrates as being anthropologically voluntaristic, ontologically violent and biopolitically pessimistic, Milbank re-narrates natural law as a hylozoistic theory of divine government. Despite this ostensibly theocentric focus, I investigate the possibility that Milbank's overt and covert preoccupation with the secular *mythos* is disclosive of the fact that his 'new theology' cannot make sense without it. In other words, he, too, needs his 'enemies' – the secular *mythos* – in order to identify and champion his theological 'friends'.

Deconstructing the 'unsaid(s)'

The three analyses presented in this book aspire to make contributions to knowledge in their own right. This is because they investigate the understudied interconnection between natural law discourse and different genealogies of the secular *mythos*. While the nature of any discourse presupposes some diversity of views and some level of disagreement, what stands out here is that, despite drawing on the same philosophical-theological and Christian-Catholic heritage, Finnis, Porter and Milbank deploy its language to communicate contradicting understandings of what natural law *is* and what it *ought* to be used for. In fact, such is the disconnect that the 'three voices' effectively talk past each other.

Beyond the examination of the 'three voices', the general fragmentation and dissent within current debates in natural law reflect a discordant amalgam of interpretations, hinting at possible misunderstandings or misinterpretations of the tradition. Recognizing this is vital because the fragmentation and dissent taking place *within* the tradition cast doubt over the Catholic Church's institutional ability

5. John Milbank, Catherine Pickstock and Graham Ward, 'Introduction', in *Radical Orthodoxy*, ed. John Milbank, Catherine Pickstock, and Graham Ward (Abingdon: Routledge, 1999), 1–2.

to substantiate the universality of its own moral discourse to those *outside* the tradition. Remarkably, however, it is a fact seldom acknowledged or sufficiently described and, therefore, remains largely unaccounted for. A possible reason for this is that such an admission might be viewed as a contradiction of the Catholic Church's claim to be able to speak objectively and authoritatively as to the 'specific precepts of the *natural law*' by 'proclaiming to men what they truly are and reminding them of what they should be before God'.[6] Nevertheless, the failure to demonstrate the sociocultural transcendence of the Church's message reflects a discoursal anxiety that cannot be explained away by adverting to some extramural factor like the predicament of the 'culture wars'. Pointing to causes outside the natural law tradition cannot, ipso facto, explain the fragmentation taking place within the natural law tradition.

The conspicuous silence on this matter, both institutionally and intellectually, is itself insightful and informs how I intend to address this lacuna. In his fairly recent book, *The Kingdom and the Glory*, the 'postmodern' philosopher Giorgio Agamben asserts that 'in every theoretical work – and maybe in every human work – there is something like an "un-said"'.[7] Some authors, he says, 'attempt to approach this "un-said" and elusively evoke it, while others knowingly leave it unspoken'.[8] I intend to appropriate this deconstructive insight in order to interrogate, specifically, how it is the construction of the secular *mythos* which suppresses (or, in certain instances, instrumentalizes) certain theo-cultural presuppositions that have, heretofore, remained largely 'unsaid'. Each of the three analyses will provide a detailed account of how these 'unsaid(s)' actually serve a strategic purpose that inflects the literary *oeuvres* of each of the 'three voices'. In the process, the contextual contingency and solipsistic character of the secular *mythos* will also be exposed, illuminating the existence of what I will refer to as the presence of several different 'inner audiences'.

Part Two will endeavour to move beyond the deconstruction of the 'unsaid(s)' within current debates in natural law by highlighting the reconstructive horizons that have surfaced in light of Part One. Chapter 5 draws attention to how constructing the natural law tradition in reaction to the secular *mythos* culminates in a series of disremembering aporia. I limit my discussion to three in particular: (1) alethiological, (2) anthropological and (3) genealogical. I understand the identification of an aporia not as an insuperable dilemma but as a moment from where the discourse is behoved to 'state perplexities well' in order to discern a new way forward – to move from aporia into euporia.[9]

6. The Holy See, 'Catechism of the Catholic Church', 1993, https://www.vatican.va/archive/ENG0015/_INDEX.HTM. Accessed 1 May 2019. (See: No. 2036.) (IAITT).

7. Giorgio Agamben, *The Kingdom and the Glory* (Stanford, CA: Stanford University Press, 2011), 22.

8. Ibid.

9. Raymond Younis, 'Euporia', in *Reconstructing Social Theory, History and Practice*, ed. Harry Dahms and Eric Lybeck (Bingley: Emerald Group, 2017), 90. My discussion of the definition of aporia and euporia, especially in Chapter 5, is indebted to this text.

Building upon this discussion, Chapter 6 elucidates how the raising of the theological 'unsaid(s)' changes and restores the inherent dialogical dimension of natural discourse. Again, as a gateway to further research, I reconsider how a long-perceived 'enemy' of natural law, namely, Jacques Derrida, can actually be reconsidered, heuristically, as a potentially fruitful 'friend', although he is what we might call a 'pharmakonic friend'. This is because, on the one hand, I will demonstrate how his reconstructive consociation of the act of memory with the desire for justice can help raise the theological 'unsaid(s)', culminating in the recognition of the need for the discourse to address its – often disremembered – relationship with theological eschatology. On the other hand, Derrida's 'eschatology' outworks itself to be an atheological euphemism for the endless experience of deferral and *différance* – a 'work of mourning'.

The abridged discussion of Derrida's jurisprudential contribution is not meant to act as a 'fourth voice' in this book. Rather, I intend to highlight how his own search for justice allows for an 'eschatological epiphany', the retrieval of which can potentially contribute towards the euporetic reorientation of current debates in natural law. The book concludes by intimating how natural law can be reconstructed as a 'work of memory' – a theory of 'dialogical *anamnesis*', which, drawing upon Aquinas's theological anthropology, recognizes the intrinsically soteriological and immanently eschatological dimension of the natural desire for justice – the 'original memory' and 'ontological tendency' of natural law.[10] Fleshing out in detail what this approach might look like will be a project for a later time.

Chapter 1 will lay some of the groundwork by arguing that, at a meta-level, the fragmentation that characterizes current debates in natural law is largely a tragic recapitulation of ancient debates found at the origins of jurisprudence. To substantiate this contention, I revisit the (pseudo)-Platonic dialogue of the *Minos*, one of the inaugurating texts in Western jurisprudence.[11] Although frequently lampooned as un-Socratic, argumentatively abrupt and philosophically truncated, I proffer a more promising reading, especially of those points where the dialogue appears vaguest and unfinished. I contend that this much-neglected dialogue can offer a valuable hermeneutical framework with which to illuminate some of the deeper theo-cultural issues that shape current debates in natural law.

10. C.f. Joseph Ratzinger, 'Conscience and Truth', *Communio*, vol. 37 (Fall 2010), 534.

11. I am aware of the scholarly disputation over whether or not the dialogue should be considered part of the Platonic corpus. However, I will follow Leo Strauss in referring to the text as 'Platonic'. See: Michael Crowe, *The Changing Profile of the Natural Law* (The Hague: Martinus Nihjoff, 1977), xi.

Chapter 1

THE 'WINDY MYSTICISM'

Section I: The ancient Minos

Ὁ νόμος ἡμῖν τί ἐστιν;[1]

Jurisprudence, rooted in the inquiries of the Western philosophical tradition, commenced with what Leo Strauss identified as the 'gravest of all questions': 'Tell me, what is law?'[2] In Plato's *Minos*, Socrates poses this question to his Athenian Companion [ἑταῖρος], catalysing a dialogical exchange that concentrates on the finding and formulating of a mutually concordant response.[3] The Companion initially asserts, albeit in very imprecise and undeveloped terms, that law should be defined positivistically as whatever decree is 'loyally accepted' or 'accepted by custom'.[4] In this answer, law is presented as something intrinsically contingent – artificially constructed, formally promulgated, and subsequently enforced by a recognized political authority for the sake of sustaining sociopolitical harmony in the *polis*. This definition emphasizes an unbridgeable epistemic disjunction between the factuality of the law and more value-laden notions such as the good and the just. Such an extreme brand of legal positivism, which has become a prevailing philosophical motif, effectively leaves no room for philosophical-theology to contribute. Hence, in the continued opinion of many contemporary legal positivists, to speak of an 'ontology of law', or of its 'nature', or even just to invoke the term 'natural law' is to articulate nothing more than a 'windy mysticism'.[5]

1. Plato, 'Minos', in *Plato XII*, trans. W. R. M. Lamb, ed. Jeffrey Henderson (Cambridge, MA: Harvard University Press, 1955), 385.

2. Leo Strauss, *Liberalism: Ancient & Modern* (Chicago: University of Chicago Press, 1995), 65.

3. C.f. Lewis V. Bradley, 'Plato's "Minos"', *The Review of Metaphysics*, vol. 60 (September 2006), 17, fn. 1; Claire McCusker,'Between Natural Law and Legal Positivism', *Yale Journal of Law & the Humanities*, vol. 22, no. 1, Article 3 (2010), 83–4.

4. Plato, 'Minos', 391.

5. An expression I have appropriated from Gilbert Ryle's influential review of Martin Heidegger's *Being and Time*. Gilbert Ryle, 'Heidegger's "Sein und Zeit"', in *Critical Essays. Volume 1* (London: Routledge, 2009), 222.

In contrast, Socrates proffers a loftier definition of law as that which 'tends to be discovery [the finding] of reality' and, therefore, 'something distinct from things loyally accepted.'[6] While he never explicitly uses the term 'natural law' [φυσικός νόμος] in the *Minos*, the metaphysical foundations of Socrates' theory support it being described as an inchoate example of a natural law epistemology.[7] (Despite potential disagreements, there is broad agreement that the dialogue was at least critical for the augmentation of the natural law tradition within Western jurisprudence).[8] This is because the presence of the word 'discovery' and the affirmation that 'true opinion' is dependent upon 'reality' (being) infers that the truth of law is something to be apprehended ontologically by perceiving and participating, insofar as is humanly possible, in the very structure(s) of existence itself.[9] The law is thus something akin to speaking, hearing, and seeing – it is something we seek and do by nature.[10]

Of course, the philosophical coherency of Socrates' definition presupposes an axiomatic confidence in humankind's capacity to know the reality of being *qua* being – a subject of immense philosophical and theological conjecture.[11] Indeed, this is the very objection raised by the Companion: 'How is it if law is discovery of reality, that we do not use always the same laws on the same matters, if we have thus got realities discovered?'[12] Much to the chagrin of philosophers, Socrates never explicates the exact epistemological process by which an individual can discover law's essence, nor does he explain how its sociopolitical reproduction should actually take place. Instead, as Jeffrey Henderson observes, 'we are abruptly told that our ignorance is shameful, and the discussion is clumsily broken off.'[13]

Despite the apparent absence of these explicative details, the perspectival and definitional juxtaposition between Socrates and his Companion still provides an illuminating compass for the purposes of this book. I will draw attention to three aspects of the *Minos* that can help frame the forthcoming analyses of the 'three voices': (1) jurisprudence is an inherently dialogical discourse; (2) jurisprudence is a fragmented discourse; (3) jurisprudence is always haunted by the theological 'unsaid' of divine government.

6. Plato, 'Minos', 391, 395.

7. C.f. Leo Strauss, *Studies in Platonic Political* Philosophy (Chicago: University of Chicago Press, 1983), 137.

8. Mark J. Lutz, *Divine Law and Political Philosophy in Plato's Laws* (DeKalb: Northern Illinois University Press, 2012), 14.

9. Plato, 'Minos', 395.

10. C.f. Ibid., 391. Steven Thomason, 'Philosophy and Law', *The Journal for Ancient Greek Political Thought*, vol. 3, no. 5), 61.

11. Plato, 'Minos', 396.

12. Ibid., 395, 397.

13. Jeffrey Henderson, 'Introduction to the *Minos*', in *Plato XII*, trans. W. R. M. Lamb, ed. Jeffrey Henderson (Cambridge, MA: Harvard University Press, 1955), 387.

Jurisprudence as dialogical elenchus

The first aspect worthy of note is that the *Minos* presents jurisprudence as a dialogical discourse. Each of the perennial questions asked in the dialogue are never simply rhetorical or proposed in splendid isolation. Rather, each of the opinions advanced by the two protagonists is explained, explored, and evaluated in and through learned conversation(s) – the process of Platonic elenchus. Hence, Socrates' insistence that definitional concurrence with respect to the nature of law can only be achieved if 'we study the matter jointly', thereby avoiding the inimical trap of lapsing into soliloquys or what he describes as 'lengthy speeches'.[14] The aim of jurisprudential speech, then, is to foster the 'we' – that is to say, a collective understanding of the communicability, intelligibility, and universality of the truth of law.

This point illuminates what was already imbedded within Socrates' asseveration that '[l]aw *tends* [*βούλεται*] nonetheless to be discovery of reality.'[15] Claire McCusker rightly argues that, although this translation is by no means incorrect, a more complete translation of the word *βούλεται* is 'to will, wish, be willing' – law *wishes/aspires* to discover and, ultimately, to reflect the truth of reality *qua* reality.[16] This, I would suggest, brings jurisprudence within the realm of philosophical-theological anthropology since the dialogical process itself is instigated and animated by a desire seeking teleological fulfilment. Hence, 'law is unified not by its discovery of reality, but only by [a mutual] aspiration to discover reality.'[17] This teleological aspiration not only legitimates the existential hope of discovering a universal (natural) law, but also subsequently reframes the function of language within the dialogical *modus operandi* of jurisprudence. Language is now put at the service of this desire, and so rhetoric is employed to abet the philosophical movement towards knowing and articulating the common reality of law *qua* law.

Undoubtedly, some have deemed this approach to be both uncomfortable and unpersuasive since the history of jurisprudence is fraught with definitional disagreements and a growing philosophical insistence upon 'Wittgensteinian silences' – 'What we cannot speak about we must pass over in silence.'[18] However, over the past fifty years or so, jurisprudence has become anything but a discourse of elongated silences. Costas Douzinas, Professor of Law at the University of London, speaks of a surprising 'renaissance' within the discipline:

> The legal system is going through a serious crisis while jurisprudence is enjoying something of a renaissance. At the turn of the millennium, law faces a crisis of

14. Plato, 'Minos', 399.

15. Ibid., 395.

16. McCusker, 'Between Natural Law and Legal Positivism', 92.

17. Ibid.

18. Ludwig Wittgenstein, *Tractatus Logico-Philosophicus*, trans. D. F. Pears and B. F. McGuiness (London: Routledge, 2006), 89.

> form and a demand for ethics … [and] [t]he moral deficit of the law goes hand in hand with the crisis of legal form.[19]

It is noteworthy that this 'renaissance' has coincided with the accession of postmodern hermeneutics in the Academy and the emergence of what has been described as a 'new jurisprudence', a discourse that is being sustained and enlivened by the assimilation of a plethora of creative interpretive methodologies within legal studies.[20] This underscores why the dialogical character of jurisprudence should not be underestimated or dismissed. In fact, it should be recovered with renewed interest.

Modern phenomenology has also contributed to this jurisprudential awakening by heightening an awareness of how anthropological 'authenticity' – the coming to terms with what it means to be a human being in a specific cultural context – is unattainable unless existence is understood in coincidence with 'co-existence'.[21] To be a human being is to be in fellowship with other human beings; it is to coexist in a community and, more importantly, to be mutually recognized as a part of that community. This point coheres with what is also a central consideration of the 'new jurisprudence' outlined by Douzinas, which begins neither with the consciousness of the individual nor with abstract epistemological-ontological claims, but with an 'ethics of alterity' – meaning, it begins with 'the other' without whom we would never have 'come to law' in the first place. For '[c]oexistence places a limit on infinite responsibility'.[22]

Obviously, in order for coexistence to be guaranteed and our human dignity protected, society perforce requires the establishment of positive law. This logically necessitates the prior articulation of a public philosophical anthropology. Since this anthropology (even if conceptually thin) provides the edifice for the development of the social order and the extrapolation of specific legal norms, the *logos* by which we formulate it and the language we use to describe it become immensely important. Socrates clearly believed that both the *logos* and the language had to reflect reality and that, ideally, this reality should be determined through a constructive dialogical discourse, which, when truly authentic, is a dialogue about the nature of our human identity. If this is correct, then the implication of Socrates' thesis is that the nature of law can only be discovered by first discovering something of the nature of humankind.[23] This presupposes a turning away from the epistemic isolation of the thinking subject in order to appreciate how reason

19. Costas Douzinas, 'Law and Justice in Postmodernity', in *The Cambridge Companion to Postmodernism*, ed. Steven Connor (Cambridge: Cambridge University Press, 2004), 196.

20. Ibid., 200.

21. W. Lujipen, *Phenomenology of the Natural Law* (Pittsburgh: Duquesne University Press, 1967), 17, fn. 2.

22. Douzinas, 'Law and Justice in Postmodernity', 213.

23. Although, this does not mean, as the Socratic dialogues demonstrate, that it is not possible to have law and to live by the law without knowing the nature of the law.

and language are sociologically conditioned since both are semantically tied, and philosophically grounded within, a specific cultural narrative and political context. At least on this point, therefore, the 'new jurisprudence' is actually quite old.

Jurisprudence as parodic fragmentation

The second aspect I want to draw attention to is how, historically speaking, jurisprudence has always been a fragmented discourse. The disjunction we find in the ancient text of the *Minos* closely resembles the disjunction we find within contemporary discourse. Although the philosophical and theological landscapes are certainly different, jurisprudence is still frequently dichotomized into two antithetical schools of thought: various expressions of legal positivism, on the one hand, and various expressions of natural law theory, on the other. Nevertheless, at a practical level, positivistic and naturalistic theories of jurisprudence are seeking to achieve the same thing: the public legitimation of a particular way of knowing the law and substantiating respect and obedience to it for the sake of preserving sociopolitical harmony in the *polis*.[24]

A cursory examination of the history of jurisprudence reveals that the discourse has continued to swing like a pendulum between these two pre-eminent traditions. Often what propels the transposition of the pendulum is the arrival of a decisive sociopolitical event or the resurgence of a prevalent ideology, metaphysic, or epistemology. Thus, if we were to chart the chronological lineaments of jurisprudence as it has developed since the time of the *Minos* (fourth-century BCE), the contours of the trajectory would appear to be more cyclical rather than strictly linear. You could say, then, that jurisprudence has become an aeonian parody of its own historical crisis.

Inevitably, jurists throughout history have had to decide at some point whether to affirm, as with Socrates, that nature exists and that reality can be known, and thus form a suitable basis for jurisprudential reflection, or, alternatively, to follow the Companion, whose pious scepticism towards speculative-metaphysical realism prefigures the critical philosophies of Immanuel Kant and Ludwig Wittgenstein, and decide that the 'essence [of law] is always hidden from us'.[25] Another possibility is to view the Athenian Companion as the proponent of a proto-postmodern philosophy that declares 'essence' to be either a non-existent category or, following Friedrich Nietzsche, something that can never be captured linguistically, thereby necessitating the creation of an alternate substructure for establishing the authority of law so as to maintain social cohesion within the *polis*. Both the proto-modern/Kantian and postmodern/Nietzschean perspectives share

24. Of course, traditionally speaking, natural law theory wants to go beyond this as it is ultimately concerned with the deeper harmony of the world; the apperception of the cosmic ordering of *nomos* (νόμος) to *physis* (φύσις).

25. Ludwig Wittgenstein, *Philosophical Investigations*, trans. G. E. M. Anscombe (Oxford: Blackwell, 1968), 109.

a methodological similarity in that both repudiate the ontological naturalism or moral realism of Socrates as a starting point for common jurisprudential reflection. Most importantly, both enforce a hermetic-ideological disjunction between theoretical and practical reason. The question is: can jurisprudence do without ontology – specifically, an ontology of nature?

Jurisprudence as divine government

In many ways, this question also appertains to the relationship between theology and jurisprudence, which is a third aspect I want to highlight from the *Minos*. Although it is evidently possible to dialogue philosophically about the practice of law-making, to what extent can we leave our theological presuppositions 'unsaid' in order to dialogue truthfully and persuasively about what is good for human flourishing?

Even though Socrates and his Athenian Companion agree to 'coexist' as they enter into a process of elenchus, they ultimately come to realize that their dialogue is being undermined by the presence of a theological 'unsaid'. Socrates initially tries to persuade the Companion of the unchanging reality of law without explicitly crossing the threshold into metaphysical speculation. He does this by arguing analogously from empirical observation. Doctors, gardeners, and even cooks are governed by knowledge of certain 'internal laws', which are seemingly timeless and universally accepted as real.[26] Socrates concludes that, since the art of law-making is the work of state governance, the best government or king will be the one 'whose laws are best for the souls of men'.[27] Thus, he asserts that the best laws are the ones tradition declares to be of divine origin and thus are part of the provenance of divine government.

It is only after the failure to discover the law through the art of deductive and analogical reasoning that the dialogue gives way to the recognition of the centrality of the theological 'unsaid'.[28] In the same abrupt fashion with which the discourse commenced, the denouement of the theological grounds of the law is catalysed by a question: '[T]ell me ... who by tradition has shown himself a good lawgiver among the ancient kings, so that to this day his ordinances remains, as being divine?'[29] What is particularly interesting about this question is that it re-orientates the discourse away from the authority of the empirical or the rational to recognizing the authority of the tradition. Furthermore, it also ushers in the realization that the

26. I have appropriated the phrase 'internal laws' from: McCusker, 'Between Natural Law and Legal Positivism', 99.

27. Plato, 'Minos', 409.

28. However, it is important to note that this realization does not negate the value of the dialogical process. For it is only through the dialogical encounter of the 'we' that the 'unsaid' that resides within the 'I' is able to surface.

29. Ibid., 410.

realism of law requires a legitimating perspective that is 'beyond the law', so-to-speak. A divine (theological) perspective.

Socrates brings these considerations together by raising what has become a perennial debate within contemporary discourse. How should one narrate the story of the genealogical origins of the (natural) law? For how we account for the unwritten origins of law has an inevitable impact upon how the language of the law is inscribed upon, and secured within, the socio-cultural fabric of the *polis*. Although Socrates and his Athenian Companion agree that the most ancient laws come from Crete, their particular interpretations of the tradition are fragmented on account of their acceptance of two incommensurable *mythoi* about the law-giver. The Companion has imbibed a *mythos* of 'Attic tragedy' told by the 'tragedians' (the tragic poets) which decries King Minos, the Ordinator of the laws, as 'harsh and unjust', whilst esteeming King Rhadamanthus, the guardian of the laws, as a 'just man'.[30] Socrates endeavours to correct the fictional 'impiety' of this tragic *mythos* by proposing an alternate *mythos* from the Greco-heroic tradition told by the epic poets, Homer and Hesiod. The 'impiety', which has been diffused to 'the multitude', extends from the proliferation of a devious lie about King Minos, which subsequently destabilizes the link between the citizens and their gods. Socrates avows that Minos was a divine human being and a hero, one who was chosen to mediate the law to the *polis* after 'consorting and discoursing' with Zeus. Given that Minos was the only one to be afforded this honour, he is worthy of 'praise unsurpassable'.[31]

It is, therefore, through a specifically theological elenchus that the eternal laws of Zeus are disclosed to Minos, who then as King ordained laws to govern his people, laws which made the people of Crete and Sparta 'happy through the length of time'.[32] But Socrates' appeal to the theological 'unsaid' of divine government does not negate the elenchus about the law, but, rather paradoxically, it is this 'unsaid' which grounds the ontological possibility of discovering the reality and the reason of law itself. In the *Odyssey*, Homer bears witness to this paradox by describing King Minos as holding a golden sceptre in his hand whenever performing his duties as judge. An ornamental privilege that he never ascribed to King Rhadamanthus. Since the golden sceptre is a symbol of his education in divine government, according to which he then governed and directed Crete, its public (or even narratological) display is synonymous with the raising and remembering of the theological 'unsaid' – that the language of the law is intrinsically informed by, and thus ordered to, the eternal law of Zeus.

The subtle, yet significant, distinctions being made in the epic *mythos* between King Minos and King Rhadamanthus also have interesting philosophical-theological implications. 'Rhadamanthus was a good man indeed', says Socrates, 'for he had been educated by Minos'.[33] But his education was limited to but

30. Ibid., 411.
31. Ibid., 415.
32. Ibid., 417.
33. Ibid., 417.

one subsidiary part of the kingly art – that of 'presiding in law courts'.[34] Thus, Rhadamanthus acted within, and judged according to, a pre-established order.[35] One might say that he upheld the positivistic, immanent, and, in modern parlance, 'secular' character of the law. In contrast, Minos is the one who founds the law upon the reality of that which goes beyond the law. Furthermore, it is Minos who charges Rhadamanthus with the authority of judging in the city and to Talos, the 'brazen man', the authority of judging in the villages of Crete.[36] Talos had the law inscribed upon brazen tablets that he would carry in procession three times a year to all the villages in order for all its inhabitants to see and so remember its decrees. But one can extrapolate that these written tablets are a pharmakon. Whilst the inscriptions have a mnemonic effect, imparting knowledge of the precepts of the law which brings remedic stability to the *polis*, they can also have a disremembering effect since the inscriptions are now detached from the colloquial genesis of the law. This explains why it was possible for Rhadamanthus to be eulogized in the tradition as a just ruler whose perduring ordinances gave the impression 'as being divine'. For these just ordinances were actually being promoted by a theological 'unsaid' – the authoritative speech of Zeus – mediated by the divine King Minos who, as Socrates acclaimed, 'discovered aright the truth of reality in regard to the management of state' in the mystery of divine government.[37]

Socrates' raising of the theological 'unsaid' draws attention to a deeper theological-semiotic predicament. After riposting the tragedians' *mythos* as a politically motivated retaliation for Minos's war on Athens, he must, nevertheless, utilize their most powerful tool, poetry, in order to narrate a more believable tale. This dependence accentuates the power of language, the power not only to communicate reality but also to construct it. In other words, poetry is never just employed to portray 'objects "objectively"'.[38] It may indeed be the noetic device with which we conflate *nomos* with *physis*. Furthermore, from a theological perspective, Socrates reminds us of the need for the language of law to be continually refined with an apophatic-like humility in the light of revelation. This is implied by the fact that King Minos would return to the cave of Zeus to continue the anamnetic dialogue about divine government – 'to learn some things, and to show his knowledge of others that he had learnt from Zeus in the preceding nine years'[39] – the point being that the dialogue must always continue. For, as Socrates concludes, we can continue to disremember those things within the soul 'on which its good and abject state depends'.[40]

34. Ibid.

35. Michael Davis, 'Plato's *Minos*: The Soul of the Law', *The Review of Politics*, 78 (2016), 358.

36. Plato, 'Minos', 417 fn. 1.

37. Ibid., 419.

38. Davis, 'Plato's *Minos*', 362.

39. Plato, 'Minos', 415.

40. Ibid., 421.

Whilst some scholars deride this ending as unhelpfully abrupt, I would argue that it is being deliberately left open-ended. One could interpret the apparent failure and concluding silence of the *Minos* as actually being instigative of a potentially propitious moment of ongoing self-reflection upon one's hidden assumptions. This being the case, the activity of dialogical elenchus, particularly within jurisprudential discourse, is thence as much about self-disclosure (the 'unsaid') as interpersonal persuasion (the 'said'). Silence itself becomes a linguistic sign that something important has been disremembered and, hence, left 'unsaid' – a point I will return to in Part Two of this thesis.

Section II: The contemporary dilemma

'Tell me, what is secular?'

Drawing upon this three-fold consideration of the *Minos*, the following three chapters will explore the dialogical, fragmenting, and theological character of natural law, as found in the contributions of Finnis, Porter, and Milbank. It will quickly become apparent that each of these 'three voices' are trying to retrieve something about natural law from the past in order to try and revolutionize natural law in the present. However, as I have already intimated, it will also become apparent that their retrievals of the tradition are being intoned and inflected by certain theo-cultural 'unsaid(s)'. I will investigate whether it is the failure to attend to these 'unsaid(s)' that has led to the intramural fragmentation over how Thomas Aquinas's theology of natural law should be reclaimed and re-presented.

Aquinas certainly embodied the spirit of Socrates in the *Minos* by instigating his 'Treatise on Law' by inquiring of the 'essence of law'. As the Angelic Doctor explained, 'the law, as to its essence, resides in him that rules and measures; but by way of participation, in that which is ruled and measured … so that every inclination or ordination which may be found in things subject to the law, is called a law by participation.'[41] But since the truth of law depends upon its derivation from the eternal law of God, to partake of (and, thus, express) 'right reason' must also mean to participate in (and, thus, express) something of the universal plan of divine government. Hence, in concurrence with Augustine, Aquinas concludes that '*in temporal law there is nothing just and lawful, but what man has drawn from the eternal law.*'[42] Nevertheless, our ability to discern and apply the natural law can indeed be hindered on account of original sin.[43] It is for this reason that it was necessary for God to illuminate the natural law by imparting the divine law, 'for it is certain that such a law cannot err.'[44]

41. ST. I-II q.91, art.6.
42. ST. I-II q.93, art.3. (IAITT)
43. ST. I-II q.94, art.6.
44. ST. I-II q.91, art.4.

Each of the three analyses will address two interrelated points of inquiry. The first involves identify the underlying contextual and intellectual factors that influence the different ways in which Finnis, Porter, and Milbank construct the secular *mythos*. The second is to then explore how this *mythos* is invoked and to evaluate the extent to which it informs ('hinders') their reading of Aquinas. Through this three-way conversation, it will then become possible to attempt to answer the pre-eminent question at hand. Is the intramural fragmentation within current debates in natural law a consequence of the fact that the way in which the secular *mythos* is being narrated is also fragmented? Is it because Finnis, Porter, and Milbank are all reacting to this tragic *mythos* that certain critical elements of the natural law tradition are being disremembered in accordance with the false hope of translating a theory of divine government into a theory (or, anti-theory) of 'secular reason'? Thus, rather than beginning jurisprudential inquiry by asking the gravest question, 'Tell me, what is (natural) law?', perhaps contemporary natural law theorists need to begin by asking the 'unsaid' question, 'Tell me, what is secular?' It is to Finnis that I shall pitch this question first.

Chapter 2

ON ('NEW') NATURAL LAW: JOHN FINNIS'S ANALYTICAL RESPONSE TO ITS 'CULTURED DESPISERS'

Section I: Framing the analysis

A new natural law

It would not be too hyperbolic to suggest that current debates in natural law are a series of footnotes to John Finnis's *magnum opus*, *Natural Law & Natural Rights* (1981). Admittedly, this is a provocative and prodigious contention considering the book was published now close to forty years ago and was even characterized by the author at the time as 'no more than introductory'.[1] Of course, Finnis writes not as a theologian but as a legal philosopher – a vocational distinction he is keen to reiterate lest his substantial employment of Thomistic principles and his intermittent references to the Catholic Church's teachings be misconstrued as diffident appeals to an ecclesiastical authority.[2] The arguments that constitute the so-called New – or Neoclassical – Natural Law Theory (NNLT) are thought to have won the 'attention of secular philosophers' precisely because they are 'secular', that is to say, strictly the product of integral philosophical reasoning alone.[3] In other words, they 'stand or fall by their own reasonableness or otherwise', a conviction based upon a theoretical denial of the need for any real metaphysical or transcendent reference, but a denial made possible by the sharp distinction Finnis makes regarding the *duplex operatio* of the speculative and practical intellect.[4] After all, a sound theory of natural law, says Finnis, 'has never been anything other than an appeal to public reasons' and 'nothing other than the account of all the reasons-for-action which people are able to accept, precisely because these are

1. John Finnis, *Natural Law & Natural Rights* (Oxford: OUP, 2011), v. (*NLNR*).

2. Finnis, *NLNR*, vi.

3. C.f. Gerard V. Bradley and Robert George, 'A Reply to Jean Porter', *The American Journal of Jurisprudence*, vol. 39 (1994), 303.

4. Finnis, *NLNR*, vi.

good, valid and sound as reasons.'[5] Importantly, therefore, the principles of natural law are not 'expressions of God's will' for they only include:

> (i) a set of basic practical principles which indicate the basic forms of human flourishing as goods to be pursued and realized … (ii) a set of basic methodological requirements of practical reasonableness (itself one of the basic forms of human flourishing) which distinguish sound from unsound practical thinking … (iii) a set of general moral standards.[6]

With very few exceptions, *NLNR* has been received by legal philosophers as a 'freestanding' account of the nature of practical reasoning, which, broadly speaking, Finnis believes is synonymic with what defines jurisprudential and legal reasoning, albeit in a slightly more restricted sense.[7] This strategic enterprise has drawn consummate applause from many Christian theologians committed to identifying a purely philosophical register with which to defend intelligibly the Catholic Church's teaching on the existence of exceptionless moral norms. For instance, that performing direct abortions, engaging in homosexual activity, using artificial contraception, or telling lies are *always* morally illicit. At the same time, the NNLT has been the subject of intense opprobrium from many other philosophers/theologians, especially those who Finnis describes as 'Conservative Thomists'. These philosophers/theologians believe the NNLT represents an egregious betrayal of the authentic tradition, losing touch with nature *qua* nature by erroneously trying to synthesize Thomistic natural law with liberal jurisprudence, thereby constructing a theory that is so 'new' that it is questionable whether it can accurately be called a theory of natural law.[8]

What more can be said?

In a recent interview, Finnis lamented that he has personally learnt precious little from engaging with his many critics and attributed a large part of their dissension to just a series of unfortunate semantic misunderstandings and theoretical misrepresentations.[9] For this reason, he understands his ongoing task as 'clarifying

5. John Finnis, 'Natural Law and the Ethics of Discourse', *Ratio Juris*, vol. 12, no. 4 (December 1999), 370. John Finnis, *Human Rights & Common Good* (Oxford: OUP, 2011), 97.

6. Finnis, *NLNR*, 402, 23.

7. 'Legal reasoning is, broadly speaking, practical reasoning.' John Finnis, 'Natural Law and Legal Reasoning', *Cleveland State Law Review*, vol. 38, no. 1 (1990), 1.

8. C.f. Kevin M. Staley, 'New Natural Law, Old Natural Law, or the Same Natural Law', *The American Journal of Jurisprudence*, vol. 38, no. 1 (1993), 109.

9. Oxford Conversations: John Finnis, 'Critics, God, and the Human Function', 2016, https://www.youtube.com/watch?v=gB5z2BSTdyo. Accessed on the 10th December 2017.

what I've already said', believing the basic moves of his theory to be sophisticated and sound and the calls for conceptual reform unfounded and unnecessary.[10] I will focus my analysis in this chapter on what has been left 'unsaid' by exploring the programmatic relationship between the theological 'unsaid(s)' that undergird his NNLT, his philosophical anthropology, his re-narration of the 'practical meaning' of the secular, and his own methodological and strategic confidence in the intelligibility and persuasiveness of his contribution. The pre-eminent 'unsaid' I will focus on is Finnis's ascription to theological extrinsicism and to a *duplex-ordo* ontology, which, put simply, means that 'Beatitude is twofold: the first is "natural" and the second is "supernatural"'.[11] These two tiers are separated ontologically with human nature conceived independently of the realm of the supernatural and the workings of grace.

I will argue that these theological principles animate Finnis's protreptic methodology and legitimate what I call the three 'critical moves' of the NNLT. Particular attention will also be given to examining how Finnis's interactions with H. L. A. Hart shaped not only the structure and content of *NLNR*, but also his understanding of what a 'modern secular' argument should look like. I will then discuss how Finnis's discovery of Germain Grisez's influential – even if controversial – reading of Aquinas became the 'critical moment' whence he found a way to retrieve and reconstruct the Thomistic natural law tradition without contravening the (anti-metaphysical) rules of his secular interlocutors. This reading was also supported by his utilization of certain hermeneutical tools, which enabled Finnis's NNLT to fit within the parameters of his liberal-secular milieu. I will discuss three principal tools: (1) genealogical claims, (2) theological economy, and (3) the exercise of the 'art of writing.'

Finnis has recently declared that the fundamental *élan* behind his contribution can only be correctly discerned by taking into account his intellectual milieu.[12] Given its programmatic importance, I will begin this analysis by identifying the contextual origins and the intended audience of *NLNR*; taking a coincidental interest in what he must have left 'unsaid' – and, more importantly, 'why?' – for a generation of Thomists to have supposedly arrived at a 'faulty exegesis' of what remains the most famous contribution to current debates in natural law.[13]

10. Ibid.

11. C.f. Henri de Lubac, 'Duplex Hominis Beatitudo', *Communio*, Vol. 35 (Winter 2008), 599–612.

12. John Finnis, 'Grounding Human Rights in Natural Law', *The American Journal of Jurisprudence*, vol. 60, no. 2 (2015), 204.

13. Ibid.

Section II: A liberal secular milieu

A protreptic 'speech' to its 'cultured despisers'

'Every author has his milieu.'[14] Finnis has expressed surprise and umbrage at his critics, but especially the 'tradition-based' critics 'from the more or less Thomistic tradition', for failing to take into consideration the full import of this ostensibly incontrovertible remark made in the preface of *NLNR*.[15] In consequence, 'these reviewers and readers, seeing things done quite out of traditional orders of treatment, and reading occasional programmatic declarations more or less in isolation from contexts, endnotes, and later argumentation, all too quickly wrote the book down or off as a sell-out.'[16] A quintessential example of this alleged oversight can be found in the review article composed by Ernest Fortin, titled, 'The New Rights Theory and the Natural Law' (1982), which Finnis recognizes as 'one of the most, and most enduringly, influential' appraisals of his *magnum opus*.[17] Responding some thirty-four years hence, he attributes Fortin's essay with exposing his 'failure of foresight' with 'special clarity'.[18] In particular, he laments that 'scholars who thought of themselves as guardians of the tradition, or of classical wisdom, would turn out to be readers whose comprehension was blocked by questionable presuppositions-as far-reaching, or nearly so, as the errors and oversights of those who think of themselves as moderns.'[19] The most consequential of such 'questionable presuppositions' is borne out of an exegetical inattentiveness to the closely intertwined relationship between milieu and methodology.

The contextual circumstances surrounding the publication of *NLNR* in 1981 share a didactic affinity with those which prompted Friedrich Schleiermacher's *Speeches* on religion. Although certainly dissimilar in terms of style and form, it would not be unhelpful to think of the course of Finnis's argument on natural law as being akin to a protreptic speech to its 'cultured despisers'. To borrow Schleiermacher's own turns of phrase, *NLNR* was certainly an 'unexpected undertaking'.[20] Within Anglo-American jurisprudence, natural law theory had

14. Finnis, *NLNR*, vi.

15. Ibid., 416.

16. Ibid.

17. Finnis, 'Grounding Human Rights in Natural Law', 199, 201.

18. Ibid., 201.

19. Ibid.

20. The entire quotation reads as follows: 'It may be an unexpected undertaking, and you might rightly be surprised that someone can demand from just those persons who have raised themselves above the herd, and are saturated by the wisdom of the century, a hearing for a subject so completely neglected by them … From time immemorial faith has not been everyone's affair, for at all times only a few have understood something of religion while millions variously played with its trappings with which it has willingly let itself be draped out of condescension.' Friedrich Schleiermacher, *On Religion: Speeches to Its Cultured Despisers* (Cambridge: CUP, 1996), 3.

become 'so completely neglected' that one would 'rightly be surprised' that Finnis was able to solicit 'a hearing for a subject so completely neglected' by those 'saturated by the [purported and predominant] wisdom' of the modern school of analytical jurisprudence, the most significant architect of which was Finnis's own mentor, H. L. A. Hart, a founding father of modern legal positivism and Chair of Jurisprudence at Oxford University from 1952 to 1973.[21] Legal positivism and analytical jurisprudence were still very much considered methodologically antithetical to natural law. Writing in 1971, Thomas Cowan, the then Professor of Law at Rutgers University, characterized natural law as the 'natural enemy of both legal positivism and analytical jurisprudence', declaring that:

> When cornered, natural law theorists admit that any law that is not in accordance with the will of God or of right reason is not law at all … Legal positivism and analytical jurisprudence emphatically deny to natural law the quality of being law-lawyer's law … This radical secularization of law completes its emancipation from religion, erecting a wall of separation that legal positivism and analytical jurisprudence mean to preserve intact.[22]

Modern analytical jurisprudence

In a certain sense, analytical jurisprudence is still prepared to ask the 'gravest of all questions', 'What is law?', but reframes that question in accordance with the logic of Hume's Guillotine (the illicit derivation of normative 'ought's' from descriptive accounts of what 'is') and Moore's naturalistic fallacy (the illicit epistemological move of inferring moral values or making third-order claims on the basis of one's observations of natural facts or from first-order claims) – a logic that was, heretofore, presumed destructive and inimical to the very idea of natural law. The 'modern phase' or 'second phase' of this analytical tradition was inaugurated by the powerful assimilation of Ludwig Wittgenstein's philosophy of language. The so-called 'late Wittgenstein' attributed metaphysical puzzlement to the misuse of ordinary language, which prompted him to move away from the pursuit of an idealized language to investigating the appropriate use of ordinary language in instances where such puzzlement emerged.[23]

Hart believed that Wittgenstein provided 'the main stimulus' for addressing 'some gnawing problems' within jurisprudence, problems that he believed would 'drop away' if jurists ceased to ask, 'What is law'? (a question that Hart, via

21. For a rather uncontroversial definition of legal positivism, see: H. L. A. Hart, *The Concept of Law* (Third Edition) (Oxford: OUP, 2012), 185–6; John Finnis, 'The "Natural Law Tradition"', *Journal of Legal Education*, vol. 36 (1986), 493.

22. Thomas A. Cowan, 'Law without Force', *California Law Review*, vol. 58, no. 3 (1971), 687.

23. I am indebted here to: Carl A. Auerbach, 'On Professor H. L. A. Hart's Definition and Theory in Jurisprudence', *Journal of Legal Education*, vol. 9, no. 1 (1956), 39.

Wittgenstein's influence, 'abjures') and based their inquiry instead on trying to answer 'What sort of statement is a statement of law?'[24] This modification reflects an underlying doubt as to whether the ever-recurring search for a determinate ontology or the essence of law can lead to anything more than a 'windy mysticism'. It also reflects an attempt to adjudicate two interconnected philosophical conundra: the conundrum of (moral) realism and the conundrum of historicism, both of which have far-reaching implications for advancing a philosophy of natural law.

With respect to the former, the shadow of Immanuel Kant and David Hume obviously looms large. Analytical jurisprudence sought to disassociate jurisprudential inquiry from an ontological or isomorphic theory of truth as correspondence, which, in this instance, specifically refers to the idea that legal words or concepts mirror pre-existing objects and realities in the world.[25] Corollary to this, as Cowan intimates, all modes of (overt) theological and metaphysical thinking about the nature of law are eschewed as 'strange', 'fantastic', and, ultimately, 'unacceptable' to 'most modern secular thought'.[26] Hence, according to Finnis, the 'central methodological insight' of modern analytical jurisprudence is that, '"as a descriptive legal or social theorist", one can and must "[hold] apart one's own commitments, critical morality, group membership or non-membership."'[27] In other words, jurisprudence is delineated as a science in its own right,[28] dedicated to expounding a radically 'secular' analysis of fundamental legal concepts with an emphasis on elaborating upon the 'open texture' of legal language and its 'performative' function.[29]

However, can either the texture or the performance of legal language be properly understood without recourse to the historical development of jurisprudential thought? The model of analytical jurisprudence dominant when *NLNR* was published implied that there was no methodological prerequisite that

24. H. L. A. Hart, 'A Review of Jerome Frank's "Law and the Modern Mind"', 270. Quoted in: Sybil Schlesinger, 'Working Definitions: A Critique of H. L. A. Hart's Use of Wittgenstein in *The Concept of Law*', *ARSP*, vol. 83, no. 1 (1997), 105.

25. 'There is nothing which simply 'corresponds' to … legal words.' H. L. A. Hart, *Definition and Theory in Jurisprudence* (Oxford: OUP, 1983), 24; Anthony Carty, *Philosophy of Law. Second Edition* (Edinburgh: Edinburgh University Press, 2017), 105.

26. Hart, *The Concept of Law*, 189; H. L. A. Hart, 'Problems of the Philosophy of Law', in *Essays in Jurisprudence and Philosophy*, ed. H. L. A Hart (Oxford: OUP, 1983), 112.

27. John Finnis, 'On Hart's Way: Law as Reason and as Fact', *The American Journal of Jurisprudence*, vol. 52, no. 1 (2007), 25.

28. C.f. H. L. A. Hart, 'A Reply to Professor Bodenheimer', *University of Pennsylvania Law Review*, vol. 105 (1957), 953–75.

29. Hart appropriated the phrase 'open texture' from Friedrich Waismann to refer to the linguistic and definitional indeterminacy of legal concepts. H. L. A. Hart, 'Jhering's Heaven of Concepts and Modern Analytical Jurisprudence', in *Essays in Jurisprudence and Philosophy*, ed. H. L. A Hart (Oxford: OUP, 1983), 275–6.

it should: 'The purpose of analytical jurisprudence is to analyse, without reference either to their historical origin or development or to their ethical significance or validity, the first principles of law.'[30]

Meeting them where they are

It is within the 'modern' milieu of analytical jurisprudence that Finnis grounds the identity of his own natural law theory. He states this explicitly, and no doubt strategically, in the preface to *NLNR*.[31] For it is precisely to those saturated by the apparent 'wisdom' of this milieu, long-considered antithetical to, and deleterious of, the natural law, that he pitches the medium and the message of his approach. However, Finnis also states that his interest in analytical jurisprudence antedates his own gradual realization that there might be more to natural law theory than just 'superstition and darkness'.[32] Reflecting on this transition of perspective in the postscript to the second edition of *NLNR*, Finnis recollects the disconcertment he felt as a law student at the 'inability or unwillingness' of contemporary natural law theorists to 'meet modern secular students as and where they are'.[33] As a former atheist, who spent his teenage years grappling with the scientific determinism and utilitarianism of Bertrand Russell and eventually David Hume's ethical non-cognitivism, Finnis was sensitive to the proscribing power that such philosophies had over academic discourse.[34] In an article written in 1960, two years prior to his conversion to Catholicism, it is clear that his own convictions about the relationship between political and religious discourse were emblematic of such influences:

> As children of the Twentieth Century we fear the conjunction of power and moral certitude. We are not impressed by religious claims to superior wisdom … We think that faith is prejudicial to clear thought about the needs of society; that the religious jargon of 'right', 'God's law' and so on make impossible political debate in a common language, let alone on even similar assumptions. On all these grounds we are satisfied with the usual modern belief in Australia that politics and religion are two compartments of man's social existence that are better kept separate.[35]

In his response to Fortin's review article, Finnis reveals that every chapter of *NLNR* was formulated with the intention of re-presenting to 'secular students'

30. John Salmon, *The First Principles of Jurisprudence* (London: Steven & Hayes, 1893), 5.

31. Finnis, *NLNR*, vi.

32. Ibid., 415.

33. Ibid.

34. See: Germain Grisez, 'About John Finnis', Publication Date Unknown, http://www.twotlj. org/Finnis.html. Accessed 10 April 2018.

35. John Finnis, 'Religion in Politics', *On Dit*, vol. 28, no. 4 (14 April 1960), 6.

and 'modern readers' the fundamental truths of classical political philosophy.[36] The principal challenge to this re-presentation was the prevailing intellectual predisposition to rebuke anything that relates to, or derives from, magisterial teaching or speculative theology. 'Every part of *NLNR*', says Finnis, 'is shaped and marked by a consciousness of this challenging fact.'[37]

The rise of liberal secularism

Throughout his literary *oeuvre*, Finnis frequently describes his secular-analytical interlocutors as 'liberals', or as 'liberal secularists', or as persons who inhabit 'liberal secular' societies. Furthermore, he referred to Hart, his principal interlocutor within the academy, as 'always liberal', and he engages extensively with the *Political Liberalism* of John Rawls, whose work he 'scorns' in *NLNR*.[38] Conscious that such nomenclature is often definitionally contingent and contextually inconsistent, Finnis nevertheless regards the philosophical attitudes of liberal secularism to be of particular importance to appreciating his distinct milieu.[39] In his essay, 'Unjust Laws in a Democratic Society', he gives two reasons for this.[40] First and foremost, liberal secularism – especially within Western countries – has progressively sought to extricate sociopolitical discourse from the historical influence of the Christian faith, giving rise to a cacophony of conflicting conceptualizations and judgements about reality and the morality of the common good. Secular liberals call the resultant sociopolitical framework 'pluralist', but Finnis suggests that it would be more accurate to just call it ' "discordant" or "divided about essentials" '.[41]

The second reason he gives is in many ways the ideological justification for endorsing the first reason. In light of the liberalist disavowal of a universal or transcendent foundation for truth, personal autonomy is turned into the pre-eminent sociopolitical 'virtue'. This kind of thinking obviously prescinds from the notion of objective 'truth' and is replaced – at least in terms defended by Rawls – by the idea of the 'reasonable', allowing for the possibility that a plethora of different political policies might be 'reasonable' even if they are untrue.[42] The obvious sociological problem with this is that the ability to pursue what an individual might want necessitates the co-operation of one's fellow citizens – a partisanship that is unlikely to be agreed to if acknowledged as a purely instrumental relationship. For this reason, proponents of secular liberalism give a new 'secularized' meaning

36. Finnis, 'Grounding Human Rights in Natural Law', 200.

37. Ibid.

38. John Finnis, *Philosophy of Law* (Oxford: OUP, 2011), 257; C.f. Finnis, *NLNR*, 76; Finnis, 'Grounding Human Rights in Natural Law', 204 fn. 13.

39. Ibid., 201.

40. John Finnis, 'Unjust Laws in a Democratic Society', *Notre Dame Law Review*, vol. 71, no. 4 (1996), 596.

41. Ibid., 597.

42. C.f. John Finnis, *Religion & Public Reason* (Oxford: OUP, 2011), 113.

to the 'pre-secular' language of the 'common good', 'human rights', and 'human dignity' in order to advance one's 'self-asserting and self-protecting *will*'.[43] Finnis believes that this translates into a 'secular nihilism', sustained by an ideological alliance between democracy and relativism, which gradually engenders a host of systematic injustices. The most notable of which include the exclusion of the rights of the unborn, the disabled, and the dying.[44] Critically, therefore, in liberal democracies a *lingua* of rights naturally triumphs over a *lingua* of the (common) good.

Furthermore, 'liberal secularists' consider Roman Catholics – and especially Thomists – to be mental slaves, a conclusion that denotes what Finnis calls a flagrant '*petitio principii*' since it is 'covertly and overtly' predicated upon the supposition that both Catholicism and Thomism are irrational and fatuous.[45] Finnis argues that if the secularists are to hold this position coherently, then they must be open to considering the possibility that the central principles of Thomistic philosophy and jurisprudence are true – that is to say, they can be established and tested through the autonomous exercise of natural reason. Although this point was left 'unsaid' in *NLNR*, Finnis later acknowledged that he 'tacitly proceeds on this basis'.[46] Thus, even if his exculpatory comments about deferring to natural reason alone – rather than yielding to, or referencing, an authority – are 'sincere and true', he also reveals that they are rhetorically strategic.[47]

The collapse of neo-Thomism

The desire to emphasize carefully the practical and autonomous character of natural reason also reflects a definitively theological aspect of Finnis's milieu, which, although left 'unsaid' in *NLNR*, is made explicit in his reply to Fortin. Therein he states that the book was composed contemporaneously to '"the pseudomorphic collapse of Neo-Thomism in the wake of Vatican II."'[48] Finnis associates neo-Thomism (and neo-scholasticism more generally) with the manualist tradition of moral theology, which he reproves for promoting a plethora of philosophically spurious principles in the name of Aquinas. In consequence, Aquinas' natural law theory more specifically, and the classical moral tradition more generally, had been unfairly written off by the 'cultured despisers' as falling prey to a host of Enlightenment and post-Enlightenment objections. Two of the most significant principles or propositions of neo-Thomism/neo-scholasticism that Finnis attributes to the unfortunate eschewal of the authentic classical tradition are: (1) the espousal of a neo-Suarezian naturalism and (2) the 'commingling

43. Finnis, 'Unjust Laws in a Democratic Society', 597. (IAITT).
44. Ibid., 598.
45. Finnis, 'Grounding Human Rights in Natural Law', 203.
46. Ibid., 202.
47. Ibid., 203.
48. Ibid., 202 fn. 9.

of historical interpretation and philosophical construction', particularly with respect to interpreting the relationship between Aquinas's treatise on law and his eschatological doctrine of the ultimate end.[49] Again, in the spirit of Schleiermacher, Finnis underscores to the 'cultured despisers' of natural law that, actually, 'few have understood something' of the classical jurisprudential tradition, whilst many, especially the neo-Thomists, have 'played with its trappings'.[50]

For this reason, Finnis interpreted the post-conciliar dethronement of neo-scholastic and neo-Thomistic rationalism as a propitious opportunity to investigate afresh whether an Aristotelian-Thomistic approach to natural law can find a way to circumvent the objections of modern analytical jurisprudence and liberal secularism. A key part of this process is arresting the critical suppositions of those within modern liberal jurisprudence, such as Lon Fuller, Hans Kelsen, Joseph Raz, and Hart, all of whom, he claims, have either misjudged Aquinas's philosophical framework as inextricably moored to a disguised theological provenance or misunderstood it as a form of rationalist essentialism that reduces the practical order to an elaboration of an a priori theory of human nature.[51] Responding to these intellectual and cultural predicaments became a powerful undercurrent that shaped the protreptic face of Finnis's 'new' methodology.

Section III: A methodological reaction

A protreptic Thomism

What is Finnis's response to this milieu? At this juncture, it suffices to introduce two key clarificatory elements in light of the preceding discussion. First, in keeping with the ahistoricism of modern – especially English – analytical jurisprudence, Finnis attests on the first page of the Preface of *Natural Law & Natural Rights* that his NNLT does not proceed by way of genealogy. 'No effort is made to give an ordered account of the long history of theorizing about natural law and natural rights.'[52] This expressed methodological disassociation from history and genealogy emulates Hart's juxtapositional distinction between an analysis of law *qua* law and theories of and about the law – a distinction Finnis believed to be of significant importance. 'There can be a history of theories, doctrines, and accounts of matters that have no history', writes Finnis, '[a]nd the principles of natural law ... have no history.'[53] Since natural law concerns itself with timeless

49. John Finnis and Germain Grisez, 'A Reply to Ralph McInerny', *The American Journal of Jurisprudence*, vol. 26, no. 21 (1981), 31.

50. See the epigraph at the beginning of this chapter.

51. C.f. Lon Fuller, *The Meaning of Law* (New Haven, CT: Yale University Press, 1963), 63; Hans Kelsen, *Pure Theory of Law* (Oxford: OUP, 2007), 5; Joseph Raz, *The Authority of Law* (Oxford: OUP, 2009), 158.

52. Finnis, *NLNR*, v.

53. Ibid., 24.

truths, Finnis discountenances any attempt to try and conflate or associate it with a political ideology, regardless of whether it be liberal or conservative.[54] However, lest this objectivism be confused as a surreptitious attempt to smuggle in a return to metaphysical essentialism, Finnis clarifies that his interest lies in identifying the constitutive forms of human flourishing, purified of historical and political excesses. Abstract debates regarding whether human nature is ontologically determinate or indeterminate are considered by him to be extraneous to the NNLT.[55]

The 'essential distinction' between natural law theories and the theory of natural law also bespeaks to Finnis's complete disinterestedness in engaging with postmodern interpretivism and his professed refusal to enter 'the game' of situating the truth of 'What is law?' as a matter of 'era, period, age or epoch.'[56] Such a trajectory is a dangerous foundation for ethical relativism since it implies that all knowledge is merely the product of 'taking a look'.[57] Such a perspective systematically displaces one of the key methodological ingredients of analytical jurisprudence – the disjunction between the ontological (the *is*) and the normative (the *ought*). In reply, Finnis defends philosophy as a process of reasoning and understanding that, although has certain empirical foundations in our perceptions of the world, quickly and necessarily exceeds the 'spatially dominated metaphors of "perspective"'.[58] For this reason, he draws the conclusion that the supposed 'heavy artillery' of the postmodern critique of knowledge is actually 'aimed (if at all) at itself', and, therefore, he is confident that it will 'silence itself soon enough.'[59] This explains, then, why there is not even a single reference to either postmodernism (as an historical epoch) or postmodern philosophy (as a school of thought) in *NLNR*. Yet, it also becomes clear that it remains an unspoken epistemological enemy, one that is indirectly critiqued if one reads between the foundationalist lines of Finnis's analytically free-standing NNLT. For in a later essay, Finnis acknowledges that although Nietzsche's 'name may be absent from it, *NLNR* is conceived in part as a response to him.'[60] You could say that Nietzsche is the sceptical interlocutor who has been left 'unsaid'!

An analytic-Thomistic transmogrification

The second clarificatory element of Finnis's contextual methodology clarifies his turn to the one he refers to as 'the first liberal', the 'first Whig', and even if jocosely, 'the postmodern Parisian intellectual', Thomas Aquinas.[61] Aquinas escapes the

54. Finnis, 'The "Natural Law Tradition"', 493.
55. C.f. Finnis, *NLNR*, 50, Notes II. 1.
56. Ibid., 58.
57. Finnis *Philosophy of Law*, 333.
58. Ibid., 332.
59. Ibid.
60. John Finnis, 'Grounds of Law and Legal Theory', *Legal Theory*, vol. 13 (2007), 322.
61. John Finnis, *Aquinas: Moral, Political, & Legal Theory* (Oxford: OUP, 1998), vii.

postmodern power play of contesting meta-narratives precisely because his contributions were not 'ideological'.[62] Rather, all of his presuppositions are said to be intelligible to anyone who engages in a process of rational discernment – they are universally accessible.[63] Hence, before moving to re-present this theory in Part II of *NLNR*, he affirms that:

> the reason for making the attempt is that a theory of practical reasonableness, of basic forms of human good, and of practical principles, such as the theory Aquinas adumbrated but left insufficiently elaborated, is untouched by the objections which Hume (and after him the whole Enlightenment and post-Enlightenment current of ethics) was able to raise against the tradition of rationalism eked out by voluntarism.[64]

The methodological complication is that, on the one hand, Finnis states that his approach is one of faithfully re-presenting the classical-Thomistic natural law tradition, signalling a desire to respect and recover it historical roots and foundational principles. Yet, on the other hand, he also intends to develop the main elements of that tradition in order for it to be found useful to those interested in 'the history of ideas' or by scholars and students open to 'forming or reforming' their understanding of its merits.[65]

In a pivotal explicatory essay, written in collaboration with Germain Grisez and Joseph Boyle in 1987, Finnis clearly states that the NNLT 'uses some language common in the (broadly speaking, Thomistic) natural law-tradition' out of which the theory was formulated.[66] However, he then adds a caveat that the use of such language 'differs in various ways from the theories articulated by Aristotle, Thomas Aquinas, and others'.[67] This invites speculation over whether the NNLT is utilizing Thomistic language but, in a methodological sleight of hand, transmutes its meaning, possibly by emptying it of its theological content in order to make it more palatable to a liberal-secular audience. It also raises the hermeneutical problem of when 'development' becomes a euphemism for a philosophical-theological 'reformation' or strategic 're-formulation'. More importantly, according to whose philosophical standards do you measure this 'developed' restatement to be both sound and successful? How far can you depart from Aquinas before you are no longer considered 'Thomistic'?

62. Ibid., vii.

63. Ibid.

64. Finnis, *NLNR*, 46–7.

65. Ibid., v–vi.

66. John Finnis, Germain Grisez and Joseph Boyle, 'Practical Principles, Moral Truth and Ultimate Ends', *The American Journal of Jurisprudence*, vol. 32, no. 32 (1987), 99. (Hence Forth, 'PMU'.) Similarly, in *Aquinas*, he says that: 'My exposition quite often goes beyond what Aquinas says.' (Finnis, *Aquinas*, viii).

67. Ibid., 99.

Finnis would no doubt respond to such concerns by referring to his book *Aquinas*. Here we find a restatement of the fundaments of the NNLT, only this time with meticulous and fastidious referencing to Aquinas's corpus. Given his intended audience, it is likely for strategic reasons that Finnis was careful not to do this in *NLNR*. With the exception of chapter two in Part One,[68] references to Aquinas's works are predominantly found in the endnotes situated at the end of each chapter (written in significantly smaller font) rather than more perspicuously in the footnotes.[69] In his reply to Fortin, Finnis admits that only the *careful* reader would realize that what is being left 'unsaid' here is his intention to delicately impress the point upon his readers that his NNLT is that of Aquinas's and vice versa.[70] However, this admission only intensifies the methodological confusion. For in his clarificatory essay, Finnis declared that *NLNR* cannot be understood aright unless one clearly recognizes that, with few expressed exceptions, his references to Aquinas are always to be interpreted as an accurate adoption of his viewpoint.[71] But if such a recognition is essential for interpretive accuracy, why leave it inconspicuous or 'unsaid'? What, therefore, is the logic behind this second element of Finnis's methodology?

When evaluated in light of his milieu, it is evident that a delicate balancing act is taking place underneath the textual surface of *NLNR*. Lest he confirm the secularists' suspicion that Catholic natural law theorists are mental slaves of the Angelic Doctor, Finnis is cautious to accentuate the 'freestanding' epistemological character of the NNLT – its foundation in reason alone.[72] At the same time, Finnis was overtly aware of Aquinas's importance within the tradition of natural law and clearly desired his work to be judged 'Thomistic'. In his reply to Fortin, he disclosed his anticipation that those attuned to the book's secular milieu, especially other Christians and Thomists, would pay close attention to the numerous references to Aquinas in the endnotes. This, I would argue, was done to press the exegetical

68. In this section, Finnis critiques popular misrepresentations of the Thomistic natural law tradition.

69. It is important to clarify that I am referring specifically to when Finnis turns in Part Two (which he says is at the 'core' of *NLNR*) to exposit the most crucial aspects of NNLT in Chapters III, IV, and V. In Chapters III and IV where he makes his case for the basic goods of human flourishing, twenty-one of the twenty-six references to Aquinas are found in the endnotes and not in the footnotes.

70. Finnis, 'Grounding Human Rights in Natural Law', 203.

71. 'To understand this book [*NLNR*] aright, one should note that whenever Thomas Aquinas is quoted or cited, the author is to be taken (except in a few cases where he expresses a reservation) to mean to adopt Aquinas' view.' Finnis, Grisez and Boyle, 'PMU', 150.

72. Perhaps this also lends a further tactical explanation for the preference for endnotes rather than footnotes.

integrity of his approach such that it would be deemed 'neo-classical' rather than 'new'.[73]

The three 'critical moves'

The theoretical propinquity between historical milieu and this rhetorico-politically nuanced methodology prompts a critical inquiry into the compatibility and reconcilability of Finnis's strategical 'unsaid' with some of his more pronounced statements. For instance, statements such as the 'principles of natural law … have no history',[74] or that '[i]t scarcely makes sense to talk of a natural law tradition', or that 'being concerned with truth, natural law theory is quite distinct from political movements?' would seem to undermine his strategical emphasis upon context.[75] Once again, there appears to be another discreet balancing act operating *sub rosa* within the NNLT. On the one hand, Finnis describes his theory as 'classical' to signify not only his chronological dependence, but also his normative conviction that, irrespective of intellectual fashions, the 'classical' understanding of natural law is objectively true and, thus, timelessly sound. On the other hand, Finnis admits that the intelligibility of his 'neo-classical' approach is firmly situated within the 'modern tradition' and, therefore, indissociable from the historical particularism of his liberal secular milieu. At the very least, such a balancing act would seem to render questionable how historically and politically 'freestanding' the NNLT actually is.

From an exegetical perspective, it is also valuable to assess the impact that this balancing act has had upon his re-presentation and development of Aquinas's thought. Is Finnis justified in claiming that this 'freestanding' approach takes off at every point from Aquinas? Or, would it be more accurate to say that his reading of Aquinas takes off from his analytical construction of secular liberalism?[76] To what degree is Finnis guilty of replicating the same neo-scholastic *modus operandi* he forcefully rebukes by 'commingling historical interpretation and philosophical construction'?[77]

An instructive place to begin is with what I call the three 'critical moves' of the NNLT. I call these moves 'critical' not just because they are fundamental to the epistemological coherency of the NNLT, but because they reflect robust methodological responses to Finnis's construction of his liberal secular milieu. It is my contention that Finnis employs these 'critical moves' to demonstrate how

73. Finnis is bitterly opposed to the labelling of his basic value account of practical reason as 'new', rather than 'neoclassical'. See: John Finnis, 'Reflections and Responses', in *Reason, Morality, and Law*, ed. John Keown and Robert P. George (Oxford: OUP, 2013), 532.

74. Finnis, *NLNR*, 24.

75. Finnis, 'The "Natural Law Tradition"', 493.

76. What Finnis does say, however, is that Aquinas' theory was 'left insufficiently elaborated'. Finnis, *NLNR*, 46–7.

77. Finnis and Grisez, 'A Reply to Ralph McInerny', 31.

the truth of natural law can still be legitimated according to the rules prescribed by 'those whose rules they are' – namely, the 'cultured despisers' – whose primary disposition we can now summarize as being one of 'scepticism', especially towards 'religious revelation' and 'authoritarian sacredness'.[78]

(1) In defence of human freedom: A poly-teleological riposte of God as the Summum Bonum[79]

The first critical move is one of philosophical anthropology and involves negotiating between the Charybdis of teleological naturalism and the Scylla of self-determination in human freedom.[80] To insist upon a determinate teleological conception of human nature would, according to Finnis, enslave the individual to a form of (divine) voluntarism, which, he believes, is incompatible with the philosophical presupposition that human beings have a 'radical capacity for free choice.'[81] This is because the notion of a single *ultimus finis* would reduce the exercise of practical reasoning to the pushing and pulling of an extrinsic force, which would reduce the act of choosing to a selection of means rather than the free selection of (ultimate) ends.[82] True freedom, says Finnis, is to be the author of one's own flourishing – to be one's own destiny, to be 'an end in oneself'.[83] Hence the stated importance for Finnis of keeping Aquinas's treatise on law and his eschatological reflections completely distinct. This fundamental point finds expression in Finnis's requirement that, as a requirement of practical reasonableness, 'an individual self' should live according to a 'coherent plan of life.'[84] Thus, human fulfilment involves each person's rational discernment and existential pursuit of a poly-teleological yet 'harmonious set of purposes and orientations.'[85]

78. Finnis, 'On Hart's Way', 25. At various junctures in *NLNR*, Finnis engages in a series of hypothetical arguments with a character he calls the 'sceptic'. I will return to this in Chapter 5. Furthermore, the three 'critical moves' could be considered broader, textually more encompassing, extrapolations of what Finnis described as 'preliminary clarifications.' Finnis, *NLNR*, 24.

79. It was Benedict M. Ashley who used the term 'polyteleologism' to characterize this aspect of Grisez's thought. C.f. Benedict M. Ashley, 'What is the End of the Human Person?', in *Moral Truth and Tradition*, ed. Luke Gormally (Dublin: Four Corners Press, 1994), 68–96.

80. A poignant objective of Finnis work is to demonstrate how Aquinas's natural law theory is successful in avoiding the 'Scylla of "absolutism" and the Charybdis of "relativism"', even if he defends the existence of exceptionless moral norms. C.f. John Finnis, *Reason in Action* (Oxford: OUP, 2011), 188.

81. Finnis, Grisez and Boyle, 'PMU', 101.

82. Finnis, *Aquinas*, 170.

83. Ibid., 170. C.f. Finnis, 'Grounds of Law and Legal Theory', 342.

84. Finnis, *NLNR*, 103–4.

85. Ibid.

According to Finnis, this position is by no means new. In fact, NNLT rejects the idea that Aquinas accepted the Aristotelian supposition that human nature is teleologically oriented to a single *ultimus finis* or *summum bonum* in God ('the First Mover' in the case of the Stagirite, for whom, of course, this single orientation was sheerly natural, as it was not for Aquinas).[86] Finnis contends that whenever Aquinas speaks of a single end (*telos*) of human flourishing, he is actually referring to a plurality of basic reasons for action or 'human goods' ('*bona humana*'), which are incommensurable (prior to choice), universally identifiable, and, by logical necessity, 'equally our basic ends.'[87] In other words, the existence of free choice depends upon having '*motives* for choosing and doing each of two or more incompatible options.'[88] However, Finnis adds the caveat that 'these motives are not determinative' because 'not even the motives which are necessary … settles the free choice, save one's own very act of making it, that act is truly creative.'[89] This means that the choices that are truly 'basic' and shape a person's life history are not the mere by-product of one's antecedent dispositions or pre-rational desires; they are a participation in, and an understanding of, the value of the basic goods, which not only create new wants and desires but even shape a new (although not entirely new) identity or character.[90] This hermetic disjunction between choice and what we might call our pre-rational nature finds expression in Finnis's equally disjointed understanding of the relationship between human nature (*physis*) and human culture (*nomos*). 'Culture', he asserts, is simply 'what we add, by our choices to nature, that is to all that we find … prior to human decisions to believe, plan, make, and do.'[91]

(2) In defence of 'Imperfecta Beatitudo'*: The social and political integrity of human nature as* 'Natura Pura'

The second critical move, which is corollary to the first, asserts that Aquinas repudiated the idea that every human being has a natural, *in corde*, desire for the beatific vision.

86. C.f. Finnis, Grisez, Boyle, "PMU", 132–3; Finnis, *Aquinas*, 170, 314-315; Finnis, *NLNR*, 89, 401 401 -byly Finnis' meant by assering that n no be gleanded except from milieu: mental slaves.een milieu and methodology; there 401. From a purely exegetical perspective, this is a surprising claim. Finnis position is seemingly irreconcilable with the following references in the *Summa Theologica*: ST I q.2 a. 1 ad. 1; ST I-II q.1 a.4; ST I-II q.1 a.5; ST II q.3 a.1.

87. C.f. Finnis, *Aquinas*, 80 fn. 92.

88. John Finnis, *Moral Absolutes* (Washington, DC: Catholic University of America, 1991), 58. (IAITT).

89. Ibid., 58.

90. John Finnis, *Fundamentals of Ethics* (Washington, DC: Georgetown University Press, 1983), 138. (Henceforth *FoE*).

91. Finnis, *Religion & Public Reason*, 328.

> Since human persons cannot naturally be actualised by divine goodness without ceasing to be human … human persons cannot naturally be actualized by divine goodness. And so, the human will can have *no natural disposition to fulfilment in divine goodness* … [T]he hearts of human persons, considered precisely according to their nature, are not made for God.[92]

Finnis avows that, since the truth of the first principles of practical reason is unmediated – for they are self-evident, grasped by *synderesis* – and because friendship with God is *not* something that human beings naturally desire but something we discover through revelation and the reception of supernatural grace, human fulfilment can, and indeed should, be envisaged in abstraction from the Creator.[93] For this reason, Finnis strongly defends what he calls 'the life of practical reasonableness' as a path to *beatitudo*, albeit *imperfecta*.[94] It is around the principle of this purely natural end of 'integral human fulfilment', which is itself predicated, a priori, upon the existence of a theory of pure nature, that Finnis believes Aquinas organized his social and political theory. (Although, he also asserts that Aquinas never clarified exactly what 'imperfect human fulfilment' is since he dedicated most of his time to exploring perfect fulfilment.)[95] This gives further philosophical justification for bracketing out God, theology, and metaphysics from the fundaments of his NNLT and considering the natural law 'strictly and integrally' within the epistemological parameters of practical reason.[96] This resituating of natural law within a metaphysically restricted system would seem to suggest that Finnis is borrowing from the fundamental categories of Immanuel Kant.[97]

(3) In defence of practical reason: Natural law has nothing to do with nature

Although the previous two 'critical moves' of the NNLT denote highly controversial interpretations of Aquinas's theory of natural law, it is arguably the third critical move that has attracted the most intrigue and consternation. In the final chapter of *NLNR*, Finnis acknowledges his discontent with the phrase 'natural law', describing it as an 'unhappy term'.[98] The unhappiness arises because the presence of the word '*natura*' implies, *a priori*, that the logic of a 'natural law theory' must rest upon the

92. Finnis, Grisez and Boyle, 'PMU', 134.
93. Finnis, *NLNR*, 103.
94. Finnis, *Aquinas*, 109.
95. Ibid.
96. Finnis, *Religion & Public Reason*, 58, 82.
97. C.f. Russell Hittinger, *A Critique of the New Natural Law Theory* (Notre Dame, IN: University of Notre Dame Press, 1987). In response to this accusation, Finnis has said that Kant, himself, takes over some of the deontology of Christian moral doctrine and so if there are any similarities between Kant and the NNLT they are simply a coincidence of results. I will return to this point in Chapter 5.
98. Finnis, *NLNR*, 374.

necessary inference of normative values from empirical/metaphysical facts about (human) nature – or, the derivation of a moral '*ought*' from a theoretical discourse about what '*is*'. Such a supposition, he avows, is either a 'myth or a misreading' of the classical tradition.[99] For in the context of the philosophy of law, natural law 'is just another name for legal philosophy' and that 'the argument of this book [*NLNR*] does not rely, even implicitly, on the term "human nature"'.[100]

At the risk of 'widespread dissatisfaction', Finnis asserts that, contrary to popular perception, the classical exponents of natural law, most notably Aquinas, never even dreamt of attempting such a derivation:

> [I]t is simply not true that 'any form of a natural-law theory of morals entails the belief that propositions about man's duties and obligations can be inferred from propositions about nature.' Nor is it true that for Aquinas 'good and evil are concepts analysed and fixed in metaphysics before they are applied in morals.' On the contrary, Aquinas asserts as plainly as possible that the first principles of natural law are *per se nota* (self-evident) and indemonstrable ... They are not inferred or derived from anything.[101]

It is important to remember that Kant's riposte of an ontological (correspondence) theory of truth – *adequatio rei et intellectus* – is thought to pose a seemingly insuperable problem for defending a properly Thomistic account of natural law. This was because the truth value of the natural law was thought to be grounded upon a metaphysical inquiry into the essence of human nature. In seeking to correct this common form of reductivism, Finnis explains how Aquinas's theory of truth in fact overcomes both Kant's epistemological roadblock and Hume's guillotine on their own terms.

With respect to natural law, the principal question can be phrased as follows: In what way do the principles of practical reasonableness correspond with, or relate to, the intelligible order of reality? Finnis acknowledges that this is fundamentally a question of philosophical anthropology. A sound theory of natural law must be attentive to the four-fold distinction between the orders of reality or, perhaps more accurately, to how the different orders of cognition relate to reality.[102] Although Finnis does make reference to this in *NLNR*, a more succinct summary of this distinction can be found in his book *Aquinas*.[103] What is controversial about this metaphysical schema is Finnis's further contention that Aquinas avowed that the four orders are 'irreducibly distinct',[104] the principal implication being

99. Finnis, 'The "Natural Law Tradition"', 493.

100. John Finnis, 'What Is the Philosophy of Law?', *The American Journal of Jurisprudence*, vol. 59, no. 2 (1014), 138; Finnis, *NLNR*, 50.

101. Ibid., 33–4.

102. Finnis, 'Natural Law and Legal Reasoning', 5.

103. Finnis, *Aquinas*, 21; Finnis, *NLNR*, 136–8.

104. Finnis, *Aquinas*, 21; Finnis, Grisez and Boyle, 'PMU', 24–5.

the methodological proscription of any attempt to deduce moral or third-order conclusions about the human good from first-order or descriptive accounts of human nature. In other words, NNLT insists upon a logical separation of moral cognition, which occurs when one is thinking practically, from an ontological or teleological study of human inclinations, which occurs when one is thinking speculatively.[105]

This leads to two sub-aspects of the third critical move that are worth highlighting. The first is 'a cardinal principle of Aristotle's and Aquinas's methodology', the absence of which in *NLNR* accounted for a 'serious weakness' in the book's original presentation of the argument:

> That is the principle, pervasive in their work but conspicuously lost to view in the work of their modern would-be representatives, that we do not know natures of things without knowing those things' capacities, which in turn we cannot know without knowing their actualization in activity, which in turn we cannot understand with any adequacy except by knowing the activities' objects.[106]

What this epistemological axiom attests to is that, although ontologically speaking, objects of volition are contingent upon the human nature we possess (generally speaking, 'what one is to be' is grounded upon what one 'naturally is'), epistemologically, knowledge of human nature is contingent upon our first coming to know the objects of human willing (the 'reasons for action').[107] Finnis denounces any suggestion that this would reduce human nature to a mere 'rhetorical flourish'.[108] What he does say is that an adequate understanding of human nature cannot be discerned '*except by that practical pursuit that Aristotle called ethics*.'[109] 'Aquinas' moral arguments', says Finnis, 'never run from "natural" to "therefore reasonable and right" but always from "reasonable and right" to "therefore natural."'[110] To emphasize this conclusion, Finnis clarifies that, according to the 'mainstream' natural law theorists, the word 'natural' in 'natural law' should be understood as '"of reason", as in "the law of reason" or "the requirements of reason."'[111] He reiterates

105. To be fair, Finnis does desist from any suggestion that there is an *absolute* separation between theoretical and practical reason. In *NLNR* he asserts that there is 'a mutual though not quite symmetrical *interdependence* between the project of describing human affairs by way of a theory and the project of evaluating human options with a view, at least remotely, to acting reasonably and well.' C.f. Finnis, *NLNR*, 19. (IAITT) See also: Finnis, *FoE*, 12.

106. Finnis, *NLNR*, 416.

107. C.f. Finnis, Germain Grisez, Boyle, 'PMU', 116.

108. Finnis, *FoE*, 20.

109. Ibid., 20. (IAITT).

110. Finnis, *Aquinas*, 153 fn. 91; Finnis, *Human Rights & Common Good*, 354 fn. 4.

111. John Finnis, 'Natural Law Theories', 2007, https://plato.stanford.edu/entries/natural-law-theories. Accessed on 10 March 2018.

this again in his article 'On "Public Reason"', stating that the principles of 'natural law' are 'natural' 'because, *and only because*, they are rational – requirements of being practically reasonable – and thus accessible to beings whose nature includes rational capacities.'[112]

But how exactly does objectivity relate to truth? A second sub-aspect to the third critical move is Finnis's avowal that one must overcome the illusion of objectivity that the correspondence theory of truth affords, an illusion that he believes is at the root of reductivism (whether it takes the form of ethical naturalism or philosophical empiricism) and significant instances of moral scepticism. Ironically, it is the apparent objectivity of the correspondence theory of truth that, he believes, also undermines it – the idea 'that to which true judgments have their truth by corresponding ('the facts', 'the world', 'the reality' …) somehow lies open to an inspection conducted otherwise than by rationally arriving at true judgments of the type in question.'[113] In order to understand the truth particular to the principles of natural law, one must restate the distinction between the truth of 'theoretical knowledge' and the truth of 'practical knowledge'. Put simply, practical knowledge, which concerns itself with what one ought to do, follows from a rational consideration of what it is good to be.[114] Prior to this practical syllogism, practical knowledge has no reality; but by exercising our practical reason, we are able to bring 'something into reality' – that is, a possible future way of *being*.[115] Speaking analogously, one can speak of the truth of practical knowledge as an *adequatio* in a more limited sense: as the 'conformity of *what is to be* through knowing to the *knowledge* which will help to bring it about.'[116]

Section IV: Intellectual influences

Theo-cultural osmosis: Herbert Hart and Germain Grisez

In attempting to heed Finnis's critical response to his 'tradition-based' critics, I have sought to examine the interplay between his liberal-secular-post-conciliar milieu and his adoption of a modern-analytical-post-metaphysical methodology. With this discussion in mind, I now embark on a deeper investigation of the theological 'unsaid' in Finnis's NNLT. To illuminate this dimension of his thought, it is necessary to discuss the deeper influence of two intellectuals, Herbert Hart and Germain Grisez, upon the formulation of the three 'critical moves' of the NNLT and upon the structure and content of *NLNR*. Although I have already mentioned Hart's general influence within Finnis's intellectual milieu, I now want to explore his specific influence upon how Finnis constructs the secular *mythos*

112. Finnis, *Reason in Action*, 259. (IAITT).
113. Finnis, *FoE*, 64.
114. Finnis, Grisez and Boyle, 'PMU', 117.
115. Ibid., 116.
116. Ibid., 117. (IAITT).

and what he considers to be a secular – 'purely philosophical' – argument in *NLNR*. I then examine the extent to which Grisez's controversial reading of Aquinas gave Finnis an 'unsaid' theological justification for formulating such an argument, that justification being Finnis's theological ascription to a *duplex-ordo* theory and to an anthropological extrinsicism which, rather paradoxically, also gives a theological intelligentsia to his construction of, and engagement with, the secular *mythos*.

Natural law as 'reasons for actions'

I previously touched upon the impressive role that Herbert Hart played in engendering the modern-analytical phase of legal positivism within Anglophonic jurisprudence in the post-1950s. As I explained, Hart abjured the ontologically imbued question, 'What is Law?', because he had come to the conclusion that 'nothing concise enough to be recognized as a definition could provide a satisfactory answer to it.'[117] Nevertheless, despite upholding the archetypical conviction of legal positivism (that there is no necessary connection between law and morality, which Finnis believes was a criticism directed at Aquinas),[118] Hart famously avowed that '[l]aw is surely not the gunman situation writ large, and legal order is surely not to be thus simply identified with compulsion.'[119] This recognition stemmed not from any moralistic observation, but because he realized that trying to understand the law simply as that which obligates habitual obedience just does not 'fit the facts.'[120] The paradigmatic importance of *The Concept of Law* was that it sought to shift jurisprudence away from both obscuring metaphysical myths and authoritative threats by providing 'an explanatory and clarifying account of law as a complex social and political institution with a rule-governed (and in that sense 'normative') aspect.'[121] This shift displaced the ontological implications of the question, 'What is law?', and sought to replace it with an elucidatory and methodological reproduction of the way in which the rules of law 'function in the lives' of its adherents.[122]

One of the principal reasons why the NNLT was given popular attention within the academy was that it seemed to reflect something of the spirit behind Hart's jurisprudential shift. In particular, *NLNR* challenged the popular impression that natural law was indissociable from a host of metaphysical-theological presuppositions and/or authoritative decrees. To make this point clear, Finnis expressed critical umbrage at the metaphysical inquiry that inaugurated the discourse of the *Minos*. 'Legal theory', he said, 'gets off to a shaky start' because Socrates makes the wrong move of treating the end that is the human good as if

117. Hart, *The Concept of Law*, 16.
118. Finnis, *Philosophy of Law*, 163.
119. H. L. A. Hart, 'Positivism and the Separation of Law and Morals', *Harvard Law Review*, vol. 71, no. 4 (February 1958), 603.
120. Hart, *The Concept of Law*, 80.
121. Ibid., 239.
122. Ibid., 90.

it were something to be produced by following a theoretical recipe or blueprint – illegitimately moving from 'is' to 'ought'.[123]

Finnis believed that he had found a way to bring natural law within an analytical-modern framework of jurisprudence, and he did not shy away from attributing the roots of this realization to Hart. It was Hart, he says, who put jurisprudence 'firmly on the road back – or rather, forward – to the point where it will re-join the classical [Aristotelian] tradition.'[124] Where the roads of the modern-analytical and the classical tradition meet is in Hart's recognition that the rule of law provides 'good reasons for action', thereby inaugurating a 'laborious recovery' from the Hobbesian-styled voluntarism of Jeremy Bentham.[125] From this intra-psychic viewpoint, Hart was prepared to accept that the law can be 'rationally grounded'.[126] He would even go on to recognize what he termed as 'the core of good sense' in the natural law tradition, even if he was only prepared to accept what he calls the 'minimum content of Natural Law.'[127] Hart also made a subsequent genealogical claim that the historical origins of the classical expression of natural law were 'quite secular', which he esteems as its most enduring quality and the reason for its longevity:

> Natural Law … have their roots in Greek thought, which was … quite secular. Indeed, the continued reassertion of some form of Natural Law doctrine is due in part to the fact that its appeal is independent of both divine and human authority, and to the fact that despite a terminology, and much metaphysics, which few now accept, it contains certain elementary truths of importance for the understanding of both morality and law. These we shall endeavour to disentangle from their metaphysical setting.[128]

Finnis would later state that he viewed Hart's founding insights as a 'standing invitation' to re-present a 'neo-classical' theory of natural law.[129] The whole ambition of *NLNR*, says Finnis, is to consider the internal viewpoint from the perspective of the 'practically reasonable' person (the *spoudaios*) – that is to say, the person who deliberates upon and seeks to act in accordance with and for 'the flourishing of all human persons and groups'.[130] This explains why he framed his

123. Finnis, *Philosophy of Law*, 51.

124. Finnis, 'Reflections and Responses', 464; Finnis, *Philosophy of Law*, 119, 234.

125. Hart, *The Concept of Law*, 313; Finnis, *Philosophy of Law*, 120.

126. Hart, *The Concept of Law*, 313.

127. Ibid., 193. It is a truism, says Hart that, in general, humankind desire to live. Thus, one can infer that human survival is a 'contingent fact' and should, therefore, be protected by law. Ibid., 191.

128. Ibid., 188.

129. Finnis, *The Philosophy of Law*, 256.

130. Ibid., 120; Finnis, *NLNR*, 15.

own seminal contribution to natural law in terms of 'reasons for action'.[131] In fact, this proposition becomes what is arguably the theoretical fulcrum of the NNLT.

Hart's Titular Imperative

Besides influencing the epistemological (non-metaphysical) roots of Finnis's NNLT, it is no secret that Hart had an instructive influence over *NLNR*. In fact, in his capacity as the then editor of the Clarendon Series, Hart prescribed its title, making it emphatically clear to his former student that he wanted a book on *Natural Law* that also addressed the notion of *Natural Rights*.[132] The instruction to include the conjunction – *&* (*Natural Rights*) – is itself significant even if, on first blush, it might appear rather inconsequential. In the postscript to *NLNR*, Finnis revealed that Hart had once met with the Catholic legal philosopher and historian, Michel Villey, and received a copy of *Lecons d'histoire de philosophie du droit* (1957), which he read and then passed on to Finnis. Through a sophisticated genealogical analysis, Villey considered the subjectivism of natural rights to be a parasitical corruption of the objectivism of scholastic-Thomistic natural law. Although this debate is complex, the underlying point of contestation is surprisingly simple: either the tradition of natural law is antithetical to the contemporary notion of natural rights and it is, therefore, extraneous to the thought of Aquinas, or natural law and natural rights can be harmoniously reconciled with each other and with the Thomistic tradition.[133]

Beyond specifying that the book on natural law address the topic of natural rights, Finnis says that Hart 'never gave the least indication of what he hoped the book would or would not say.'[134] Nevertheless, the conjunction within the prescribed title certainly had a programmatic effect. For Finnis states that '[a]lmost everything in this book [*NLNR*] is about human rights ('human rights' being a contemporary idiom for 'natural rights').'[135] In keeping with his strategy of meeting his secular interlocutors as and where (he thinks) they are, defending the value of

131. As Robert George has observed: 'Much of what Finnis would go onto achieve in legal and political philosophy would be rooted in critical engagement with Hart's thought.' This is because 'Finnis takes on board Hart's key insights … and pushes them to their logical conclusions.' Robert George, 'The Achievement of John Finnis', in *Reason, Morality, and Law*, ed. John Keown and Robert P. George (Oxford: OUP, 2013), 3.

132. Finnis, *NLNR*, 414–15.

133. For a good overview of this debate from the perspective of a Catholic theologian who believes rights are antithetical to natural law see: Tracey Rowland, 'The Case Against the Marriage of Natural Law & Natural Rights', in *The Cambridge Handbook of Natural Law and Human Rights*, ed. Tom Angier, *Iain T. Benson* (Cambridge: CUP, 2023), 74–87.

134. Finnis, *NLNR*, 415.

135. Ibid., 198. However, in his reply to Fortin, Finnis acknowledges that his attention to 'natural rights' only occupies a 'small part (albeit a very important one)' of his book. C.f. Finnis, 'Grounding Human Rights in Natural Law', 205 fn. 16.

the ubiquitous modern grammar of rights would no doubt be warmly received by Hart *et al.* Certainly, there is nothing inherently problematic with maintaining an openness to the dialogical advantages of using such a widely recognized phrase. Nevertheless, it is valuable to consider the extent to which Finnis's strategic rapprochement between natural law and natural rights is primarily motivated by his wish to gain Aquinas a seat at the 'jurisprudential table'.[136]

Fortin's principal grievance with *NLNR* was that he considered the introduction of natural rights to be a pernicious attack on the metaphysics of the natural law tradition, arguing that it originated out of libertarian – Hobbesian –voluntarism. But what Fortin takes to be an illegitimate blurring of philosophically irreconcilable discourses, Finnis defends as simply the elucidation of the fact that Aquinas had already *'got there first'*, that is to say, the language of 'rights' is of Thomistic provenance.[137] For even if Aquinas never used the term 'human rights' or 'natural rights', according to Finnis, 'he clearly has the concept.'[138] 'For he articulates a series of precepts or norms of justice which concern, he says, what is owed to everyone alike.'[139] A correct translation of '*ius*', then, is subjective 'rights',[140] which Aquinas uses to denote the conclusions of practical reason and the 'demands of justice'.[141]

By bringing the language of law and rights together, Finnis is proffering a genealogical challenge against the popular narrative that interlinks the advent of rights with the advent of 'Enlightenment secularism.' He believes that it is Aquinas's theory of justice, where rights are considered to be correlative with duties and *vice versa*, that was usurped and eschewed by Hobbes and his regressive philosophical successors. It is the task of *NLNR* to demolish Hobbes's notion of rights whilst simultaneously explaining to its secular enthusiasts that Aquinas already spoke their language in a more logical and rational manner, owing to the fact that his account of rights is underpinned by basic values, which, rather than being predicated upon something akin to a Hobbesian will-to-power or speculative metaphysics, reflects 'aspects of the real well-being of flesh-and-blood individuals.'[142]

Regrettably, according to Finnis, such intricacies were disregarded, especially by those Thomists who remained obdurately inattentive to his conscious efforts to discern an appropriate linguistic register – one that might serve to circumvent the hostility that the modern 'cultured despisers' associate 'with the past'.[143] Yet, this acknowledgement suggests that Finnis's strong desire to harmonize natural law and natural rights within the Thomistic tradition was a rhetorical precaution lest

136. Brian Leiter, 'The End of Empire', *Rutgers Law Journal*, vol. 36 (2004–5), 165.
137. Finnis, 'Grounding Human Rights in Natural Law', 200. (IAITT)
138. Finnis, *NLNR*, 206; Finnis, *Aquinas*, 136.
139. Finnis, *Philosophy of Law*, 107.
140. Finnis, 'Grounding Human Rights in Natural Law', 214.
141. Finnis, *NLNR*, 210.
142. Ibid., 225.
143. Finnis, 'Grounding Human Rights in Natural Law', 201.

an exclusive recourse to the parlance of natural law be too sullied by its purported religio-metaphysical inheritance.[144]

For love or for approval?

To what degree did Hart's forced titular conjunction inform Finnis's own expectations as to how he can bring natural law back into vogue within his liberal-secular milieu? A preliminary clue can be gleaned from the original and unpublished project outline of *NLNR*, drafted in 1968. In this early document, Finnis says that the book will be 'guided by the view, thoroughly developed by recent historians, that…human rights have developed by way of 'differentiation' of the primitive concepts of the order of the world and of law.'[145] The brevity of the outline only serves to intensify the prominence of this statement, indicating how conscious Finnis was of the Hartian-secular attitude that championed human rights as a concept of 'differentiation' from the 'primitive' concept of natural law. Finnis reacts to this sensibility by strategically trying to dissolve this point of 'differentiation' by explaining how '[n]atural law stands to natural rights, not as something "quite different", but as premises stand to entailments.'[146] Could this not be interpreted as an astute attempt to convey the religio-metaphysical independence of natural law by translating its conclusions into the more universally acceptable 'liberal-secular' discourse of human rights?

Subsequent remarks signal towards the possibility that Finnis's re-presentation of Thomistic thought is, once again, being controlled here by his engagement with Hart and the secular *mythos*. In his reply to the criticisms levelled at his theory by 'Conservative Thomists' like Fortin, Finnis becomes relatively coy about his interest in natural rights, stating in the first line that '*NLNR* says nothing about rights until the eighth of its thirteen chapters.'[147] One might conclude, then, that the book is unbalanced, especially considering that the titular conjunction gives the impression that natural law and natural rights will be afforded an equivalent treatment in terms of length and scope. However, when addressing the 'cultured despisers' in *NLNR*, Finnis is quick to declare that almost everything in *NLNR* is about human rights.[148] This disparity gives clear indication of the way in which his intended audience influences and inflects the way he reads and re-presents the tradition.

144. Ibid.

145. John Finnis, 'Outline of the book on Natural Law and Natural Rights' (1968), reproduced and published as an Appendix in: Santiago Legarre, 'HLA Hart and the Making of the NNLT', *Jurisprudence*, vol. 8, no. 1 (2017), 97.

146. Finnis, 'Grounding Human Rights in Natural Law', 199.

147. Ibid., 199.

148. It is worth reciting the quotation referred to above where Finnis states that '[a]lmost everything in this book [*NLNR*] is about human rights ('human rights' being a contemporary idiom for 'natural rights').' Ibid., 198.

Returning to *NLNR*, the fact that the discussion of natural/human rights is left to one of the latter chapters makes one suspicious about whether its inclusion is more of a 'signal to the secular' than an organic development of his NNLT. For the upshot of this conclusion is that the language of liberalism (by which I mean the liberal penchant for a *lingua* of human rights) need not be rejected but can find an alternative derivation from within the tradition of natural law itself. Finnis seems to admit to the newness of this language when he asserts that '[t]he fact that theology is now *articulated* in terms of rights as well as duties changes its propositional content not at all.'[149] However, if this is the case, does it not imply that the inclusion of natural rights is merely a linguistic trope designed to guise 'theology' so as to capture the approval of the secular imagination? Again, in principle, there is absolutely nothing wrong with wanting to find new and innovative ways to express ancient truths. The concern I am raising here is not so much what Finnis describes as the marrying of natural law and natural rights 'for love', but whether 'for love' is in fact a euphemism for 'secular approval' – motivated by a programmatic desire to marry Catholic political thought with political liberalism.[150] If so, then one can rightly question the legitimacy and tenability of this arranged marriage since it would wholly depend upon the legitimacy and tenability of Finnis's construction of the secular *mythos*, not to mention the legitimacy and tenability of using the natural law tradition for such purposes. The fundamental point is that there is strong evidence to suggest that Hart's titular imperative became a reactionary focal point with which the story of Thomistic natural law could be rewritten as the story of the wedding between Catholicism and secular liberalism.[151] '[T]his is not polygamy', exclaims Finnis.[152] For Thomistic natural law and the popular *lingua* of natural rights 'are not two distinct realities'; rather, they are 'two aspects of – two ways of talking about – one and the same fruitful object of reasonable love and devotion.'[153]

Is god really necessary?

What is left 'unsaid' by Finnis is that there is a discernible price for marrying these two ways of speaking within contemporary jurisprudence according to the terms he has seemingly embraced. For even if natural law and natural rights are simply two, almost synonymous, expressions for one objective level of reality,

149. Ibid., 218. (Underlining is my own.) (IAITT) Has Finnis accidentally let 'theology' slip in here?

150. Ibid., 213.

151. My claim would even be supported, rather ironically, by Ryan Anderson and Daniel Philpott's recent collaborative essay, which defends Finnis' position on natural rights. C.f. Daniel Philpott and Ryan T. Anderson, 'Introduction', in *A Liberalism Safe for Catholicism* (Notre Dame, IN: Notre Dame University Press, 2017), 17.

152. Finnis, 'Grounding Human Rights in Natural Law', 213.

153. Ibid., 214.

the structure of *NLNR* nevertheless attests to the existence of a *duplex-ordo* understanding of reality. In the postscript to *NLNR*, Finnis touches upon the controversy surrounding the final chapter, which is also the *only* chapter of Part III. The title of the chapter, 'Nature, Reason, and God', provides a formidable clue as to why it became a notable point of conversation between Finnis and Hart. Influencing its final place within the book's structure was one of the substantive interventions that Hart made.[154]

The central argument of Chapter XIII is that, whilst it is not logically necessary, it would nevertheless not be unreasonable to aspire to go beyond the limitations of an exclusively analytical understanding of the basic values and moral requirements of the natural law. Having recourse only to 'natural reasoning', he says, 'leaves somehow "subjective" and "questionable" the whole structure of basic principles and requirements of practical reasonableness and human flourishing.'[155] Following Francis Bacon's avowal 'that a little philosophy inclineth man's mind to atheism; but depth in philosophy bringeth men's minds about to religion', Finnis says that the final chapters of his significant texts (*NLNR* and *Aquinas*) offerexplicit argumentation for such a conclusion.[156] This is because there is a level of rational instability that impels one to postulate in practical terms about what Finnis rather floridly calls '[f]urther questions about the point of human existence.'[157]

In a characteristically Kantian fashion, natural reasoning can 'speculatively postulate that the uncaused cause exists in something like the mode of personal life', which then 'permits the speculating thinker to hope that the uncaused cause might reveal itself to be lovable, and that the "ideal observer" which practical reasonableness postulates as a test of arbitrariness might prove to have a real and substantial counterpart.'[158] The point being that such theological postulates about the divine authorship and causality of the natural law, without deflating or contradicting the free-standing normative conclusions arrived at through the free-standing exercise of practical reason, nevertheless, provide a deeper reason for 'the point of living according to the requirements of practical reasonableness'.[159] Is this not, then, an example of understanding seeking faith?

Hart didn't buy the noumenal medicine. In a letter written to Finnis in April 1977, he expressed concern over the 'God-chapter', which was originally to be chapter ten. 'Is God (I mean the chapter on) really necessary?', he asked.[160] A motivating reason for Hart's apprehension was that he found the chapter to be

154. Finnis, *NLNR*, 415.

155. Ibid., 405.

156. Finnis, *Religion & Public Reason*, 1. In nearly all of Finnis' major works on natural law, the final chapter is dedicated to addressing further, theologically imbued, questions.

157. Finnis, *NLNR*, 371.

158. Ibid., 406.

159. Ibid., 405.

160. See Legarre, 'HLA Hart and the Making of the NNLT', 92.

'*tremendously difficult*', which, from a commercial perspective, 'may deter readers (lawyer) *buyers* by making them fear they cannot understand I–IX without…X.'[161] He then suggested that this religio-metaphysical chapter should be disentangled from the book proper and, if it had to remain, be placed as an appendix. Finnis's compromise was to structure the book as it is found in its current form. Chapter X became Chapter XIII, the final and only chapter of what is an entirely separate 'Part' to the book (Part III).

Some might think the coercing influence of Hart on this matter to be, again, rather innocuous. Yet, there is a powerful theological 'unsaid' at work here, the implication of which is that the reality of natural law is, even on Thomistic grounds, ontologically detachable from both reference to the eternal law and to divine governance. In a conversation for Hart's biography, Finnis acknowledged that he was indeed originally trying to present 'a theological basis for the book's argument' but was worried that this 'might undermine the book as a work of philosophy.'[162] Thus, Finnis's impression of the secular *mythos* clearly inflects the understanding conveyed in *NLNR* regarding the disciplinary relationship between philosophy and theology. It is a relationship of 'either-or' not 'both-and'. Conclusively, whilst Finnis might be justified in his claim that *NLNR* is not an example of epistemological polygamy, he might not be able to altogether dismiss the presence of an extra-ontological affair. Specifically, an affair between Aquinas, now being read as the 'first liberal', and the liberal-secular *mythos*, now being constructed – in implicit accordance with Hart's coercing directive – as a metaphysically dissociated and theologically dissevered hermetic reality.

Germain Grisez's insight(s)

One could summarize the influence that Hart had over Finnis's NNLT by saying that he stipulated (even if just implicitly) a basic criterion that (Thomistic) natural law would need to meet in order to be reconciled with modern-analytical jurisprudence – the most obvious criterion being that natural law should rediscover its secular roots so as to disentangle and detach itself from a theological-metaphysical setting. If so, should Finnis have declined the invitation to sup at the 'jurisprudential table' on such terms?

Mark C. Murphy, another prominent natural law theorist, certainly believes so. Murphy contends that if the invitation demands the espousal of a jurisprudence detached from its theological presuppositions, then one should refuse to dine.[163] Yet, Murphy also makes two conjunctive claims, specifically about the 'God chapter' in *NLNR*. The first claim is interpretative: that, within the context of *NLNR*, Chapter XIII is best read as being largely detached from its otherwise jurisprudential and

161. Ibid., 92, 94. (IAITT).

162. Nicola Lacey, *A Life of H. L. A Hart* (Oxford: OUP, 2006), 347.

163. C.f. Finnis, 'Grounds of Law and Legal Theory', 339–44; Mark C. Murphy, 'Finnis on Nature, Reason, and God', *Legal Theory*, vol. 13 (2007), 187–209.

ethical content. The second claim is evaluative: that the philosophical arguments presented in Chapter XIII have proven to be unpersuasive. According to Murphy, recognition of these two points instigated an unacknowledged change in the direction of Finnis's post-*NLNR* trajectory. Interpretively, Finnis's subsequent work on natural law exhibits the cessation of trying to detach theism from natural law. Evaluatively, given that Finnis was already trying to find a way to situate and stabilize his basic goods theory in a wider theistic context, he was right to go on to make the intrinsicality of that explanatory relationship explicit.[164]

With certain nuances, Finnis responded positively to Murphy's assessment. First, he agreed that *NLNR* declined to make an explicatory argument that linked the basic goods to the '*goodness*' of God. Second, he also concurred that in his later work (especially in *Aquinas*), he does explain in more robust – non-detached – terms how our pluralistic and diverse participation in the basic goods is also expressive of our participation in the divine nature.[165]

These issues point towards the pre-eminent 'unsaid' I am wanting to raise in this chapter: Finnis's ascription to an extrinsicist anthropology and a *duplex-ordo* ontology. Here, it is important to discuss the influence of Germain Grisez upon the composition of *NLNR* and on Finnis's post-*NLNR* work. *Contra* Murphy, I will argue that there actually was no substantive change towards non-detachability in Finnis's later work. Once Grisez's influence is adequately appreciated, it will become clear that there was only a continuing attachment to the secular *mythos* and the distillation of the same theological 'unsaid' that was already at work in *NLNR*, albeit in incipient form. If Hart prescribed the criteria for developing a genuinely 'secular' theory of natural law, I will show that it was Grisez who supplied Finnis with the theological insight(s) he needed to reconcile Aquinas's theory of natural law with this criterion. Such was the significance of this insight that it would become known as the 'critical moment' in the development of his NNLT.

A theological principle for secular engagement

Bernard Lonergan said that 'only the theologian can affirm a natural desire to see God; a philosopher has to be content with paradox.'[166] In the same way that Finnis would swiftly move to rebuke any suggestion that his approach to natural law was 'new', equally, he would rebuke any suggestion that this approach ends in 'paradox'. One way he might respond to this is by drawing attention to the thought of Grisez, a theologian, who he believes proffered a philosophically coherent – that is to say, unparadoxical – interpretation of Aquinas that affirms the existence of a free-standing natural end to human life.

164. Ibid., 202.

165. Finnis, 'Grounds of Law and Legal Theory', 342.

166. Bernard Lonergan, *Collected Works of Bernard Lonergan: Collection*, ed. Frederick E. Crowe and Robert M. Doran (Toronto: University of Toronto Press, 1988), 84.

Grisez's influence upon Finnis's contribution to natural law is well-documented.[167] In terms of his intellectual biography, his encounter with Grisez's work in 1965 was 'the critical moment' that made it possible for him to deploy Aquinas's treatise on law in a manner that, he believed, would be found palatable by Hart and his other analytical colleagues.[168] This is because Grisez provided 'the outlines of an adequate theory of first principles of practical reason, principles which [Bernard Lonergan's] *Insight* had spoken of but manifestly failed to articulate or even accurately to conceive.'[169]

The philosophical character of Finnis's recourse to such principles has recently been questioned by Nicholas Bamforth and David Richards. Frustrated by a general insouciance towards exploring the dependence of *NLNR* upon Grisez's work, they have sought to redress this oversight, arguing that the logical force of Finnis's professedly 'secular' approach is thwarted by an underhanded collusion with what are inexorably 'theological' and 'doctrinal' presuppositions.[170]

Although I share Bamforth's and Richard's fundamental supposition, it is perhaps slightly churlish to argue for the non-detachability of *NLNR* from Grisez's contribution as a theologian by focusing upon the fact that Finnis and Grisez (i) have collaborated extensively together and (ii) both affirm interpretations of Catholic moral teachings that they (and many others) find 'sexist', 'homophobic', and, therefore, 'unappealing'.[171] As they state in their conclusion, for example, 'As our analyses show … Finnis's scheme of basic goods and requirements of practical reasonableness, as set out in *NLNR*, is very largely an application of the scheme devised by Germain Grisez.'[172] The implication is that Finnis is attributed 'guilt by association', an argument which even the feminist natural law theologian, Cristina Traina, challenged as tending towards 'overkill'.[173] As she rightly points out, such an investigation is only useful to the extent that it serves to illuminate the critical moves in Finnis's own jurisprudence.[174]

This is the intention for including Grisez in this discussion. For what Bamforth and Richard overlooked is what has continually been left 'unsaid' in nearly all of the major responses to *NLNR* – namely, that Grisez's account of practical reason provided Finnis with the *theological* principle he needed to legitimate what he believed a 'secular' natural law argument should look like. In what is arguably the foundational essay of the NNLT, 'The First Principle of Practical Reason', Grisez

167. See, for instance, Finnis, *NLNR*, vii.

168. George 'The Achievement of John Finnis', 2.

169. Finnis and Grisez, 'About John Finnis'.

170. Nicholas Bamforth, David A. J. Richards, *Patriarchal Religion, Sexuality and Gender: A Critique of New Natural Law* (Cambridge: CUP, 2009), 3.

171. Ibid., 228.

172. Ibid., 335.

173. Cristina Traina, 'Book Review of *Patriarchal Religion, Sexuality and Gender*', *Journal of Law and Religion*, vol. 25, no. 1 (2009–10), 311.

174. Ibid.

boldly asserts that 'Natural law does not direct man to his supernatural end.'[175] In fact, a faithful exegesis of Aquinas would render any interpretation to the contrary absurd since natural law consists exclusively of a series of self-evident precepts of natural reason which direct man to a free-standing and indeterminate natural end. As he writes, 'Because the specific last end is not determined for him by nature, man is able to make the basic commitment which orients his entire life.'[176]

In his theological *magnum opus*, in the preparations for which he was closely assisted by Finnis, Grisez would go on to affirm a quintessentially extrinsicist or two-tiered anthropological position on the *desiderium naturale*:

> My contention is that the human heart is not naturally oriented towards adoption as a child of God and the heavenly inheritance which goes with this status. It is naturally oriented towards human fulfilment, which is found in human goods in which one naturally can participate more and more. Most important, the Christian need not accept an Augustinian or Thomistic version of Neo-Platonism, with its supposition that the human heart is naturally insatiable by human fulfilment, and naturally drawn to fulfilment in the Beatific Vision of God.[177]

Since human beings are created without the *capax Dei*, the capacity to choose one's 'ultimate concrete end' is not only dependent upon a strict *duplex-ordo* understanding of the relationship between the natural and the supernatural end, but it also necessitates that doing natural law is understood as a distinctly practical activity – operationally autonomous from the exercise of, or recourse to, theoretical reason/knowledge.[178]

This two-tiered understanding of both human destiny and the human intellect also translates into a two-tiered understanding of the human good. Grisez elucidates that, while Aquinas 'emphasises end as a principle of natural law', he also held that such end(s) 'cannot be identified with moral goodness itself.'[179] Grasping this distinction is considered by Grisez to be of critical importance both

175. Germain Grisez, 'The First Principle of Practical Reason: A Commentary on the *Summa Theologiae*, 1–2, Question 94, Article 2', *Natural Law Forum*, vol. 168 (1965), 184.

176. Ibid., 200.

177. Germain Grisez, *The Way of the Lord Jesus. Volume 1* (Chicago: Franciscan Press, 1997), 809–10.

178. As I noted in the discussion of the three 'critical moves', the bifurcation of the practical and speculative intellect, which neatly corresponds with the distinction in jurisprudence between 'ought' and 'is', is necessary to preserve the poly-teleological character of human choice. Finnis, *NLNR*, 37. It is also noteworthy that Finnis was also attracted to this reading of Aquinas because he believed that secular modern philosophy was concurrently taken a second look at what is meant by 'practical knowledge'. C.f. Finnis, *FoE*, 2.

179. Grisez, 'The First Principle of Practical Reason', 187.

to understanding Aquinas's treatise on the end of humankind and to understand why advocates of the NNLT detach natural law from theology. In relation to the aforestated quotation, a distinction is developed between the pre-moral (meaning that which is not the product of moral reflection and possessing no moral significance prior to choice), self-evident, first principles of practical reason – the master principle of which is, 'Good is to be done and pursed, and evil is to be avoided' – and the first principles of morality. The former concerns the intelligibility of the human good (the practical truth of the basic goods), whereas the latter concerns human fulfilment (moral truth). Furthermore, on Grisez's reading, Aquinas's natural law presupposes that 'the first principle of practical reason is the last end' and 'expressly identifies the principles of practical reason with the ends of the virtues pre-existing in reason.'[180] Such (ultimate) end(s), nevertheless, provide an 'extrinsic foundation' for directing moral courses of action.[181]

Integral human fulfilment

Grisez would develop the idea that our knowledge of the first principles of practical reason (what *might* be done) specifies the first principle of morality (FPM) (what *ought* to be done). According to the 1987 formulation, the FPM states, 'In voluntarily acting for human goods and avoiding what is opposed to them, one ought to choose and otherwise will those and only those possibilities whose willing is compatible with a will toward integral human fulfillment.'[182] The important phrase to highlight here is 'integral human fulfilment'. This 'ideal', as the ultimate object of the moral will, is clarified by Grisez as the 'ultimate end' of a 'potentially universal community.'[183]

Yet, clarity gives way to complexity when Grisez proceeds to make a number of subsequent caveats. For instance, that 'integral human fulfilment' 'is not a supreme good, beyond the basic human goods' and that it 'cannot refer to a purpose to be pursued as a concrete objective of cooperative human effort.'[184] Thus, on the one hand, the decision to incorporate a defined 'ultimate natural end' into the FPM answers to the practical need for a teleological orientation with which to measure the moral implications of our participation in the basic goods. Hence, the NNL theorists describe 'integral human fulfilment' as 'the nearest thing to what morally

180. Ibid., 183.

181. Ibid.

182. Finnis, Grisez and Boyle, 'PMU', 128.

183. Germain Grisez, 'Natural Law and the Transcendent Source of Human Fulfilment', in *Reason, Morality, and Law*, ed. John Keown and Robert P. George (Oxford: OUP, 2013), 450–1.

184. John Finnis, Joseph M. Boyle and Germain Grisez, 'A Sounder Theory of Morality', in *The Historical Development of Fundamental Moral Theology in The United States*, ed., Charles E. Curran and Richard A. McCormick (New York: Paulist Press, 1999), 207; Finnis, Grisez and Boyle, 'PMU', 132.

good people mean by happiness.'[185] In this sense, the function of 'integral human fulfilment' is analogous, albeit now in theologically abstracted ('secular') terms, to the *ultimus finis* in Aquinas.[186] Yet, on the other hand, the practical purpose of this ideal – that is to say, its rectification of the order of the will – is seemingly undone by their insistence that it is an 'unrealisable ideal', and, in that sense, it doesn't exist.[187] At best, therefore, we are back to Kantian territory of postulating regulative ideals so that practical reason can find conclusive, non-theological, grounds to deliberate morally about what ought to be done.

The difficulty with this position is that it lacks any teleological basis with which to bridge the movement from self-evident first principles to very specific moral norms.[188] How does one logically progress from an irreducible and incommensurable plurality of pre-moral basic goods to an elaborate defence of moral absolutes? This dilemma has caused some legal scholars, Pauline Westermann being a notable example, to question whether the identification of the basic goods is actually predetermined by an 'unsaid' speculative-theological vision of what constitutes human perfection. To put this another way, it is '[b]ecause they are perfective of man's nature, they are regarded as intrinsic values'.[189] Westermann is suspicious that the NNL theorists are actually clandestine perpetrators of the naturalistic fallacy, believing they are 'pretending that the basic goods are first selected on the basis of their "self-evidence", and only afterwards 'happen' to be perfective of human nature.'[190] But the issue I would raise here is whether this two-tiered account of the human good is actually what allows for the basic goods to be understood anthropocentrically, without necessary regard for one's (supernatural) vocation and dignity as *imago Dei*. From a theological perspective, the attraction of embracing this extrinsicist position is that it would allow for an anthropocentric natural law to exist even within Christian theology.

185. Finnis, Grisez and Boyle, 'PMU', 132.

186. But contrary to Grisez's and Finnis' claims, the *ultimus finis* in God forms the foundation of our freedom. For '[f]inal and perfect happiness can consist in nothing else than the vision of the Divine Essence' (ST I-II q.3 a.8). It is for this reason that Aquinas speaks of our natural inclination towards the ultimate good as an *instinctus rationis* – the first expression of the natural – since it provides the inner light that moves the will towards true freedom in eternal beatitude. C.f. Servais Pinckaers, *The Pinckaers Reader* (Washington, DC: Catholic University of America, 2005), 170.

187. Finnis, Grisez and Boyle, 'PMU', 133. I am grateful to Fulvio Di Blasi's essay for helping me to phrase this problematic. C.f. Fulvio Di Blasi, 'Ultimate End, Human Freedom, and Beatitude', *The American Journal of Jurisprudence*, vol. 46 (2001), 122 fn. 33.

188. C.f. Tracey Rowland, *Catholic Theology* (London: Bloomsbury, 2017), 76.

189. Pauline Westermann, *The Disintegration of Natural Law: Aquinas to Finnis* (Leiden: Brill, 1998), 254.

190. Ibid., 255.

Finnis's 'freestanding' Aquinas

Finnis's encounter with Grisez's work had a powerful influence upon his decision to incorporate and affirm a dualistic or two-tiered structure in *NLNR*. A significant piece of confirmatory evidence for this can be extrapolated from a consideration of the original structure outlined in the 1968 schema for the book. The important point to note is that, according to the1968 schema, Finnis had originally intended to dedicate the sixth of fourteen chapters to a discussion of 'Man "in the image of God"', wherein he would imbed, among other things, a discussion of the first principles of practical reason.[191] One might reasonably speculate that, at this particular juncture, Finnis was attempting to maintain an integrated understanding of how the goodness of God relates to and informs the intelligibility of the natural law. However, by 1977, the original schema had been radically reshaped. (As noted, an entirely separate 'God chapter' was written, and it was extricated to the end – rather than remaining at the structural heart – of the book.) Given that it was during 1974–1975 that Finnis had the opportunity to work closely with Grisez on overtly theological matters, it is very likely that it was during this time that he became increasingly familiar with his thoughts on the *desiderium naturale* and, implicitly perhaps, the idea of a *duplex-ordo* account of the natural law.[192]

One could say that if Hart influenced the way in which Finnis constructs the secular *mythos*, then it is the influence of Grisez which gave him the intellectual tools he needed to engage it. For, ostensibly, a *duplex-ordo* understanding of reality, which corresponds to a strict renunciation of an *ultimus finis* in God, gives a theological justification for disentangling the secular from the metaphysico-religious in natural law theory, a task which Hart's genealogy of the origins of natural law deemed worthwhile. But perhaps most importantly, it was this fundamental 'unsaid' that underscored Finnis's conviction that his protreptic speech on natural law – predicated upon the philosophical intelligibility of the three 'critical moves' – would be found compelling to its erstwhile 'cultured despisers'.

Theologically entwined

Contra Murphy, I do not believe there is any evidence to suggest that Finnis has deviated from this original conviction in his later work. This is because I do not believe Finnis's later work evidences a shift away from detaching theology from natural law. In the Preface to *Aquinas* (the book that Murphy cites as proof of this shift), Finnis not only reveals the fact that *NLNR* is rooted in Grisez's 're-presentation' of classical thought, but that, since 1965, 'Grisez's major writings have not claimed to be interpretations of Aquinas.'[193] Rather, he has regarded Aquinas' work 'as the

191. Finnis, 'Outline of the book on Natural Law and Natural Rights' (1968) in Lazarre, 'HLA Hart and the Making of the NNLT', 97.

192. See: Germain Grisez, 'My Collaboration with John Finnis', Publication Date Unknown, http://www.twotlj.org/Finnis.html. Accessed on 2 February 2019.

193. Finnis, *Aquinas*, ix.

point of departure for a free-standing philosophical treatment of ethical theory'.[194] Finnis then goes on to say that he has 'collaborated extensively with Grisez in this free-standing work' and that writing this book, *Aquinas*, 'has confirmed my previous understanding of the foundational principles (and Aquinas' subscription to them).'[195]

Even a cursory examination of the contents of *Aquinas* attests to an ongoing employment of a two-tiered structure. The first nine chapters focus exclusively on those aspects of Aquinas's thought which are 'purely philosophical', and only the final chapter is dedicated to discussing 'some elements of his theology, and of the case for accepting them as the philosophical inquiry's appropriate completion and supplement'.[196] Hence, the same theologically detached structure employed in *NLNR* is also employed in *Aquinas*. The only difference is that the deliberately detached final chapter of *Aquinas* includes a more explicit and expansive treatment of pending theological questions, such as why practical reason is (paradoxically) oriented to *beatitudo imperfecta*?[197]

Structural issues aside, Finnis's *Aquinas* does include a much clearer and comprehensive attunement to the theological principles that underpinned the philosophy of detachment in *NLNR*. Two points are of particular relevance. First, after admitting that Aquinas's interest actually centred upon *beatitudo perfecta*, he still gives overarching attention to distinguishing and clarifying *beatitudo imperfecta*. This denotes a clear instance where Finnis has chosen to follow Grisez over Aquinas. For whilst Aquinas did accept that the natural end and the supernatural end are distinct, and therefore different, this distinction is an epistemological abstraction and not the reification of two *separate* realities. Aquinas still held that every human being is in concrete reality ordained to an eternal happiness that is not proportionate to our natural faculties:

> [I]f man were ordained to no other end than that which is proportionate to his natural faculties, there would be no need for man to have any further direction on the part of his reason besides the natural law and the human law which is derived from it.[198]

A second point of close attunement to Grisez's thought found in *Aquinas* is the detailed incorporation and further elaboration of the idea of 'integral human fulfilment'. Finnis admits that his decision not to include this ideal in *NLNR* was influenced in part by a desire not to offend the pluralistic tastes of his liber-secular audience.[199] However, in *Fundamentals in Ethics*, published in 1983, Finnis

194. Ibid.
195. Ibid.
196. Ibid., vii.
197. Ibid., 295.
198. ST I-II q. 91, a. 4.
199. Finnis, Grisez and Boyle, 'PMU', 150.

acknowledged that he had been looking for a way to develop Aquinas' moral theology of natural law into a complete philosophical ethics, calling this ideal 'the gap which Aquinas failed to fill.'[200] Finnis explains that Aquinas evidenced the moral intelligibility of the normative precepts of the natural law by referring to the witness of revelation. Hence, for reasons likely pertaining to historical circumstance, he never felt the need to formulate an integrally philosophical exposition of practical wisdom.[201]

The history of moral philosophy (as distinct from moral theology) is, according to Finnis, the search for the 'missing intermediate principles.'[202] In *NLNR*, Finnis referred to nine 'requirements of practical reasonableness' and admitted in an endnote that he is indebted to Grisez for the differentiation and analysis of these requirements, describing his contribution as representative of 'a major advance in the philosophical analysis of natural law.'[203] Initially, Finnis had stressed a strong reluctance to proffer a master moral principle as a basis with which to unify these principles, fearing that it would be misinterpreted as a return to is–ought reductivism.[204] But by the time he wrote *Aquinas*, Finnis includes discussion of what he terms 'the highest morally binding principle' – not God but, in agreement with Grisez, 'integral human fulfilment'.[205] Practically speaking, Finnis believes Aquinas orientated the moral life around 'virtue in action' as opposed to the *summum bonum* (divine end).[206] Unlike Grisez, who is at least prepared to admit that his view on practical reason diverges from that of Aquinas, Finnis argues that wherever Aquinas ties human fulfilment to contemplation of God, he is actually referring to a complete and integral synthesis of all of the basic goods.[207] In his 'Aquinas Lecture' delivered at Blackfriars, Oxford, in 1985, he warned against reading Aquinas's 'elliptical' remarks on God as the ultimate end 'literally', reiterating instead that 'man's true last end is integral human fulfilment.'[208] Even more recently, Finnis reiterated 'how a strictly philosophical moral philosophy (ethics) needs and has a unifying "last end"'.[209] He then continued to elaborate that this 'last end' is 'not an end-state whether in this world or the next, but an ideal of practical reason – integral human fulfilment, not as goal of any plan or project, but as an ideal against which options can be measured as open to such fulfilment

200. Finnis, *FoE*, 69.

201. Ibid., 69.

202. Ibid., 70.

203. Finnis, *NLNR*, 100–27, 129.

204. Finnis, *FoE*, 70.

205. Finnis, *Aquinas*, 104, 117.

206. Ibid., 107.

207. Ibid., 85–6. Finnis and Grisez admit to this divergence, suggesting that Finnis' view is closer to that of Aquinas. C.f. Finnis, Grisez and Boyle, 'PMU', 151.

208. John Finnis, 'Aquinas Lecture 1985: Practical Reasoning, Human Goods and the End of Man', *New Blackfriars*, vol. 66. no. 784 (October 1985), 443, 445.

209. Finnis, *Reason in Action*, 12.

or not open to it, and thus as fully reasonable (morally sound) or more or less unreasonable (immoral).'[210] This interpretation represents another balancing act between wanting to be received as a faithful Thomist and wanting Aquinas to be respected by his liberal-secular interlocutors.

In light of this discussion, there comes to the surface a theological 'unsaid', which, rather ironically, renders Murphy's otherwise erroneous claim coherent. For what my analysis has shown is that Finnis's position has always been, and has increasingly become, theologically entwined, but entwined with a theologically extrinsicist anthropology that ripostes the traditional Augustinian position on the *desiderium naturale*, as well as being dependent upon a *duplex-ordo* reading of Aquinas's theory of the *summum bonum*, the fundaments of which he has appropriated from Grisez's account of practical reason. These questionable theological perspectives illuminate the strategic thought that lies behind the three 'critical moves', giving them a theological intelligibility that they would otherwise lack even if the origins of that intelligibility have been left 'unsaid'.

Section V: Hermeneutical tools

A hermeneutical proceduralism

Finnis's clear but unspoken ascription to a two-tiered or *duplex-ordo* construction of reality supports and mirrors his perception of what he previously called the 'secular measure' and later, after his conversion, describes as the 'perennial Catholic doctrine' – according to which 'the secular and religious realms exist in parallel, within the heart and mind of the believer and in public forms – church and state – each free from the supervisory management of the other.'[211] Given what has already been discussed, it is not hard to see why he esteemed this distinction as 'perennial' and why he would want to claim it as 'Catholic'. Without it, his strategic defence of the public character of natural law as a theory of reasons for action would be threatened if not entirely undone. Hence, it is also unsurprising that Finnis believes the 'first condition' for a Catholic to be able to participate in 'public policy deliberations and debates' is to be 'quite clear about the relations between faith and reason'.[212]

To understand the theo-cultural significance of this point, I now want to draw attention to a series of hermeneutical tools which (although left 'unsaid' in *NLNR*) Finnis utilizes to augment an extrinsicist reading of faith and reason in Aquinas. This will reveal, even more conspicuously, the rules of the secular *mythos* that regulate Finnis's reading of the tradition. I will focus upon three interpretive vignettes: (1) genealogical claims, (2) the employment of theological economy, and (3) the exercise of the 'art of writing.'

210. Ibid., 12.
211. Finnis, *Religion & Public Reason*, 5.
212. Ibid., 114.

Genealogical advertence

The first hermeneutical tool is genealogical. Although Finnis says he abstains from speculating about the genealogical development of natural law and natural rights, *NLNR* is not entirely immune from making controversial genealogical claims. Chief among these is his depiction of Hugo Grotius's (1583–1645) contribution to natural law.

In what is possibly an attempt to thwart, proleptically, what has nevertheless become a common supposition – that his professedly 'Thomistic' position is actually a secular 'sell out' – Finnis challenges the common supposition that Grotius 'inaugurated a new, modern, and secular era in natural law theorising by his '*etiamsi daremus*" '[213] The so-called impious hypothesis was an epistemological affirmation that the principles of the natural law would retain a 'degree of validity even if we should concede [*etiamsi daremus*] that which cannot be conceded without the utmost wickedness, that there is no God'[214] This speculative conjecture has typically been identified with instigating an epochal shift away from the scholastic-Thomistic understanding of natural law as a theory of divine government towards the modern understanding of natural law as a detached form of philosophical reasoning. But Finnis insists that this standard reading actually results from a complete misreading of Grotius. Instead, he makes an alternate genealogical claim that:

> Grotius must be assumed to have known (if only from his reading of Suarez) that, for the purpose of discussing the roots of obligation, the hypothesis of God's non-existence (or indifference) had been a commonplace of theological debate since, at the latest, the mid-fourteenth century.[215]

Two critical remarks are pertinent here. First, in hoping to deflect the attribution of advancing a 'secular position' propelled by the canon-like influence of Grotius, Finnis relocates the genesis of the '*etiamsi daremus*' form of thinking to 'very many' of the scholastics who, purportedly, utilized it to the same effect as Grotius.[216] A footnote or reference to verify this contentious claim would have been helpful. Unfortunately, neither is provided. Second, the reason for this absence might be another strategic move, reflecting a desire not to distract from the protagonist Finnis wants to impress as the real genealogical villain in the tradition of natural law, Francisco Suarez. Suarez, not Grotius, says Finnis, eschewed Aristotle's and Aquinas's natural law by erroneously asserting that the obligation to follow its moral precepts extends not from their inherent reasonableness but from the

213. Finnis, *NLNR*, 43.

214. C.f. Hugo Grotius, *De Jure Belli ac Pacis*, trans. Francis W. Kelsey (Oxford: Clarendon Press, 1925), 13.

215. Finnis, *NLNR*, 43.

216. Ibid.

ordinances of the divine will. Hence, the first principle of a neo-Suarezian natural law is '[f]ollow nature', which culminated in the 'perverted faculty' argument that remained popular in Catholic seminaries up until the 1960s.[217] Even though Finnis ultimately puts Grotius on the same side of the watershed as Suarez, his decision to focus the critical spotlight on Suarez's theoretical naturalism (whilst challenging the conventional genealogical suppositions about Grotius as the intellectual father of a 'new' and 'secular' natural law) would presumably prick the ears of his liberal-secular audience.

Nevertheless, there is a duplicitousness to Finnis's genealogical claims. Even though Finnis is right to criticize Suarez's notion that natural law is founded on a reading of normative facts of theoretical nature, he wrongly assimilates Aristotelian *phronesis* to Kantian practical reason. Yet, ironically, the theological coherence of this seemingly philosophical assimilation is underpinned by an unspoken appropriation of a Suarezian – extrinsicist – anthropology with its concomitant rejection of a *desiderium naturale* in God.[218] Thus, Finnis's circumscribing of natural law to the confines of practical reason is equally as problematic as Suarez's circumscribing of natural law to the confines of theoretical reason. For in both instances, Suarez and Finnis have fragmented reason in a way that Aquinas did not, thereby creating an epistemological duality that is emblematic of a dualistic understanding of the relationship between nature and grace, as well as approximating (already and after) Kant's separation of *phenomena* from *noumena*.[219]

Newman's economy

Finnis's desire to disentangle the philosophical from the theological in Aquinas required the strenuous employment of what I have denominated here as a second hermeneutical tool, the use of which is conveniently left 'unsaid' in all of his major works. The fact that nowhere in Aquinas's vast literary output can the same separatist structure or abstracting methodology be found obviously presented Finnis with a great exegetical challenge. For Aquinas, philosophy was always the 'handmaiden'. Its linguistic and explicative categories were helpful for the purpose of making theology clearer.[220] What he said philosophy cannot do is make the theological fit within the bounds of the philosophical. 'On the contrary,

217. Ibid., 49.

218. For an influential critique of Francisco Suarez's extrinsicism see: Henri de Lubac, *Augustinianism and Modern Theology*, trans. Lancelot Sheppard (London: Geoffrey Chapman, 1969), 158–9.

219. Aquinas never maintained such a sharp divide between theoretical and practical reason, rather, he believed the difference between them to be merely "accidental": ST I q.79, a.11; ST I q.73, a.3; ST I q.79, a.11.

220. ST I q.1 a.5.

philosophy should be brought within the bounds of faith.'[221] How, therefore, or, on what basis, can Finnis legitimate his strategy? Moreover, on what grounds could he still consider it 'Thomistic'?

In what was originally an unpublished address delivered at the University of Princeton in 2004, titled, 'Telling the truth about God and Man in a Pluralist Society', Finnis revealed to his audience that *NLNR* involved the procedural application of another theological principle known as 'economy'.[222] Whilst originating out of the thought of the Alexandrian Church Fathers of the third century AD, it was John Henry Newman who gave it recent attention. He defined 'economy' as a prudential hermeneutic or praxis, which states that, when articulating 'religious conduct or statement', one should express the truth in its most 'expedient and most suitable' form 'at the time for the object in hand'.[223] The principle is said to be imitative of the gradualness with which the economy of salvation is revealed by God in history. Whilst of evident pastoral value, Newman warned that it could easily be abused by becoming a means to justify insincerity or political cunning.

Considering that this is perhaps the central hermeneutical tool employed in *NLNR*, Finnis's description of 'economy' is surprisingly terse. Following Newman, he says that it involves 'the adapting of exposition to the receptiveness, the state of mind, of one's expected audience' but 'withholding no more of the relevant truth than the ignorance or prejudices of one's hearers would prevent them from properly understanding and assessing.'[224] But unlike Newman, Finnis refashions what is a theological principle into a political game of 'post-pone my theism'. Hence, he presses the point that his mentor, Hart, was far more economical with his atheism than he is with his theism. For Hart left his atheism completely 'unsaid' in his major works, whereas Finnis allows his theism to surface in Chapter XIII.[225]

What Finnis did leave 'unsaid' is how he practiced this principle 'strenuously' in his exegesis of Aquinas, acknowledging, for instance, that he deliberately 'abstracted from' and 'passed over in silence' the 'theological concerns and foundations' of 'the great theologian's theological' insights.[226] This economical practice of bracketing out theology from natural law also allowed him to delineate several other important conceptual boundaries between faith and reason, nature and grace, practical and theoretical knowledge. The preface to *NLNR* hints at this approach,

221. Thomas Aquinas, *Faith, Reason and Theology. Questions I-IV of his Commentary on the De Trinitate of Boethius*, trans. Armand Mauer (Ontario: Pontifical Institute of Mediaeval Studies, 1987), 49.

222. Finnis, *Religion & Public Reason*, 43.

223. John Henry Newman, *The Arians of the Fourth Century* (London: Longman, Green, 1908), 269; John Henry Newman, *History of My Religious Opinions* (London: Longman, Green, 1865), 343.

224. Finnis, *Religion & Public Reason*, 43.

225. Ibid.

226. Ibid.

with Finnis advising readers 'whose concerns are limited to jurisprudence [that they] may omit [the 'God-chapter'] Chapter XIII.'[227]

Although left 'unsaid' in *NLNR*, Finnis's interest in the practice of boundary drawing is also of curious provenance. In the epigraph to an essay originally published in 1970, 'Reason, Authority and Friendship in Law and Morals', Finnis quoted the following words from Wittgenstein:

> How should we explain to someone what a game is? … We do not know the boundaries because none have been drawn. To repeat, we can draw a boundary – for a special purpose. Does it take that to make a concept usable? Not at all! (Except for that special purpose.)[228]

Finnis returned to this remark some thirty-seven years hence, commenting that he was particularly drawn to the idea that the demarcation of conceptual boundaries was indissociable from one's (theoretical) purpose.[229] 'That thought', he writes, 'lies behind a good deal in *NLNR*.'[230] Considering Finnis's methodological objectives, appeasing the political economy of the secular *mythos* appears to be the 'special purpose' behind his bracketing out of Aquinas's theological economy from his NNLT.

The 'art of writing'

This 'special purpose' is informed by an explicitly exoteric aspect of Finnis's approach: to demonstrate how Aquinas's theory of natural law actually elaborates and defends all of the highest political ideals esteemed within the current liberal-secular milieu. Hence, his avowal that 'Aristotle and Aquinas had got there first, so to speak, and can, now too, be philosophically helpful.'[231] Finnis insists that times have since changed and secular-liberals are not, or need not be, so adverse to classical-Thomistic thought (and *vice versa*).[232]

However, Finnis faces a challenge in reconciling these conciliatory sentiments with his deliberate recourse to a third hermeneutical tool he employed in *NLNR*. In his essay responding to Fortin, Finnis admits that, in the hope of mollifying the antagonsim of his secular-liberal interlocutors, he made strategic use of the 'art of writing'.[233] This is because the secular *mythos* is also described by Finnis as

227. Finnis, *NLNR*, v.

228. Ludwig Wittgenstein, *Philosophical Investigations*, §61. Quoted in: Finnis, *Religion & Public Reason*, 104.

229. Finnis, *Grounds of Legal Theory*, 318.

230. Ibid.

231. Finnis, 'Grounding Human Rights in Natural Law', 200.

232. Ibid.

233. Ibid., 201, 204.

promotive of a climate of religious 'indifference', of 'materialist assumptions', and of a 'clear-cut willingness … to *kill* the unborn child'.[234]

Whilst he does not specifically acknowledge the source of this hermeneutic, he almost certainly appropriated it from Leo Strauss, despite his desire to rebuke Strauss's bifurcation between liberalism and Thomism.[235] Taking for his subject matter the notion of 'writing between the lines', Strauss explored how certain forms of persecution encourage authors to disguise the forbidden fruit of socially heterodox (anti-liberal) opinion(s) by developing peculiar techniques of writing, which, consequently, occasions the development of peculiar forms of literature. Strauss explains this 'art' as follows:

> That literature is addressed, not to all readers, but to trustworthy and intelligent readers only. It has all the advantages of private communication without having its greatest disadvantage – that it reaches only the writer's acquaintances. It has all the advantages of public communication without having its greatest disadvantage – capital punishment for the author.[236]

Thus, what is being said in writing can become a surreptitious medium with which to communicate a deeper 'unsaid', which can only be grasped by the 'intelligent' or 'trustworthy' reader. For 'thoughtless men are careless readers, and only thoughtful men are careful readers.'[237]

Finnis's discussion of the 'careful reader' in his response to Fortin's criticisms echoes these Straussian undertones.[238] He specifically rebukes those Thomists who remained insensitive to the rhetorical predicament of *NLNR* and its intent of re-presenting Aquinas natural law. However, his emphasis on the natural reconcilability of secular-liberalism with natural law Thomism is seemingly contradicted by the fact that *NLNR* is also an expression of the 'art of writing'. One possible explanation is that Finnis is trying to re-narrate the secular by appealing to, and developing, the idea of practical reason as a foundation for natural law, now cautiously parlanced by the 'art of writing' and yet theologically informed by a *duplex-ordo* theory. The difficulty with this hermeneutical strategy is that it engenders a conceptual difficulty within the NNLT itself. It seems far too much

234. See: John Finnis, 'On the Practical Meaning of Secularism', *Notre Dame Law Review*, vol. 73, no. 3 (1998), 491–516; Finnis, *Religion & Public Reason*, 330.

235. In the Preface to *NLNR*, Finnis quotes Strauss' belief that 'the issue of natural right presents itself today as a matter of party allegiance. One is occupied by the liberals of various descriptions, the other by the Catholic and non-Catholic disciples of Thomas Aquinas.' It is in opposition to this sentiment that Finnis introduces his own theory. Leo Strauss, *Natural Right and History*, 7. Quoted in: Finnis, *NLNR*, 7.

236. Leo Strauss, 'Persecution and the Art of Writing' (1941), *Social Research*, vol. 82, no. 1 (Spring 2015), 82.

237. Strauss, 'Persecution and the Art of Writing', 81.

238. Finnis, 'Grounding Human Rights in Natural Law', 203.

has been left 'unsaid'. One has to either be part of the intellectual elite or a very careful and well-informed reader to perceive what is being 'written between the lines', which, on Finnis's own admission, necessitates an understanding of how exactly he constructs his milieu and his methodology.

Section VI: NNLT in action

Bringing the threads together

It is time to explain how all these ariadnean threads come together in the exposition of the NNLT itself and to then draw some preliminary conclusions. Leaving an account of the practical fundaments and application of the theory to the end of this chapter would certainly seem to go against 'traditional orders of treatment'. But in keeping with the hermeneutical focus of this book, I have deliberately given primordial attention to what Finnis has left 'unsaid' in order to shed new light on what has been said. As such, this discussion can afford to be significantly shorter than it would otherwise have been. Following this brief outline of the NNLT, I will give one example of how Finnis has employed his theory to defend the intelligibility of one of the Catholic Church's most contested moral teachings – the use of artificial contraception. The chapter will then conclude with some brief evaluatory remarks.

NNLT in a nutshell

The NNLT begins with Finnis, drawing 'squarely' upon Grisez's controversial interpretation of Aquinas's first principle of practical reason (I-II q.94 a. 2), explicating a neoclassical science of practical reasonableness.[239] Focusing upon practical reasonableness, which Finnis conveniently calls 'the natural law written on the heart', illuminates the practical meaning of secularism itself, an understanding that secularism has itself, heretofore, obscured or forgotten by erroneously conflating sub-rational emotions/passions/pleasure with the basic human goods.[240] According to Aquinas, every rational human being is naturally inclined to move towards the good since every acting person acts in a manner that is congruent with his intention to pursue 'integral human fulfilment'. Hence, the first precept of the natural law, which directs all purposeful human action, is that the 'good is to be done and pursued, and evil is to be avoided'. This first principle is a product of *synderesis* and is self-evident, that is to say, 'known just by knowing the meaning of their terms'.[241] It is, therefore, indemonstrable and is directive of end-oriented behaviour, behaviour that pursues an intelligible purpose. As the determination of intelligent reasons for action, the natural law is neither mediated

239. Finnis, *NLNR*, vii.

240. Finnis, 'On the Practical Meaning of Secularism', 501.

241. Finnis, Grisez and Boyle, 'PMU', 106.

by, nor deduced from, a speculative inquiry into human nature. In fact, it has nothing to do with human nature, only the reasonableness of the human good.

The most expeditious way to uncover such purposes, the basic goods, is to enter into a process of epistemological self-reflection by asking, 'Why are you doing that?'. If we remain persistent with this line of inquiry, we will eventually arrive at (about) seven basic goods – basic because they require no further explanation as to why an individual would purposefully pursue them. A distinction is then made between substantive and reflexive basic goods. The substantive goods, which include (1) life itself, (2) knowledge, and (3) excellence in work and play, are substantive because their instantiations do not require choices. In contrast, the reflexive goods, which include (4) friendship, (5) aesthetic experience, (6) practical reasonableness, and (7) religion, are instantiated by the nature of the choice according to which one pursues them. (Finnis would later include marriage between a man and a woman as an eighth basic good.)[242]

As a theoretical bulwark against the moral calculus that is intrinsic to proportionalist or consequentialist forms of reasoning, Finnis argues that the basic goods are rationally incommensurable since they are 'nothing other than aspects of human persons, and human persons cannot be weighed and balanced'.[243] Practically speaking, as irreducible and, therefore, primary principles of action, the basic goods cannot be put into a moral hierarchy by specifying the *summum bonum*. A crucial factor animating Finnis's staunch defence of the 'pre-moral' character of the basic goods is his poly-teleological emphasis upon the existential importance of creative free-choice – the first critical move. It is up to the individual to determine how they will integrate these diverse and attractive reasons for action into a rational and harmonious 'plan of life'. Living in accordance with this 'plan of life' is a 'significant part' of how the NNLT defines 'happiness',[244] or at least 'the happiness for which they are prepared to settle' by willing 'integral human fulfilment.'[245]

Since the practical principles of the natural law underlie the reasoning's of 'good people and bad people alike', they are not themselves moral 'oughts'.[246] In other words, both moral and immoral people always act in pursuit of one or more of the basic goods. What is needed, therefore, is a set of intermediary principles – 'modes of responsibility – which can provide 'determinate [moral] guidance' to ensure the 'plan of life' is practically reasonable.[247] In *NLNR*, Finnis enumerates nine 'requirements of practical reasonableness', which are said to be expressive of the method of natural law.[248] These requirements or modes presuppose, and are

242. Finnis, *NLNR*, 448 fn. 25.
243. Finnis, *Reason in Action*, 195.
244. Finnis, *NLNR*, 103.
245. Finnis, Grisez and Boyle, 'PMU', 133.
246. Finnis and Grisez, 'A Reply to Ralph McInerny', 27.
247. Finnis, *Reason in Action*, 249.
248. For a detailed explication of these nine requirements see: Finnis, *NLNR*, 100–25.

derived from, the underived and self-evident FPM. Unlike the first principle of practical reason, these intermediary principles can supply a response as to what 'ought to be done' since they articulate something of what is meant by the good. To will the integral fulfilment (the good) of oneself and one's neighbour.

Absolute moral norms are the rational deductions of the requirements of practical reason and are fully specific explications of the original normativity of the 'good that is to be done and pursued.' This is 'practical reason in action', which Finnis equates synonymously with 'virtue in action', virtues being the embodiment of moral truth in and through the performance of choice by 'a good person' – one who, with a 'fully integrated personality', intends to act in accord with 'integral human fulfilment.'[249] Moreover, these moral norms also provide the generative platform for identifying human rights and human responsibilities (the objects of natural justice), both in relation to oneself and in relation to others.[250] Finnis argues that because all human beings can share in the excellence of the basic goods, it can be inferred that there is an objective recognition that because these goods are *good for me*, they must also be good for everyone else.[251]

As an illustrative example, take the issue of contraception. Finnis is one of the staunchest champions of the Catholic Church's teaching that the use of artificial contraception is 'intrinsically evil'. In fact, Finnis has gone so far as to suggest that, among Catholics, the widespread attack on the existence of absolute moral norms was precipitated by the issue of contraception.[252] The NNL argument is surprisingly simple. Using artificial contraception is always intrinsically evil because it involves an intentional attack on the basic good of human life. This is because when a couple agree to use artificial contraception for the sake of engaging in sexual activity, they deliberately intend to prevent the conception of new human life, thereby acting against one of the substantive basic goods and, thus, contradicting the FPM. It is in this sense that Finnis asserts that contraception is 'anti-life' and, hence, always wrong. But is this argument persuasive?

Appraising the NNLT

Before trying to answer that question, it is helpful to recapitulate some of the archetypical themes covered in this chapter. One of the original elements of this analysis has been to explore how the excavation of the theo-cultural 'unsaid(s)' behind *NLNR* gives a clearer picture as to how Finnis enters into current debates in natural law. This analysis has exposed the lineaments of the programmatic – yet 'unsaid' – relationship that exists between Finnis's construction of the secular *mythos* and his re-presentation of 'Thomistic' natural law. 'Many if not all of us', says Finnis, 'live as secularists.'[253] And it is as 'secularists', conscious of our

249. Finnis, *Aquinas*, 107; Finnis, Grisez and Boyle, 'PMU', 130.
250. Ibid., 138.
251. Finnis, *Human Rights & Common Good*, 5.
252. Finnis, *Moral Absolutes*, 85.
253. Finnis, *Religion & Public Reason*, 333–4.

responsibility to shape the sociopolitical landscape for the common good, that, he believes, we must reflect upon the public reality of 'liberal secularism'.[254] It is out of this reflection, animated by various intellectual interlocutions and cultural assessments, that the fundamental impetus of *NLNR* is borne: 'to give an account of natural law that is philosophically sound, untouched by Humean and all subsequent philosophical and cultural objections, and at the same time to the extent permitted by philosophically critical criteria – is more authentically in line with St. Thomas's thought than were his most influential sixteenth-century commentators and followers.'[255]

Once this methodological intent is viewed through the modern-analytical prism of his contextual milieu, Finnis's speech to the sceptical 'cultured despisers' appears to hit all the secular notes to gain Aquinas a seat at their jurisprudential table, beginning with the three overarching 'critical moves' that get the NNLT methodology off the ground, so to speak. With respect to the first critical move, although Finnis decries the discordant pluralism of liberal secularism, he nevertheless renounces an ultimate teleology or a hierarchical ordering to the basic goods, thereby allowing a poly-teleological scope for a pluralist individualism and political liberalism. Thus, when Aquinas spoke of the life of practical reason as being teleologically ordered to a common eschatological fulfilment in God, Finnis clarifies that he was actually referring to our individuated participation in the unrealizable – wholly terrestrial – ideal of 'integral human fulfilment'. Unexpectedly, there is a perceptibly relativistic streak to Finnis's natural law theory. Since the conceptual principles of natural law are without an essence or an ultimate end according to which their value can be determined and measured, their content is subject to how they are conveyed and employed in a particular context – according to our own 'plan of life'.

With respect to the second critical move, although Finnis decries the liberal secular attempt to secularize the 'pre-secular' language of human dignity, human rights, and the common good, he nevertheless renounces the natural desire for God in order to allow for the sociopolitical integrity of 'nature' and the 'natural end'.

With respect to the third critical move, although Finnis decries the pervasive influence of Kantian and Humean presuppositions within secular liberalism, he not only affirms a Kantian view of the rational self as predicated upon *Willkür*, but he also maintains the operative independence of practical reason from speculative reason, a move that underpins the NNLT's respect for the Humean inspired fact-value distinction, which in analytical jurisprudence is as close to an incontrovertible dogma as you could find.

It is also worth recalling three further features of the NNLT that, ostensibly, would be found attractive by scholars whose values reflect Finnis's construction of his liberal-secular milieu. First, by focusing on the free-standing structure of the first principles of practical reason, Finnis can instantiate Hart's genealogical claim

254. Ibid.

255. Finnis, *Grounding Human Rights*, 203.

that natural law can disentangle itself from a metaphysical or theological setting. This feature would ostensibly be found attractive within secular legal theory because it liberates natural law from a consideration of pre-rational (biological) human nature, a line of argument that has, ostensibly, been rendered intellectually obsolete after Darwin's theory of evolution.

Second, by declaring the basic goods to be incommensurable prior to the exercise of existential choice, and by disassociating the constitution of the moral virtues from a specification of the ultimate end, Finnis avoids any association of the perfectionism of virtue ethics.[256] In fact, Finnis effectively reduces the virtues to *bonum mihi* rather than *bonum honestum*. The virtues are no longer constitutive of common ends, but are rather a means to individualized ends. Furthermore, Finnis wants to stay away from dealing explicitly with virtue understood as a habitual inclination to act for the good, because it necessarily crosses the is–ought distinction. This feature would, ostensibly, be found attractive to secular legal theory in that the idea of the moral life is largely an individual concern and does not extend in any significant way into political decision-making, avoiding the political perfectionism associated with paternalism or collectivism.

Third, in all of his major presentations of the NNLT, Finnis avoids presenting an anti-modernity narrative or constructing an anti-secular genealogy. In opposition to those who would write off the secular as being entirely synonymous with the 'culture of death', Finnis re-narrates it on the basis of what he takes to be the 'perennial Catholic doctrine.'[257] Similarly, in opposition to those who would write off subjective natural rights as a modern eschewal of objective natural law, Finnis presents a moral theory that marries both 'for love'. This feature would, ostensibly, be found attractive within secular legal theory as it enables the normative conclusions of the natural law to be presented in the more popular – less theological imbued – language of subjective rights.

Recognizing these various points of continuity suggests an abiding methodological dependence upon, and a reactionism to, Finnis's account of the secular *mythos*. One might conclude, therefore, that he constructs the secular *mythos* as a narrative of potential – as a discourse that can be redeemed from liberalist and postmodern infiltration. Yet, one might also conclude that this desire to save the secular ideal is precisely what infiltrates and inflects his methodological reading of the Thomistic tradition – in particular, his protreptic belief that he can defend the integrity and normativity of the natural law without needing to cross the threshold into the realm of the theological.

Whilst Finnis might indeed be right to call attention to some of the 'questionable presuppositions' of both admirers and despisers of the natural law, it seems fair, in light of this discussion, to turn that same criticism back on Finnis. For all of

256. I am grateful to Dr Mark Retter who alerted me to this conclusion. Though I have since noted that this issue is also discussed by Hittinger. See: Hittinger, *A Critique of the New Natural Law Theory*, 162.

257. Finnis, *Religion & Public Reason*, 328. See Supra note 145.

the NNLT's pretensions to be theologically and metaphysically 'free-standing', it is questionable whether the theory would remain purposeful or coherent unless one accepts Finnis's presuppositions about his liberal-secular milieu. Hence, it seems he is indeed guilty of doing the very thing he criticizes the neo-scholastics of, namely, 'commingling historical interpretation' with 'philosophical construction'. As I have also argued, there is an underlying tension between Finnis's desire to 're-present' Aquinas's natural law on Aquinas's own terms and his use of a variety of hermeneutical tools with which to adapt Aquinas's natural law to the 'receptiveness, the state of mind' of the 'cultured despisers'.

A conflicting reception

This tension gives some explanation as to the mixed reception of Finnis's NNLT. Certainly, there is evidence to support the judgement that Finnis has been successful in attracting the interest of the 'modern secular' legal community. For instance, a search of the online legal database, *LexisNexis*, reveals a dramatic increase in citations to Thomas Aquinas since the publication of *NLNR* in 1981.[258] Furthermore, within the academy itself, Finnis's NNLT is often taught as the only account of natural law worth considering. In the words of Jonathan Crowe, Senior Lecturer in Law at the University of Queensland, '[m]ore than one generation of law students has been taught to believe that contemporary natural law begins and ends with Finnis … [because] the only natural law ethical framework students encounter is that defended by Finnis.'[259]

Whilst such indicators suggest that the NNLT has been found intellectually stimulating and compelling, this does not necessarily infer that it has also been found persuasive. This is obviously hard to quantify. But the evidence suggests that those who actually found the NNLT persuasive were not the intended 'secular' audience. A deeper analysis of the exact sources which have bolstered the number of references to Aquinas within legal scholarship (post-*NLNR*) reveals that the top five highest concentrations originate from journals of Catholic provenance or association.[260] Tied for sixth place is the first 'secular' journal to rank – namely, *The Michigan Law Review* – and the *Yale Law Review* is the only other 'non-Catholic' journal to feature in the top ten.[261] Such indicators question the rational, *ergo* universal, basis for Finnis's normative claims and cast doubt over the ability of his NNLT to operate as a *lingua franca*.[262]

258. The exact numbers are traced in: Eugene Rogers, *Aquinas and the Supreme Court* (Chichester: Wiley-Blackwell, 2013), 4.

259. Jonathan Crowe, 'Natural Law Beyond Finnis', *Jurisprudence*, vol. 2, no. 2 (2011), 295, 296.

260. Rogers, *Aquinas and the Supreme Court*, 8.

261. Ibid.

262. Moreover, whilst this would take another thesis to properly substantiate, it is hard to identity a single instance where a Neo-classical Natural Law argument has been successfully run in legal court. One example is *R v Morrow* (1981): Finnis tried to run a

I believe that Finnis's contribution has been found unpersuasive because he, too, has failed to bridge the gap between the general (supposedly self-evident) first principles of practical reason and the specification of moral norms. Take the issue of contraception mentioned above. One can expect to find near universal agreement with the NNLT's starting point that life itself is a basic good. But to then oppose the use of contraception because it contradicts the seventh requirement of practical reason since it purportedly involves an intentional choice to prevent the conception of new life is a very weak line of reasoning. Irrespective of one's religious dispositions, a reasonable person could rightly point out that, through the use of contraception, there is no life to be destroyed or impeded. Furthermore, what if a contracepting couple stated that their intention was to respect the basic good of life by doing all they could to only bear children when they were in a position to provide for a child's needs (food, education, support)?

In hindsight, Finnis's defence of 'orthodox' Catholic teaching is actually quite 'unorthodox'. This is because, by virtue of its philosophical predicament, it is incapable of arguing from the same premises commonly used by the Catholic Church. There are two principal reasons for this. First, because Finnis has inexorably tied his construction of natural law to his construction of the secular *mythos*, he is unable to articulate the fact that the Church's teaching on contraception is intertwined with its teaching on the sacramentality of marital love: that God has empowered human beings with a unique capacity to participate or to share in the creative love of God through the procreative and unitive act of sexual intercourse – itself protected by the unique bond of marriage. Thus, contraception is said to suppress the unitive, procreative, and the sacramental dimensions of marriage. Second, because Finnis does not share the Church's vision that the ultimate end of humankind is God, he has to find a purely philosophical way to establish the 'universal viewpoint' of the Pauline Principle – the seventh requirement of practical reason.[263] However, to say that something like the Pauline Principle is known by reason is not the same thing as saying that something is known by reason alone. For once the Word of God is revealed to us, reason is in a privileged position. On this score, I think Westermann is right to be suspicious of whether Finnis's epistemology of the basic goods is, genealogically speaking, already situated within, and, thus, illuminated by, a theological context – in particular, by Finnis's own Catholic faith.

'NNLT' argument in defence of Fr James Morrow, a Catholic priest who tried to stop an abortion and was charged with assault and other offences and was convicted. I am grateful to Jamie Carr, Barrister, for assisting with the identification of this example.

263. Finnis position on the ultimate end clearly contradicts the teaching of the first encyclical of moral theology ever published, *Veritatis Splendor*. 'God, the supreme good and ultimate end *(telos)* of man' (No. 12) Pope John Paul II, *Veritatis Splendor*, 1993, http://www.vatican.va/holy_father/john_paul_ii/encyclicals/documents/ hf_jp-ii_enc_06081993_veritatis-splendor_en.html. Accessed on 1 March 2018.

Underlying all these issues is the pre-eminent theological 'unsaid' of Finnis's contribution – his ascription to a *duplex-ordo* theory and his riposte of the Augustinian understanding of the '*cor iniquetum*'. Finnis's NNLT goes even further than the earlier scholastic *duplex-ordo* theories did in prescinding not just from the orientation to the beatific vision, but even from a necessary reference to God as creator. As a theory about the *bonum mihi* rather than the bonum *honestum*, he builds the relational-dialogical component of natural law on friendship as a basic good, rather than the other way around by defining forms of friendship by reference to the common goods to be pursued. This, to my mind, touches upon the principal issue. On Finnis's own admission, his understanding of 'liberal secularism' reflects the consideration of a conglomeration of ideas rather than a dialogical consideration of human beings and human destiny as such.[264] Arguably, this is the fundamental reason why it has not been found anthropologically persuasive, even if it remains intellectually engaging and philosophically sophisticated.

264. Finnis, 'On the Practical Meaning of Secularism', 493.

Chapter 3

JEAN PORTER'S SCHOLASTIC DEFENCE OF ETHICAL NATURALISM: NATURAL LAW AS A THEOLOGICAL LOCUS FOR CONTEMPORARY MORAL REFLECTION

Section I: Framing the analysis

A bête noire

Jean Porter is not persuaded. Although a fellow Catholic and, more pertinently, a fellow natural law theorist, Porter remains firmly convinced that Finnis's NNLT is neither an accurate nor an attractive interpretation of Aquinas.[1] Even if on first reading it comes across as 'thoroughly traditional', affirming quintessentially 'Catholic' imaginings of Thomistic natural law as a secular *lingua franca*, she believes the theory is quintessentially 'modern' and ultimately incongruent with the tradition.[2] For similar reasons, Porter also does not accept that Finnis's explication of a philosophically autonomous account of both practical and pure reason is capable of yielding specific moral norms of universal import. She asserts that only those who accept, *a priori*, his theoretically circumscribed synthesis of Aristotelian phronesis with a Kantian impression of the *bonum rationis* would stand even a remote chance of arriving at his normative conclusions – that, for example, contraceptive and homosexual acts are always intrinsically evil. Incidentally, Porter not only does not share Finnis's unwavering opinions on such matters, but she actually believes there are grounds within the natural law tradition to challenge them.

From the perspective of Finnis and his closest collaborators, Porter's critical reactions are quite typical of the misrepresentations that have become commonplace amongst their 'tradition-based' opponents. This has led to the likes

1. Jean Porter, *Ministers of the Law* (Grand Rapids, MI: W. B. Eerdmans, 2010), 67. (Henceforth *MOL*).

2. Jean Porter, '"Direct" and "Indirect" in Grisez's Moral Theory', *Theological Studies*, vol. 57 (1996), 611; Jean Porter, *Nature as Reason* (Grand Rapids, MI: W. B. Eerdmans, 2005), 39. (Henceforth *NasR*).

of Robert George and Gerard Bradley, who have both sought to reply to Porter's purported confusions, to assume that her rejection of at least some of their normative conclusions extends from her misreading of the NNLT itself, rather than providing the ideological impetus for performing an already prejudiced misreading.[3] Nevertheless, this interpretive disputation actually serves to raise a further concern with the NNLT. If a Catholic theologian, one who is deeply versed in the Thomistic natural law tradition and critically engaged in contemporary jurisprudence, can so readily misconceive what Finnis is actually saying, what hope do we have that those outside the tradition will find the NNLT any more accessible and intelligible? For is not 'accessibility' a prerequisite for 'intelligibility', and 'intelligibility' a test for 'universality'?

A 'not so paradoxical' story

A key element of Porter's strategy is to contest how scholars like Finnis narrate the story of natural law. In what is an unequivocal challenge to Finnis's avowal that the principles of natural law 'have no history', Porter asserts that natural law is, inexorably, a 'historically situated' form of moral inquiry. Prima facie, this is an 'intolerably paradoxical' position since it would completely undercut the so-called 'traditional' veneration of natural law as a 'tradition independent' system of moral knowledge, upon which its secular appeal was thought to depend.[4] Porter argues, however, that it only appears 'intolerable' and 'paradoxical' because Catholic moral theology has embraced and maintains certain questionable assumptions about contemporary sociopolitical ('secular') discourse. These assumptions, fortified by the pervasive influence of the NNLT, have confounded those committed to defending the natural law tradition into thinking that there is but one way to face an aggressive secularism without lapsing into moral relativism – namely, through an interpersonal and intercultural exchange on the level of reason alone. Instead, we must reassess the validity of these modern assumptions, realizing that the promise of deriving specific moral norms from indubitable and immutable first principles in a manner that is universally compelling is a fictional chimera that has been found wanting.[5]

A peculiar twist to Porter's contribution is the insistence that the contemporary instauration of natural law does not require its reinvention *de novo*. Although a paradoxical move on both counts, she argues that the recovery of the theologically

3. Ibid., 127.

4. Jean Porter, 'A Tradition of Civility', *Scottish Journal of Theology*, vol. 56, no. 1 (2003), 28. Joseph Boyle, a staunch defender of the NNLT, speaks of natural law as a theory that argues for the 'tradition independence of moral knowledge'. Joseph Boyle, 'Natural Law and the Ethics of Tradition', in *Natural Law Theory: Contemporary Essays*, ed. Robert P. George (Oxford: Clarendon, 1992), 15.

5. Jean Porter, *Moral Action & Christian Ethics* (Cambridge: CUP, 1999), 200. (Henceforth *MA&CE*).

grounded ethical naturalism of the medieval scholastics of the eleventh and twelfth centuries can provide a 'cogent and supple' basis even for secular jurisprudential reflection.[6] The tenability of her argument centres upon both a genealogical and theological reappraisal of how the manifest diversity within contemporary secular ethics actually relates to the historical particularity of scholastic moral reflection. She summarizes her core argument as follows:

> Moral commitments that are so basic to late-twentieth-century Western moral thinking that they now seem self-evident were in fact mediated to modernity through the scholastic concept of the natural law ... It may be that our common secular morality is in fact more Christian than either its critics or its defenders are prepared to admit.[7]

The principal purpose of this chapter is not simply to establish the obvious fact that the contributions of Finnis and Porter talk past each other. Rather, it is to begin to examine the less obvious and 'unsaid' reasons as to why they *do* talk past each other. Thus, although I am interested in clarifying her position on the value and purpose of natural law, this too is epiphenomenal to discerning the forces and factors that gave rise to the particular lineaments and contours of her theory in the first place, in particular, her distinct construction of the secular *mythos*. To that end, the critical thrust of the chapter remains the same as Chapter Two: to deconstruct what has been said by disinterring the theo-cultural 'unsaid(s)'. Through this analysis, an interesting paradox will surface. Despite their obvious exegetical and normative differences, I will argue that Porter's contribution is animated by the same theological 'unsaid' I identified in Finnis's project – an ascription to a *duplex-ordo* theory and a disavowal of a natural (ontological) desire for God. Porter refers to this central thesis as representing a 'theological loss' for the sake of a valuable 'theological gain'. In the course of this chapter, I will refer to this 'unsaid' as the 'programmatic *logos*', which, like Finnis, is ultimately a programmatic reaction to her own account of the secular *mythos*.[8]

6. Jean Porter, *Natural & Divine Law* (Ontario: Saint Paul University Press, 1999), 18. (Henceforth *N&D*).

7. Porter, *N&D*, 166.

8. In a conversation with William Meyer, Porter acknowledges a continuity between her original arguments in the *Recovery of Virtue* and her later works on natural law. This leads Meyer to refer to the *Recovery of Virtue* as the 'programmatic' text of her contribution. I believe there is another – rarely commented upon – text that is 'programmatic' of the theological 'unsaid', which sustains both the coherence, and the strategical development, of her theory of natural law, namely, the first essay she ever published, titled, 'Desire for God: Ground of the Moral Life in Aquinas', *Theological Studies*, vol. 57 (1996): 611–32. (Henceforth *DFG*).

Section II: Baptizing the secular

Asking the right questions

This section is dedicated to analysing how Porter's interpretation of her sociopolitical and intellectual milieu informs her methodological interest in the secular *mythos* and, ultimately, her pluralistic reconstruction of natural law. Porter's contribution is framed by a desire to reassert the centrality of reason in Thomistic natural law whilst responding to a 'fuller story' concerning the breakdown and fragmentation of reason within Catholic, ecumenical, and secular discourse. On this score, she acknowledges her indebtedness to, and appropriation of, Alasdair MacIntyre's diagnosis of secular moral discourse.[9] In a reflection on MacIntyre's tradition-constituted cognitivism, she makes the following claim:

> In order to understand MacIntyre's theory of rationality as tradition- guided inquiry, it is necessary first of all to realize that the immediate context of that theory is to be found, not in the classical or medieval thought to which he devotes so much attention, but in the debates over the nature of rationality and the meaning of truth that have dominated philosophy since the seminal work of Wittgenstein and Quine.[10]

This statement illuminates the deeper significance of Porter's own diagnosis of her 'immediate context'. Thus, before turning to identify how she constructs the 'secular', it is useful to summarize her detailed analysis of current debates in natural law by focusing upon three critical questions that, in many ways, frame her contribution.

The first critical question arises from her analysis of the acrimonious dispute over the rational tenability of defending intrinsically evil acts within Catholic moral theology.[11] On one end of the spectrum is the 'radical interpretation' of Aquinas's natural law theory espoused by Grisez and Finnis. As I discussed in the last chapter, the NNLT bases its epistemology upon certain 'self-evident' first principles of practical reason, which form the foundation for the discernment of objective moral norms. On the other end of the spectrum are the exponents of proportionalism, a system of ethics that proposes an alternate basic maxim of 'choose the lesser evil', which is also declared to be a 'self-evident' principle of practical reasoning that they consider to be 'beyond debate'.[12]

9. C.f. Alasdair MacIntyre, *After Virtue. Third Edition* (Notre Dame, IN: University of Notre Dame Press, 2007).

10. Jean Porter, 'Openness and Constraint', *The Journal of Religion*, vol. 73, no. 4 (1993), 517.

11. Jean Porter, *Recovery of Virtue* (Louisville, KY: John Knox Press, 1990), 20. (Henceforth *ROV*).

12. C.f. Richard A. McCormick, 'Ambiguity in Moral Choice', in *Doing Evil to Achieve Good*, ed. Richard McCormick and Paul Ramsey (Chicago: Loyola University Press, 1978), 38.

Porter identifies here a significant impasse within Catholic moral theology since both NNL theorists and proportionalists invoke the idea of 'self-evidence' to defend contradicting understandings of the anatomy of the moral act. Recognizing this polarizing dilemma motivates Porter to want to recalibrate how we ground the rational character of the discourse by recontextualizing it within its 'proper arena' of 'philosophical and theological anthropology'.[13] It is from this robustly metaphysical perspective that she raises a first critical question for research: 'Can we arrive at moral truths which are rationally compelling to all well-disposed persons, whatever their specific beliefs, commitments, and social/cultural location?'[14]

The second critical question derives from her observation of how a growing number of Protestant theologians are reacting against the purely philosophical character of Catholic natural law ethics. Eugene Rogers is cited as an influential example. He argues that if we read Aquinas 'in terms of his own usages and not in ours', then it becomes incoherent to try and detach natural law from a theological doctrine of saving grace.[15] On a similar front, Porter also surveys the thought of those she calls 'contemporary pacifist theologians', especially the contributions of Stanley Hauerwas and John Milbank. Both these theologians emphasize the 'distinctiveness' of the Christian message as a foundational criterion for assessing its theological adequacy.[16] This leads to a wholesale rejection of any attempt to try to harmonize a Christian natural law morality with the values of secular liberalism, declaring such a project to be nothing more than a delusive Kantian spell.[17] Although she believes these theories represent a 'salutary corrective' to those who would like to believe that Aquinas composed a *Summa Philosophiae* as opposed to a *Summa Theologiae*, she expresses strong concerns over the dialogical implications of this trajectory.[18] Acquiescing to the idea, for example, that moral theologians must 'remain within the particular' of the Christian narrative would infer that there is 'no hope of real conversation even with other sorts of Christians, much less the world'.[19] This assessment raises a second critical question in Porter's *oeuvre*: 'To what extent does a sound account of the natural law depend on particular theological perspectives, and how is this reflected in our interpretation of its universality?'[20]

13. Jean Porter, 'Basic Goods and the Human Good in Recent Catholic Moral Theology', *The Thomist*, vol. 57, no. 1 (January 1993), 47–8.

14. Jean Porter, 'Moral Ideals and Human Nature', in *Universalism Vs. Relativism*, ed. Don S. Browning (Plymouth: Rowan & Littlefield, 2006), 59.

15. Eugene Rogers, *Thomas Aquinas and Karl Barth* (Notre Dame, IN: University of Notre Dame Press, 1995), xi; Eugene Rogers, 'The Narrative of Natural Law in Aquinas's Commentary on Romans', *Theological Studies*, vol. 59 (1998), 254–76.

16. Porter, *N&D*, 287.

17. Porter, *ROV*, 29.

18. Jean Porter, *Justice as Virtue* (Grand Rapids, MI: W. B. Eerdmans, 2016), 51.

19. Porter, *ROV*, 28, 31.

20. Porter, *NasR*, 44.

Already, a recurring motif is emerging. Current debates in natural law are characterized most fundamentally by the persistence of a series of polarizing either/ors: 'Either we can establish a purely Christian morality grounded in the distinctive narratives of a tradition or we must fall back on the universally valid morality of the Enlightenment.'[21] This is where Porter makes a significant intervention. In the spirit of Hegelian dialectics, the identification of an antithesis occasions the formulation of a thesis capable of negating or transcending what is sometimes referred to as the 'law of an excluded middle'. With respect to Porter's contribution, I contend that her 'thesis' takes the form of her own theo-cultural and genealogical construction of the secular *mythos*. For both strategically and methodologically, her 'selective retrieval' and development of the scholastic tradition is intended to illuminate the 'considerable degree of overlap between Christian ethics and secular morality.'[22] To do this, Porter re-presents the concept of 'tradition'.[23] It is this concept above all that enables her to subvert the floundering and under-determining dichotomy between, say, nature and reason and replace it with a dialectical alternative that is instead based upon what she considers to be the more integral relationship between nature and history.[24] This informs a third critical question that animates Porter's trajectory: 'What is the proper relationship between Christian and non-Christian sources in theological ethics?'[25]

Porter's 'liberal secularism'

Implicitly or explicitly, the notion of the 'secular' hovers over each of these three critical questions and features prominently throughout Porter's literary corpus. I believe an unacknowledged reason for its recurrence is that her attempt to re-narrate the story of natural law (by answering these questions) is concurrently an attempt to also re-narrate the secular *mythos* through the eyes of a Catholic (and self-described feminist) theologian. By explaining how these two, heretofore conflicting, narratives are actually historically intertwined, Porter believes she can facilitate the discoursive dissolution of the 'law of an excluded middle' and thereby riposte the misleading impression that her contribution is 'intolerably paradoxical'. Given that the Church is both a contemporaneous and historically

21. Porter, 'A Tradition of Civility', 46.

22. Porter specifically contrasts this more irenic viewpoint of the secular with the political eristics that lurk behind Finnis' NNLT. Porter, *N&D*, 165.

23. 'I refer to tradition of natural law reflection as a way of indicating that prior to self-reflective theorising on the natural law we find an extended history of reflection and commentary on the natural law, mediated through texts and developed through a process of self-conscious appropriation, commentary, critique, and revision of earlier approaches.' Porter, *NasR*, 7.

24. Porter, *N&D*, 43–4.

25. Jean Porter, 'The Subversion of Virtue', *The Annual of the Society of Christian Ethics*, vol. 12 (1992), 40.

situated institution, it will always be 'continuous' to some extent – both physically and culturally – with the particular society and age in which it is located.[26] Hence, '[t]he boundaries between the church and the world will always be permeable, and for this reason the task of Christian ethics will always necessarily involve appraisal and selective affirmation.'[27] This alludes to an early point of methodological differentiation between how Finnis and Porter construct the 'secular' in relation to natural law. Whereas Finnis seeks to illuminate the public reality of the secular by focusing upon the purportedly ahistorical and autonomous character of practical reason, Porter seeks to illuminate its 'hidden theological assumptions' by tracing the historical genesis of secular moral values to scholastic reflections on the natural law.[28]

On first glance, one might associate Porter's inquiry into 'hidden theological assumptions' as a nod to John Milbank's rendering of the secular as just a 'bad theology' in disguise, a topic I will discuss in Chapter Four. However, this would be a hasty and highly erroneous interpretation. Porter is actually highly critical of what she describes as 'the remarkably negative attitude towards secular society' that typifies this type of thought.[29] To treat the secular as something 'alien and hostile' to Christianity or to treat Christian ethics as something 'self-contained' and 'self-justifying' is 'as unrealistic as the Enlightenment ideal of universal morality that is its mirror image':[30] unrealistic, because both positions are unsustainable when evaluated in the light of scholastic history. For this reason, the study of history is deemed by Porter to be the constitutive element for the constructive endeavour of theological ethics, precisely because it opens up the horizon of forgotten possibilities with which theologians can engage the secular and, in particular, to realize that there is indeed another way to do 'natural law' outside of the assumed framework of a fundamental either/or.[31]

Nevertheless, Porter does not shy away from arguing that the fundaments of the natural law theory that she, herself, wants to propose are 'distinctively theological'.[32] In fact, if Porter insists that Christian theological ethics must rediscover its pedagogical constitution in the historical evolution of the Christian moral tradition, she is equally concerned that Christian theological ethics should become 'even more robustly and resolutely theological than it already is'[33] – a refreshing conviction, but a conviction she denies as being in conflict with her

26. Porter, *NasR*, 137.

27. Ibid., 332.

28. Porter, *N&D*, 18.

29. Ibid., 286.

30. Porter, 'A Tradition of Civility', 47.

31. See: Jean Porter, 'Mere History', *The Journal of Religious Ethics*, vol. 25, no. 3 (1997), 103.

32. Ibid., 30.

33. Jean Porter, 'Christian Ethics and the Concept of Morality: A Historical Inquiry', *Journal of the Society of Christian Ethics*, vol. 28, no. 2 (2006), 17.

dialogical opinion that a genuine Christian ethic must be able to meet certain criteria that, for all intents and purposes, are 'external to that tradition', that is to say, 'secular'.[34]

Murray's methodology

It is here that Porter's alternate narratological thesis about the secular is of underappreciated significance. The most informative insight is found in a single, yet rather revealing, footnote in her book, *Ministers of the Law*, published in 2010. The footnote corresponds with Porter's conscious recognition that espousing a 'theology of law' would indeed seem counter-intuitive and counterproductive given her desire to 'engage secular jurists and philosophers'.[35] Again, she swiftly moves to clarify that it only seems counter-intuitive and counterproductive if a 'theology of law' is presumed to be in hopeless opposition to things such as the 'civic ideal of religious neutrality' or 'the institutional arrangements through which this ideal is sustained.'[36] Porter argues to the contrary, asserting that such arrangements are 'just and exigent' since they reflect the specific 'histories and circumstances of the societies in which they are embedded.'[37] For such reasons, she declares in the corresponding footnote that she is 'broadly in agreement with John Courtney Murray's defence of contemporary liberal secularism on natural law grounds.'[38]

Although a relatively pithy and easily overlooked remark, it is of immense hermeneutical interest to disinterring what is being left 'unsaid' within Porter's contribution. Therefore, it is worth repeating. Following the influence of John Courtney Murray, Porter is wanting to use natural law theory to *defend* contemporary 'liberal secularism'.[39] Recognizing this relationship is very important because Murray is often thought to have provided the intellectual background for what Elizabeth Mensch and Alan Freeman have called 'the Catholic embrace of the "secular city"'.[40] At the same time, it is also of significant interest that Finnis's neo-classical approach is considered by several scholars (including Porter herself) to be the consummate expression of Murray's 'pure reason' approach to natural law.[41] Cristina Traina, another Catholic-feminist natural law theorist, has also traced this rationalistic trajectory, arguing that:

34. Ibid., 28.

35. Porter, *MOL*, 5, xvi.

36. Ibid., 5.

37. Ibid.

38. Ibid., 5 fn. 7.

39. John Courtney Murray (1904–1867) was a Jesuit priest and theologian who made significant contributions to Catholic social and political thought.

40. Elizabeth Mensch, Alan Freeman, *The Politics of Virtue* (London: Duke University Press, 1995), 91.

41. Porter, *NasR*, 35–7.

> Since Murray's influential writings in the 1950's and 1960's, the political appeal of Roman Catholics scholastic natural law … has been that its theological foundations … permit or even compel it to operate politically in the realm of human reason, without formal or even implicit reference to revelation.[42]

Even though Porter rejects Murray's rationalistic reading of natural law, she still defends the prophetic relevance of his political thought, especially his recognition and discussion of the 'fundamental domestic problem' of 'sustaining civic unity in the face of irreducible pluralism.'[43] On this point, she retains what she considers to be Murray's fundamental strategy, namely, to vindicate the value of natural law by using it to vindicate the value of contemporary liberal secularism. This desire, she asserts, should come as little surprise. After all, she describes herself as 'a twenty-first-century woman with strong liberal sensibilities.'[44] Similarly, in an article on the prospects of using Aquinas's thought to formulate a Catholic feminism, she states that 'It is no part of my thesis that liberalism as such is radically flawed, or that we should abandon it.'[45] Again, to the contrary, she holds that the core ideal of secular liberalism, that is to say, its focus upon the 'rational moral individual', is 'sound and should be reaffirmed.'[46]

Denouncing generalities

A further level of Murray's influence is reflected in Porter's prerogative of allowing her analysis of her secular-liberal context to inform her methodology. In so doing, she heeds Murray's thought about respecting the dynamic nature of the Catholic intellectual apostolate:

> The initial responsibility of the Catholic intellectual is, then, that of undertaking a comprehensive analysis of the present intellectual, cultural, and spiritual situation in its totality. If we are to interpret the world, as we must, even to itself, our first duty is to understand it, in detail, with full realism, under abnegation of the easy generalities with which the world is ordinarily denounced.[47]

42. Traina, 'Book Review of *Patriarchal Religion, Sexuality and Gender*', 311.

43. Jean Porter, 'In the Wake of Doctrine', in *John Courtney Murray & the Growth of Tradition*, ed. J. Leon Hooper and Todd David Whitmore (Kanas City: Sheed & Ward, 1996), 25.

44. Porter, *MOL*, 337.

45. Jean Porter, 'At the Limits of Liberalism', in *Thomas Aquinas*, ed. John Inglis (Aldershot: Ashgate, 2006), 391.

46. Ibid.

47. John Courtney Murray, 'Reversing the Secular Drift', 1949, https://www.library.georgetown.edu/woodstock/ murray/1949. Accessed on the 21 May 2019.

Porter certainly tries to avoid and even looks to abnegate the 'easy generalities' that have typically framed current debates in natural law. Such generalities have resulted in theologians becoming preoccupied with defending theological breaches that are no longer under secular attack or even of secular interest. It is already clear that her contribution 'flies in the face' of what she refers to as 'the most cherished assumptions' of modern philosophers and theologians alike.[48] Arguably, there are three principal generalities and paradoxical assumptions that Porter seeks to invert through her comprehensive analysis of her 'secular' milieu: (1) that natural law is unintelligible without a teleological conception of human nature; (2) that natural law is unintelligible unless theologically grounded; and (3) that natural law is unintelligible unless it admits to, and allows for, a plurality of possible interpretations. It is helpful to examine these three inversions in turn.

Defending human nature

When framing her evaluation of current debates in natural law, I noted Porter's belief that the breakdown of rational discourse within both Christian and secular ethics might find a common resolution if their respective debates were reframed as debates principally about competing philosophical-theological anthropologies. (Or, more specifically, competing visions about the nature of the human good and about human nature itself.) Ascribing normative value or ethical relevance to the so-called 'prerational aspects of human nature' (even if morality is 'under-determined' by nature alone and always requires the interpretive moves of reasoned reflection) is certainly a controverted and, prima facie, paradoxical strategy.[49] Besides the various philosophical objections that I have already discussed, it would also appear embarrassingly antiquated in the light of modern evolutionary biology. Unsurprisingly, therefore, theologians have been reticent to afford moral significance to the pre-rational aspects of human nature, surmising that such lines of argument have been irrevocably tarnished by the now highly ridiculed 'perverted faculty' sexual ethic.

If 'easy generalities' were maintained, particularly with respect to the dogma-like status of the naturalistic fallacy, then a metaphysical excursus into human nature would rightly be denounced as irrelevant to contemporary concerns in ethics as well as in jurisprudence. Porter recognizes this, stating that, until recently, any recourse to metaphysical biology would have been swiftly rejected. However, as she rightly points out, 'A great deal has happened since the days of Moore and Ayer.'[50] Within the contemporary academy, an increasing number of scientists – who, more often than not, have no obvious theological allegiances – are beginning to speak again in terms of 'natural teleologies'. This is particularly true, says Porter, of an area of scientific research known as evolutionary psychology which she

48. Porter, 'Moral Ideals and Human Nature', 61.

49. Porter, *NasR*, 49; Porter, *N&D*, 141.

50. Porter, 'Moral Ideals and Human Nature', 62,

describes as being 'built on the premise that human behaviour [inclusive of our moral behaviour] can be explained, at least in part, as an expression of species-specific nature that can be interpreted in terms of evolutionary adaptations'.[51] Porter claims that a similar move towards reconsidering ethical naturalism and even Aristotelian essentialism has also received renewed attention within moral philosophy and the philosophy of science:

> Recent work in the philosophy of biology makes a strong case that an Aristotelian approach need not be incompatible with our understanding of the evolutionary process, and moral philosophers are once again turning to an Aristotelian teleology as a starting point for a theory of the virtues.[52]

Hence, Porter feels confident she is able to invert the accusation of paradox by contesting the assumed reign of the naturalistic fallacy. Ironically, the ethical naturalism of the scholastic natural law tradition, which theologians have been reluctant to embrace, continues to live on in the secular academic discipline of evolutionary psychology. To compound the irony, Porter believes that the credibility of natural law has ultimately suffered a 'sharp decline' amongst 'secular philosophers' as a result of Finnis's apologetical defence of the naturalistic fallacy.[53] For by equating human nature with the operations of practical reason alone to the exclusion of both biological anthropology and even metaphysics, the concept of natural law has become extraneous from the 'distinctive concerns' of contemporary jurisprudence.[54] Far from engaging the secular imagination, natural law has become even more synonymous with Catholic thought and yet, paradoxically, even from within this theological context, it is still typically parroted as a codified set of moral rules discernible through the exercise of 'pure reason'. The unfortunate consequence of this is that Christian philosophers and theologians have unwittingly sidelined what she describes as 'a most significant point of contact between Christian thought and other elements of the wider intellectual culture.'[55] In response, Porter wants to show how a 'plausible account of human nature' in both 'philosophical and scientific terms' can 'widely be, albeit not universally, accepted among our contemporaries.'[56] This notwithstanding, Porter quickly moves to stress that her account of ethical naturalism will nevertheless be 'theological rather than strictly philosophical'.[57]

51. Porter, *N&D*, 26. In *NasR*, Porter distances herself a little from evolutionary psychology, focusing instead on 'anthropological and comparative studies of other primates' which, she asserts, 'can be of more value …' Porter, *NasR*, 106.

52. Porter, *MOL*, 84.

53. Porter, *NasR*, 32.

54. Jean Porter, *MOL*, 83.

55. Porter, *NasR*, 55.

56. Porter, *N&D*, 56.

57. Ibid.

Defending natural theology

Surely, however, her claim that natural law must become even more robustly theological would undermine this interesting point of interdisciplinary confluence with respect to ethical naturalism? To the contrary, Porter says that she is committed to defending the legitimacy of doing 'natural theology', specifically for the sake of harnessing credibility within the intellectual academy and across the wider sociopolitical setting,[58] though she distinguishes her understanding of natural theology from what she calls the 'full blown' natural theology of the neo-scholastics.[59] At the same time, she does not believe that the aspiration to universalism should or could be dismissed *tout court*. This judgement reflects, at least in part, her observation of the surprising development of a pseudo-natural theology amongst secular scientists.[60] For instance, Porter cites the work of Paul Davies who proffers a controversial thesis that scientific investigation provides a surer pathway to God than theology itself. Davies heralds the arrival of a 'new physics' that is increasingly oriented towards reformulating questions such as the existence of God or the meaning of human existence in the light of recent investigations into such things as human psychology (consciousness) and quantum mechanics.[61] Whilst Porter readily admits that such conclusions will never be completely reconcilable with Christian doctrine, she urges that it would be foolish for theologians not to try and learn from and develop this kind of natural theology.

Turning again to the scholastics, Porter champions this integrative approach on the basis that Christian theologians have 'reasons, implicit in their own tradition, to take the project of natural theology seriously.'[62] On this score, Aquinas's moral theology is especially pertinent because it 'presupposes that the content of morality can be derived from independent non-theological grounds.'[63] Correlatively, it is Aquinas's ethics of virtue, which, according to Porter, completes his ethics of natural law, which is of particular relevance precisely because it 'shares much in common' with the contemporary resurgence of theories of virtue, a resurgence taking place within both Christian and secular ethics.[64]

58. Porter, *The ROV*, 175.

59. Neo-scholasticism sought to retrieve the *philosophia perennis* of Thomas Aquinas in order to navigate an epistemological pathway to God and to the natural law via the so-called *praeambula fidei*.

60. Porter, *ROV*, 175.

61. See: Paul Davies, *God and the New Physics* (New York: Simon & Schuster, 1983).

62. Porter, *ROV*, 175.

63. Porter, 'DFG', 65.

64. Porter, *Justice as Virtue*, ix, 4.

Defending moral pluralism

The contemporary validity and defensibility of Aquinas's position does not necessarily extend to his entire moral theory. It is unlikely, says Porter, that it will always be found 'rationally compelling.'[65] Nor should it. This leads on to the third paradox that she hopes to dismantle: that because natural law is a culturally and historically mediated tradition, it is unintelligible and unsustainable unless it allows for a plurality of legitimate interpretations. Obviously, this flies in the face of the popular practice of tying the universality of natural law to a transcultural and trans-epochal consensus regarding specific and objective moral norms. In contrast to Finnis who has expressed aversion to the phrase 'natural law', Porter esteems it. 'It survives', she suggests, 'precisely because the idea of natural law is not tied to any particular construal of nature or any one account of the relation between natural principles and social conventions.'[66]

As I noted in the first chapter, jurisprudence has stereotypically been generalized as an either-or response to an 'ever-recurring' question: 'Are you a positivist or a natural law theorist?' Porter notes that, in recent decades, this sentiment has been reconsidered within secular jurisprudence, with scholars becoming progressively more historically conscious. As a result, many have started to question the legitimacy of their own assumptions about jurisprudence. To support this observation, Porter references the writings of the legal philosopher, Neil MacCormick.[67] Referring to the disputation between legal positivism and natural law, he wrote that 'various contemporaries have pretty convincingly established that there is a need for improvement' and that '[i]t is better to reject the aforesaid dichotomy [between natural law and legal positivism] as based on a misleading account of the history of legal ideas.'[68] Remarks such as this indicate that secular legal scholars are ready and willing to take another look at natural law jurisprudence, particularly in order to adjudicate the relationship between moral universalism and moral pluralism.[69]

Porter believes that it is the scholastic natural law tradition that best demonstrates how it is possible to respect coherently the 'diverse social forms through which our shared human nature is expressed.'[70] Even though Aquinas is the central protagonist in her 'tradition bound' story of the natural law, she accentuates the fact that her own contribution should, in the first place, be understood as a reformulation of the scholastic approach. The most important aspect of this reformulation involves the dialectical reclamation of natural law as a universal, but subjective, capacity or power for moral analysis and discernment – as opposed to a determinate theory of universal moral norms.

65. Ibid., 56.

66. Porter, *MOL*, 63.

67. Porter also references several other Anglophonic legal theorists. See: Ibid., 17, 63.

68. Neil MacCormick, *Institutions of Law*, 278–9. Quoted in Porter, *MOL*, 66.

69. Porter, *NasR*, 326.

70. Ibid., 338.

Section III: Scholastic natural law theories

A 'selective retrieval'

In order to unveil the relevance of the scholastic natural law tradition, we must first challenge our own contemporary assumptions and eschew popular generalizations. This explains why Porter never begins by engaging with the theologians of the past or even with the Christian tradition per se. Instead, she introduces all of her major works with an overview of contemporary thought, which, she explains, is done to 'set a context for my reconstructive remarks.'[71] Hence, it is only in light of the previous section that the rationale for Porter's 'selective retrieval' of the scholastic natural law tradition can be discerned. This 'selective retrieval' serves to show, directly and indirectly, how a secular-philosophical understanding of nature and a theological-metaphysical understanding of scripture can be brought together 'through a dialectical interpretation of the two that harmonises the two while respecting the integrity of each.'[72] Porter hastens to clarify that the scholastics were not motivated by a desire to accommodate a 'secular worldview'.[73] For, as she, herself, acknowledges, the category of the 'secular' is, itself, a historically contingent concept. Rather, the scholastics' positive and irenic stance towards the authorities of the world extends from a specifically theological and doctrinal commitment to respecting the integrity, intelligibility, and natural goodness of creation.

This is another highly significant remark with which to preface the forthcoming discussion: first, because it hints at how Porter understands the nature of theology, and second, because it hints at the way she understands how grace – as a principle of activity – relates to natural principles. Third, and most importantly, it hints at how Porter will accommodate her account of the liberal-secular *mythos* within her theological account of natural law. In this section, I will touch upon several constituting elements of her interpretation of the scholastic natural law tradition, which, both individually and accumulatively, suggest that her 'selective retrieval' of scholastic natural law is being guided by a programmatic reaction to her account of the secular *mythos*. I begin with her foundational interest in prioritizing the scholastics' doctrine of creation, since it is her interpretation of this foundational doctrine that justifies Porter's belief in the possibility of a natural law pluralism.

A doctrine of creation

To disinter how Porter understands the doctrine of creation, we must first disinter how she understands the relationship between nature and grace. In a manner that mirrors Finnis's decision to extricate the 'God Chapter' to the end of *NLNR*, Porter also leaves any discussion of the theological relationship between nature and grace to the end of her seminal work, *Nature as Reason*. The only exception to this is

71. Porter, 'At the Limits of Liberalism', 390.

72. Porter, *ROV*, 293.

73. Porter, 'Christian Ethics and the Concept of Morality', 18.

found in the concluding paragraph of the Introduction to that same text, where she gives a brief – yet programmatic – insight into what will prove to be a vital historical and hermeneutical contention:

> The scholastics' positive attitude towards the natural world, and their readiness to interpret it in theological terms, might suggest that they did not draw the sharp distinction between nature and grace we find in later Catholic thought ... Nonetheless, they did insist on a distinction between nature and grace ... I will argue that this distinction is still valid, and in fact theologically indispensable.[74]

What is left 'unsaid' here is how she distinguishes, definitionally, a 'distinction', from a 'sharp distinction', from a 'dichotomy'. What is said, however, is her intention to ground and situate this 'distinction' within Christian doctrine. In this instance, the focus is on how she believes the scholastic understanding of nature and grace gives a logical priority within ethics to a doctrine of creation as opposed to, say, a doctrine of Christology. This helps to explain Porter's remark that it is good to treat moral theology as an entirely separate discipline from systematic theology.[75] Moreover, it sets the scene as to how a 'more robustly and resolutely theological' account of the natural law can still require the pursuit of what she calls a 'more purely philosophical account of nature' and the natural law.[76] The paradox is that this 'more purely philosophical account of nature' is being subtly supported and reinforced by what she declares to be distinctly Christian beliefs. For Porter also avows that it is because of such doctrinal presuppositions that the scholastics did not delineate a 'sharp line between the philosophical and theological aspects of the scholastic concept of the natural law.'[77]

Porter readily admits that she was attracted to the scholastic account of the doctrine of creation because it cuts across and transcends typical ideological and political dichotomies.[78] On this point, she positions her contribution to natural law within a wider trajectory of wanting to reaffirm the scholastic 'motif of the goodness of the natural', which, she believes 'is making a comeback outside of traditional Catholic circles.'[79] In light of her ambition to demonstrate the historical harmony between Christian and secular ethics, it is not difficult to discern why Porter would want to interpret and esteem the scholastic doctrine of creation in such terms. Not only does it establish a theological foundation for thinking about natural law according to what she considers to be the more promising motif of natural goodness, it also provides a purportedly traditional theological

74. Porter, *NasR*, 52.
75. Porter, 'Christian Ethics and the Concept of Morality', 17.
76. Porter, *N&D*, 123.
77. Ibid., 122.
78. Ibid., 21.
79. Porter, *RoV*, 27.

justification for separating natural law away from the tradition-dependent doctrines of Christology and eschatology.

Ironically, this line of thought creates an early dichotomy between creation and Christology. Porter even states that creation and Christology are the two poles with which Christians can narrate the story of the moral life.[80] But these two poles can be isolated – perhaps even dialogically polarized – from each other because 'we experience the one God in diverse ways, which from our standpoint stand in paradoxical tension with one another.'[81] It is on such grounds that Porter launches a critique against Karl Barth and the pacifist theologians whose work he has influenced, though her principal line of critique is rather enigmatic. She contends that such theologians believe that 'an adequate account of morality must be not only theological but specifically and distinctively Christological.'[82] In contrast, for the scholastics, 'their Christology is not directly formative for their understanding of the natural law.'[83] What is mystifying here is that Porter wants to create a disjunction between the 'theological' and the 'Christological', whereby the 'theological' includes only the doctrine(s) she considers relevant to her reconstruction of natural law – specifically, the doctrine of creation. This leads Porter to conclude, for example, that 'morality should be understood first as a 'natural' phenomenon', that is to say, 'natural' in contrast to being 'transcendentally grounded' or 'implicitly divine'.[84] A theological-doctrinal foundation that legitimates the development of a 'secular morality' is thus secured.

Philo or the stoics?

It is very plausible that Porter's aspiration for a secular-theological rapprochement, particularly by emphasizing the integrity and independence of the order of nature, also had some bearing over how she locates the sources which shaped the scholastics' approach to natural law. On this matter, Porter states her staunch reliance upon the work of Richard Horsley.[85] Horsley sought to reaffirm the common genealogical assumption that the scholastics were essentially borrowing and adapting principles that were Stoic in origin.[86] This reaffirmation was prompted by the work of biblical scholar Helmut Koester, who had begun to challenge this thesis, arguing instead that it was the Judaic scholar, Philo of Alexandria, who originated and mediated the foundations from which the Christian natural law tradition would develop.[87]

80. Porter, *MOL*, 57.

81. Ibid., 57.

82. Porter, *N&D*, 171.

83. Ibid.

84. Porter, *NasR*, 126.

85. Porter, *N&D*, 66–7.

86. Richard A. Horsley, 'The Law of Nature in Philo and Cicero', *The Harvard Theological Review*, vol. 71, no. 1/2 (January–April 1978), 35–59.

87. Helmut Koester, 'The Concept of Natural Law in Greek Thought', in *Religions in Antiquity*, ed. Jacob Neusner (Ledien: Brill, 1968), 523–41.

What is distinctive about Philo's thought is that he challenged the cosmological immanence of the Stoics by believing the 'law of nature' to be authored and ruled by the Divine *Logos* who is transcendent.[88] The ontological 'law of nature' is thus merged with a theo-political one of divine government – *physis* is thereby blended inexorably with Biblical Torah, thence uniting the very realms of human experience that Porter wants to separate.[89] Koester argued that, with respect to moral values, 'Stoicism has not overcome the deep-rooted antithesis of *Nomos* and *Physis*.'[90] For although Stoicism affords nature a divine dignity, it never has what Koester refers to as the 'status of a divine legislator.'[91]

Although Porter is open to the possibility that the scholastics were aware of Philo's theory of divine government, her genealogy focuses solely upon their appropriation and preservation of the Stoics' philosophical ideals.[92] This discussion is also meant to explore how the scholastics' own turn to the sources reveals something about their historically situated context. For whilst the scholastics incorporated the archetypically Stoic notion of natural law as nature in accordance with right reason, and the metaphysical grounding of both in a 'transcendent *noetic* reality', such philosophical ideas were recontextualized within what Porter describes as 'the sophisticated apparatus of twelfth- and thirteenth-century philosophies of nature.'[93] The heightened interest in natural law theory during the twelfth century was linked to what Charles Haskins refers to as the 'discovery of nature' – referring to the prominent ascendancy of natural philosophy within university curriculums, denotive of a 'new understanding of the religious significance of the natural world.'[94] Porter asserts that this 'new understanding' is underscored by a shift away from the traditional 'symbolic-speculative' accounts of nature towards promoting confidence in the power of human rationality to interpret the meaning (the intelligibility) inherent within the constitution and structure of the autonomous natural order.[95]

Such notions were only given further momentum by the rediscovery of Aristotelian natural philosophy, which, to a certain extent, either displaced or refined the anterior commitment to decoding the *Timaeus* (which ultimately involved trying to reconcile the Platonic propensity to personify 'Nature' or to speak of a 'world-soul' existing independent of the God-Creator with the creation narrative given in the book of Genesis), which had become influential in the early decades of the twelfth century.[96] Porter believes this positive emphasis upon the

88. Koester, 'The Concept of Natural Law in Greek Thought', 522.

89. See: Agamben, *The Kingdom and the Glory*, 9; Samuel Sandmel, *Philo of Alexandria: An Introduction* (Oxford: OUP, 1979), 122, 124.

90. Koester, 'The Concept of Natural Law in Greek Thought', 530.

91. Ibid.

92. Porter, *N&D*, 66–70.

93. Ibid., 69.

94. Ibid., 71.

95. Ibid.

96. Ibid., 72.

independent intelligibility of nature, which affirmed the priority of a doctrine of creation, 'proved to be central to the development of scholastic thinking on the natural law.'[97] However, it will also prove central to her intellectual *détente* between natural law and her positive account of the secular *mythos*.

Neither pristine nor homogeneous

Porter's promotion of the philosophical integrity and intelligibility of nature is not for the sake of establishing a universal foundation for the derivation of one pristinized or homogeneous definition of natural law. She argues that neither theologians nor jurists of the medieval era ever attempted to do this.[98] An illustrative case in point is the summary formulated by the canonist, Stephen of Tournai. Writing in the middle of the twelfth century, Tournai was the 'first' scholar of his time to describe 'four senses' (with an added 'fifth understanding') of the natural law. He writes:

> And it should be noted that the natural law is spoken of in four senses. For we speak of natural law which is introduced by nature itself, and is not placed only in the human person, but also in animals ... The law of nations, which takes its origin from human nature alone, as it were beginning with it, is also said to be a natural law. The divine law, which our highest nature, that is, God, taught us, and placed before us through the law and the prophets and the gospel, is also said to be natural law. We also speak of a natural law which includes at once both human and divine law, and also that law which is placed in all animals by nature. And according to this last understanding, something is established 'by natural law, that is, by divine, and that other primitive law.' Or, if you can stand a fifth understanding ... the natural law which is placed in the human person alone ... namely, [a faculty directed towards] doing good and avoiding evil. This is, as it were, a part of the divine law.[99]

Contrary to common perceptions, the scholastic concept of natural law 'does not begin with a fully determinate account of human nature, on the basis of which they [the scholastics] deduce moral conclusions.'[100] Nor did they begin with an autonomous understanding of practical reason. Reason was always expressed in continuity with a 'more general theory of intelligibility of the natural world' or upheld as 'the distinctive aspect of human nature' that is the capacity for 'rational discernment in drawing moral conclusions from reflections on human nature.'[101]

97. Ibid., 75.

98. Ibid., 13.

99. Stephen of Tournai, Weigand. Quoted in: Porter no. 244–46. Quoted in: Porter, this a finite goodnessve thetes a point oft to note that she with natural law is that it *N&D*, 76. See also: Huguccio of Ferrara, Lottin, 109–10. Quoted in: Porter, *NasR*, 14–15.

100. Porter, *N&D*, 79.

101. Porter, *NasR*, 71; Porter, *N&D*, 63.

At the same time, medieval accounts of naturalism and reason were guided by a theological commitment to scripture as the interpretive key to grasping the central importance of certain human inclinations, which then informed communal reflection on what should be considered normative to human nature and human reason.[102] Furthermore, the scholastics had no theological inhibitions about appropriating from non-Scriptural or non-Christian sources. Instead, they expounded a natural philosophical-theology that understood human reason and scripture to be 'complementary and mutually interpreting, in such a way that reason enables us to comprehend and interpret scripture even as scripture completes and corrects the deliverance of reason.'[103]

The retrieval of this contextualizing aspect of scholastic history is of particular interest to Porter because it 'can remind us that moral pluralism within the Christian community is inevitable and probably healthy.'[104] Whilst modern moral theology has a tendency to 'leave history behind', the scholastics remained attuned to the historical character of the 'act of interpretation'[105] – that, by its very nature, the interpretation of scripture or even a major historical text is never a 'passive process' because 'our agenda in reading scripture [or any text for that matter], our sense of what is central and what is marginal, and our assumptions about what would count as a plausible reading are all shaped by prior interpretations.'[106] By allowing space for 'social and historical factors' they could legitimately speak of 'multiple natural laws',[107] differentiated depending on whether they construed the relationship between nature and reason as 'more as nature, or more as reason, or equally as nature and reason.'[108]

A substantive point that Porter is trying to impress is that the genius of the scholastics is being obscured by the fact that they did not circumscribe the natural law in consonance with the 'centrally important' presuppositions of modern philosophy and theology.[109] In particular, that a theory of natural law is invariably constituted by the epistemological derivation of 'a set of precepts derived deductively from … self-evident rational axioms.'[110] As Porter is at pains to point out, such an understanding 'was quite foreign to the authors under

102. Ibid., 136, 141.

103. Porter, *NasR*, 17; C.f. Porter, *N&D*, 124, 145–6. To reiterate, according to Porter, the scholastics were certainly conscious of the Scriptural particularity of their natural law framework. Yet, they did not believe this negated its potentially universal appeal.

104. Porter, 'Mere History', 116.

105. Ibid., 106.

106. Ibid., 155.

107. Porter, 'A Tradition of Civility', 36; Porter, 'Christian Ethics and the Concept of Morality', 12.

108. Albert the Great, *De Bono*, 5.1.2. Quoted in: Porter, 'A Tradition of Civility', 36.

109. Porter, *NasR*, 24.

110. Jean Porter, 'Contested Categories', *The Journal of Religious Ethics*, vol. 24, no. 2 (Fall 1996), 212.

consideration.'[111] In *Natural & Divine Law*, a distinction is made between the scholastic theologians, who understood natural law, first and foremost, as a set of precepts, and the scholastic canonists, who tended to think of natural law as principally a capacity for judgement. But Porter goes on to add a clarification, lest one over-exaggerate the difference:

> [T]he natural law in its primary sense is understood [by the scholastic theologians] as comprised of the fundamental norms by which the power of moral discernment operates, rather than as the power itself; but neither they nor the canonists consider the natural law in its primary sense to be comprised of specific moral rules.[112]

In another place she elaborates further on this definition:

> [T]he natural law is fundamentally a capacity or power to distinguish between good and evil; it is intrinsic to the character of the human soul as made in the Image of God, and therefore it cannot be altogether obliterated.[113]

This does not mean that the scholastics never referred to the existence of specific moral norms. Indeed, they certainly did.[114] Yet, it is misleading to assume that such precepts were extrapolated from a set of philosophically determinate – tradition-independent – first principles of practical reason.[115] The formulation of moral norms or precepts was never a 'deductive' process, but, rather, an 'analogical' or 'interpretive and associative' one.[116] As Porter explains, 'The starting points from which the scholastics argued could not be rendered consistent with any conclusion whatever, but they did underdetermine their conclusions, in such a way as to provide room for social and historical factors to shape those conclusions in fundamental ways.'[117] For this reason, the scholastics happily accommodated not just a plurality of definitions of natural law, but a plurality of different normative interpretations of its normative conclusions.

Gratian's Decretum

Based on these disparate remarks alone, one may still wonder how such an eclectic collage of definitions might provide persuasive points of *entrée* into contemporary

111. Ibid.

112. The one textual exception to this is the 'Tractaturus magister' of unknown authorship. See: Porter, *MOL*, 79 fn. 23.

113. Porter, *NasR*, 13.

114. Porter, *N&D*, 90.

115. Ibid., 136, 146.

116. Porter, 'A Tradition of Civility', 36.

117. Ibid.

secular discourse. Porter is certainly conscious of this. Moreover, she, herself, repeatedly notes that, ostensibly, such a 'distinctively theological' framework appears 'confused, incomplete, and unsophisticated' when it then tries to speak of 'reason', or 'nature', or the 'natural order'.[118]

At this juncture in her narrative, Porter reclaims a further distinction that is pivotal to her genealogy: the distinction between 'the natural', which, as already highlighted, can be defined in a multiplicity of ways, and 'the conventional', referring to the development of cultural customs and decrees. Porter is of the firm opinion that a renewed appreciation for the scholastics understanding of the intrinsic – as opposed to dichotomous – relation between 'natural' and 'conventional' principles can provide an invaluable point of correspondence with contemporary secular jurisprudence.[119]

To emphasize the strategic importance of this point, Porter repeats in several places throughout her literary corpus a quotation taken from the beginning of Gratian's *Decretum* that not only is thought to have put natural law on the theological agenda of the scholastics, but, in many respects, forms another starting point for Porter's own reconstruction. As such, it is worth quoting here:

> The human race is ruled by a two-fold rule, namely, natural law and custom. The natural law is that which is contained in the law and the Gospel, by which each person is commanded to do to others what he would wish to be done to himself, and forbidden to render to others that which he would not have done to himself. Hence, Christ [says] in the Gospel, 'All things whatever that you would wish persons to do to you do the same also to them. For this is the law and the prophets.'[120]

To a contemporary reader, Gratian's 'two-fold rule' would appear to commingle two irreducibly distinct provenances of moral knowledge: the law of reason and the law of the Gospel. However, this judgement, says Porter, is both 'contestable' and 'unjustified' with respect to the scholastic paradigm of natural law because, again, it involves the employment of a system of evaluation that is 'not their own'.[121] When situated within a 'tradition', one can begin to understand the importance of the classical distinction between 'the natural' and 'the conventional' in bringing consistency, systematization, and unity to scholastic reflections on the natural law and the relationship between nature, reason, and revelation.

118. Porter, 'Contested Categories', 207.

119. Porter, *MOL*, 67.

120. Porter quotes this passage throughout her corpus which emphasises its importance. Ibid., 72; Porter, *NasR*, 346; Porter, *N&D*, 129; Porter, 'A Tradition of Civility', 33; Porter, 'Contested Categories', 213.

121. Porter, *NasR*, 29.

On this point, Porter asserts that the scholastics aligned themselves more closely to Cicero than to Aristotle insofar as they were conscious of how human society, inclusive of its practices and social institutions, encompasses a 'long-standing process of human reflection and invention', as opposed to being the immediate expression of human inclinations or 'pre-conventional givens'.[122] Thus, the 'natural' in 'natural law' was able to include not only that which exists prior to 'human customs and enactments', but also the practices and conventions that have their genesis in a series of 'naturally given starting points'.[123] In fact, because of the flexibility of the tradition, '[t]he scholastics quickly saw that almost any originating principle of human life can be regarded as 'nature', corresponding to the law embodied – actually or ideally – in social conventions.'[124]. This reading of Gratian clearly embodies her understanding of the doctrine of creation. When this relationship is appreciated, one can begin to perceive how her liberal-secular rapprochement with scholastic theology can be rendered clear and coherent: that all these elements, 'scripture, reason, truth, and sound judgment', can be mutually considered to form a 'pre-conventional natural law' and, as such, be mutually and plurally considered as instantiations of 'divine wisdom and will'.[125]

Identifying this scholastic conviction underscores Porter's genealogical avowal that Grotius's 'impious hypothesis' most certainly '*is* an innovation'.[126] For unlike Finnis, who deemed the principle of the '*etiamsti daremus non esse Deum*' to be a legitimate philosophical commonplace (even if it was employed within theological debates), Porter contends that it was actually being espoused as a legitimate theological commonplace. She asserts that Grotius was a theologian who, following the scholastics, saw no disconsonance between theology understood as a doctrine of creation and natural law understood as reason itself. The fundamental innovation he introduced was that these two sources were considered epistemologically distinct. Revelation, therefore, tended to be viewed as something confirmatory, correctional, or supplementary to the determinations of reason alone. A practical corollary of this theoretical shift towards a new epistemological foundationalism is that natural law is gradually reinvented as a philosophical mechanism with which to extrapolate, evaluate, and codify specific moral norms, a reinvention Porter laments since it negates the key strength she identifies in the scholastic tradition – its ability to incorporate a diverse range

122. Ibid., 11.

123. Porter, *N&D*, 77; Porter, *NasR*, 12.

124. This also speaks to the methodological relationship between natural law as a 'product of reason', natural law as a 'substantive account of [the good] of human nature', and natural law as a 'distinctively theological' expression of the teachings of revelation/cripture. Ibid., 13.

125. Porter, 'Christian Ethics and the Concept of Morality', 10.

126. Porter, *NasR*, 27. (IAITT).

of 'legitimate' definitions of the natural law, even under its primary rubric as a principle of order.[127]

A theological loss and a theological gain

I want to conclude this section by returning to Porter's retrieval of the 'theologically indispensable' distinction between nature and grace – the 'programmatic *logos*'. The distinction between nature and grace is no doubt attractive to Porter because it provides her with a metaphysical foundation with which to legitimate the integrity of the natural order in relative isolation from Christology. Nevertheless, she still describes this position as 'theological' as it gives priority to a doctrine of creation. This denotes the principal reason why Porter believes the scholastic natural law tradition can be made relevant to both contemporary theological and secular ethics. The principal reason being that it allows nature and reason to be brought together – rather than juxtaposed – within a theological framework.[128] But this move comes at a theological cost, a cost that is mitigated by a corresponding theological gain:

> The loss is that, for the scholastics, morality is desacralized; it is seen as a natural phenomenon, as an expression of the human person's continuity with the rest of the world, and not as in itself a medium for transcendence. In compensation, however, the scholastics offer a theological interpretation of this naturalistic morality, precisely because they interpret the natural world itself theologically ... This does not imply for them that the moral life in itself offers a way to salvation; on the contrary, they insist that it does not.[129]

In the following section, I will explain how this purportedly scholastic insight becomes a hermeneutical key to discerning the 'unsaid' that governs her further reclamation of Aquinas's natural law. The fundamental problem with this position is that, theologically speaking, it seems almost indistinguishable from Finnis's 'desacralized' and 'freestanding' position, which she ripostes. After promising to reclaim a 'robustly theological' account of the natural law, she ultimately admits that, from a certain perspective, 'a theological justification for endorsing the value of human existence is not needed.'[130] But if the argument I have been making thus far is sound, then a theological justification is needed that guides Porter's 'selective retrieval' of scholastic thought. That theological justification is the 'programmatic *logos*'. It's just being left 'unsaid'.

127. Porter, 'A Tradition of Civility', 35.

128. Referencing the research of the historian D. E. Luscombe, Porter notes that, particularly during the first half of the Twelfth century, nature and reason were often used interchangeably. Porter, *N&D*, 86–7.

129. Ibid., 100.

130. Porter, *NasR*, 135.

Section IV: Resituating Aquinas

A man of his time

Porter believes that it is ignorance of the mediating influence of scholastic natural law theories that has augmented the unfortunate tendency to read Aquinas' contribution as an ahistorical and philosophically self-contained system. This approach belies the fact that, as with the scholastics before him, Aquinas's understanding of such fundamental concepts as 'nature' and 'reason' were already influenced by a host of Christian and pre-Christian sources. Similarly, since Porter argues that Aquinas shared the scholastics' irenic disposition towards his 'secular' authorities and the natural world, he, too, was 'very much a man of his time'.[131] He must, therefore, be read through the eyes of the scholastics, not the eyes of Grotius or Kant. But I will show that, when interpreted against her desacralized reading of the scholastics, the secular *mythos* plays an especially powerful role in destabilizing her reading of Aquinas. I will begin by examining how Porter relocates the roots of Aquinas's ethical naturalism in the metaphysical-teleological world view of the scholastics. I will then attend to what she believes is the 'cornerstone' of Aquinas's natural law – his account of human happiness. Strategically, human happiness is considered in abstraction from Aquinas's eschatology, which, as with Finnis, is left 'unsaid'.

A contradicting ambiguity

Like the scholastics' approach, Aquinas's natural law is also said to be 'paradoxical' since it straddles divisions – fundamental 'either-or's' – by simultaneously affirming 'that the natural law reflects universal aspects of human existence' and, yet, 'it can only be fully understood in theological terms.'[132] Thus, at several points throughout her literary corpus, Porter makes promising remarks that suggest she is wanting to reclaim an interesting synthesis of philosophy and theology. For instance, in the *Recovery of Virtue*, she states that the only text she will consider of Aquinas is his 'mature theological synthesis' (the *Summa Theologiae*).[133] Similarly, in *Moral Action & Christian Ethics* she asserts that 'I have not attempted to draw sharp distinctions between the theological and the philosophical' because 'it does not seem to me there is much to be gained in the way of clarity or persuasiveness.'[134] In her article on 'The Subversion of Virtue' in Thomistic thought, she states her resistance to 'the distinction between theology and moral philosophy set by the academy'.[135] In one of her more recent works, *Justice as Virtue*, she describes how a renewed appreciation for Aquinas's theologically imbued world view offers

131. Porter, *Justice as Virtue*, 53.
132. Porter, *NasR*, 324.
133. Porter, *ROV*, 32.
134. Porter, *MA&CE*, 2.
135. Porter, 'The Subversion of Virtue', 40.

a 'salutary corrective to earlier attempts to draw a sharp line between Aquinas' supposedly pure philosophy and his theological aim and convictions'.[136] Thus, when considered in coincidence with her recurring claim to be developing a 'theological account of natural law' or to be undertaking a 'theologically informed account of legal authority', one would think it safe to presume that she is reacting against those who argue that you can extricate natural law from its theological roots and context.[137]

However, such a conclusion is ultimately rendered ambiguous and uncertain. As I have already noted, there remains a definitional ambiguity – an 'unsaid' – surrounding how she distinguishes a 'distinction', from a 'sharp distinction', from a 'dichotomy'. This ambiguity only intensifies further when she turns to Aquinas. A close analysis of the same texts just cited reveals the presence of an alternate, seemingly contradictory, line of interpretation. For instance, in the *Recovery of Virtue*, Porter reveals her intention to restrict her analysis of Aquinas to 'the more philosophical components' of the *Summa Theologiae* and to have 'generally bracketed its more properly theological components'.[138] Why? Because she believes it is his philosophical formulation of the 'natural end' and the 'natural human good' that is 'most illuminating to contemporary Christian ethics.'[139] The exact hermeneutic is replicated in her article on the unity of the virtues: 'In what follows, I will focus on the philosophical aspects of Aquinas's theory of the virtues, bracketing the more distinctively theological aspects of that theory.'[140] Similarly, in *Moral Action & Christian Ethics*, she also states that her approach will be to 'start on the philosophical side', which likely correlates with her claim that 'one of the most attractive implications of Aquinas' account of the moral life' is that, by allowing 'God to be God', it 'frees us to be our limited individual selves.'[141] In her article on 'The Subversion of Virtue', she describes how Aquinas's 'whole theory of morality presupposes sharp distinctions between the natural and the supernatural.'[142] Such distinctions allows one to affirm that 'the natural order is good and complete in itself' and can, thus, be interpreted philosophically.[143] In her latest book, *Justice as Virtue*, we are told that she has focused her study 'on the fundamental rational structure and the philosophical implications of Aquinas' theory of virtues' because he distinguishes 'reason and nature' from 'revelation and grace' in order to 'safeguard' their 'relative integrity and independence'.[144]

136. Porter, *Justice as Virtue*, 52.

137. Porter, *NasR*, 5; Porter, *MOL*, xvi.

138. Ibid., 32.

139. Porter, *ROV*, 32.

140. Jean Porter, 'The Unity of the Virtues and the Ambiguity of Goodness', *Journal of Religious Ethics*, vol. 21, no. 1 (Spring 1993), 141.

141. Porter, *MA&CE*, 5, 110.

142. Porter, 'The Subversion of Virtue', 38–9.

143. Ibid., 39.

144. Porter, *Justice as Virtue*, 51, 52.

A conflicted choice

Evidently, there is a palpable conflict that continues throughout Porter's literary *oeuvre* between, on the one hand, wanting to reclaim the robustly theological framework of the scholastic-Thomistic natural law tradition, and, on the other hand, wanting to eschew that same tradition by reinstating a dichotomous distinction between philosophy and theology, nature and grace, reason and revelation. It is interesting to note that in an essay published in 2009, written in hindsight of her seminal contributions on natural law, Porter reveals that, whilst she still maintains 'that the natural law cannot be adequately understood outside a theological context', she has only *now* come to realize 'that the dichotomy between a theological and a philosophical account of natural law is too simplistic.'[145] This is a perplexing admission. For was it not the case, as I have demonstrated above, that a defining mark of her earlier contribution, particularly in *Nature as Reason* (published 2005), was to negate such a dichotomy? But now she appears to be implying that it is only in hindsight that she has come to realize that this dichotomy was 'too simplistic'. Does this infer that she was previously an exponent of such a dichotomy? In light of all that has been said, one would think that Porter would be quick to follow her admission by reaffirming the essentiality of proffering a 'theological account' of Thomistic thought. Howevever, such is not the case. Instead, she writes that Aquinas's persuasiveness is tied to his philosophical accessibility:

> In my view, Aquinas's account of the natural law depends in part on philosophical claims, more specifically on a broadly Aristotelian philosophy of nature, which implies the actuality, the epistemic accessibility, and the normative significance of a shared human nature. As such, it does offer resources for defending and evaluating substantive moral claims on the basis of rational considerations that we might reasonably hope to be persuasive, even across the boundaries of distinct traditions of rational inquiry.[146]

Earlier I argued that Porter's desire to re-narrate natural law away from a series of historically questionable dichotomies was interlinked with her desire to re-narrate popular assumptions about the liberal-secular *mythos*. Hence, I suggested that the secular *mythos* was akin to a Hegelian thesis which heralds a dialectical transcending of the 'law of an excluded middle.' In reality, however, the strategic wish to baptize her vision of liberal-secularism only serves to instate another fundamental either-or: Either you reclaim the theological robustness of

145. Jean Porter, 'Does the Natural Law Provide a Universally Valid Morality?', in *Intractable Disputes about the Natural Law*, ed. Lawrence S. Cunningham (Notre Dame, IN: Notre Dame University Press, 2009), 90.

146. She does go on to say that the natural law, at least in terms formulated by Christians, does require theological specification since many of its normative conclusions rest upon theological presuppositions. Ibid., 90–1.

the authentic natural law tradition, including its eschatological dimension, or you dress-up 'dichotomies' as – theologically supported – 'distinctions' in a bid to stay relevant and credible within the secular *polis*. The ambiguity that runs throughout her work thus gives voice to the tension that this 'either-or' creates. This suggests that what is being left 'unsaid' here is that Porter is unable to reframe the natural law tradition in the way she originally sets out to do, namely, as a philosophical and theological synthesis. Arguably, this is because she has allowed her reconstruction of the tradition to be framed, dialectically, by her underlying construction of the secular *mythos*.

The closest Porter ever comes to recognizing or revealing this dilemma is in relation to a comment she makes in *Nature as Reason* concerning how, from a Christian perspective, the virtue of justice is 'ambiguous':

> The city of God and the city of the world are two separate realms, and the Christian will have to choose at some point where her final allegiance will lie. The scholastics, including Aquinas, tended to affirm the goodness and value of the earthly city and its constitutive ideal of justice, even while they relativized its claims.[147]

If, as this passage suggests, a Christian must choose her final allegiance, Porter's choice is already apparent. But to suggest that Aquinas, himself, was faced with the same 'either-or' is anachronistic. Perhaps this marks a significant instance of what she describes as 'reading Aquinas against himself' for contemporary purposes by exploiting the 'seeds of his own revision'.[148] At the very least, it seems to contradict, unequivocally, the metaphysical continuity that her account of the doctrine of creation was thought to instantiate. Nevertheless, once we appreciate the fact that this 'choice' does operate as a starting point for Porter's reclamation of natural law, it is no longer surprising that her 'Thomistic' reconstruction of natural law is centred upon less soteriologically and eschatologically imbued themes such as the 'natural end', 'natural desire', and the 'natural virtues'. In order to illuminate more fully how this choice is both underpinned and illuminated by the theological 'unsaid' and how it inflects her reading of Aquinas, I will now elaborate briefly on each of these 'natural' notions in turn.

The natural end

Porter believes that Aquinas appropriated the scholastics' general metaphysical framework within which they developed a naturalistic account of ethics that, she argues, is 'credible and persuasive', even when scrutinized by 'contemporary biological science'.[149] The most important consequence of this is that Aquinas,

147. Porter, *NasR*, 220.
148. Porter, 'At the Limits of Liberalism', 389.
149. Porter, *NasR*, 322.

like the scholastics, was a metaphysical realist who had no trouble setting forth an account of the moral good based upon an inquiry into the nature of creation itself. That is to say, to know the good for humankind presupposes that there is a human nature that, in principle, is knowable. To know the good to be pursued, therefore, is dependent upon knowing what it means to instantiate the nature that is peculiar to a particular creature's form of existence. Thus, knowledge of the moral 'ought' is indeed dependent upon knowledge of the anthropological 'is'. More specifically, it is by reflecting theoretically upon the intelligibility of the human inclinations with 'the light of natural reason' that one can analyse and discern their normative (obligatory and forbidden) significance (ST I-II 91.2).[150] This is expressed in the emergence of 'certain ideals of virtue', which are thence considered 'naturally desirable.'[151] Porter concludes that, for Aquinas, there is 'no gap to be bridged' between facts and values because his theory of the human good is able to integrate harmoniously a speculative account of human nature with the practical judgements of human reason.[152]

Since we can bring various theories of human nature to bear upon our practical considerations, Porter believes that Aquinas remained agnostic as to whether the normative content of the natural law can be 'equally known to all' (ST. I-II 94. 4). As such, the precepts of the natural law must remain general. In order to give concrete force to these precepts, Porter argues that we must allow for a process of communal reflection, which allows room for both 'rational persuasion' as well as 'the formation of custom'.[153] However, what Aquinas brings to communal reflections about the natural law is a unique synthesis of the scholastics' metaphysical framework of goodness with an Aristotelian emphasis upon *eudaimonism*. Why this is significant is that it further extends the point that the natural law is not a reductivistic analysis of 'close-in' telelologies of human biology, but is, rather, a theoretical reflection upon a creature's teleological orientation towards ultimate fulfilment and perfection.[154]

The 'cornerstone' of Aquinas's natural law, says Porter, is his theory of human happiness, which is defined in accordance with the determination of the *ultimus finis*. Porter is conscious that to orientate the discernment of moral norms around a consideration of a final end would likely be considered inimical to contemporary philosophical thought. Furthermore, like Finnis, Porter laments the fact that Aquinas's most detailed discussion on human happiness is centred upon the supernatural end (the contemplation of God) of human existence.[155] In order to remedy this 'obstacle', Porter narrows her attention to what she refers

150. Porter, 'Does the Natural Law Provide a Universally Valid Morality?', 77.

151. Porter, *NasR*, 322.

152. Porter, *ROV*, 44.

153. Porter, 'Does the Natural Law Provide a Universally Valid Morality', 88.

154. Porter, *NasR*, 322. I have appropriated the phrase 'close-in' teleologies from: Steven A. Long, *Natura Pura* (New York: Fordham University Press, 2010), 157.

155. Porter, *NasR*, 144.

to as 'connatural' or 'terrestrial' happiness by reconstructing Aquinas's terse and undeveloped remarks on the natural end. Hence, she reformulates Aquinas's first principle of practical reason as follows: 'all persons naturally seek happiness, that is, the fullest possible enjoyment of the good(s) that each believes will perfect and fulfil him or her as a human being.'[156]

To defend the legitimacy of this reformulation, Porter takes critical aim at Henri de Lubac who, she asserts, 'denies that we need speak of a natural end of human life' or that 'there is any relation between natural law and beatitude.'[157] De Lubac is accused of downplaying the distinction that is absolutely essential to Porter's reconstruction of Aquinas' natural law – the distinction between nature and grace.[158] This, I would argue, is a misreading of de Lubac (and of Aquinas too). De Lubac certainly affirms the existence of a natural end in Aquinas's thought.[159] The more exegetically complex question is whether that natural end is free-standing, that is to say, ontologically independent of, and unmediated by, a single divine *telos*. On this point, Porter acknowledges that she might be misreading Aquinas.[160] Yet, throughout her vast literary output, the impression is given that references to a supernatural *telos* are irrelevant to doing natural law. This is because the 'natural fulfilment' of the 'natural end' is 'good and complete', meaning we would not be left unsatisfied or 'tormented by unfulfilled longings' even if we were not called to a supernatural end.[161] This being the case, it is hard not to see how Porter's distinction between the natural and the supernatural end can be considered to be simply epistemic, rather than ontologically reified into a *duplex-ordo*.

The natural desire

The 'programmatic' clue that Porter does ontologically reify the distinction between the natural end and the supernatural end is found in her anthropological disavowal of 'an actual, positive desire for God.'[162] Her most detailed defence of this point is actually found in the first essay she ever published, 'Desire for God'. Despite the historical nascency of this essay, it has remained 'programmatic' to the extent that, even when left 'unsaid', its fundamental claim continues to substantiate the *logos* behind her commitment to a theological *duplex-ordo* and justifies her 'philosophical' reaction to the secular *mythos*.

156. Porter, *ROV*, 86. Porter shares Finnis' poly-teleological understanding of the ultimate end of human life. 'Aquinas', she writes, 'does allow for the possibility that the goal of human life might be inclusive rather than a dominant end.' Ibid., 78.

157. Ibid., 379, fn. 64, 104 fn. 70.

158. Ibid., 383 fn. 69.

159. De Lubac, 'Duplex Hominis Beatitudo', 599–612.

160. Porter, *NasR*, 380.

161. Ibid., 158 fn. 24.

162. Porter, 'DFG', 52.

At the heart of the essay is how to understand what Aquinas meant by the doctrine of the *desiderium naturale* and how this doctrine informs his relationship between the natural and supernatural economy. According to Porter, the first step to an accurate exegesis is to read the doctrine of the *desiderium naturale* through the prism of the scholastic-Thomistic doctrine of creation. Creation itself is orientated by divine decree towards a perfection of form. Since the notion of perfection/goodness is intrinsically linked to the notion of desirability (ST I q. 5. 3), all creatures, rational or irrational, can be said to have a natural desire for the fulfilment of their 'capacities through the enjoyment of a completely satisfying good.'[163] But the nature of that desire needs to be carefully nuanced. When Aquinas speaks of a creature possessing a natural desire for God he is simply affirming the presence of a natural, dynamic tendency to attain a connatural good, that is, 'to be themselves', perfectly, as God intended.[164] It has nothing to do, says Porter, with 'some special divine intervention into creation', or that all creatures have an innate desire for a supernatural *telos*.[165] 'For precisely this reason, Thomas is able to maintain a qualitative distinction between the desire for God inspired by grace (which *is* an actual, positive desire) and the natural desire for God that grace presupposes.'[166]

Imbedded within this quotation is an explicit endorsement of a two-tier structure that pivots upon a qualitative distinction between a purely formal desire for God (i.e., natural human fulfilment) and an actual desire for God in the beatific vision.[167] This qualitative difference in desires translates into a corresponding qualitative difference in the conceptualization of ends. The object of the formal desire for God is natural happiness, which is defined by Porter as a 'life of moral and intellectual reasonableness, culminating in the philosophical contemplation of the first cause of everything',[168] whereas actual happiness is only attained in the beatific vision.[169]

The inherent exegetical difficulty with this position is that Aquinas does avow that actual happiness (direct union with God) is the true ultimate end of the moral life. Porter certainly recognizes this point.[170] However, she believes it is possible to 'reconstruct' Aquinas in such a way as to preserve a sharp theoretical distinction between the natural and supernatural ends, whilst simultaneously protecting the inner integrity of the moral life within the 'overall economy of grace'.[171] The doctrinal consequences of this reconstruction, however, are manifest. First, Porter

163. Ibid., 53.
164. Ibid., 52.
165. Ibid.
166. Ibid., 52. (IAITT).
167. Ibid., 55.
168. Ibid.
169. Ibid.
170. Ibid., 55.
171. Ibid., 58, 56.

rejects any theological anthropology that holds that the dynamism of human nature is in any way conditioned by a natural desire for supernatural beatitude. Second, she suggests that there is nothing theologically incoherent about positing the possibility that human nature could be fulfilled without being supplanted by the call to a supernatural end through the bestowal of supernatural grace. Believing herself to be following Aquinas's thought on the matter, she writes:

> [T]here is no reason to deny that the proper operations of the rational creature could function quite well without the supernatural transformation of grace and glory … For most persons, it would be a life in which the natural inclinations of the human person are all attained in a balanced, orderly way, without injury to one's fellows; imagine the life of a happily married, inoffensive professor of philosophy with a pleasant social life and a bent towards civic affairs.[172]

Clearly, this position requires the construction of a 'two-tiered' – or *duplex-ordo* – theory of reality. Even though Porter would possibly contest this, it is hard to imagine how her theological justification for developing a moral theology that is 'self-contained' is possible without asserting a naturalism that is predicated upon a philosophical integralism, even if that integralism can be theologically justified.

The natural virtues

In her more recent work on natural law, Porter reveals that she has come to accept that 'human desire, choice, and action can be analysed in terms of inclinations towards basic goods, which can be grasped by reason, independently of any kind of speculative theoretical account of human nature' – a position that, prima facie, is synonymous with the NNLT[173] – though she does qualify this remark by saying that this does not imply that our entire understanding of human nature is contingent upon 'spontaneous rational apprehension[s]', thereby maintaining – at least to some degree – her previous position that, for Aquinas, our speculative knowledge of human nature does inform our practical judgements about the moral life.[174] Nevertheless, even in spite of this qualification, Porter's exegesis of Aquinas has progressively come to align itself more closely with that of her bête noire. Yet, what does remain distinctive about Porter's contribution is the way she interlinks terrestrial happiness as the 'proximate norm' for the natural law with terrestrial happiness as the 'practice of the virtues.'[175]

Porter's interest in virtue ethics is animated in part by her recognition of its historical persistence and popularity.[176] As she points out, secular ethicists are

172. Ibid., 68.
173. Porter, 'Does the Natural Law Provide a Universally Valid Morality?', 81.
174. Ibid., 83.
175. Porter, *NasR*, 162.
176. Ibid., 177.

'running towards' virtue-based moral theories as a balancing corrective to ethical legalism.[177] The ideals we associate as being paradigmatic of particular virtues are themselves a product of perduring communal reflection upon human experience, which involves, of course, a level of theoretical speculation concerning what constitutes the 'teleological ideal of human nature.'[178] It is important to accentuate, that, according to Porter, the virtues are principles of unity in the moral life. They connect and reflect the intelligibility of 'nature as nature' with the principal expression of natural law as 'nature as reason.'[179] By reason of this conceptual link, a life practicing the virtues is a life in pursuit of terrestrial happiness. Once approached in this way, Porter believes we can begin to understand how a theory of natural law is incomplete without a theory of virtue since it is the 'life of virtue' which provides the *telos* for the precepts of the natural law.[180] In fact, from a Thomistic perspective, a 'theory of natural law *is* a theory of virtue.'[181]

An important reason for Porter's interest in exploring how Aquinas's virtue ethics relates to his theory of natural law is that she believes it can illuminate even more clearly how theology and philosophy should relate in relation to his overall account of the moral life. The critical move here is, of course, very familiar. In order to safeguard the philosophical integrity of the natural virtues for the sake of secular import, Porter repeats and reiterates the perennial value of Aquinas's 'clear distinction' or 'sharp distinction' between nature and grace, the natural and the supernatural.[182] This 'distinction' takes on heightened significance here because it structures and informs a corollary two-fold distinction in Aquinas's virtue ethics. First, between the ontological integrity of the acquired and the infused virtues, and, second, between virtues that are orientated to a purely rational good and virtues that are orientated to God.[183] To understand exactly what Porter is trying to reclaim here, it is important to note that she distances herself specifically from de Lubac and Rahner, who, she asserts, are reluctant to interpret these distinctions in such 'sharp' terms.[184] This reluctance, she argues, is a tragic mistake. For it is only by maintaining the sharpness of these distinctions that we can preserve, theologically, certain 'insights we cannot afford to lose.'[185]

Although Porter leaves 'unsaid' what these indispensable insights are, it is not hard to determine what those insights might be in light of her defensive construction of the liberal-secular *mythos*. From an exegetical perspective, she

177. Porter, 'The Subversion of Virtue', 33.

178. Porter, *NasR*, 177.

179. Ibid., 178.

180. Ibid., 50.

181. Ibid., 323. (IAITT).

182. Jean Porter, 'Virtue', in *The Oxford Handbook of Theological Ethics* (Oxford: OUP, 2007), 217; Porter, *NasR*, 389; Porter, 'The Subversion of Virtue', 38–9.

183. Ibid., 38–9; Porter, 'Virtue', 214.

184. Porter, 'The Subversion of Virtue', 39.

185. Ibid.

asserts that, by virtue of the aforestated distinctions, Aquinas must be committed to rejecting 'any continuity' between the infused virtues, which are bestowed by God, and the acquired virtues which result from natural human effort.[186] In other words, not only are they rationally distinct from each other, but Porter also believes you *cannot* have both at the same time – the theological implication being that there is no continuity, either anthropologically or ontologically, between the natural and the supernatural end. However, this discontinuity is interpreted positively. It provides a methodological impetus for preserving a 'purely philosophical analysis of the virtues'.[187] Porter believes that Aquinas gives us an example of this. His distinction between acquired and infused virtues demonstrates a point of overlap between Christian and secular ethics.[188] More fundamentally, since the distance between the natural and supernatural end 'exceeds every standard of comparison', a theological interpretation of natural law must preserve the ethical autonomy of a desacralized natural order and of finite forms of moral goodness.[189] Accumulatively, such points begin to make explicit in her later work what has been the implicit argument running throughout the course of this analysis: that, although left 'unsaid', Porter's natural law defence of secular-liberalism is dependent upon the authority of a hidden theological 'unsaid', her ascription to a *duplex-ordo* theory – the 'programmatic *logos*'.

Section V: Re-deploying Aquinas

The incommensurability thesis

After exploring Porter's 'selective retrieval' and development of certain theoretical components of Aquinas's natural law, I will now address how she believes this framework can be deployed effectively within her construction of liberal-secular discourse. There are two key developments that ground what she calls the 'permanent significance' of Thomistic thought within both Christian and secular ethics. First and foremost, the nature of Aquinas's metaphysical claims must be recalibrated by Alasdair MacIntyre's 'tradition-guided' understanding of rationality. Second, Aquinas's theory of 'the right' must be matured into a doctrine of subjective natural rights, which, despite the Catholic Church's objections, can be used to support something like same-sex marriage.

I previously alluded to how Porter's commitment to doing natural theology is interlinked with her commitment to demonstrating how a specifically Christian ethic can and should be open to being found credible according to criteria that

186. Ibid., 41.

187. Ibid.

188. In the sense that he then uses Aristotelian categories as a basis with which to then speak analogically and qualifiedly about the acquired virtues and the life of grace. Ibid., 41.

189. Porter, 'Virtue', 218.

are 'external' to the tradition. A distinguishing feature of Porter's contribution is how she believes these criteria should be discerned. In *The Recovery of Virtue*, Porter explicitly affirms her commitment to a highly nuanced version of what she refers to as the 'incommensurability thesis'.[190] Unlike Aquinas, who established the objective intelligibility and the universal knowability of things in themselves within a common (Aristotelian) 'metaphysical biology', Porter argues that 'there is no way to show that one scheme is simply wrong, without presupposing the foundational beliefs of another scheme.'[191] This is because 'there is no neutral standpoint from which to evaluate schemas' because all theories of the good are located within distinct, culturally specific, narratives; the 'rival schemes are incommensurable'.[192]

It is important to clarify that, although she acknowledges her departure from Aquinas's conviction that 'at least the central tenets of morality are knowable to all (I-II. 94. 4–6)', Porter would demur at any attempt to conflate her thesis of incommensurability with that of either relativism or perspectivism.[193] This reflects her carefully nuanced revision of MacIntyre's 'third alternative', an alternative which tries to eclipse the epochal 'either-or' of modern epistemological foundationalism and postmodern perspectivism. Porter states emphatically that 'incommensurability not only does not exclude a generally agreed upon body of knowledge', but it also 'presupposes it.'[194] This is because the very idea of two (or more) perspectives being 'incommensurable' necessitates that they must, as a descriptive minimum, be based upon a mutual recognition of that same object. In other words, there must be, however general, some shared judgement about 'what sort of something this is'.[195] Therefore, Aquinas's general theory of goodness, which depends upon the intelligibility of the different kinds of species, remains valid and defensible even if one embraces the incommensurability thesis. But she hastens to add that this basic validity and defensibility does not necessarily mean that Aquinas's entire moral theory will always be found 'rationally compelling'.[196] 'To the contrary', she argues, 'there is good reason to believe it would not be' because it 'presupposes the whole structure of his philosophical and theological beliefs.'[197]

It is here that we come to the more advanced level of what she means by 'incommensurability'. As different cultures develop and diversify within their respective historical frameworks, we obviously find significant variations in the way these perspectives reflect upon and try to articulate the truth of whatever it is they are trying to grasp or understand. Reason is itself conditioned and

190. Porter, *ROV*, 54.

191. Ibid., 83, 54.

192. Ibid., 54.

193. Porter, *NasR*, 56, 63.

194. Porter, *ROV*, 55.

195. Ibid., 55–6.

196. Ibid., 56.

197. Ibid.

remains contingent upon the practical and intellectual tradition – the 'core commitments' – out of which it has evolved and continues to evolve.[198] What Porter appreciates and appropriates from MacIntyre's analysis is his acute sensitivity for a putatively paradoxical point – that it is precisely by becoming cognisant of the incommensurability of rational discourse that we can finally begin to discern more compelling and imaginative starting points for harnessing effective cross-cultural and intra-cultural dialogue. In the words of MacIntyre, 'reason can only move towards being genuinely universal and impersonal in so far as it is neither neutral nor disinterested.'[199]

This does mean that Christian natural law theorists should not try to offer a philosophically persuasive account of the world. According to Porter, one can aspire to attain a practical consensus regarding the 'truly human', but only through a non-coercive, yet pragmatic, negotiation with those who reason within other traditions.[200] This is why she speaks of her account of natural law as balancing ethical naturalism with cultural pragmatism.[201] In a certain sense, this represents the dialogical expansion of the scholastics' dialectical distinction between nature and convention or between 'genuine rationality' and 'genuine incommensurability'.[202] The normative conflict that arises when two different traditions clash will never be fully resolved on the basis of a purely rational or theoretical exchange alone. Rather, it will also require what she describes as an evaluation in terms of the 'liveability' or 'practical workability' of each respective tradition.[203] Whilst Porter does not expand in any significant detail as to how this existential criterion is to be cashed out into a clear criteria, it is obvious that she believes 'liveability' must reflect something of how 'we observe' our common human nature in its pursuit of common ideals.[204] Hence, she concludes that 'there need be no inconsistency between a strong version of metaphysical or epistemic realism and a secular-pragmatist account of reality.'[205]

Aquinas's permanent significance

We are now in a position to understand what Porter means when she affirms the 'permanent significance' of Aquinas.[206] Despite Porter's intention of returning

198. C.f. Jean Porter, 'Disposition of the Will', *Philosophia*, vol. 41 (2013), 299.

199. Alasdair MacIntyre, *Three Rival Versions of Moral Inquiry* (Notre Dame, IN: University of Notre Dame Press, 1990), 59–60.

200. Jean Porter, 'The Search for a Global Ethic', *Theological Studies*, vol. 62 (2001), 120.

201. Porter, 'Openness and Constraint', 535.

202. Ibid., 59; Jean Porter, 'Review: Three Rival Versions of Moral Enquiry', *The Journal of Religion*, vol. 72, no. 1 (January 1992), 134; Porter, *ROV*, 54; Porter, *N&D*, 141.

203. Porter, 'Openness and Constraint', 534.

204. Ibid.

205. Porter, 'Moral Ideals and Human Nature', 69–70.

206. Porter, *ROV*, 172–3.

natural law to its metaphysical and theological roots, her broader dialogical aspirations ultimately eschew the foundationalist authority of these claims, asserting instead their tradition dependence. Insofar as these metaphysical ideals are found to be rhetorically persuasive and are considered to have 'practical workability' by a political community, they can still retain a regulative force. Influenced by the rhetorical turn within secular jurisprudence, Porter distinguishes between natural law as a 'strategy of justification' and natural law as a strategy of 'rhetorical persuasion'.[207] Porter discounts the former (an example of which might be Finnis's explication of the universal 'modes' or 'requirements of practical reasonableness') because it mistakenly assumes that people reason solely on the basis of 'universal rational considerations alone'.[208] In contrast, the political-dialogical medium of 'rhetorical persuasion' aspires to engage one's interlocutors anthropologically, 'as they actually are … on the basis of [and in ongoing continuity with] their actual perceptions and desires'.[209]

This is where a scholastic-Thomistic natural law theory, informed (broadly) by an Aristotelian-metaphysical account of human nature, remains relevant – it can help to identify certain 'natural desiderata' or 'natural objects of the will' that, almost invariably, reflect what human beings 'spontaneously desire'.[210] Similar to how Finnis enumerates a list of basic goods, Porter develops a list of *desiderata*, which include to live, to experience the pleasures associated with basic human activities, to be healthy, to be free to pursue one's own spontaneous desires, to establish a close sexual bond, and to participate in public life.[211] Although these natural *desiderata* are insufficient in and of themselves to establish a universal moral polity built around a comprehensive and concrete set of norms, it can at least prescribe the general limits of tolerable behaviour and help support the establishment of a theory of subjective human rights.[212]

Defending subjective rights

Porter's re-narration of the scholastic-Thomistic natural law culminates in her staunch defence of subjective natural rights. The important word here is 'subjective'. Although she recognizes that Aquinas did not explicitly espouse a theory of subjective rights, she believes he came very close to it.[213] This is an important genealogical move in her strategic attempt to establish a point of dialogical irenicism between Christian and secular ethics. Porter traces the genesis of the

207. Porter, *MOL*, 177.
208. Ibid., 172.
209. Ibid., 173.
210. Ibid., 176–7.
211. Ibid., 176–7.
212. Ibid., 340.
213. Jean Porter, 'From Natural Law to Human Rights: Or, Why Rights Talk Matters', *Journal of Law and Religion*, vol. 14, no. 1 (1999–2000), 85; Porter, *NasR*, 356.

'modern' predilection for a *lingua* of rights to the convictions of the scholastic-Thomistic natural law. In particular, to how the scholastics defined natural law, first and foremost, as a personal power or capacity for moral discernment. From here, Porter (following Brian Tierney) asserts that we are but a 'short step' to the idea of a 'subjective right', also understood as a personal power.[214] Theologically speaking, the scholastics considered this capacity to be a constitutive element of what it means to be created in the *imago Dei*, along with the capacity for self-determination, self-mastery, and rational autonomy. All of which are, coincidentally, consistent with Porter's secular-liberal understanding of rational equality and of human rights.[215]

This genealogical illumination is a paradigmatic example of what Porter means by exposing the 'hidden theological assumptions' that continue to govern 'secular' thinking.[216] 'Western liberal ideals of equality and the commitment to fundamental rights reflect the pervasive influence of what were originally Christian ideals and practices – an influence so pervasive as to be almost invisible.'[217] This raises an important question. If this theological influence has since become invisible, in what way does it remain necessary? In her most recent work, Porter asserts that the 'critical point' for Aquinas is that the fundamental principles of morality do not depend on Christian revelation,[218] though they can be interpreted and endorsed theologically, meaning, they can be said to reflect the wisdom of God's creation. But it is no part of her argument that without this theological perspective, modern societies will descend into 'nihilism' or succumb to a 'radical utilitarianism'.[219] For although a theoretical defence of human rights might ultimately require recourse to a theological justification, the ubiquity and extensive employment of the term indicates that it encapsulates something inherent to human nature.[220] For this reason, theologians have a vested interest, says Porter, in being open to the possibility of defending human rights on 'philosophical grounds'.[221]

Although Aquinas did not directly equate natural rights with discrete moral powers, Porter believes that his teleological account of authority gives considerable moral liberty to the individual person. The key, she says, is to appreciate his conviction that human nature naturally desires its final end, which necessarily involves the capacity to freely pursue, through self-determining choice, 'one's natural aims.'[222] Since this capacity is itself teleologically justified on the basis of a common natural end, Porter concludes that we possess a natural authority to make 'right claims' because 'we share equally in the same status, an honourable

214. Ibid., 350.
215. Ibid., 351.
216. See above, fn. 52.
217. Porter, *MOL*, 338.
218. Porter, *Justice as Virtue*, 57.
219. Porter, *NasR*, 135.
220. Ibid., 371.
221. Ibid., 372.
222. Porter, 'From Natural Law to Human Rights', 460.

status attached to the human estate itself.'[223] But, to reiterate, that 'honourable status' derives not from a common desire for a supernatural *telos* in God; rather, it is justified on the authority of the normative force of a self-contained, poly-teleological and inclusive, natural *telos*.[224] This distinction helps to explain what it means to be 'rhetorically persuasive'. Porter would see no exigent reason to bring Christological or eschatological reflections to bear on the way in which we speak about human nature or human rights because human nature is not, by nature, orientated towards supernatural beatitude. (Such language is linguistically, if not existentially, tradition specific.) Instead, she appeals to those aspects of the tradition that secular-liberals would find more accessible, credible, and, thus, intelligible: the independent value of human freedom, the capacity for self-direction and self-determination, the inclusiveness of a poly-teleological *telos* to human life, and, of course, the preservation and promotion of natural rights.

A natural law defence of SSM

This reclamation and development of a Thomistic-scholastic account of natural law and natural rights is considered by Porter to be 'very far' from depending upon the Church's magisterium 'for knowledge of the moral law'.[225] Furthermore, since the scholastics interlinked and honoured the exercise of human freedom with the pursuit of right moral behaviour, she believes that there should be some theological recognition of the rights that individual Christians have 'over against' the Church[226] – for instance, and by way of an example, the right of a same-sex couple to not be prevented by the sociopolitical intrusions of the Catholic Church from entering into a civil marriage.

In opposition to the Catholic Church's official position, which has been defended by Finnis on natural law terms, Porter supports the recognition of same-sex marriages, but also on natural law terms. Of course, for the scholastics, marriage was thought to give clear institutional expression to the natural desire to procreate. But even if this was considered to be the primary or paradigmatic starting point for defining the purpose of marriage, it was never considered its only purpose or starting point. Returning to the distinction between 'nature' and 'convention', Porter argues that the moral realism of sexual relations ('nature as nature') is mediated through social expressions, which are themselves mediated through a process of rational deliberation ('nature as reason').[227] Since the process of rational deliberation is itself dialectical, the inquiry into what purposes constitute a marriage must always be left 'open-ended'.[228] Other purposes can

223. Ibid., 459.

224. Ibid., 459; Porter, *Justice as Virtue*, 145.

225. Porter, *N&D*, 316.

226. Ibid., 317.

227. Jean Porter, 'The Natural Law and Innovative Forms of Marriage: A Reconsideration', *Journal of the Society of Christian Ethics*, vol. 30, no. 2 (Fall/Winter 2010), 83.

228. Ibid., 84.

and do come to light 'through communal experience' and 'through theoretical reflection' according to the pragmatic exigencies of the current historical and sociocultural context.[229] Within contemporary discourse, Porter believes that the right to marry can and has been extended to legitimate and promote other relationships 'so long as they do not undermine the orientation of the institution toward procreation'.[230] For instance, she cites the example of heterosexual couples incapable of having children.[231] Therefore, a similar extension could be made again on natural law terms to same-sex relationships, since such relationships can serve to promote other purposes of marriage 'as an expression of deep interpersonal love' and 'mutual fidelity', and do so without diminishing the primary purpose of marriage as a 'framework for reproduction.'[232] To not extend this socially embodied institution in this way, Porter concludes, would only be 'arbitrary and therefore unjust'.[233]

Section VI: Unfurling the banner

Answering the right questions

At the start of this chapter, I identified three critical questions that serve as methodological starting points for Porter to open up the discoursive boundaries of natural law beyond the 'law of an excluded middle'. In light of this analysis, it is appropriate to begin this concluding section by summarizing how she answers these questions.[234]

The first question cast doubt upon what is arguably the primary assumption behind how natural law is typically portrayed within Catholic moral discourse – as a philosophical *lingua franca*, with which, through the autonomous exercise of practical reason, we can discern and affirm certain universal moral truths. There are three basic elements to Porter's critique of this position. The first element is genealogical. Contrary to popular perception, she argues that neither the scholastics, more broadly, nor Aquinas, more specifically, ever sought to derive a set of universal moral norms from the operations of practical or pure reason alone. Second, the genius of the scholastic-Thomistic system was precisely its ability to

229. Ibid., 88.
230. Ibid., 90.
231. Ibid., 92.
232. Ibid., 95.
233. Ibid.
234. The three questions were as follows: (1) 'Can we arrive at moral truths which are rationally compelling to all well-disposed persons, whatever their specific beliefs, commitments, and social/cultural location?' (2) 'To what extent does a sound account of the natural law depend on particular theological perspectives, and how is this reflected in our interpretation of its universality?' (3) What is the proper relationship between Christian and non-Christian sources in theological ethics?'

respect and integrate various interpretations of natural law because natural law (as a capacity for moral reflection rather than a means for moral argument) was for them mediated by a dialectical interplay between a teleological understanding of human nature and the sociopolitical expression of cultural convention. Third, influenced by MacIntyre, reason itself is socially and historically conditioned. This suggests that an alternate set of criteria is needed to establish and assess the intelligibility of moral norms in a manner that also respects one's interlocutors 'as they actually are'. Nevertheless, even if such resources can be used to establish the intelligibility of certain general moral truths about human nature, Porter does not believe they will yield a discrete set of specific moral norms that are of universal and timeless import.

Porter's answer to the second question continues this line of genealogical critique by challenging the assumed legitimacy of dichotomizing philosophy and theology, nature and grace, the natural and the supernatural. She attributes such oppositional thinking to neo-scholastic apologetics, which has then been projected, anachronistically, back onto scholastic-Thomistic thought. Since the medieval natural law tradition was informed by a doctrine of creation, it upholds a positive interpretation of the temporal order and advanced a natural theology that respected the integrity, intelligibility, and goodness of the natural world. The moral life, informed by the natural law, reflects this natural theology since it is teleologically focused on an understanding of terrestrial happiness as the practice and pursuit of natural virtue. Consequently, the moral life was considered to be simply a natural expression of our creaturehood – it is neither 'sacred', nor 'a means of transcendence', nor a 'locus for transcendence', nor 'a way to salvation'.[235] Nevertheless, since this position preserves and promotes the 'motif of the goodness of the natural', it remains, says Porter, 'robustly theological'.[236]

In response to her third question, Porter sets out to reject how the academy's strict delineation of moral philosophy from moral theology has dichotomized the relationship between Christian and non-Christian sources. After calling attention to the way in which the scholastic theological tradition allowed and encouraged the creative interplay between scripture and a plethora of other Christian and non-Christian textual sources (out of which a variety of natural law *theories* emerged), Porter makes the surprising claim that many of the liberal-secular ideals about the moral life are essentially the reifications of scholastic 'theological assumptions and commitments'.[237] Unfortunately, because moral theologians have tended to leave history behind, they have continued to try and harmonize their theological commitments by atrophying them, constrained by the assumption that moral theology must reconcile itself with the purported demands of the philosophical monolith that is secular reason.

235. Porter, *N&D*, 100–1.

236. See fn. 114.

237. Porter, 'Christian Ethics and the Concept of Morality', 15.

Whilst there is much to commend about this approach, it is important to remember that she substantiates the value of her 'selective retrieval' of the scholastic tradition by referencing the congruency of each of these points with the prevailing intellectual sentiments within the 'secular' academy.[238] If I am correct in making this connection, does it imply that Porter is using the idea of natural law to give 'cosmic legitimacy' to her historically-situated construction of the secular *mythos*? If so, it raises the leitmotif that is at the core of this work: Is it theologically cogent and dialogically coherent to allow one's construction of the secular *mythos* to regulate the hermeneutical starting points for a contemporary re-narration of the natural law tradition? If this is the case, does the foundational relationship between milieu and methodology mirror the strategic 'unsaid' – that you cannot credibly re-narrate the natural law without also re-narrating the credibility of the secular *mythos*?

Desacralizing the natural law

Throughout my analysis, I have tried to illuminate how Porter's contribution is regulated by a desire to marry the ideals of secular-liberalism with Christian moral theology on natural law grounds. I believe this desire is methodologically informed by John Courtney Murray's attempt to reverse the 'secular-drift'; a strategy that Porter admits to being in broad agreement with. What is being left 'unsaid' is that this strategy is dependent upon the theological tenability of separating nature from grace. For despite Porter's expressed ambition of overcoming dichotomies and dualisms, this analysis has exposed the presence of another narratological trajectory, the story of *duplex-ordo*, which conflicts with and undermines this ambition.

A plausible explanation for the concurrence of these two competing stories begins to surface once we examine the role played by the secular *mythos*. I argued that Porter's irenic construction of the liberal-secular *mythos* was intended to operate like a Hegelian thesis with which to synthesize the fundamental 'either-or's' that propel the fragmentation within current debates in natural law. Yet, it soon became apparent that, by reconstructing natural law in reaction to – even if in defence of – secular-liberalism, Porter ultimately reinstated the same fragmenting dichotomies, declaring her allegiance to the 'city of the world' construed in separation from 'the city of God'. Rather paradoxically, this allegiance is adjudged to be theologically legitimate since the scholastic-Thomistic 'distinction' between nature and grace affords a logical priority to a doctrine of creation. This, in turn, liberates Porter to bracket out natural law from divine government; to autonomize the natural end from the supernatural end; and to desacralize the moral life – erecting a shocking either-or between Christ and creation, nature and eschatology, theology and philosophy.

238. I have appropriated the phrase 'cosmic legitimacy' from: Stephen D. Smith, 'Book Review, *Ministers of the Law*', *Ethics*, vol. 122, No. 10 (2011), 205.

Is this theological loss truly an expression of divine wisdom, or is this loss theologically necessary to engage the secular *mythos*? If the latter, does this not represent a perspicuous example of how the secular *mythos* is clandestinely defining the 'robustly theological' roots of the natural law tradition? Murray declared that '[t]he secularist has always fought his battles under a banner on which is emblazoned his special device, "The Integrity of the Political Order." '[239] Similarly, Porter's natural law defence of the conventions of liberal-secularism and the independence of the natural order develops under a banner upon which is emblazoned her special device of 'desacralization'. It is telling that Alain Badiou once equated this very device with 'the secularism of argumentation', which raises another important question. Is Porter's notion of 'desacralization' a quasi-theological trope for 'secularization'? Badiou would seem to think so:

> For any truth that accepts its dependence with regard to revelation and narration is still caught in mystery, and philosophy's whole being consists in wanting to tear apart mystery's veil ... Now philosophy cannot begin except by a desacralization: it installs a discursive regime that is its own, purely earthly legitimation. Philosophy demands that the mysterious and sacred authority of proffered profundity be interrupted by the secularism of argumentation.[240]

One can trace within Porter's literary trajectory how her quiet commitment to defending the liberal-secular *mythos* by desacralizing the scholastic-Thomistic natural law tradition has brought her project into closer and closer affinity with Finnis's NNLT. Porter has acknowledged this in her reply to a critique composed by Martin Rhonheimer, revealing that her position, once 'carefully qualified', has 'come closer to the "new natural law" '.[241] After having brought these 'two voices' into a successive conversation, this 'closeness' can be evinced on several counts, including their mutual affirmation of a poly-teleological conceptualization of the natural end; their mutual commitment to distinguishing the speculative realm of salvific-eschatology from the practical realm of the moral life; their mutual openness to discerning a purely philosophical register with which to defend human rights; and their mutual desire to reconstruct natural law in a missionary manner, that is to say, in a manner that will be found intelligible and credible by their 'secular' interlocutors. Such levels of congruency make sense when one appreciates the fact that Finnis and Porter share a mutual, but heretofore 'unsaid', ascription to a theological *duplex-ordo* theory.

239. John Courtney Murray, *We Hold These Truths* (Oxford: Rowan & Littlefield, 2005), 37.

240. Alain Badiou, *The Age of Poets* (London: Verso, 2014), 36.

241. Jean Porter, 'A Response to Martin Rhonheimer', *Studies in Christian Ethics*, vol. 19, no. 3 (2006), 383.

Another insight that has emerged from this successive conversation is that Finnis and Porter share a common inheritance in the thought of John Courtney Murray. Although Finnis leaves this point 'unsaid', I noted the wide scholarly opinion (supported by defenders of the NNLT like Ryan Anderson) that the NNLT is the philosophical successor to Murray's theory of natural law.[242] Although time and space prevent me from developing this insight in detail, I do believe there is strong evidence to suggest that there is a deeper level to this inheritance than simply a mutual appreciation for Murray's prophetic analysis of the political milieu. In what James Rooney refers to as the final phase in his intellectual trajectory (after Vatican II), Murray intensified his interest in 'secularism' and, coincidentally, began to intensify his interest in the 'dual orders' of 'human history', on the one hand, and 'salvation history', on the other.[243] One contemporary interpreter of Murray, Leon Hopper, asserts that this kind of language reflects Murray's commitment to a 'Gelasian Dyarchy': 'Each of the two orders is differently based (in creation and redemption) and is directed toward different ends (civic friendship and eternal beatitude). Each can legitimately claim its own autonomy.'[244] This is why Murray has been called the 'careful compartmentaliser', especially with regards to separating the secular from the sacred.[245]

How exactly Murray, himself, understood the relation between these two orders remains somewhat ambiguous. Nevertheless, the point I want to raise is well articulated by Rooney. He argues that a decisive reason for Murray's 'non-reception' in the post-Conciliar years lies in how his understanding of nature and grace has been received. Leaving aside the theological tenability of this construction, the more pressing issue is whether, by assimilating Murray's theo-cultural analysis of secular-liberalism, Finnis and Porter have also inherited a theological anthropology that is unsound (contradicted by the Second Vatican Council) and, as such, eschews the way they construct and speak to their interlocutors. For what if the 'secular' is *not* like this? What if their 'secular' interlocutors are not creatures of a *duplex-ordo* ontology? What if, as de Lubac argues, human beings do share a natural desire for God that is more than a velleity? Would this change the way we read and speak about the natural law? One philosophical theologian who has sought to ask and answer such questions is John Milbank. It is to his contribution, as the 'third voice', that I will now move to analyse, asking whether the banner of 'Radical Orthodoxy' offers more promise for natural law than Porter's banner of 'desacralization'.

242. James Dominic Rooney, 'Murray's Balancing Act', *Journal of Church & State* (May 2015), 19.

243. Ibid., 16.

244. J. Leon Hooper, 'General Introduction', in *Religious Liberty. By John Courtney Murray*, ed. J. Leon Hooper S.J. (Louisville, KY: Westminster/ John Knox, 1993), 25.

245. Mensch and Freeman, *The Politics of Virtue*, 91.

Chapter 4

JOHN MILBANK'S GENEALOGICAL RIPOSTE: NATURAL LAW AS A HYLOZOISTIC RE-NARRATION OF DIVINE GOVERNMENT

Section I: A transition

The end of natural law?

The decision to consider the contribution of John Milbank to current debates in natural law will strike some as surprising for two reasons in particular. First, unlike Finnis and Porter, Milbank is yet to publish a dedicated monograph on the subject. Second, and more importantly, he is often accused by contemporary natural law theorists of being unequivocally opposed to the very idea. For instance, Graham McAleer refers to Milbank as the 'most recent promoter' of a Barthian inspired 'theological critique', which, he avows, 'amounts to nothing less than a rejection of natural law.'[1] Gregory Baum, in his essay, 'For and Against John Milbank', denounces Milbank's purportedly postmodern inspired riposte of 'universally shared values' because this necessarily precipitates an unfortunate willingness to 'abandon the ancient tradition of "natural law"'.[2] Similarly, Bernard Mulcahy bristles at Milbank's theological integralism, arguing that it 'must inevitably call the traditional notion of 'natural law' into question.'[3]

My decision to consider Milbank's comparatively diasporic contribution to natural law are three-fold. First, even though he is yet to publish a worked-out alternative to popular imaginings on the natural law, he nevertheless refers to the notion both implicitly and explicitly throughout his vast literary corpus. Such references, I will argue, are by no means merely incidental asides. They form an inexorable part of the distinctive genealogical analysis that gives rise to

1. Graham James McAleer, *Ecstatic Morality and Sexual Politics* (New York: Fordham University Press, 2005), 62.

2. Gregory Baum, 'For and against John Milbank', in *Essays in Critical Theology* (Kansas City: Sheed &Ward, 1994), 52.

3. Bernard Mulcahy, *Aquinas's Notion of Pure Nature and the Christian Integralism of Henri de Lubac* (New York: Peter Lang, 2011), 210.

and fortifies his critique of the so-called 'secular order' and all configurations of modern 'secular reason'.

Second, Milbank's repudiation of deploying natural law as a dialogical stratagem and his insistence that theological apologetics must give way to the discursive practice of 'out-narration' is increasingly viewed within certain quarters as the most theologically viable alternative to Finnis's NNLT.[4] Thus, it is within the parameters of this thesis to explore whether – or to what extent – this approach represents a philosophically-theologically superior alternative to reclaiming or reconstructing the epistemological edifice of natural law theory.

This leads to a third reason for engaging Milbank as the 'third voice' in this thesis. Although at times Milbank seems to cleave to a neo-orthodox dismissal of natural law as being symptomatic of what Karl Barth described as the 'secular misery' that is now adulterating modern Christian theology from within, I contend that there is actually something more positive to be intimated, something that has generally been overlooked and, accordingly, still remains to be formally identified and its implications adequately explored.[5] I will argue that, contrary to common perception, Milbank *is* a natural law theorist, but a theorist whose theory – or anti-theory – is still in the 'making'. Not simply because it remains something of a lacuna in his current scholarship, but, by virtue of an underlying commitment to upholding a 'Vichian'-inspired hylozoistic metaphysic, it must remain a theory suspended within a state of ongoing artifice and dynamic contingency.

In his book, *Beyond Secular Order* (2013), Milbank stated his intention of composing a sequel titled, *On Divine Government*, in which he hopes '[m]ore will be said about natural law'.[6] The fact that this text is yet to be published constitutes an indisputable impediment to establishing the finer lineaments of his interpretation and appropriation of the tradition. However, Milbank has published a six-part series on natural law and natural rights via an online journal, 'Church Life'. Broadly speaking, Milbank's approach to natural law involves two components: the diagnostic and the reparative. Although these articles still tend to focus on the diagnostic dimension of his thought, they do give valuable indicia of what the reparative dimension of his contribution might look like.

Illuminating the secular sub-plot

Since a defining aspect of Milbank's 'Radical Orthodoxy' is to articulate the unacknowledged theological presuppositions that enliven theories of secular reason, one might suspect that his voice is included simply to corroborate the

4. This is especially true of scholars associated with '*Communio*'. C.f. Tracey Rowland, 'Natural Law: From Neo-Thomism to Nuptial Mysticism', *Communio*, vol. 35 (2008): 374–96.

5. C.f. Karl Barth, *Church Dogmatics* 1/1, trans. G. W. Bromiley and T. F. Torrance (Edinburgh: T&T Clark, 1975), xiii.

6. John Milbank, *Beyond Secular Order* (Chichester: Wiley Blackwell, 2013), 119, fn. 11. (Henceforth *BSO*).

voice of this thesis.[7] However, the principal objective of this chapter is to elucidate another fundamental and problematic 'unsaid'. I will argue that, whilst Milbank certainly makes a valuable contribution in terms of wanting to reconnect natural law with a theology of divine government, his contribution is only rendered coherent ('made strange') by his unacknowledged dependency upon, and reaction to, his genealogical narration of the secular *mythos*. I will demonstrate that Milbank's acknowledged inability to broaden the horizons of 'Radical Orthodoxy' beyond the 'secularisation issue' is indicative of the constricting power that this 'unsaid' has on his contribution. For this reason, I assert that Milbank's noble attempt to raise the theological 'unsaid' of natural law is gnostically controlled and, thence, fragmented by his ongoing collusion with the very *mythos* he says that he wants to riposte.

In order to uncover this theo-cultural collusion, I will show how several of the architectonic themes that define the programme of 'Radical Orthodoxy' originated in reaction against the philosophical-theology of Donald MacKinnon. I argue that MacKinnon bequeathed a particular interpretation of Kant that, by genealogical extension, bequeathed a particular impression of the secular *mythos*, which Milbank has perpetuated. Furthermore, a reconsideration of Milbank's paper, 'A Critique of the Theology of Right', delivered at a conference in honour of MacKinnon in July 1986, reveals the surprising extent to which the thematic origins of 'Radical Orthodoxy' were shaped by debates in natural law.

Section II: Donald MacKinnon

Kant and Cambridge

Donald MacKinnon was the Norris-Hulse Professor of Divinity in Cambridge between 1960 and 1978. He is widely celebrated as one who forged a new and impactful trajectory for doing theology in the British academy, a trajectory generated by the conviction that if the theologian is to continue to have a place within the University, he/she must be attentive to the pressures coming from the 'philosophical frontiers' of human knowledge and be prepared to form a participative, dialogical, kinship with those who would otherwise seek to 'make protesting raids upon the theologians' cherished homeland.'[8] In his revealing essay, 'Theology as a Discipline of a Modern University', MacKinnon admitted that this

7. By referring to 'Radical Orthodoxy' in inverted commas, I am distinguishing Milbank's political program or cultural manifesto from *Radical Orthodoxy* the book series. Milbank, himself, makes a developmental distinction between Radical Orthodoxy as an originally 'academic movement' to Radical Orthodoxy becoming an 'embryonic cultural and political movement.' C.f. John Milbank, 'Radical Orthodoxy's First Decade', in *The Radical Orthodoxy Reader*, ed. John Milbank and Simon Oliver (London: Routledge, 2009), 367.

8. Donald MacKinnon, *Borderlands of Theology and Other Essays*, ed. George W. Roberts and Donovan E. Smucker (London: Lutterworth Press, 1968), 54.

metaphysical vision was greatly inspired by his own attempts to negotiate the interdisciplinary borders with philosophers in Cambridge.[9] Through these negotiations, he became acutely aware that, at least within Anglophonic philosophy, Continental philosophy had stopped with Kant; the force of his 'Copernican revolution' against speculative metaphysics could not be circumvented without enduring the intellectual opprobrium of the Philosophy Faculty. This obviously raised a pivotal question for any theologian interested in sustaining a philosophical gateway to dialogue with the 'secular' academy: What should one do with the tradition of Kant? Is he the villain – the one who insidiously demolishes Christian ontology and relegates religious language to the hermetic homeland of the Divinity Faculty? Or, alternatively, is he the necessary ally – the one whose transcendental turn, when understood as being reconcilable with his transcendental idealism, sustains a subspecies of theological apophaticism, or negative theology, that keeps the idea of God as an irreducible 'Ideal of Reason'?[10]

Although the taxonomy of villain and ally is always going to be somewhat superficial, the virtually uncontested reading of MacKinnon's philosophical-theology positions him firmly on the side of embracing Kant as an apophatic ally. MacKinnon speaks of the ontological prophylactic emanating out of the *First Critique* as an epistemological bulwark against the 'peculiar indulgence' of linguistic anthropomorphism, an intellectual error that he considered to be worse than metaphysical agnosticism.[11] The prophylactic shock of the *grenzen* is valued as something positive to the extent that it keeps the theologian cognisant of the 'limits of human discourse' and so able to converse intelligibly with those who are otherwise sceptical of the cognitive import of religious credenda and its speculative metaphysical utterances.[12]

Unsurprisingly, as someone who embraced the 'spirit of the *Aufklärung*' (which he says was 'baptized into Christ' via Kant's 'urgently needed' chastening of the metaphysical pretensions of pure reason), he maintained a formal commitment to the separation of disciplines:[13] 'The world of philosophy is one world', he said, and 'the world of faith is another.'[14] One would assume that, as a corollary to this apparent dualism, MacKinnon would have also jettisoned the propriety of trying

9. Donald MacKinnon, 'Theology as a Discipline of a Modern University' (1972), in *Philosophy and the Burden of Theological Honesty* (London: T&T Clark, 2011), 64–74.

10. This discussion – hero or villain? – was influenced by my attendance (2014) at Sarah Coakley's series of lectures, titled, 'On the Very Idea of Philosophical Theology: The Cambridge Tradition'.

11. Donald MacKinnon, 'Kant's Philosophy of Religion', in *Themes in Theology* (Edinburgh: T&T Clark, 1987), 20–39.

12. Ibid., 37–8. See: Mackinnon, *Borderlands of Theology and Other Essays*, 250–1; Donald Mackinnon, *The Problem of Metaphysics* (Cambridge: CUP, 1974), 57.

13. Donald MacKinnon, 'Aspects of Kant's Influence on British Theology', in *Kant and His Influence*, ed. George MacDonald Ross (London: Continuum, 1990), 360.

14. MacKinnon, *Borderlands of Theology and Other Essays*, 72.

to bridge these worlds by engaging in natural theology. Yet, he remained cognisant of how Kant's strict circumscription of intelligible discourse to the realm of the phenomena would ultimately 'evacuate Christian faith of any serious intellectual content.'[15] Liberal-modern theology risked a continued devolution into a 'facile Kantianism', where a realist Christology gives way to, and is subordinated by, a purely technical and subjective triumph of the moral over the dogmatic.[16] For this reason, MacKinnon endeavoured to surmount this tension by eclipsing the philosophical-cum-theological either-or that informed Karl Barth's entire theological enterprise: 'The Word or existence?'[17]

A man of the borderlands

Although within the academy the theologian must parlay according to the rules prescribed by the Kantian language game, MacKinnon also carved out a space known as the 'borderlands', a place where literature becomes the crucible in which the interdisciplinary boundaries that normally separate philosophy from theology are dissolved and subsequently transcended.[18] MacKinnon was particularly sensitive to the idea that, especially when confronted by tragedy, we arrive at a form of metaphysical and conceptual excess which allows for us to project our questioning beyond the realm of the subject and out unto the theo-ontological.[19] On this score, the supra-liminal space of the borderlands gives existential acknowledgement to how, within the mind of the individual, the worlds of philosophy and theology, the secular and the sacred, 'continually interpenetrate', and according to MacKinnon, 'it would be an illusion to deny the reality of the conflict.'[20] In a certain sense, theological truths are once more brought within the bounds of so-called natural thought, even if only upon its peripheral cusp.[21] As a result, philosophy must allow for a carefully nuanced level of 'openness of texture or porosity', thereby countermanding the suggestion that pure reason alone can capture the transcendent quality of all human (particularly tragic) experience.[22] Theologically speaking, the subjectivity of our existential reflection must

15. Ibid., 30.

16. C.f. Donald MacKinnon, 'Revelation and Social Justice' (1941), in *Philosophy and the Burden of Theological Honesty*, ed. John McDowell (London: T&T Clark, 2011), 139.

17. Barth, *Church Dogmatics* I/1, xiii.

18. See: Andrew Bowyer, *To Perceive Tragedy Without the Loss of Hope*, 2016 (Accessed through ProQuest Dissertations Publishing), 162–3.

19. Kevin Vanhoozer, 'Once more into the Borderlands', in *Transcending Boundaries in Philosophy and Theology*, ed. Kevin Vanhoozer and Martin Warner (Aldershot: Ashgate, 2007), 32.

20. MacKinnon, *Borderlands of Theology and Other Essays*, 72.

21. Ibid., 153.

22. Ibid.

ultimately find objectivity in the 'theodramatic realism' of the tragic, embodied most auspiciously in the *theologia crucis*.

MacKinnon's natural law

Given MacKinnon rejected philosophical apologetics, it is interesting that he sought to uphold the value of a natural law ethic. Moreover, he demonstrated a strong preference for this tradition over the more modern and ubiquitous language of (natural) rights understood as claims.[23] Natural law, he argued, concerns itself with discerning an ethic built upon 'constraints and limitations', whereas natural rights focuses upon making 'demands and permissions.'[24] However, he was clear that natural law is not something we discover in a metaphysical vacuum, but always something we are finding in the light of a 'transcendent reality'. For Christians, this *finding* element of the tradition of natural law has 'always been complemented in practice by the tradition of a *unum necessarium*, of a union with God in Christ.'[25] For this reason, says Andrew Bowyer, MacKinnon believed 'it is the particular burden of the Christian moral theologian to see the incarnate Christ as a definitive feature of this "natural law." '[26]

MacKinnon ascribed the complexity of natural law discourse to the communicative problem of establishing a universal metaphysic of the 'good life'.[27] It is on this issue 'where practical and theoretical perplexity meet' and where the subject of natural law and the problem of metaphysics are conjoined.[28] In response, MacKinnon returns to the philosophy of Kant. For he believes it is Kant who puts communication at the very core of his theory of knowledge. MacKinnon inverts Kant's confounding of the cognoscibility of the ontological order to suggest, more positively, how his position actually bears a surprising affinity with the school of natural law in contradistinction to that of natural rights.

Although his transcendental philosophy demands that one remains silent on the identity of things in themselves, it is still possible to enter into a process of communicative discernment about what constitutes the dignity of our human nature. Natural law becomes something of a 'bridging' idiom for MacKinnon. Insofar as it is predicated upon a Kantian theory of knowledge, and, therefore, respects the autonomy of practical reason, it opens up the theoretical possibility of employing a natural law idiom as a means to articulate an international ethic of politico-ethical restraint. This idiom can be continually enhanced and developed by drawing upon the conversational insights of the borderlands regarding the

23. Donald MacKinnon, 'Natural Law', in *Philosophy and the Burden of Theological Honesty* (London: T&T Clark, 2011), 122.

24. Ibid., 120.

25. MacKinnon, 'Natural Law', 119.

26. Bowyer, *To Perceive Tragedy without the Loss of Hope*, 194.

27. MacKinnon, 'Natural Law', 120.

28. Ibid., 127.

metaphysical conundrum of the good, especially with reference to the surd character of the tragic. This enforces what is arguably the fundamental lesson MacKinnon derives, and sought to imitate, from Kant, namely, his ability to hold in balance certain alternatives that have otherwise been considered contradictory or mutually exclusive. The former Norris-Hulse Professor, Sarah Coakley (a professed continuant of MacKinnon's 'both-and' approach), describes this 'more excellent way' as follows:

> Outright rejection of secular philosophy is as dangerous an alternative as outright submission: there has to be a 'more excellent way' than the two false alternatives (fideism versus secularism) that currently feature large in theological culture wars. Ironically, Barth's dogmatics and ordinary language ('analytic') philosophy – perhaps the most important developments in the twentieth century for theology and philosophy, respectively – have together combined in a pincer movement to entrench this false disjunction. Interestingly, MacKinnon tried to learn from both, obviously in search of this 'more excellent way'.[29]

Section III: Out of the borderlands

MacKinnon's ghost: 'A critique of the theology of right'

In the preceding section, I highlighted, in very truncated terms, MacKinnon's influential construal of the relationship between philosophy and theology, paying special attention to his purported espousal of Kant as an apophatic ally and his predisposition to inhabit the interdisciplinary borderlands of literary ontology. If MacKinnon's reading of Kant is accurate, then it implies that, at least 'in the last resort', the relationship between 'is' and 'ought' cannot be as 'positively inimical' as is often assumed.[30]

With this in mind, I now turn to substantiate the significance of an assertion I made earlier: that the architectonic themes that inaugurated the 'hermeneutical disposition' known as 'Radical Orthodoxy' were in many ways catalysed by a paper given by Milbank at a conference (July 1986) that was dedicated to honouring the work of Donald MacKinnon.[31] I believe that a reconsideration of this early critique of modern theology will illuminate the powerful role that MacKinnon's thought has had on how 'Radical Orthodoxy' constructs and deconstructs the secular *mythos*. On a stylistic note, the paper is prototypical of what is now considered the quintessential characteristic of the 'Milbankian' approach to theological discourse – he tells a story. In this instance, he expounds a story that unearths

29. Sarah Coakely, *God, Sexuality and the Self* (Cambridge: CUP, 2013), 18.

30. MacKinnon, 'Natural Law', 88.

31. Catherine Pickstock, 'Radical Orthodoxy and the Mediations of Time', in *Radical Orthodoxy: A Catholic Inquiry*, ed. Laurence P. Hemming (Abingdon: Routledge, 2000), 63.

the history behind 'the post-Kantian character of modern theology.'[32] Yet what is seldom commented upon is the prominent role that the idea of natural law plays in this story not only in positioning Milbank's own response to 'Kant in Cambridge' (and beyond), but also in shaping the theo-linguistic character of his approach to natural law.[33]

I will limit my commentary of Milbank's story to four fundamental elements that I believe evince a hidden, yet highly influential, diagnostic and constructive collusion, even if via negation, with MacKinnon's thought: (1) that the assimilation of Kant's metaphysical agnosticism, which is an inversion of the Thomistic *analogia entis* and the 'way of eminence' (metaphysics of participation), is always at least 'partially reducible' to an anarchist priority of the liberal right over the common good; (2) that a careful exegesis of Kant's otherwise slippery delineation and disjunction of theoretical and practical reason (the fact/value distinction) reveals his perpetuation of the Suarezian secularization of natural law; (3) that MacKinnon is insufficiently aware of how Aristotelian hylomorphism, upon which natural law was traditionally constituted, can paradoxically transmute into a practical Kantianism; and (4) that despite the Kantian backdrop, MacKinnon's approach 'still retains an inescapable value' in that his theology of the borderlands gives rise to an alternate – postmodern – vision of the relation between theology and the secular through a blurring of boundaries.

(1) 'Liberal rights': A false theological apophaticism

At the start of every story, the audience must ask themselves a two-fold question: Why is the narrator telling this particular story? From what 'position' does the narrator speak?[34] Such questions are especially important to appreciating why Milbank's address at the 1986 Conference was far more than simply an exercise in theological polemics. Even if unwittingly at the time, it helped instigate a process of intense fragmentation in Cambridge – and ultimately in British – theology. In this subsection, I will explain the first part of this story: how Milbank tries to destabilize MacKinnon's asseveration of Kantian transcendentalism as a negative theology by exposing it as a foundation for a natural law of negative right rather than a natural law of (and for) the common good.

Even though he claims to have only ever exchanged about 'two words' with MacKinnon, Milbank was certainly inspired by his commitment to creedal orthodoxy at a time when modern theological discourse was beguiled by

32. John Milbank, 'A Critique of the Theology of Right', in *Christ, Ethics, and Tragedy*, ed. Kenneth Surin (Cambridge: CUP, 2008), 161. (Henceforth *CofR*).

33. C.f. John Milbank and Simon Oliver, 'Radical Orthodoxy: A Conversation', in *The Radical Orthodoxy Reader*, ed. John Milbank and Simon Oliver (London: Routledge, 2009), 29.

34. Graham Ward, 'Cultural Hermeneutics and Christian Apologetics', in *Imaginative Apologetics*, ed. Andrew Davison (London: SCM, 2011), 115.

the 'pathos' of a 'false humility'.[35] Milbank's diagnosis of this 'fatal disease' of theological acquiescence to the constructs of secular liberalism is intertwined with his robust resuscitation of the 'question of metaphysics', a phrase he appropriates from MacKinnon.[36] Considering that Finnis and Porter both sought to resituate their approach to natural law away from the apparent dubiousness of making substantive metaphysical claims about reality, Milbank avows definitively that the Christian *ethos* will always be found 'unconvincing if it's not connected to an entire coherent intellectual vision.'[37] This coherent vision does not necessitate a 'totalised vision'.[38] What it does necessitate is a homological re-imagining of how religious practice and belief are connected integrally to nature, law, historical hermeneutics, and descriptive accounts of sociocultural *praxis*.[39]

It is from this perspective that he launches his reproach of Kant as the metaphysical villain in modern theology and his riposte of MacKinnon's 'more excellent way' as a baptism into secular reductionism. In the first lines of the 1986 paper, Milbank explicates what would become one of the defining tenets of the 'Radical Orthodoxy' manifesto: that the pervasive attempts to accommodate Kant's transcendentalist philosophy within theological discourse be reviled and eradicated. Milbank moves swiftly to take critical aim at Kant's metaphysical agnosticism, arguing that it conceals a suppressed metaphysico-political dogmatism (which he declares to be even 'more sheerly dogmatic than much of the metaphysics of the Middle Ages'), predicated upon a demarcation of an epistemological boundary between the noumenal and the phenomenal.[40]

Although this prophylactic stabilizing of the intelligibility of human discourse exudes an air of epistemological humility (even having the semblance of a theological *via negativa*), Milbank avows that it belies an egregious arrogation of metaphysical knowledge that is far from innocent. For example, he asserts that the ability to grasp the existence of an ontological boundary presupposes that 'one must in some way stand outside it.'[41] Even if this 'standing outside is for Kant very minimal', human reason can know with absolute certainty that this distinct realm exists, even if one will always remain incognisant of its noumenal content.[42] He refers to this philosophical system as essentially an aesthetic or metaphysics of the sublime. When one stands on the precipice of cognition between understanding and reason, the faculty of the imagination, which is proscribed by the schematizing limits of formal human experience, gives way to a theoretical domain where the finite categories of the understanding no longer apply. Similarly, the formality of the

35. Milbank, *T&ST*, 1.
36. Ibid., 1; Milbank and Oliver, 'Radical Orthodoxy: A Conversation', 31.
37. Ibid., 29.
38. Ibid.
39. Ibid.
40. Milbank, *CofR*, 165.
41. Ibid., 164.
42. Ibid.

experience of beauty gives way to the amorphous experience of sublimity – human knowing 'becomes overwhelmed by the imitation of the materially formless, and infinitely total'.[43]

The principal concern is that Kantian sublimity celebrates the ostensible triumph of the subjectivity of pure reason over our fearful response to the magnitude of nature, which is an aesthetic judgement. This is because Kant understood the sublime as the 'awakening of a supersensible faculty within us', which results from an internal reflective judgement concerning the inadequacy of the imagination to lay hold of the infinite.[44] However, 'this thrusting aside of the sensible barriers gives it a feeling of being unbounded; and that removal is, thus, a presentation of the infinite.'[45] While constrained by transcendental idealism, this presentation must always be a 'negative presentation'. But it is precisely this formlessness which still 'expands the soul'.[46] According to Kant, this 'expansion of the soul' (which basically refers to the way the supersensible faculty of practical reason transcends the deficiencies – the limitedness – of the imagination) liberates humanity from the humiliation it experiences before the aesthetic forces of nature.[47]

Establishing the pre-eminence of the sublime mind of the human subject over nature as an aesthetic judgement is a pivotal, yet paradoxical, move. For when the epistemological imperceptibility of sublime reasoning is coalesced with an ontological agnosticism towards 'things in themselves', one can easily overlook how crucial this transcendental relation is to Kant's critical philosophy. For despite the epistemological emptiness of the sphere of the noumenal, it is upon the transcendental character of the sublime that he constructs the 'centrepiece of his philosophy' – 'a natural moral law derived sheerly from the self-establishing of the rational will.'[48] The perception of the sublime, therefore, is a catalyst for the transformation of the interiority of the subject, whereby the experience of aesthetic humiliation is overcome by a heightened awareness of one's inward moral freedom, or in Milbank's words, 'fears of the overwhelming and pleas for grace are transformed into awesome respect for the moral law within us.'[49]

The recrudescence of interest in Kantian sublimity in recent decades is at least attributable in part to the influence of MacKinnon, whose thought 'straddled the boundary of the sublime … with more perplexity and more intensity than anyone else's.'[50] Milbank repudiates the infiltration of a metaphysics of the sublime within modern theology as being instigative not only of a misconstrued theological

43. Ibid., 164. See: Immanuel Kant, *Critique of Judgment*, Walker trans. James Creed Meredith, ed. Nicholas Walker (Oxford: OUP, 2008), 80–1.

44. Ibid., 104.

45. Ibid.

46. Ibid

47. Ibid., 92.

48. Milbank, '*CofR*', 165.

49. Ibid.

50. Ibid., 174.

diffidence, but of presaging and abetting the advent of an 'anti-theological nihilism' cleverly disguised as an innocuous expression of negative theology.[51] In his 1986 paper, Milbank explicates the relationship between Kantian sublimity and Kantian agnosticism, arguing that, although it gives the impression of epistemological prophylacticism, it in fact enforces a robustly determinate ontological dogmatism that transcribes the '*very mode of being* of our practical and political existence'.[52] For although the empirical sciences are cognitively impuissant when inquiring into 'things-in-themselves', it is precisely this epistemological vacuity that becomes the theoretical edifice for the abstraction of human rights.[53]

What homogenizes human relationships, 'both 'personal' and "political" ', is that we all stand as rational equals on the frontiers of the *grenzen der vernuft*, equal in the sense of sharing in a common inability to transcend the *grenzen* and claim to know the good in itself. In other words, no one has the *right* to cross the boundary and proclaim knowledge of a universal common good. This, in turn, becomes the organizing principle of liberal conceptions of both personal subjectivity and human freedom, which are symptomatic of a metaphysical foundation that promotes a moral and political order of negative human rights, as opposed to one founded upon the classical transcendentals of Plato and Aquinas (truth, beauty, and goodness) which promotes a content-specific moral law.[54]

Despite his expressed esteem for MacKinnon's desire to preserve and promote Christian theological orthodoxy, Milbank's critical exposition of Kant's modern metaphysic of the sublime as a heretical injunction against divine revelation leads him to wonder whether 'MacKinnon did not altogether escape the "theology of right".'[55] One of the more palpable consequences of this prophylactic injunction is the devolution of the positive pull of the natural law towards transcendent illumination into a subjective discourse of negative natural rights. Even if MacKinnon believed natural rights to be 'parasitic' on the Christian tradition of natural law, his description of natural law as a theory of 'constraints and limitations' and his fondness for its 'elusiveness' is suggestive that his thought continued to be subsumed under Kantian categories and, as a consequence, had very little room to move beyond an intense affirmation of human finitude. Unsurprisingly, opposition to Kant and the *lingua* of rights would become central to the project of 'Radical Orthodoxy' and Milbank's reconstruction of natural law.

51. I have taken the expression, 'anti-theological nihilism', from: Randi Rashkover, *Revelation and Theopolitics* (London: T&T Clark, 2005), 112, fn. 18.

52. Milbank, '*CofR*', 166. (IAITT).

53. 'Ethics is not derived from an ontology of nature; it is the opposite, a meontology, which affirms meaning beyond being, a primary mode of non-being (*me-on*).' Emmanuel Levinas, Richard Kearney, 'Dialogue with Emmanuel Levinas', in *Face to Face with Levinas*, ed. Richard Cohen (Albany: The State University of New York Press, 1986), 25.

54. For a helpful and succinct account of this aspect of Milbank's thought, see: D. Stephen Long, *Divine Economy: Theology and the Market* (London: Routledge, 2000), 247.

55. Milbank, '*CofR*',174, 178.

(2) A Perpetuation of Suarezian theoretical naturalism

The second hallmark of Milbank's riposte of MacKinnon's natural law reflects a genealogical inquiry into the genesis of the theological propensity to situate ethics within a secular framework of pure reason. In his 1986 essay, Milbank draws a genealogical connection between the proto-transcendental character (that is say, 'transcendence without participation') of Scotus's univocal account of Being, which effects an epistemological dualism between theology and ontology, and the transpiration of Suarezian metaphysics, which effects an epistemological dualism between theoretical and practical reason.[56] In locating the critical turn to epistemology as already latent in Scotus and inherited by Suarez, Milbank is actually formulating the incipience of a counter-narrative against the usual modern metanarrative of the history of philosophy that makes Kant pivotal. This enacted an innovative and juxtapositional challenge to MacKinnon's prevailing dialogical insistence that theology within the academy be linguistically restrained by the epistemic conditions proscribed by transcendental idealism.[57] For if Kant is in fact an elaborator of Scotus, then it leads one to question why modern theology should acquiesce to the vanguards of Kantian philosophy, especially if Kantian philosophy is itself unwittingly being structured and surreptitiously regulated by an underlying metaphysical theology.

At this juncture, I want to return to MacKinnon's contention that natural law arises at the point 'where practical and theoretical perplexity meet' and the corollary claim that the relationship between 'is' and 'ought' might not be as 'positively inimical' for Kant as is often thought. Although Milbank does not reference either of these assertions explicitly in his 1986 essay, he does appear to be responding to them implicitly. Following on from his deconstruction of metaphysical sublimity as an ideological instantiation of negative right, he turns to examine how this inflects the politico-ethical relationship between theoretical and practical reason. Milbank emphasizes the need for exegetical caution since one can misconstrue Kant's purportedly universalist epistemology as a 'secular groundwork' for securing a form of moral realism.[58] For instance, whilst MacKinnon certainly appreciated Kant's renunciation of ethical naturalism, his interest in developing a communicative *theoria* – predicated upon the purported universalism of the conditions for knowledge – forms the basis for transforming theoretical reason from an inquiry into speculative ontology (that is to say, 'what *is*') into the formation of a semantic idiom (that is to say, 'how we articulate how

56. C.f. John Milbank, 'Stanton Lecture 4: Transcendence without Participation', 2011, http://theologyphilosophycentre.co.uk/papers/Milbank_StantonLecture4.pdf. Accessed on 6 April 2017.

57. C.f. John Milbank, *Theology & Social Theory (Second Edition)* (Oxford: Blackwell, 2006), xxv. (Henceforth *T&ST*).

58. The phrase, 'secular groundwork', refers to any philosophical or theological framework that operates, either procedurally or substantively, on the basis that 'ethics has some extra-theological and well-grounded autonomy.' Milbank, '*CofR*', 161.

we *know*'). The speculative 'is', therefore, is redefined as a linguistic expression of an epistemological outcome that is itself circumscribed according to a particular philosophical system of intelligibility, yet can still masquerade as a quasi-theoretical conclusion of a common dialogical finding from which certain moral 'ought's' (or negative expressions of natural right) might be freely extrapolated and promulgated.[59]

Milbank's main concern here is that the language and content of natural law is being disassociated from any formal contingency upon a practical deliberation of human nature in light of our theological destiny (or divine revelation), even if MacKinnon allowed for the supplementary inclusion of theological insights for the sake of expanding dialogical horizons. Consequently, a theologian would still have to endorse a 'secular' conception of reality with its 'empty, abstract notion of the individual subject, from which it is impossible to derive any concrete notion of desirable human goals'.[60] Furthermore, because Kant grounds his natural law of negative right upon the 'theoretically known conditions of rational nature', Milbank evinces the perpetuation of a post-Suarezian conceptualization of natural law.[61] The notion of a properly 'modern' and 'secular' natural law is attributed by Milbank to Suarez's reading of normative facts off from nature and *nomos* being projected back into nature (an interpretation he shares with Finnis). Kant perpetuates this disjunction by establishing the ideological supremacy of epistemological 'right' over ontological 'good' in a way that parodies the post-Suarezian metaphysical severance of Aristotelian practical reason from speculative natural law. Natural law is thereby 'secularised' with divine revelation being reduced to a 'supplementary legal system of essentially practical injunctions.'[62]

Thus, even prior to the formal establishment of 'Radical Orthodoxy', it is apparent that its 'most radical and fundamental of all the claims' – that Kant is actually beholden to, and an unwitting exponent of, the dualistic metaphysics that 'flows from Scotus through Suarez'[63] – was being formulated as a genealogical alternative to MacKinnon's purported instrumentalization of Kantian reason as a means to establish both a 'secular groundwork' for ethics, more generally, and for natural law, more specifically.[64]

59. Thomas Sören Hoffmann draws a similar conclusion: 'After Kant natural law becomes rational law founded on semantic autonomy of the idea of right.' Thomas Sören Hoffman, *Georg Wilhelm Friedrich Hegel – A Propaedeutic*, trans., David Healan (Leiden: Brill, 2015), 124 fn. 27.

60. Milbank, '*CofR*', 182.

61. Ibid., 168.

62. Ibid., 175.

63. C.f. John Milbank, 'Stanton Lecture 1: The Return of Metaphysics in the 21st Century', 2011, https://www.abc.net.au/religion/stanton-lecture-1-the-return-of-metaphysics-in-the-21st-century/10101748. Accessed on 1 May 2019.

64. Milbank and Oliver, 'Radical Orthodoxy: A Conversation', 36.

(3) From Aristotelian hylomorphism to Kant's things-in-themselves

By virtue of Milbank's reproach of the Suarezian severance of theoretical knowledge and natural law from Aristotelian practical reason, one might be inclined to think that this reflects an underlying wish to reclaim an Aristotelian metaphysics of substance – which, incidentally, traditional natural law was thought to be grounded upon. Yet such a deduction would be much mistaken. In fact, it is precisely with respect to this issue that we find a third point of departure in the subplot of Milbank's riposte of MacKinnon's 'more excellent way' and his theory of natural law, namely, a belief that the 'truth is made' and that there are 'no substances in creation, no underlying matter, and no discrete and inviolable "things"'.[65] Instead, Milbank would later assert that 'a modified form of Spinozistic materialism would be preferable' to the unfortunate introduction of Aristotelian hylomorphism into Christianity.[66]

In conjunction with his appreciation and appropriation of Kant's epistemological prophylactic, MacKinnon also inherited and renewed Aristotle's ontology, believing the category of 'substance' to be a categorical bulwark against an all-encompassing 'metaphysics of 'pure' process'.[67] On this point at least, Milbank is in agreement. However, he takes critical aim at the way in which substance tends to become conflated with a kind of logical atomism that stabilizes things and entities into determinate forms. 'The tendency of this doctrine', he argues, 'is to insist that things can be adequately known and distinguished as they are in themselves without believing that their full determination awaits upon the infinity of relations they may have to everything else.'[68]

What Milbank is responding to here is profoundly important because it challenges the essence and character of how truth has largely been understood within the Christian tradition and how it has been relationally configured to provide a 'secure identity' for secular thought.[69] A key point I want to emphasize is the proposition that there exists a peculiar economic and political equivalence between an Aristotelian metaphysics of substance and a Kantian transcendental philosophy of things-in-themselves. As can be gleaned from the quotation above, Milbank connects the truth (the 'full determination') or ultimate reality of particular things to a network of cosmic relationality as opposed to a theory of epistemological stability. Paradoxically, says Milbank, the more the truth of an object of metaphysical inquiry is defined according to its determinate form, the more its 'concreteness' evades our cognition. Consequently, particularity becomes its '*only* remaining property'.[70] But in the same way that Kantian sublimity leads to

65. Milbank, *T&ST*, 424.

66. Ibid., 210. Quoted in: McAleer, *Ecstatic Morality and Sexual Politics*, 33.

67. Milbank, '*CofR*', 176.

68. Ibid., 176.

69. C.f. John Milbank, 'The Thomistic Telescope: Truth and Identity', *American Catholic Philosophical Quarterly*, vol. 80, no. 2 (2006), 193.

70. Milbank, *CofR*, 177. (IA).

a nihilistic evacuation of noumenal content, practically speaking, we can also say nothing about the particularity of substance – 'one particular becomes the same as all other particulars.'[71] Hence Milbank's striking assertion that a non-dialectical discourse of substance leads back to the problematic discourse of Kant's things-in-themselves, which is the 'economic and political equivalences of liberal, post-Enlightenment society.'[72]

In order to prevent 'substance' from becoming a categorical catalyst for certain expressions of secular and atheological nihilism, Milbank believes that the term must be reconstructed as a 'linguistic marker' that recognizes 'patterns of narrative consistency'.[73] It is important to stress here that language is not merely concerned with representing ideas; it is 'like God' because 'our linguistic expressions mirrors the divine creative act which is immanently contained in the *Ars Patris* that is the *Logos*.'[74] One can discern here a further shift in his reconceptualization of the relationship between truth and language away from a doctrine of the 'analogy of being' towards an 'analogy of creation'. Although Milbank remains committed to retrieving Aquinas's metaphysical framework of participation, the emphasis is now placed upon humanity's imitation of the creative inner life of the Trinity or, as Milbank puts it, our 'participation in the divine originative-expressive capacity'.[75] It is my contention that this linguistic recalibration of substance in relation to truth-theory over and against MacKinnon's pursuit of an 'underlying constant element' will translate powerfully into Milbank's reconstruction of natural law as a historicized linguistic creation inspired by a theology of Trinitarian *mimesis*.[76]

(4) 'Radical orthodoxy': It emerged from the 'borderlands'

From the discussion thus far, it is evident that natural law featured as a prominent theme in Milbank's nascent narrative against the post-Kantian character of modern theology. Furthermore, it is equally apparent that several of the (negative) architectonic themes of 'Radical Orthodoxy' were also beginning to emerge as a juxtapositional reaction to MacKinnon's 'more excellent way'. I now want to take this analysis in a slightly different direction by explicating how MacKinnon's thought still retains 'inescapable value' for Milbank.[77]

One of the striking characteristics of MacKinnon's methodology that I referred to earlier was his preference for a 'both-and' rather than an 'either-or' approach, even if this involved holding two incommensurable positions in an insurmountable tension. An obvious example of this was his attempt to balance

71. Ibid., 177.
72. Ibid.
73. Ibid., 176.
74. Ibid., 189.
75. Ibid., 189.
76. Ibid., 176.
77. Ibid., 183.

a 'baptism' of Enlightenment universalism with a desire to give expression to the cognitive interpenetration and porosity between the sacred and the secular via his theology of the borderlands. Of course, Milbank forcefully rejects this 'both-and' strategy as not only a baptism into nihilistic indeterminism, but generative and engendering of the so-called 'bastard dualisms' of reason and revelation, philosophy and theology, nature and grace, and *nomos* and *physis*.[78] A staunch reason behind Milbank's disavowal of all dualisms is that 'Christianity is the religion of the obliteration of boundaries'.[79]

Against the polarizing pressures of both Kantian sublimity and Barthian neo-orthodoxy, 'Radical Orthodoxy' takes advantage of the postmodern interest in structural relations in order to make a 'half-turn back to pre-modernity' where the borderline between philosophy and theology is 'extremely blurry'.[80] Milbank believes that, historically, there was no theological endorsement of a secularizing space of philosophical self-enclosure. All thinking was considered 'only possible through divine illumination.'[81] That said, the retrieval of such an epistemology should not be interpreted as a motion towards Christian fideism. As Milbank explains, the medieval view always understood the revelatory event of special illumination in the mind in coincidence with an external event(s) because sacred truth is always cosmically mediated by 'human relations and practices.'[82] This explains why 'Radical Orthodoxy' also refuses any dualistic understanding of the relation between nature and culture – a point I will return to.

Besides sharing an inevitable (even if circumspect) accord with the postmodern suspicion of all pretences to rational universalism or anthropological essentialism, one can also see how this position bears a conscious affinity with MacKinnon's idea of the borderlands. But what MacKinnon constructed as a proscribed space within the academy for exploring the interpenetration of disciplines on matters ordinarily excluded from philosophical discourse, Milbank develops into an all-encompassing theo-cultural movement.[83] What was for MacKinnon a literary crucible for metaphysical speculation becomes an ontological mantle for Milbank, upon which he constructs his political manifesto of definitive Christian practice. Insofar as Milbank was influenced by MacKinnon's 'postmodern' sidelining of the distinction between philosophy and theology, it is no exaggeration to say that 'Radical Orthodoxy' emerged from MacKinnon's 'borderlands'.

78. C.f. Milbank, Pickstock and Ward, 'Introduction', in *Radical Orthodoxy*, 2.

79. C.f. John Milbank, *Being Reconciled* (London: Routledge, 2003), 196.

80. John Milbank, 'Postmodern Critical Augustinianism', in *The Radical Orthodoxy Reader*, ed. John Milbank and Simon Oliver (London: Routledge, 2009), 49; Milbank and Oliver, 'Radical Orthodoxy: A Conversation', 32.

81. Ibid., 32.

82. C.f. John Milbank, 'Culture, nature, and mediation', 2010, https://tif.ssrc.org/2010/12/01/culture-nature-mediation/. Accessed on 25 October 2017.

83. C.f. Milbank, 'Radical Orthodoxy's First Decade', 367.

Section IV: A 'divine comedy'

From a Theologia Crucis to a Divina Commedia

I will now analyse how Milbank extends his response to these four architectonic themes by developing his own genealogy of the secular *mythos*. Particular attention will be given to examining the philosophical relationship he identifies between modern secular theories of natural law and the purportedly emancipatory (though actually perverse) metaphysical ontology of modern politics. The purpose of this discussion is to ascertain the historical reasons why Milbank categorically rejects the MacKinnon-like supposition, shared by both philosophers and theologians, that natural law can enact a reconciling 'both-and' rapprochement between Christian and secular-liberal ethics – a strategy that, as I have shown, both Finnis and Porter promote. Another paradoxical conclusion of this exposition is that secular-liberal ethics is, according to Milbank, already theologically reconciled and promoted, but reconciled with, and promoted by, a series of rupturing Christian heresies. Thus, it is ultimately his 'devious' construction of the secular *mythos* that frames his 'devious' *divina commedia* against the 'modern' tradition of natural law and natural rights.[84]

An invented 'factum'

In the first paragraphs of his *magnum opus*, *Theology & Social Theory*, Milbank gives an insightful synopsis of the foundational lineaments that distinguish 'modern' from 'pre-modern' (in particular, medieval) accounts of the natural law. Such lineaments are predominantly shaped and informed by an underlying structural relationship between the notion of the secular and the autonomization of political theory, which is gradually transformed into an immanent political ontology. As the idea of the secular has often been received within sociology as something ahistorical, the inevitability of this relationship has rarely been challenged. In contrast to modern interpretations, Milbank's genealogy asserts that, in the medieval era, the idea of the secular was intrinsic to Christendom because it merely referred to the time between 'fall and *eschaton*'.[85] In other words, there existed no spatial or temporal dualism that transcribed the domain proper to the Church and the domain proper to the secular/political sphere. The so-called 'natural order' was never split from the political ontology of divine government. Consequently, the notion of an independent and self-referential secular sphere had to have been 'strenuously invented', 'instituted', and 'imagined' .[86] This explains

84. See: Graham Ward, 'John Milbank's *Divina Commedia*', *New Blackfriars*, vol. 73, no. 861 (June 1992), 311–18.

85. Milbank, *T&ST*, 9.

86. John Milbank, 'A Closer Walk on the Wildside', in *Varieties of Secularism in a Secular Age*, ed. Michael Warner, Jonathan Vanantwerpen and Greg Calhoun (Cambridge, MA: Harvard University Press, 2013), 56.

why the very first words of *Theology & Social Theory*, 'Once there was no secular', gained such notoriety and why the book's subsequent argument was found to be so provocative.[87] For if once upon a time there indeed was no secular and the idea of the secular as a spatial domain was not latent, then the argument follows that there also was once no such thing as 'secular reason', upon which the dialogical confidence of modern natural law theory is thought to depend.

The pursuit of a genealogy beckons one to appreciate that we do not inhabit a spatial synchrony, but, instead, the existential reality of temporal diachrony. As such, it is the task of the genealogist to 'penetrate the shadows' that otherwise conceal the homological relationship between one's theoretical musings and one's political or pragmatic intentions.[88] For 'all meaning and all action involves genealogy.'[89] The politics of modernity is always regulated (even when heavily concealed) by what are often highly esoteric expressions of modern philosophy.[90] Milbank laments that it is precisely because this relationship is insufficiently explored that human history 'rarely comes to the light of day' and consequently 'we remain unable to clearly see ourselves.'[91] This explains why he is unconcerned by those who might be inclined to dismiss his disparate narrative of the secular *mythos* as inordinately abstruse. For if one is courageous enough to plumb the hidden depths of history, then it is likely that one's conclusions will appear equally esoteric and possibly even implausible. Hence, he concludes that theological abstruseness may indeed be the philosophical touchstones for genealogical credibility.[92]

One salient level of abstruseness is generated by Milbank's underlying conviction that the category of the secular cannot be thought of 'substractively', by which he means, it cannot be thought of as if it actually is what it proclaims itself to be, 'namely the secular':[93] a purportedly natural, ahistorical, value-neutral, spatialized, objective, epistemological sensibility or *factum*.[94] Rather, the emergence of this desacralized viewpoint was largely the coincidental outworking of a new 'political science',[95] whereby the 'political' is re-imagined as an independent sphere of 'pure liberty' and of 'pure power'.[96] Milbank consociates the invention of the secular politic as an arena of public power with the positing of a new existential vision that accords human nature its unique status by virtue of the self-determining power of the individual will. This characteristically nominalist (insofar as it translates the Ockhamite prioritization of divine will over divine intellect into human nature)

87. Milbank, *T&ST*, 9.

88. Milbank, *BSO*, 1.

89. John Milbank, *The Future of Love* (Eugene, OR: Cascade Books, 2009), 180.

90. Milbank, *BSO*, 2.

91. Ibid., 1.

92. Ibid., 2.

93. Milbank, 'A Closer Walk on the Wildside', 56.

94. Milbank, *T&ST*, xiv.

95. Ibid., 19.

96. Milbank, *The Future of Love*, 225.

and liberal constitution of social reality leads to a two-fold anthropological redefinition: first, of 'Adam's *dominium*' as a matter of 'power, property, active right, and absolute sovereignty', and, second, of 'Adam's personhood' as a matter of mere self-mastery (*homo faber*).[97] Thus, the invention of the secular political order is contingent upon the innovative construction of a new theory of human nature, ultimately necessitating a complete reconceptualization of the *imago Dei* as but a will-to-power.[98]

Gowns not tweed

Another important level of abstruseness can be identified by way of a question that Milbank raises in *Theology & Social Theory*: '[H]ow did this anthropology ever secure legitimacy in a theological and metaphysical era?'[99] His answer? '[I]t was theologically promoted.'[100] Milbank's 'devious move' is to expose, genealogically, the idea of 'secularity' and 'secular reason' to be a 'theological achievement' of medieval provenance.[101] For clarity's sake, it is worth quoting a concise summary of how Milbank traces the progressive articulation of this 'different and somewhat contrariwise theological insertion':[102]

> In a gradual process stretching from Scotus through Suarez to Banez, theology started to conclude that human beings not only have two distinct final ends (as Aquinas allows), a natural one and a supernatural one, but that the former remains substantially independent of the latter. If previously the notion of a purely rational philosophy had been overshadowed by a sense of something pagan and unredeemed, now, especially after Francisco Suarez, this was seen as an entirely legitimate exercise, within the bounds of 'pure nature' … A fully autonomous theoretical philosophy, in principles independent of any existential orientation or quest for beatitude, had at last arrived.[103]

It is important to stress that Milbank is consciously contesting the one-sided perception, popularized by the wisdom of contemporary sociology, that 'secularization' is merely the inexorable upshot of the process of 'desacralization'. According to this view, the secular sphere is considered the residue of 'the natural and self-sufficient' once 'the superfluous and additional' of the supernatural

97. Milbank, *T&ST*, 13.

98. See: Ibid., 14–15. See: John Milbank, 'On Not Quite Agreeing with Slavoz Žižek', in *The Monstrosity of Christ: Paradox or Dialectic?*, ed. Creston Davis (Cambridge, MA: MIT Press, 2009), 179–81.

99. Milbank, *T&ST*, 15.

100. Ibid.

101. Ibid., 12.

102. Ibid., 28.

103. Milbank, *BSO*, 27.

and the theological has been atrophied and then removed.[104] What this account misses, however, is that this 'de-sacralised backdrop' was itself positively instituted by medieval theologians wanting to establish a more secure foundation for the absoluteness of the divine will and the absolute gratuity of divine grace.[105] This theological tendency is catalysed by what Milbank terms 'the rupture of 1300' – referring to how Scotic voluntarism supplants the idea of participation in the eternal law; a univocal ontology supplants ontological difference, and, most notably, nature is sundered from grace.

From a jurisprudential perspective, Milbank is keen to press the point that the genesis of subjective natural rights and the idea of natural law as a subjective power can be traced not to Grotius and Hobbes, but, once again, to Scotic-Ockhamite voluntarism.[106] The rejection of cosmic mediation, concurrent with the separation of law from divinity, precipitates a doctrine of creation according to which the power of God is mediated in terms of His creatures' fundamental capacities, powers, and faculties for autonomous volition.[107] The rather comedic aspect of this abstruse narrative is that the autonomy of the philosophical and the ontological integrity of the political-jurisprudential order was not the product of 'pipe-smoking men in tweed' rebelling against 'men in clerical gowns', as one might imagine.[108] To the contrary, it was because the 'men in clerical gowns' had sundered the natural from the supernatural for the sake of 'peculiar religious reasons' that the secular finds an autonomous and univocal space, the space of 'pure nature'.[109]

A two-fold anachronism

Milbank believes that it is tragically anachronistic to want to baptize a secular vision of reality by retrieving medieval-scholastic natural theology on the auspice that it espoused a theory of 'pure nature' or a 'purely autonomous philosophy'.[110] This popular supposition is predicated upon two principal genealogical errors.[111] The first centres upon the delusion that 'natural beatitude' is broadly commensurable with the notion of 'pagan *theoria*' or 'pagan *physis*' explicated especially by

104. Milbank, *T&ST*, 9.

105. Milbank, 'Stanton Lecture 1'.

106. John Milbank, 'The History of Natural Right', 2019, https://churchlifejournal.nd.edu/articles/the-history-of-natural-right/. Accessed on 1 February 2019.

107. Milbank, *BSO*, 115; Milbank, 'The History of Natural Right'.

108. Milbank, 'Stanton Lecture 1'.

109. Ibid.; C.f. Milbank, *BSO*, 15.

110. See his critique of Joseph Kleutgen on this point. John Milbank, 'Truth and Vision', in *The Radical Orthodoxy Reader*, ed. John Milbank and Simon Oliver (London: Routledge, 2009), 70.

111. Milbank, 'Truth and Vision', 70.

Aristotle.[112] Drawing upon the work of Eric Voegelin, Milbank argues that it is anachronistic to project a theory of *natura pura* back onto pagan *physis* because even Plato and Aristotle had already begun to refer the natural to the supernatural, albeit in more immanent and 'intra-cosmic' terms.[113] It would be more accurate to consider Peripatetic philosophies as roughly foreshadowing and anticipating the 'Christian supernatural' as well as the 'Christian natural'.[114] The paradox is that the medieval rediscovery of Aristotelian philosophy actually occasioned its reinvention as a purely philosophical discourse, desacralized of its inherently religious existential dimension. The historical integration of this distorted interpretation of antique thought helped legitimate and encourage the instigation of a 'sharp distinction' between philosophical and theological discourse within Christian theology.[115] To promote this 'sharp distinction' as 'a gain', says Milbank, 'is surely naïve'.[116] As he explains:

> In many ways this rediscovery of antique thought disturbed an older Christian model ... In the case of the Greek Fathers from the apologists onwards, and of Augustine, little distinction was made between *philosophia Christiana*, 'doctrine' and 'theology' ... For with the incarnation of the *Logos* itself, and the more general descent of *Sophia* in the joint arrival in time of the *Logos-Ecclesia* ... it was considered that a more complete human reasoning, or 'philosophy' became possible.[117]

From a historical perspective, Milbank concludes that the endeavour of natural theology is also the inceptive work of that 'villain' Scotus and his nominalist successors.[118] Yet, a fundamental reason for its continuation is that it has been deemed concomitant with Aquinas's discourse on natural law.[119] This denotes a second instance of interpretive anachronism that Milbank wants to correct. As I discussed in the last two chapters, Finnis and Porter both assert that Aquinas made a 'sharp distinction' between philosophy and theology in a bid to safeguard the categorical integrity and existential sufficiency of 'natural reason' and the 'natural order'. Milbank ripostes this trajectory as an 'un-Thomistic' epistemologizing of Aquinas's theological ontology at the hands of Kantian and Cartesian rationalism. Although a straightforward exegesis of certain passages would seem to affirm the legitimacy of an autonomous philosophy illuminated solely by natural reason,

112. John Milbank, 'The Last of the Last', *Revista Portuguesa de Filosofia*, T. 58, Fasc. 2, Politica & Sociedade: Ensaios Filosoficos (April–June, 2002), 277.

113. Milbank, *BSO*, 6.

114. Milbank, 'The Last of the Last', 276.

115. Milbank, *BSO*, 22–3.

116. Ibid., 23.

117. Ibid., 22–3.

118. Milbank, 'The Last of the Last', 279.

119. Ibid.

Milbank believes a deeper interpretive analysis reveals that Aquinas's assimilation of Aristotelian philosophy was always subordinated to, and mediated by, an Augustinian Neo-Platonism.[120] For instance, Aquinas reworked Patristic teaching in Aristotelian terms, so that the ontological yearning for God was expressed in terms of the natural desire for the beatific vision.[121]

It is in the logic of the desire for deification that we rediscover the *logos* of divine government.[122] Faith and reason are gnoseologically imbedded within a single metaphysical framework of participation in the divine intellect.[123] In support, he cites the following passage from the *Summa Theologiae*: 'Hence also the intellectual power of the creature is called an intelligible light, as it were, derived from the divine light, whether this be understood of the natural power, or of some perfection superadded of grace or glory.'[124] The main point Milbank is trying to convey here is that, whenever Aquinas seems to be proffering a purely philosophical argument, it always implies and depends upon the attentive reception of divine illumination. This is why he speaks of faith and reason as 'different intensities' that are intertwined within the same historical-providential trajectory of 'coming-to know'.[125] On this view, as Simon Oliver explains, philosophy was never abstracted from the horizon of grace because it was always, at least, a 'faint illumination', an illumination thence intensified in and through the arrival of divine revelation.[126]

A theological ruse

Although he places heightened emphasis on the influence of Scotus and Ockham, Milbank also asserts that Grotius and Hobbes were instrumental to consolidating the idea of 'pure nature' and the violent anthropology that undergirds it. Whilst both of these writers posited distinctive philosophical-cum-theological political theories, they both subscribed to the fundamental idea that human nature is

120. Milbank, 'Truth and Vision', 70, 72, 108 fn. 3; John Milbank, *The Suspended Middle* (Grand Rapids, MI: W. B. Eerdmans, 2005), 20.

121. C.f. Frederick Bauerschmidt, *Thomas Aquinas* (Oxford: OUP, 2013), 68; Milbank, *BSO*, 24.

122. Matthew Levering, 'A Note on John Milbank and Thomas Aquinas', *New Blackfriars*, vol. 95, no. 1059 (2014), 529.

123. Milbank, 'Truth and Vision', 72.

124. ST I q. I a. 5. Quoted in: Ibid., 109 fn. 7.

125. Milbank, *BSO*, 25.

126. Simon Oliver, 'Introduction to Part II', in *The Radical Orthodoxy Reader*, ed. John Milbank and Simon Oliver (London: Routledge, 2009), 66. The climactic genealogical source of the anachronistic reinvention of Aquinas as an anticipator or architect of 'modern rationalism' is located by Milbank in the work of Suarez. Milbank asserts that Aquinas only '*commented* on Aristotle's *Metaphysics*: he didn't write his own: that didn't happen till the year 1600 or under the authorship of Francisco Suarez'. Milbank, 'Stanton Lecture 1'. (IAITT).

defined, first and foremost, by the *conatus* of self-preservation.[127] On one level, this conclusion extends from a Renaissance-inspired re-imagination and repossession of nature as something to be interpreted like an 'open-book', an idea which obviously animated the purportedly Suarezian *operandi* of deriving moral norms from natural facts.[128] Nature in modernity becomes a neatly transcribed and totalized category of the purely philosophical. Something that can be exhaustively comprehended 'apart from God'. In corollary to this, natural law also becomes an autonomous, yet judicially invariable, immanent order of the *polis* that charts the politico-social conventions prescribed by the evolution of the sovereign state.[129]

Milbank's genealogy is especially attentive to the influence of Grotius's 'impious hypothesis' upon modern impressions of natural law.[130] *Contra* Finnis, but in concurrence with Porter, Milbank contends that Grotius's thesis represents a watershed moment in the historical trajectory of natural law reflection. For it was Grotius who 'broke the ice' in extricating natural law from intrinsically religious forms of inquiry.[131] If it is the case that the precepts of natural law possess at least 'a degree of validity' even if there is no God (as Grotius indeed claimed), then one can assume that the foundations of the natural law are 'quite secular' and that its dialogical appeal has the capacity to transcend questions of both 'divine and human authority'.[132] Milbank is quick to reject such a supposition as a theological 'ruse' because it is predicated upon the idea that nature is a 'sealed-off totality', which infers that one can legitimately chart a boundary around 'the same' (universal), namely, our common human nature, to the exclusion of that which is 'other' (particular), namely, one's personal theological or religious convictions.[133] Not only does this incite and encourage a dualistic understanding of the relationship between faith and reason that would be consummated in Kant's metaphysic of the sublime, but it also enforces a characteristically secular divide between nature and culture – a legacy that Milbank describes as being peculiar to the political West because it is a 'specifically *secular* divide' animated by 'a naturally universalising thrust'.[134]

The secular(-izing) construal of both culture and politics as merely the contrivances of temporal and social power play also provide the conceptual ingredients for Hobbes's pragmatist recalibration of natural law.[135] Natural law is reconstructed and instrumentalized so as to legitimate the apparent exigency

127. Milbank, *T&ST*, 10.

128. Ibid.

129. Ibid.

130. Ibid.

131. C.f. J. B. Schneewind, 'Hugo Grotius: Introduction', in *Moral Philosophy from Montaigne to Kant*, ed. J. B. Schneewind (Cambridge: CUP, 2003), 88–90.

132. Hart, *The Concept of Law*, 183.

133. Milbank, 'Postmodern Critical Augustinianism', 53.

134. Milbank, 'Culture, Nature, and Mediation'.

135. Milbank, *BSO*, 128.

of a singular secular (state) power – the '*Leviathan*' – enacted to police and preserve (liberal) peace in the *polis*. The artifice of the sociocultural *factum* thereupon becomes the coercive, yet contractually imposed, detour that mollifies our otherwise violent nature.[136] Unsurprisingly, therefore, Hobbes rejected the existence of a *finis ultimus* or a *summum bonum* by asserting that such notions deliberately seek to obscure the fact that (politically redeemed) human nature is ultimately 'the art of man.'[137]

A biopolitical continuum

Milbank considers the invention of the realm of the secular to be virtually synonymous with the invention of the realm of modern natural law theory.[138] However, he also links the Grotian-Hobbesian genesis, consolidation, and justification of the modern political state with the re-emergence of a Stoic circumscription of a 'state of nature', catalysed by a rising philosophical tendency to formally abstract the animal (natural-biological) aspects of human nature from the artifice of culture and law.[139] For this reason, he refers to the Stoics as the 'precursors' of both 'the [modern] economic paradigm' as well as 'modern natural law'[140]

In many ways, Milbank's genealogical critique of the secular culminates in his identification of a 'hidden' continuum between antique Stoicism and modern secular reason,[141] a continuum now unmasked as being committed to, and propelled by, a thematic *mythos* of assumed 'original' and 'ontological' violence. This violence is then reflected in the emergence of historically specific polities and social structures.[142] The identification of this point leads him to identify a mutual subordination in both antique and modern jurisprudence to a biopolitical ethos.[143]

Biopolitics is a nebulous concept to define, given that it has been resituated and consigned different meanings according to the motivating interests of different authors. Although credited to the Jewish philosopher, Walter Benjamin, Milbank is particularly interested in Giorgio Agamben's and Bruno Latour's explication of biopolitics, both of whom are influenced by Michel Foucault's reflections on the topic.[144] In essence, biopolitics concerns the technocratic institution of regulative,

136. Ibid.

137. Thomas Hobbes, *Leviathan* (Oxford: OUP, 1998), 7.

138. Milbank, *The Future* of Love, 118.

139. Milbank, *BSO*, 178. C.f. Charles Taylor, *A Secular Age* (Cambridge, MA: Belknap Press of Harvard University Press, 2007), 115.

140. Milbank *The Future of Love*, 128.

141. Milbank, 'A Closer Walk on the Wildside', 73.

142. Milbank, *T&ST*, 5.

143. C.f. John Milbank, 'Paul against Biopolitics', *Theory, Culture & Society*, vol. 25, nos. 7–8 (2008), 15–172.

144. Milbank asserts that the tendency to consider human beings as contemptible, individualistic, and merely material structures awaiting the imposition of an artificial, yet

jurisprudential, and disciplinary structures, which are politically inscribed upon all aspects of human life and then socially policed. This obviously reflects a specifically post-Hobbesian conception of biopolitics, which, following the Stoic natural law tradition, establishes and derives moral and political *nomos* from a violent *physis* of self-governing *conatus*.[145] This thereby engenders a further and aporetic division between the belief that human nature is 'factually given' and that human nature is merely an 'artificial construct'.[146]

Milbank identifies here a precarious paradox inherent within secular liberalism. On the one hand, the advancement of a neo-Stoic reading of life as self-governing – yet, naturally red in tooth and claw – justifies the interventional manufacturing of a 'natural law' of keeping contracts. Yet, on the other hand, the erection of an artificial framework of social contractualism engenders an anarchic pattern of life that is 'intrinsically wild' – even if agonistically subdued by cultural norms – and 'dynamically creative'.[147] This paradoxical *mythos* underscores a further 'supreme contradiction' within modern thought, the importance of which has already been alluded to, that is, how the natural order is at once cultural and the cultural is at once natural even if they are considered (epistemologically) to be divided.

On this point, Milbank is strongly influenced by Foucault, Agamben, and, perhaps most especially, Latour. In his seminal work, *We Have Never Been Modern*, Latour presents an alternate understanding of modernity, one not fundamentally to do with the advent of Cartesian foundationalism or Kantian rationalism, but with the emergence of different but complementing practices of 'purification' and 'translation'.[148] The practice of 'purification' refers to the ontological separation of the human from the non-human, which is basically correlative with the establishment of a boundary that differentiates nature from culture objectively.[149] The practice of 'translation' involves the process of 'hybridization', the mixture of nature and culture, which mediates the development of new intellectual, social, and political paradigms.[150] According to Latour, it is only when these two practices

refining, cultural-political superstructure was first labelled as 'bio-political' by the Jewish philosopher, Walter Benjamin. (C.f. Milbank, *BSO*, 178). However, Sven-Olov Wallenstein attributes the term to Rudolph Kjellén who used it describe an 'organicist conception of the state' comprised of '"life-form" and "ethnic individuality."' C.f. Sven-Olov Wallenstein, 'Introduction: Foucault, Biopolitic and Governmentality', in *Foucault, Biopolitic, and Governmentality*, ed. Jacob Nilsson and Sven-Olov Wallenstein (Huddinge: Södertörn University Publications, 2013), 7.

145. Milbank, *T&ST*, 27; Milbank, 'Paul against Biopolitics', 168.

146. John Milbank, 'The History of Natural Law', 2018, https://churchlifejournal.nd.edu/articles/the-history-of-natural-law/. Accessed on 1 February 2019.

147. C.f. John Milbank, 'A Conversation', in *Political Theology for a Plural Age*, ed. Michael Jon Kessler (Oxford: OUP, 2013), 37.

148. Bruno Latour, *We Have Never Been Modern*, trans. Catherine Porter (Cambridge, MA: Harvard University Press, 1993), 11.

149. Ibid., 11.

150. Ibid.

are conceptualized independently from each other that we can continue to be modern and biopolitical for it is precisely this division that preserves the 'tortuous relations' in the *polis*: 'Relativism, domination, imperialism, false consciousness, syncretism' are all products, says Latour, of this, ostensibly, 'Great Divide'.[151]

Milbank uses Latour's analysis to expose the liberal biopolitical constitution as a reductivistic illusion. As I have already described, modern political theory tried to delineate a fixed boundary between a purified nature and a translated culture. However, this biopolitical disjunction allows for an unconstrained extension of cultural boundaries under the political auspice of '*techne*' and 'operational control'.[152] One of the striking consequences of this is that, progressively, the sovereign state and the capitalist market assume the power to experiment with 'absolutely everything', including the biosphere. For example, in an article titled, 'The Impossibility of Gay Marriage and the Threat of Biopolitical Control', which he says he frames in 'broadly 'natural law' terms', Milbank speaks unequivocally of a slippery biopolitical slope:

> There was no *demand* for 'gay marriage' and this has nothing to do with gay rights. Instead, it is a strategic move in the modern state's drive to assume direct control over the reproduction of the population, bypassing our interpersonal encounters. This is not about natural justice, but the desire on the part of biopolitical tyranny to destroy marriage and the family as the most fundamental mediating institution.[153]

Although modern philosophy sought political refuge in the objectivity of nature in displacement of any formal consensus about the good, ironically, nature was always a cultural construct, but a construct born out of the machinations of a 'machinic organism' or sovereign power. Aporetically, knowledge (or that which is most 'knowable') becomes increasingly tied to the contrivance of a cultural-experimental pacification of nature and nature's conflictual instincts. Yet, in consequence, the extent to which human beings can control and manipulate nature becomes strangely adumbrative of our own nature at work. In other words, does the advent of the political Leviathan or the modern automaton reflect our 'psychic mastery of nature', or does it reflect 'the natural mechanisation of the psychic?'[154]

151. Ibid., 11–12.

152. John Milbank, 'John Milbank Interview', 2017, https://www.gold.ac.uk/faithsunit/current-projects/reimaginingreligion/landmark-interviews/john-milbank/. Accessed on 10 December 2017.

153. John Milbank, 'The Impossibility of Gay Marriage', 2013, https://www.abc.net.au/religion/the-impossibility-of-gay-marriage-and-the-threat-of-biopolitical/10099888. Accessed on 10 December 2017.

154. Milbank, *BSO Order*, 179.

An ontology of peace

This alludes to a fundamental similitude between the antique *polis* and the modern state. In agreement with Agamben, Milbank asserts that politics inexorably involves an ontological dimension. Nevertheless, both ancient and modern expressions of the biopolitical espouse an ontological vision that is nihilistic because being is defined immanently and without reference to the immortality of the soul or the resurrection.[155] Antique immanentism was defined against a dualistic backdrop suspended between the chaos of 'agonistic "nature" ' and the 'arbitrary divine or human law shaping "culture" '.[156] Modern immanentism restores this dualistic chaos by trying to think of *creatio ex nihilo* without God – 'a nothing that is self-generative.'[157] In both biopolitical models, human life is negatively defined over-against the finiteness of life in the face of death and, thus, a contestation ensues between 'the pursuit of my life rather than yours, the prolongation of the life of some at the expense of the life of others.'[158]

For Milbank, the sole pathway out of the nihilistic grip of biopolitics is 'an authentically religious route'[159] and, for him, that route is Christianity. Only Christianity has the power to transform the dichotomization of 'confusion and order, *hyle* and *eidos*, *physis* and *nomos*, nature and culture' into a single 'divine art of Creation' that is 'alone able to speak or produce things from nothingness'.[160] Practically speaking, then, the 'religious route' simply involves narrating the Christian *mythos* (a 'counter history', a 'counter ethics', and a 'counter ontology') since it is the only *mythos* able to out-narrate the nihilism inherent within the secular *mythos*. At the structural heart of this alternate *mythos* is what Milbank refers to as an 'ontology of peace', according to which differences are conceived as 'analogically related, rather than equivocally at variance.'[161] However, attempting to establish peace by marrying a Christian theory of natural law with a secular-liberal account of natural rights is to try and construct an illogical and biopolitical hybrid of peace and violence. To put this in Pauline terms, you cannot marry a politics of death – 'a politics without soul' – with a Christian politics of eschatological hope, that is to say, a hope that passes beyond the *theologia crucis* of life into a natural justice that relates life to the resurrection. The violence of secular biopolitical law can only be out-narrated by the supernatural vision of Christian peace – 'a natural

155. John Milbank, 'The Ethics of the Soul', 1999, https://www.firstthings.com/article/1999/03/004-the-ethics-of-self-sacrifice. Accessed on 15 December 2018.

156. John Milbank, 'Stanton Lecture 3: Immanence and Number', 2011, http://theologyphilosophycentre.co.uk/ papers/Milbank_StantonLecture3.pdf. Accessed on 1 May 2019.

157. Ibid.

158. Milbank, 'Paul against Biopolitics', 140.

159. Ibid., 135.

160. Milbank, 'Stanton Lecture 1'.

161. Milbank, *T&ST*, 279.

law of equity rooted in an eternal, divine law' – which is emboldened by a 'much better story'.[162]

Section V: Hylozoism and divine government

On divine government

We are now in a position to consider how Milbank's 'devious' *divina commedia* against MacKinnon's 'more excellent way' and his extended genealogical critique of the secular *mythos* are likely to inform the architectonic elements of his alternate account of natural law in *On Divine Government*. To emphasize the continuity between genealogical origins and political ends, I will revisit the four originating theses of 'Radical Orthodoxy' that I rehearsed at the commencement of this chapter. Only now, I will explain how Milbank is likely to re-narrate them into four reparative components through which a 'Radically Orthodox' reclamation of natural law can take place. I enumerate them as follows: (1) that the secular-liberal priority of subjective right must be genealogically out-narrated – rather than reconciled – in order to re-found the Catholic priority of natural law as a theory of objective *ius*; (2) that the post-Kantian perpetuation of a Suarezian inspired 'secular groundwork' for natural law must be permanently forestalled by concentrating instead upon Aquinas's assimilation and perpetuation of a Philonian-inspired understanding of natural law as a theory of divine government; (3) that the metaphysical stability of Aristotelian hylomorphism upon which the truth of natural law was thought to depend must give way to a hylozoistic theory of 'truth as made' (*verum-factum*); and (4) that natural law is inseparable from the law of grace and from the providential and political fusion of church and state.

(1) Natural law out-narrating natural rights

In 1725, the Italian philosopher, Giambattista Vico, sought to make a provocative intervention within the then-current debates in jurisprudence by publishing his *Scienze Nuova*, the subtitle of which announced the development of an alternate theory of natural law.[163] This alternate theory was constructed and elaborated in censorious opposition to the theories espoused by those he refers to, somewhat pejoratively, as the 'three princes of natural law': Selden, Pufendorf, and, most importantly, Grotius.[164] Vico presented two general lines of critique: first, that the

162. Ibid., 394; Milbank, 'Paul against Biopolitics', 135.

163. Walter Rech, 'History and Normativity', *Journal of the History International Law*, vol. 17 (2015), 151.

164. C.f. Leon Pompa, *Vico: A Study of the 'New Science' (Second Edition)* (Cambridge: CUP, 1990), 46.

'princes' were too rationalistic in their approaches to natural law and, second, that they were bereft of 'historical consciousness.'[165]

If Milbank publishes *On Divine Government*, it is likely that his reparative contribution will follow a similar methodological pattern of 'critique in order to construct'. Evidence of this likely emulation of Vico's stratagem can be evinced from his decision to begin his six-part series on natural law with a revisionist narratological sketch of its genealogical relationship to the idea of natural right.[166] From this historically enlightened perspective, Milbank believes we can finally see the real theologico-political predicament that undermines current debates in natural law – that both 'modern conservatism and modern liberal-leftism are locked in exactly the same rights-based paradigm.'[167] Finnis's NNLT is singled out by Milbank as a quintessential example. By ignoring the real origins of natural law in the theological-metaphysics of classical and medieval thought, he accuses Finnis of producing a 'novel, modern doctrine' that is 'much more reducible to a [socially liberal] modern natural rights doctrine' than he and his fellow NNL theorists might think.[168] Thus, it is likely that Milbank will seek to out-narrate Finnis's socially 'conservative' and Porter's socially 'liberal' contributions by rehearsing the same genealogical argument: that they are both the inheritors and transmitters of a revised theory of natural right presenting itself as a revised theory of Thomistic natural law.

Milbank's fundamental concern here is to re-narrate the history of events that led to the terminological displacement of *ius* viewed objectively as the *id quod iustum est* (the equitable or right order of things) by *ius* viewed subjectively as a *facultas* or a *potestas licita*. In agreement with Michel Villey's historical study, Milbank claims that, up until at least the thirteenth century, natural rights were always understood within an objective cosmic order of divine government and, hence, were considered within, and subordinate to, a teleological theory of natural law. Furthermore, Aquinas, he avows, never had a concept of natural rights in a subjective sense; rather, he consistently correlated individual right-claims with the specification of another person's responsibility/duty.[169] The foundation for both an individual's right-claim and a person's correlate responsibility/duty was always found in objective *ius*, which was, itself, always determined and measured by a relational and equitable consideration of 'justice as distribution'.[170]

165. Rech, 'History and Normativity', 151.

166. John Milbank, 'A Revisionist Account of Natural Law and Natural Right', 2018, https://churchlifejournal.nd.edu/articles/a-revisionist-account-of-natural-law-and-natural-right. Accessed on 1 February 2019.

167. Ibid.

168. Ibid.

169. Milbank, 'The History of Natural Right'.

170. John Milbank, 'Against Human Rights', *Oxford Journal of Law and Religion*, Vol. 1, No. 1 (2012), 216.

In seeking to defend these historical contentions, Milbank realises that he is among an intellectual minority who strongly denounce the modern paradigm of subjective rights as the bastard offspring of a 'mutated theology'.[171] This brings him into conflict with scholars who appeal to history in order to esteem subjective rights as the fruitful distillation of the liberalism already inherent within the western natural law tradition. To out-narrate this genealogy of continuity, Milbank proffers a revisionist genealogy of rupture that illustrates how modern theories of subjective right are historically contingent upon the distillation of much earlier theological moves. In defence of Villey, Milbank identifies the decisive moment of rupture in the arrival of Ockham's nominalist theology, which instates a notion of God as the sovereign possessor of absolute power (or absolute right) over creation. This catalyses the gradual superseding of *ius* as a participation in divine government by *ius* as a personal entitlement mediated by a divine authority. In other words, the definitional shift from objective to subjective occurs when *ius* is no longer considered principally as a '*relational* matter' and becomes concerned solely with the isolated will or capacities of the individual.[172] Milbank argues that, even after this shift took place in the Middle Ages, natural rights were still advanced as being demonstrative of a theory of divine government (or of natural law), albeit now presented in an etiolated and perverse form as a regime of pure power or pure volition.[173] 'In this way', he concludes, 'the link of *ius*, whether viewed as objective right (or law) or as subjective right, with conceptions of *divine government* did not immediately disappear.'[174]

From Milbank's revisionist genealogy, we can confidently infer that the drift within contemporary Catholic thought towards a modern-subjective account of natural rights not only assumes an ontological-epistemological boundary between human nature and divine grace, but secretly enacts an ancient and heretical mode of divine government – a theology of sovereign power of divine right that gradually transmutes into a modern philosophy of Kantian autonomy.[175] It is the ontological dissolution in Kant of the metaphysical interrelation between the order of the outer cosmos and the experience of one's inner moral dispositions that consummates this dogmatic ethic of 'constraints and limitations' in natural law theory (to borrow MacKinnon's definition).[176] This trajectory is then inherited and intensified within Catholic thought, says Milbank, by an evolutionary shift that occurs in the 1930s and 1940s from a 'corporatist' to a 'personalist' understanding

171. Milbank, 'A Revisionist Account of Natural Law and Natural Right'.

172. Milbank, 'Against Human Rights', 221.

173. Milbank, 'A Revisionist Account of Natural Law and Natural Right'.

174. Ibid. (IAITT).

175. Milbank, 'The History of Natural Right'.

176. Josef Bengston, *Explorations in Post-Secular Metaphysics* (New York: Palgrave Macmillan, 2015), 155.

of dignity that focuses upon the individual rather than the community,[177] an 'evolution' that 'is crucial for understanding how the unlikely marriage of rights with dignity was consecrated after the Second World War'[178] – so unlikely, in fact, that he contends that prior to 1948, Catholic moral discourse only ever mentioned rights 'scarcely'.[179]

After drawing attention to these forgotten metaphysico-historical assumptions, Milbank raises the crucial issue of what a truly 'Catholic' attitude to natural rights should look like. In the conclusion to his appositely titled essay, 'Dignity, not Rights', he observes that the Catholic Church's endeavour to defend the dignity of the unborn and of the dying by deploying a liberal rhetoric of subjective rights points to a contorted political relationship with liberalism more generally. For it is on such fundamental moral issues that the Church necessarily rejects liberalist values, *tout court*. This inconsistency cannot be explained away as merely a residual disagreement. Rather, it should, says Milbank, be interpreted as a powerful indicator that Catholicism has always been incompatible with liberalist formulations of subjective rights.[180] An important political reason for this incompatibility is that the biopolitical logic that underscores liberal rights (the reduction of the human person to an egoistic and voluntaristic individual) engenders an aporia whereby rights are construed as at once 'natural', and yet this 'naturalness' can only be secured through the constraining and conventional power of the (secular) state. In the light of this 'covert role of always arbitrary and central legislation', subjective rights are, ironically, defined by their 'transgressibility'.[181] In other words, they are always suspendable according to the whim of a sovereign will-to-power.

(2) Law and divine government: A philonian reconciliation

Although left 'unsaid', the preceding discussion on subjective rights reveals implicitly how the architectonic and inherited story of 'Kant in Cambridge' is being subtlely expanded to form an introductory basis for Milbank's reparative contribution to natural law. The contemporary 'prince(s)' and 'princess(es)' are genealogically positioned as the modern elaborators of the same villainous trajectory inaugurated (formally) by Scotus, subjectivized by Ockham, and consummated in Kant. Like MacKinnon, it is the 'both-and' constructions of the secular *mythos*, advocated by the likes of Finnis and Porter, that provides the foundational opposition with which to instantiate the revisionist *mythos* of a natural law according to 'Radical Orthodoxy'.

177. John Milbank, 'Dignity, not Rights: Against Liberal Autonomy', 2016, https://www.abc.net.au/religion/dignity-not-rights-against-liberal-autonomy/10097418. Accessed on 10 December 2018.

178. Ibid.

179. Ibid.

180. Ibid.

181. Ibid.

Of course, in keeping with his narratological approach, a *mythos* about tragic villains can only be sustained by the dialectical presentation of restorative heroes. Hence, we come to what I have delineated as the second reparative component. In order to permanently thwart the perpetuation of a 'secular-groundwork' for natural law, Milbank makes another contrasting and revisionist contention by locating the origins of the 'authentic' natural law tradition in Philo Judaeus. Contrasting and revisionist, because Catholic philosophy has, almost universally, traced the origins of its natural law tradition to Stoic ideas and ideals. Although Milbank does not deny the fact of Stoic influence, he maintains that this influence is both secondary and, in many respects, distortive.[182] He ventures that the Stoics' 'naturalisation of politics' does not actually allow *nomos* and *physis* to coincide harmoniously since the 'naturalness' of the law is tied to the belief that nature goes in certain fated ways and this prescribes the law. It is from here that a fluidity emerges between 'laws of nature', as observed in science, and 'natural law', as applied ethics, resulting in a tendency to derive moral principles by looking at (and interpreting) the facts of nature.

The modern villain, Suarez, is consequently portrayed as being closer to Stoicism than to Thomism given that, on Milbank's reading, he allows the 'naked power' of deductive reasoning to dictate the determinate and expansive normative content of the natural law.[183] Furthermore, by maintaining that the natural law is extrapolated from a set of fixed theoretical-rational facts about human nature, Suarez revivifies the Stoic emphasis upon the immanence of the individual, now considered principally as a 'biologically given natural unit', thereby reducing 'cultural relationships' to merely the artificial confirmation that natural facts do possess normative force.[184] But since the 'natural' force of the law extends from the will alone, 'human or divine', Milbank concludes that Suarez bifurcates *bios* from *polis*. Consequently, 'given powers and capacities become not so much signs of dutiful responsibilities as themselves the subjective source of now naturalized subjective rights.'[185]

Against this biopolitical backdrop, Philo is introduced as the genealogical hero of the natural law tradition precisely because he inverted the **Stoic** immanentization and desacralization of the cosmos by uniting the Hebraic notion of God as omnipotent ruler with the Greek's metaphysical ontology.[186] *Nomos* was thereby synthesized harmoniously with *ousia* since Greek being was now proclaimed as God and the cosmos interpreted as a 'divinely willed legality.'[187] In other words, the ontological is now considered concomitant with a theory of divine government.

182. Milbank, 'The History of Natural Law'.

183. John Milbank, *The Religious Dimension in the Thought of Giambattista Vico (Part II)* (New York: The Edwin Mellen Press, 1992), 132. (Henceforth, *RD2*).

184. Milbank, 'The History of Natural Law'.

185. Ibid.

186. Milbank, *BSO*, 13.

187. Ibid.

Thus, for Philo, there could be no such thing as a sheerly 'secular groundwork' for natural law. Indeed, he considered the natural law to be 'thoroughly Biblical in origin' and the revealed Mosaic Law to be its sole complete proclamation.[188] This perspective sustains both the sacralization of the cosmos and the sacralization of history as governed by providence. For the idea of divine government implies both a normative and a descriptive dimension; that is to say, it not only prescribes the norms according to which society *should* be governed, but, even more importantly, describes how history *must* go since it is governed by God.

Establishing the genealogical origins of the 'authentic' natural law tradition in Philo's fusion of nature and politics in a theology of divine government is by no means an end in itself. The meta-narratological point for Milbank is to adumbrate how it was this intrinsically theological discourse of law that was assimilated, developed, and sustained originally by the Church Fathers and then, most crucially of all, by Aquinas. Against the modern tendency to conceive natural law in contrast to the law of revelation, Milbank describes how Gregory of Nyssa, after assimilating Philo's politicization and personalization of ontology, sees the Incarnation as the restoration of the natural law, an event that Moses' proclamation merely foreshadowed. In continuity with Gregory of Nyssa and the Church Fathers, Milbank avows that Aquinas also believed that 'the proper exercise of natural law is dependent upon the Incarnation' – upon 'the *Logos* who is also *Nomos* itself.'[189]

Here we find a further indication of how Milbank's reparative contribution to natural law, although insightful, involves an underlying reaction to the story of 'Kant in Cambridge'. Following the theology of the borderlands, Milbank is in clear, but unspoken, agreement with MacKinnon's theological avowal that the practical discernment of natural law is something Christians must do in light of the Incarnation. However, in clear opposition to MacKinnon's Kantian inflection, Milbank declares that his approach to natural law will go 'clean against' any effort to render it of universal or dialogical import.[190] Besides claiming to be more exegetically faithful to Aquinas, he also asserts that it is precisely those features of his thought which many Catholic philosophers would write off as too strange that will prove to be of most value in a 'postmodern and perhaps postsecular era'.[191]

One pertinent example of this hinges upon Milbank's declaration that Aquinas was innocent of the desacralizing aporia that effects the biopolitical duality between nature and culture. Innocent, because, in continuity with the Philonian-Hebraic tradition, Aquinas also espouses a theo-cultural understanding of natural law as a participatory theory of divine government that is mediated through a hybrid of

188. Milbank, 'The History of Natural Law'.

189. Ibid.

190. Ibid.

191. Ibid.

'natural cultural processes'.[192] Whilst Aquinas accepts that 'culture "adds to" nature', this addition can still be considered 'natural' in the sense that such contributions fulfil what nature intended.[193] Consequently, 'if the natural is always already for us cultural, the cultural never exits the natural and what is 'fundamental' for culture remains an attempt to discern what is 'fundamental' for nature'.[194] Milbank argues that the 'naturalness' of the natural law refers to both our free participation in the eternal law of God – who is 'both nature and culture' – as well as our exercise of conscientious judgement through which, when in harmony with nature, we too 'mediate the divine government'.[195]

It is important to stress the revisionist implications of this 'reparative' reading of the tradition. In reaction to MacKinnon's post-Kantian ('both-and') preoccupation with formulating a secular epistemological basis for natural law, Milbank unites theoretical and practical reason, fact and value, nature and culture in a robustly theological and biblical understanding of history that is itself supernaturalized. Natural law is thereby rendered inseparable from Christology since it is through the Incarnation that something of both the 'historical as well as the ethical' is disclosed to us.[196] Milbank clearly intends to resituate natural law firmly within a theological-ontological framework of truth that is, like nature, participatory, dynamic, and always culturally mediated.

(3) Natural law is 'man-made': A hylozoistic alternative

The previous sentence offers an emblematic indication of what I expect will develop into a distinguishing component of Milbank's revisionist and reparative contribution to current debates in natural law. It is important to recall that one of the architectonic themes emerging out of Milbank's critical engagement with, and construction of, the secular *mythos* in 'The Theology of Right' was a rejection of Aristotelian hylomorphism. Broadly speaking, the Catholic natural law tradition has continued to see the assimilation of this metaphysical principle as being providential to explicating a stable ontology.[197] Moreover, building upon the Stoical understanding of the *Logos*, and the corollary identification

192. John Milbank, 'Burke's Romantic Restoration of Natural Law', 2019, https://church lifejournal. nd.edu /articles/burkes-romantic-restoration-of-natural-law. Accessed on 1 March 2019.

193. Milbank, 'The History of Natural Law'.

194. John Milbank, 'Only Theology Saves Metaphysics', 2007, http://theologyphilo sophycentre.co.uk /papers/Milbank_OnlyTheologySavesMetaphysics.doc. Accessed on 1 May 2019.

195. John Milbank, 'Stanton Lecture 5: Participated Transcendence Reconceived', 2011, http://theologyphilosophycentre.co.uk /papers/Milbank_StantonLecture5.pdf. Accessed on 1 May 2019.

196. Milbank, 'The History of Natural Law'.

197. Peter Kucer, *Truth and Politics* (Minneapolis: Fortress Press, 2014), 62.

of truth as unchanging and eternal, Christianity performed its own Philonian-like synthesis and arrived at the scholastic principle, *Verum est ens*, and the corresponding doctrine of the *analogia entis*. Milbank asserts that, because Catholic philosophy continues to remain beholden to this synthesis and to an understanding of truth as uncreated, it has become obsessed with discovering the 'general *conditioning* circumstances within which the conditioned must operate.'[198] This 'conditioning' explains why the idea of natural law is universalized as a dogmatic and unalterable moral code which, even apart from grace, is said to be discernible with a Kantian-like certainty – '*etsi Deus non daretur*'.[199]

I expect that Milbank will persist in critiquing this understanding of truth as he endeavours to construct the theological centrepiece of his 'new' account of natural law. The portentive clue is found in the final words of his fairly recent essay, *The History of Natural Law*: '[F]ar from thinking of the natural law as an unalterable code', Aquinas 'recognizes the dynamism of nature as such – the unalterable lies for him with eternity, and not with finitude or time, whose consistent measures arrive only insofar as they bend towards the eternal.'[200] What is left uncertain at this stage is how he intends to reconcile the dynamism of nature with his determinate insistence that the truth of natural law is dependent upon, and mediated by, an ontological participation in the '*Logos* who is also *Nomos*'. Nevertheless, a further clue emerges, this time from one of his earliest works – an essay penned to supplement his PhD thesis on Vico's theological significance, simply titled, 'Law'. It is on the basis of this text, in particular, that, I believe, Milbank will seek to incorporate Vico's hylozoistic understanding of 'truth as made' (*verum est factum*) into an understanding of natural law as a theory of divine government that encompasses both history as well as nature.

Despite the abundance of scholarly literature discussing Milbank's theology, there exists a notable dearth of scholarly attention given to the axiological role played by Vico's metaphysics in fomenting his idiosyncratic response to secular reason.[201] Even scarcer is the consideration of how this influence might also modulate his contribution to current debates in natural law. However, just as his favourable reading of postmodernism (as expressed in *Theology & Social Theory*)[202] likely ascends from Milbank's theo-linguistic reading of Vico's hylozoism, so it is equally likely that the originality of *On Divine Government* will ascend from Vico's 'rare and – promisingly for us, today – remarkable' understanding of natural law as

198. Milbank, *The Suspended Middle*, 101. (IAITT).

199. Milbank, 'The History of Natural Law'.

200. Ibid.

201. C.f. Alan Thompson, *Culture in a Post-Secular Context* (Eugene, OR: Wipf and Stock, 2014), 96.

202. I appreciate that Milbank goes on to qualify and question this favourable outlook in his later work.

a creative (*poesis*) practice (*praxis*).[203] This is obviously a vast and unwieldy topic. Though the question pertinent to this book remains pointed: To what extent is the jurisprudential promise embodied within Vico's metaphysics conditioned and constrained by an 'unsaid' reaction to the secular *mythos* as originally narrated in the story of 'Kant in Cambridge'?

Vico's hylozoistic metaphysics takes its theoretical origins from the ancient Heraclitan supposition that reality exists in a state of dynamic and universal flux. On the basis of this anamorphous ontology, Vico is thought to have developed an alternative account of metaphysical realism that subverts the stability of Aristotelian substances and Platonic forms with an instrumentalist theology of *semiosis*.[204] The governing axiom animating this linguistic-cultural meta-narrative is expressed (anachronistically) by Milbank as 'The True and the Made are convertible.'[205]

Whilst Milbank recognizes this to be an 'unambiguously "modern"' position, insofar as it esteems the idea of the *homo creator* and focuses upon the cultural significance of the '*factum* or *artificium*', he also believes that these contentions reflect the retrieval of a profoundly Christian element of the theological-metaphysical tradition, clarifying and illuminating what was already implicit especially in the doctrine of creation.[206] What distinguishes Vico's 'version of modernity' from the anti-metaphysical Enlightenment philosophies of his (Cartesian) contemporaries is that he understood the *factum* to be principally an aesthetic notion that is mediated in history through the progressive establishment of a rhetorical *poesis*.[207] More importantly, he (along with Nicholas of Cusa) restored the 'transcendality of the *factum*'.[208] The implication being that our *factibilitas* actually becomes both the pathway to knowledge and a 'gateway to transcendence.'[209] In other words, conceding the constructivism of culture does not supersede or negate our participation in the *bonum* of divine perfection. In fact, the human capacity for *poesis*, which Milbank extends to the 'whole realm' of human creativity, is what mediates our participation in 'God who is infinite poetic utterance' – the *Logos*, Christ![210] Thus, even though Vico disavowed epistemological 'clarity' as 'a vice of the mind', he did not yield to the abject pragmatism or unbridled relativism that has become quintessential of many postmodern ontologies.[211] As Milbank

203. Milbank, 'The History of Natural Right'; John Milbank, *The Religious Dimension in the Thought of Giambattista Vico (Part 1)* (New York: Edwin Mellen Press, 1991), 124. (Henceforth *RD1*).

204. John Milbank, 'Theology and Philosophy in Vico's Account of Human Creativity', *History of European Ideas*, vol. 2, no. 4 (1981), 299.

205. Ibid.

206. John Milbank, 'Theology without Substance', *Journal of Literature & Theology*, vol. 2, no. 1 (March 1988), 2.

207. Milbank, *RD1*, 329.

208. Ibid., 328.

209. Milbank, *T&ST*, 12.

210. Milbank, *Being Reconciled*, ix.

211. Milbank, *RD1*, 335.

explains: '[W]hen we contingently but authentically make things and reshape ourselves through time, we are not estranged from the eternal, but enter further into its recesses by what for us is the only possible route.'[212]

It is important to note the interpretive significance of this claim. Within contemporary discourse, Vico's hylozoism has typically been read as translatable into either a Kantian/neo-Kantian *mathesis* or as performative of a Hegelian teleological synthesis. Refuting both of these interpretations is paramount to ensuring Vichian linguistics can no longer be commandeered as a 'secular phenomenon'.[213] To underscore this point, Milbank asserts that, *contra* Kant, Vico's philosophy was never constrained by the foundationalist (*a priori*) categories that define transcendental idealism. The critical element of Vico's *mythos* is that he considered linguistic categories to be entirely contingent (a *factum*) – that is to say, entirely of 'human' (not divine) genesis.[214] At the same time, *contra* Hegel, the ineluctable socio-historical contingency of truth is not mitigated or constrained by an 'immanent *telos*'.[215] Milbank argues that, unlike MacKinnon, Vico had no reason to delimit 'constraints and limitations' because he had no fear of indeterminism. Instead, he posited faith in an 'immanent pressure of a transcendent reality'.[216] This faith, however, is not fideistic. It is predicated on the 'transcendentality of the *factum*' and underpinned by a 'final reference point', that of the vision of the Trinity as a 'social image'.[217] More specifically, it is 'the generation of the second person of the Trinity' that is upheld as 'the most perfect paradigm of *verum-factum*.'[218] For this reason, there exists an analogous relation – a correspondence – between the 'infinite inner creation' within the Trinity and the interpersonal linguistic constructivism of humankind.[219] In pragmatic terms, human beings make the truth when, through their own practice of *poesis*, they participate in and reflect the divine pattern of 'identity and difference' found in the Trinity.[220]

Milbank has long referred to the mimetic relationship between the *Homo Ingenium* and the inner creativity of the Trinity as an 'analogy of creation', a doctrine he proudly esteems as a 'theology without substance.' But whereas he was originally hesitant to ascribe this position to Aquinas, believing that patristic and medieval thought was unable to overcome an ontology confined to the correspondence of *ens*, a lone footnote in his later work, *Truth in Aquinas*, asserts that this hesitancy should now be 'discounted'.[221] This is because Milbank has come to the realization

212. Milbank, *Being Reconciled*, ix.
213. Milbank, *RD1*, 332.
214. Ibid., 333.
215. Ibid., 334.
216. Ibid., 335.
217. Ibid.; Milbank, *T&ST*, 12; Milbank, *RD2*, 137.
218. Milbank, *RD1*, 108.
219. Ibid., 117.
220. Milbank, *T&ST*, 307.
221. Milbank and Pickstock, *Truth in Aquinas*, 112 fn. 147.

that 'Aquinas does in effect say that we are 'co-creators' (participating in the creative act), since we do communicate *esse* in limited ways.'[222]

By recognizing this rather subtle connection, we can now envisage how Vico's hylozoism might be reconciled with Milbank's vision of Thomistic natural law as being both dynamic and, therefore, revisable, yet incarnational and, therefore, eternal. The 'peculiarity' of Vico's contribution which Milbank finds most appealing is that he was the one who historicized natural law (thereby considering it to be a 'man-made entity') by identifying it with divine providence.[223] Milbank posits that the biological order of humankind is somehow linked to the providential order of divine justice by what he calls a 'pneumatic spark' that is inherent within human nature – analogous to what Vico called the 'few eternal seeds of the true' that are buried within us.[224] In our post-lapsarian state, this spark is all but a faint glimmer, reducing the natural law to a 'rudimentary *seminalia*' that 'does not extend to details'.[225] This existential condition has a twofold impact upon the discernment of natural law. First, its imperatival content is minimal and has to be 'ceaselessly revised' as a 'work of time and culture'.[226] Second, this 'revision' is only made possible through the grace of the Incarnation since it is Christ who restores and revivifies our historico-ethical link to the divine government.[227]

I would argue that these clues suggest, proleptically, that Milbank is not going to adumbrate a *theory* of natural law, but rather intends to fabricate an alternate *mythos* about the natural law. The principal difference being that a theory of natural law can be tested, usually through a process of reasoned argument based upon certain criteria, and so its truth or falsity determined and secured. For Milbank, however, '[t]ruth is not tested in any way'.[228] To speak of 'self-evident' goods, or 'objective' reasons, or even to promote the value of 'dialectical argument' is to give credence to what are actually secular aberrations that ultimately contradict, rather than confirm, Christianity.[229] For behind such modes of expression is a refusal to appreciate Aquinas's belief that the natural law was, in this epoch, essentially 'destroyed'.[230] Hence, even on an epistemological level, we require the stories of Jesus because, as Milbank explains, it is only the words of the Gospel that reveal an alternative (non-violent) jurisprudential discourse and tradition of 'living beyond the Law.'[231]

222. Ibid.

223. Milbank, *RD2*, 135.

224. Milbank, 'Paul against Biopolitics', 160; Giambattista Vico, *Principi Di Una Scienza Nuova*, trans. Leon Pompa (Cambridge: CUP, 2002), 41.

225. Milbank, 'The History of Natural Law'.

226. Milbank, *The Future of Love*, 179; Milbank, 'The History of Natural Law'.

227. Ibid.

228. Milbank and Pickstock, *Truth in Aquinas*, 8.

229. Milbank, *T&ST*, 401.

230. Milbank, 'The History of Natural Law.'

231. Milbank, *Being Reconciled*, 202.

> Thus, Christ (the eternal *verbum* or *certum*) proposes to human beings a *heroic law*, that is (we have every reason to say in consequence of Vico's general usage) a *concrete, poetic* law, which is none other than the enacted narrative of his life … It is then a 'myth', or figurative narrative of a metaphoric, non-violent, generative kind, which best secures a vision of infinite truth and virtue which will not collapse into the totality of a rational system.[232]

After Christ, the truth of natural law is no longer bound by epistemological 'constraints and limitations'. It is secured by the creative force of *caritas* and is 'based on persuasion'.[233] Strictly speaking, there can be no criteria for natural law since truth 'declares itself'.[234] It 'shines outwards in beauty', it is 'self-authenticating', and thus a gift from Christ himself.[235]

(4) 'Living beyond the law': An ecclesiological jurisprudence

Milbank contends that Western jurisprudence is itself still trying to think through and negotiate the Christian discoursive invention of 'living beyond the Law'.[236] This invention was itself an event of grace and not a by-product of the natural order. Above all, it is the Incarnation which bequeaths to Christianity the theo-cultural stimulus to transgress and transcend the boundaries that have otherwise separated the created from the Creator, immanence from transcendence, and humankind from God.[237] At the same time, Christianity 'preserves and elevates' the law.[238] What this means in *praxis* remains relatively ambiguous. Milbank says that, at the very least, it will involve the discovery of a 'hidden mean between process and limit, between movement and stasis: in theological terms, the co-belonging of grace with Law, and not a dialectical duality of Law and Gospel'.[239] In the same way that philosophy is argued to be inseparable from theology, Milbank affirms that natural law is inseparable from the law of grace and, even more provocatively, from the economy of the Church.[240]

The borderland-like idea of a 'hidden mean' is presented as a possible reparative answer to the 'riddle of our times'. Theologically, it mediates a *tertium datur* between the religious propensity to want to delineate the law absolutely and the postmodern propensity to want to inscribe just one law: 'produce, alter, or make different, such that yesterday's transgressive innovation is today's crime of stasis'.[241]

232. Milbank, *RD2*, 175. (IAITT).
233. Milbank, *RD2*, 174.
234. Milbank, *The Future of Love*, 176.
235. Milbank and Pickstock, *Truth in Aquinas*, 9; Milbank, *The Future of Love*, 176.
236. Milbank, *Being Reconciled*, 196.
237. Ibid., 197.
238. Ibid., 198.
239. Ibid.
240. Milbank, *The Future of Love*, 306; Milbank, 'The History of Natural Law'.
241. Milbank, *Being Reconciled*, 202.

Thus, Milbank aims to reconcile an understanding of nature that is open-ended with an affirmation that certain boundaries, cultural idioms, essences, and natures are in fact 'supposed to be' because they are orientated by grace to grace.[242] In essence, Milbank intends to reconstruct natural law in order to reflect a 'theology without substance', but in a manner that, paradoxically, allows for the restoration of the 'language of substance' as a linguistic ideation of our ultimate teleology.

How is this theologically possible? On the basis of Milbank's final Stanton Lecture delivered at Cambridge University in 2011, Peter Kucer believes Milbank might be modifying his Vichian 'analogy of creation' and gradually moving towards the more Catholic idea of an 'analogy of being'.[243] To support this thesis, he cites Milbank's definitional affirmation of substance as a stabilizing concept which 'records our awareness that there is persistence and holding together of a thing despite change.'[244] Kucer extrapolates that this might indicate that he will eventually adopt a discourse of 'substance' so as to defend certain 'moral teachings' of the natural law to be both universal and ahistorical.[245] This interpretation, however, is unlikely and I would challenge it on the basis that Milbank's remarks are commensurate with the position he outlined in his programmatic essay against MacKinnon. In particular, his discussion of substance as a 'linguistic marker' for 'patterns of narrative consistency'.[246] Moreover, in the same Stanton Lecture he clearly states that the real 'bond of substance', that is to say, 'the real source of nature and stability', must remain a mystery.[247]

A more promising alternative to Kucer's thesis begins to emerge when we start to identify the 'hidden mean' of the natural law with the mediatory locus of the Church. It is the *telos* of the Church, says Milbank, that compensates for the 'protean malleability' and the 'absence of a nature', which, he says, 'uniquely defines the human animal.'[248] He supports this position by arguing that if the Incarnation restores the grace of divine counsel that enables humankind to discern and fulfil the natural law, then, we must accept that 'the Church alone fully follows and enacts on earth the natural law through her "economy" '.[249]

Like the antique biopolitical division between nature and culture, Milbank considers any attempt to separate the City of God from the City of the World to be a 'secular divide' that was equally foreign to Aquinas's theory of natural law as it was to the Church Fathers. Milbank asserts that if we must speak of the

242. Ibid., 199.

243. Kucer, *Truth and Politics*, 185.

244. Ibid., 185.

245. Ibid.

246. C.f. Milbank, *CofR*, 176.

247. John Milbank, 'Stanton Lecture 8: The Surprise of the Imagined', 2011, http://theologyphilosophycentre. co.uk/papers/Milbank_StantonLecture8.pdf. Accessed on 10 May 2019.

248. Milbank, *The History of Natural Law*.

249. Ibid.

'co-belonging' of law and Gospel, then we must also speak of the 'co-belonging of church and state'.[250] Indeed, once natural law is understood to be as much about divine government as about the discernment of divine norms, then a defence of natural law must be fused with a defence of founding the political state in the redemptive action of the Church.[251] From this perspective, there can be no secular territory from which theology must escape. The legitimacy of positive law is determined by its correspondence with the natural law, and the legitimacy of the natural law is providentially saved from sheer pragmatism by its correspondence with the grace and economy of the Church.[252] In other words, to live beyond the violence of the law is always to live within the communal and cultural *poesis* that is the community of the Church.

Although Milbank recently aligned himself with Edmund Burke's assertion in *Reflections* that natural law is 'exactly at one with the Church establishment', the theological momentum behind Milbank's position likely stems from what he believes was left latent and 'unsaid' within Henri de Lubac's metaphysics.[253] In *Beyond Secular Order*, Milbank characterizes de Lubac's theological legacy as a *via media* rejection of two theological proposals on the relation between church and state. Firstly, he rejected Giles of Rome's contention that the Church, by virtue of papal right, possesses 'direct power' over all temporal matters, arguing that it conflated spiritual authority with a secularized juridicism of rights and coercion. Secondly, he also countered Robert Bellarmine's comparatively concessionary position, which asserts that the Church only possesses an 'indirect power' over matters temporal, but only insofar as such matters relate or pertain to the spiritual.[254] (It is interesting to note that the only other name Milbank mentions here is John Courtney Murray, describing him as a contemporary continuant of Bellarmine's trajectory.[255]) According to Milbank, de Lubac rightly identified this proposal as dangerously modern since it augments a false dualism – a *duplex-ordo* – between the material and the spiritual, denying the reality that all aspects of existence possess a spiritual dimension.[256]

Whilst he commends de Lubac's *Surnatural* as having been vital to countermanding the theological infiltration of the pagan – now neo-scholastic – ontology that assumes '"capacity" or 'power' rather than 'desire' will disclose reality to us', Milbank laments that he did not allow his 'intrinsicist' understanding of nature and grace to fully inform his ecclesiology.[257] On the one hand, de Lubac clearly recognized the Church alone to be the true cultural *polis* of humankind,

250. Milbank, 'Burke's Romantic Restoration of Natural Law'.
251. Ibid.
252. Ibid.
253. Ibid.
254. Milbank, *BSO*, 203 fn. 195.
255. Ibid., 203–4 fn. 195.
256. Ibid., 203–4 fn. 195.
257. Milbank, *The Suspended Middle*, 70.

yet, on the other hand, he atrophied its politico-cultural reach by narrowing the spiritual to the 'internal' dimension of the individual, a move imitative of the belief that if grace builds harmoniously on the nature of the individual, so the Church should exercise its spiritual-cultural influence on a 'one-to-one' basis.[258] Milbank's concern is that de Lubac failed to appreciate the Church's encompassing role in directing 'secular political ends … beyond the scope of coercive law' and, thus, erroneously accentuated the disjunction between the *ecclesia* on earth and the *Civitas Dei*.[259] To illustrate this, Milbank argues that de Lubac, particularly in his interpretation of Augustine, granted too much epistemological independence to natural law, overlooking the fact that, as would be for Aquinas, the exclusive criterion for whether or not the natural law is being adhered to is 'its orientation to the law of the gospel'.[260] But this orientation is itself anthropologically grounded in a natural desire for God, which, as Milbank explains, is what unites, rather than divides, the political theologies of Augustine and Aquinas:

> One can totally agree with de Lubac that there is no unbridgeable difference between the political theologies of Augustine and Aquinas. However, if the former had almost as strong a doctrine of natural law as the latter, then the latter has almost as strong a sense as the former that the grounds of all legitimacy, including the political, lie in the human orientation to the beatific.[261]

I anticipate that Milbank's reconstruction of natural law will continue to explain how de Lubac's intrinsicist critique of a *duplex-ordo* ontology can be 'made strange' in order to disintegrate the secular boundary that separates the Church from the political sphere. This is arguably the most radical conclusion of his permanent foray into MacKinnon's existential borderlands. Yet, Milbank's ontologizing and subsequent politicization of this supra-liminal space is deemed all the more pertinent given his observation of the intensifying 'sway of secular politics away from the norms of both natural law and the gospel'.[262]

This point leads on to one final consideration. What exactly are the norms/laws of natural law on Milbank's ecclesiological-political 'borderlands'? Addressing this question is by no means straightforward. In the past, he firmly declared what he believes the Catholic tradition has always itself implied: that because the authentic Christian moral tradition is so markedly strange, 'morality cannot be Christian.'[263] It must be judged 'immoral or amoral' according to secular 'norms and codes'.[264] More recently, Milbank has asserted that his metanarrative of ontological peace

258. Milbank, *BSO*, 204 fn. 195.
259. Ibid.
260. Ibid.
261. Ibid.
262. Ibid.
263. John Milbank, 'Can Morality be Christian?', *SSCE*, vol. 8, no. 1 (April 1995), 45.
264. Ibid.

is not concerned with the provision of an 'ethics', declaring it to be undesirable to want to prescribe 'what is to be done.'[265] This coheres, for example, with his belief that Christians are 'totally wrong' to evaluate sexual issues in terms of 'what should and should not be done.'[266] 'Equally horrendous is the conservative attack on "sex outside of marriage"' (which, he argues, has 'no real warrant in the Christian tradition'), and the 'liberal slandering of romantic fidelity.'[267] Thus, he suggests that the Church should just keep silent on such matters and entrust individuals to discern these aspects of the moral law for themselves.[268]

Despite this petition for silence, Milbank has, himself, vocalized – sometimes on the basis of what he refers to as 'natural law terms' – a panoply of arguments against permitting same-sex marriage.[269] More generally speaking, he has reiterated what he considers to be the biopolitical consequences that ensue when sex is separated from procreation, a separation he asserts as being sanctioned and promoted by the neo-liberal economics of the state.[270] Outside the realm of sexual ethics, he has also vocalized a series of norm-like criticisms against the 'mean little heresy' that is capitalism, which fosters the idolatrous and liberalist cult of 'possessive individualism'.[271] 'Radical Orthodoxy' proclaims, instead, the economics of 'non-statist Christian Socialism' or a 'Socialism by Grace'.[272] He also considers the financial independence of the Church from the state, through which it sustains, first and foremost, its mission of charity to the poor and, secondly, its educational endeavour to link political discourse with knowledge of the supernatural, to also form an authentic part of the normative dimension of the natural law.[273] Furthermore, if Milbank is confident that without the restoration of 'world Christendom' we are destined to a dark and desolate future, then he must, and evidently does, take an interest in specifying certain 'Radically Orthodox' moral norms.[274] How, then, are we to make sense of this further contradiction? To try and answer this question, we must conclude by returning, once more, to what Milbank is leaving 'unsaid'.

265. Milbank, *The Future of Love*, 135.

266. Milbank, *Being Reconciled*, 205.

267. Ibid., 205.

268. Ibid.

269. C.f. John Milbank, 'Gay Marriage and the Future of Human Sexuality', 2012, https://www.abc.net.au/religion/gay-marriage-and-the-future-of-human-sexuality/10100726. Accessed on 12 March 2018.

270. C.f. John Milbank, 'John Milbank Interview'.

271. Milbank, *T&ST*, 47; Milbank, *The History of Natural Right*. C.f. John Milbank and Adrian Pabst, 'The Meta-Crisis of Capitalism', *International Review of Economics*, Vol. 62, No. 3 (2015), 197–212.

272. This is a huge topic, which, I am unable to develop here. Milbank, 'Radical Orthodoxy's First Decade', 400–10; Milbank, *Being Reconciled*, 163.

273. Milbank, 'Burke's Romantic Restoration of Natural Law'.

274. Milbank, 'John Milbank Interview'.

Section VI: The 'church' of Milbank

An evaluative conundrum

Milbank's contribution to current debates in natural law presents a unique evaluative conundrum. If, as he claims, truth cannot be tested, how is the value and viability of his alternate version (or *mythos*) of natural law to be measured and evaluated? Furthermore, on what grounds, theological or otherwise, are we compelled to listen to and accept the aesthetico-rhetorical sound of his new alternate meta-narrative?

At the interrogative heart of this chapter is a search for the theo-cultural 'unsaid(s)'. This involved plumbing the historico-theoretical depths behind Milbank's counter-ontology in order to reveal the discrete narratological influences and commitments which condition and co-ordinate the relationship between the meaning and the methodology of 'Radical Orthodoxy'. To a certain extent, this form of analysis is homologous with how Milbank, himself, portrays the task of the genealogist – to 'penetrate the shadows' of personal and collective history in order to unconceal the oft-unspoken symmetry between one's philosophical-theological narrative and one's deeper political aspirations. Since philosophical and theological language is itself imbued with, and supplemented by, the *mythos* of its own cultural genesis, any analysis of this kind will never be able to surmise all of a text's or an author's hidden presuppositions. Nevertheless, even Milbank argues that a 'reasonably informed divination' can be achieved when we consider the earlier texts that precipitated the argument found in the present text.[275] By way of an example, he asserts that:

> We cannot understand Aristotle's *Metaphysics* except as a response to his predecessors, whose position he rehearses at the commencement of his treatise. And as Alasdair MacIntyre says, the philosophy of the *Metaphysics* includes how he narrates prior philosophy, what it attempted and how it failed.[276]

In Section III, I sought to elucidate how four of the architectonic theses of what would form part of the 'Radical Orthodoxy' meta-narrative were precipitated by Milbank's earlier reaction to MacKinnon's 'more excellent way'. Accumulatively, these theses reflect Milbank's underlying desire to re-narrate the story of 'Kant in Cambridge' as a story about theology's metaphysical betrayal, rather than a story about theology's apophatic survival. What has often been overlooked, however, is the specific role that debates in natural law have played in shaping the contours of that re-narration and then, on an even deeper and 'unsaid' level, how these debates are themselves unequivocally linked to MacKinnon's bequeathal of a highly influential interpretive rapprochement of Kantian apophaticism with a tragic Christology. Hence, in a similar vein to Aristotle's *Metaphysics*,

275. Milbank, *The Future of Love*, 180–1.

276. Ibid., 181.

I have argued that it is reasonable to 'divine' that Milbank's vision of "Radical Orthodoxy"' cannot be properly understood unless it is viewed as an ongoing response to the 'programmatic' vision about modern theology he inherited from MacKinnon.

From this perspective, the genealogical story of the secular *mythos* traced in Section IV becomes a strategic attempt to proliferate an alternate meta-narrative that deconstructs the theological bulwark of Kant's critical philosophy but without having to engage with it solely on its own terms. To achieve this, Milbank re-narrates the developmental 'breaks' in the history of philosophy – seeking to expose how the apparent 'secular' orthodoxy of modern jurisprudence is often 'grounded in certain forgotten *theological* decisions that doom it to pursue a certain style of anonymous theology in the guise of philosophy.'[277] 'Radical Orthodoxy' is not simply, then, a programmatic rejection of the so-called 'critical-turn' in Kant. It is a theological 'out-narration' of the entire historical meta-narrative that is told to substantiate the veracity of the 'critical turn' – against 'the entire idea that there *is* a precritical and a postcritical phase in the history of human thought.'[278] From this purview, Kant's purportedly desacralizing position is thence genealogically re-narrated and unmasked as but 'a complex and subtle footnote' to the desacralizing revolution of Scotus, and, therefore, has deep but discrete roots in medieval theology.[279]

A[n] [un-]necessary Mythos

This conclusion returns us to an important insight. Milbank's genealogies are not just genealogies. Even more fundamentally, they empower judgements. Thus, in imitation of his reading of Vico, Milbank's 'real ambition is not 'to know' the past, but rather the Dantean one of miming the final judgment upon it.'[280] But if Milbank's genealogical meta-narrative is integral to illuminating the meaning and possibility of his theo-cultural vision, to what extent does his presuppositions about the secular *mythos* become integral to illuminating the meaning and possibility of the judgements of 'Radical Orthodoxy', especially judgements about natural law?

Another disclosive clue is found in his interpretation and, I believe, subsequent imitation, of what he upholds as the authentic Socratic-Platonic philosophical methodology. According to Milbank, Socrates and Plato recognized that a dialectic mediated by certain oppositional dualisms is, in and of itself, an insufficient grounding for the 'quest for truth'.[281] Instead they realized that philosophy must always have recourse to myth and to myth-making. Hence, in opposition to the authorless old stories of fated cruelty and conflict, they fabricated new imaginative

277. Ibid., 181. (IAITT).
278. Ibid., 194. (IAITT).
279. Milbank and Oliver, 'Radical Orthodoxy: A Conversation', 35.
280. Milbank, *RD2*, 270.
281. Ibid., 179.

stories about 'peaceful emergence and return' and of 'peaceful height and transcendence.'[282]

Milbank's genealogical story follows a similar pattern. Beginning with his programmatic 1986 essay, Milbank constructs a series of tragic intellectual villains, all of whom are then progressively negated in order to arrive at his seemingly un-negatable vision of ontological peace. Yet, for all his disdain of 'bastard dualisms', his Christian *mythos* can only be 'made strange' if it is continually narrated in definitional opposition to that which is different: peace over violence, creation over nihilism, comedy over tragedy, Aquinas over Scotus, theology over the secular, Milbank over MacKinnon. In other words, what is being left 'unsaid' is how his metaphysical villains become narratologically foundational for his re-founding and re-narration of Christian ontology by retrieving the work of his metaphysical heroes: Augustine, Aquinas, Vico, and de Lubac to name but a few.

One could take this argument a step further. What if there was no MacKinnon? And MacKinnon's Kantian apophaticism was not latent, waiting to fill the academy with the steam of his 'prophylactic Platonism'. For the borderlands had to be instituted or *imagined*, both in theory and in practice. And this instituting or imagining was, as I have argued, bound up with MacKinnon's own experience of the 'protesting raids' made by 'secular' philosophers upon the Divinity Faculty. Thus, the creative invention of the borderlands is inexorably linked to MacKinnon's 'both-and' construction of, and empirical engagement with, 'the secular'. Rather ironically, without this particular programmatic *mythos* of the secular, the *mythos* of 'Radical Orthodoxy' is likely to have never existed. Is it any surprise, therefore, that Milbank has had to admit that 'RO may, of course, have become over-obsessed with the secularisation issue' and needs to (but seemingly is unable to) 'broaden its horizons'.[283] The 'unsaid', yet foundational, reality is that it cannot be 'made strange' without it.

Students of Milbank often joke that he and his collaborators in 'Radical Orthodoxy' are offering a ' "witness protection service" for graduates who want to do theology without first genuflecting before a statue of Kant.'[284] But in order to avail oneself of this 'service', it presupposes that one has already inherited, accepted, and agreed to proliferate the Milbankian 'either-or' reaction to MacKinnon's purportedly liberal aesthetics of the sublime. Thus, if MacKinnon's 'dialogical naturalism' presupposes the acceptance of a secular-tragic-Kantian conception of reality, Milbank's 'Radical Orthodoxy' presupposes the acceptance of his theological-comedic-Lubacian conception of reality. However, what if Milbank's particular reading of Kant is no longer persuasive? Would this not necessitate a radical transformation of the aesthetic-rhetorical tune that is pied

282. Ibid.

283. John Milbank, 'Radical Orthodoxy and Protestantism Today', 2017, http://www.Sci elo .org.za/scielo.php? script=sci_arttext&pid=S1015–87582017000200004. Accessed on 11 September 2019.

284. Rowland, *Catholic Theology*, 125.

piped by Milbank from his 'literary republic' on the borderlands?[285] Christopher Insole, for instance, speaks of how theologians, bedevilled by 'Kantian anxieties', have become entrapped by the arbitrary nature of their particular solution(s) to the particular way they have 'fleshed out' the *Critique*.[286] 'Thinkers bow deeply and uncritically at the Kantian problem, and then pronounce confidently the unique indispensability of their own solution.'[287]

Insole is also a theologian who has made a significant contribution to the work now being done to demonstrate how the transcendental ego is actually fractured throughout in Kant. One example of this is his discussion of the *aporia* that would appear to undermine Milbank's 'two-realm interpretation' (that is say, a strict disjunction between the realm of the phenomenal and the realm of the noumenal) of Kant's transcendental idealism. Although there are textual instances where Kant is 'behaving himself' in ostensibly respecting this dualistic ontology, there are various other instances where he appears to contradict it, especially, for example, in his reliance upon the knowledge of ourselves as 'noumenal substances' in moral philosophy.[288] Insole develops a persuasive argument for accepting that, despite the aporetic tension which Kant, himself, recognizes, 'belief in noumenal freedom and God would not be implausible for Kant.'[289] As such, there exists a genuine and necessary porosity within his transcendental idealism.[290] Insole's scholarship gives reason to consider whether there is something *passé* in Milbank's interpretation of Kant, especially his use of MacKinnon's Kantianism as a foil with which to carve out the secular space only so as to be able to out-narrate it and, in theory, close it down.

The natural law to come

The preceding discussion obviously has powerful evaluative implications for Milbank's ongoing contributions to current debates in natural law. This is principally because of the reactionary (even if 'unsaid') continuity that I expect will fuse the older programmatic *mythos* expounded in the 'Theology of Right' with the alternate *mythos* he has begun to formulate in preparation for *On Divine Government*. When this relationship was allowed to surface, I argued that Milbank's discursive praxis of 'out-narration' is predicated upon an even deeper continuity between his re-narration of the genealogical origins of the tradition of natural law and his subsequent substantiation of a series of 'Radically Orthodox' theo-cultural and political ends.

285. I have appropriated the phrase 'literary republic' from Kucer. See: Kucer, *Truth in Politics*, 148.

286. Christopher Insole, *The Realist Hope* (Aldershot: Ashgate, 2006), 162–3.

287. Ibid., 163.

288. Christopher Insole, *Kant and the Creation of Freedom* (Oxford: OUP, 2013), 90.

289. Ibid., 120.

290. Ibid.

This conclusion is ironic given that one of the most valuable aspects of Milbank's contribution is his own attentiveness to the theological 'unsaid(s)' that, implicitly and explicitly, shape and influence the contributions of his peers. Take, for example, his theological critique of the *duplex-ordo* theory and its propagation of various governing assumptions about the secular that are often left unexamined and thus reified. Due to what he terms 'institutional reasons', Milbank has long held that the Roman Catholic Church has been unable to negate this 'false Tridentine legacy' and, in consequence, has perpetuated a discourse about natural law that is fractured (un-Thomistically) from the law of grace and charity.[291]

Even more revealing is his claim that this perpetuation is what secretly unites 'conservatives', *à la* John Finnis, and 'liberals', *a la* Jean Porter, since both assume a 'two-tier economy'.[292] Milbank argues that it is this 'two-tier economy' that frames the dilemma for the Catholic Church in terms of another either/or: 'do you speak on the basis of natural law that should be available to everybody … or do you, on the other hand, say that our positions are grounded in our entire Catholic vision'?[293] Instead, Milbank presents his Philonian-Lubacian reconstruction of Thomistic natural law as a teleological discourse that is, nevertheless, 'always situated in a kind of in-between realm'.[294] In practice, this means that 'we don't need to speak within a completely natural law-based kind of discourse: we can get people to try to see more deeply the implications of what they already think. This includes getting them to recognize that their vision isn't completely cut off from … a religious vision.'[295] At the heart of this perspective lies the retrieval of the harmonizing idea of divine government.

Whilst we can anticipate that more will be said with the release of *On Divine Government*, it is still worth acknowledging the definitional and conceptual vagueness that surrounds Milbank's contribution. On one level, this vagueness is commensurate with his contention that natural law retained only a minimal normative force in Aquinas. Never did Aquinas invoke natural law, he says, to legitimate a particular social or political arrangement.[296] (Ironically, as I've contended, Milbank does use natural law to substantiate particular socio-economic and political-ecclesiological arrangements.) On another level, the vagueness also extends from the aporetic relationship I alluded to earlier between his portrayal of jurisprudence as a hylozoistic *poesis* and the narratological concreteness of the law enacted in the life of Christ. The difficulty continues to lie in explaining how these two elements – the particularism of *poesis* and the universalism of the Gospel – are linked in order to instantiate instances of objective *ius*. Furthermore, if, as Milbank claims, beauty alone is what signs truth and if true *poesis* is always

291. Milbank, 'The Last of the Last', 279.
292. Ibid., 280.
293. Milbank and Oliver, 'Radical Orthodoxy: A Conversation', 44.
294. Ibid., 45.
295. Ibid.
296. Ibid., 131.

liturgical, then who is the judge of 'true' beauty and 'authentic' liturgy?[297] Or, is the apparently 'self-authenticating' nature of truth actually a new (gnostic) form of 'self-evidence'?

What I believe is left 'unsaid' here is how Milbank's interest in dismantling the epistemological autonomy of natural law denotes an extension of his 'devious response' to the secular *mythos*. When 'Radical Orthodoxy' was in its nascency, Milbank's theological attraction to postmodernism was tactically linked to its ability to disrupt secular truth-claims, opening the way for him to expose, more generally, how modern liberalism is constructed upon the theologically generated biopolitical *aporia* I have described.[298] Over time, however, Milbank has become increasingly cautious about leveraging this perceived advantage in postmodernism into an 'apologetical' point of departure for 'Radical Orthodoxy'.[299] For even if postmodernism obliterates boundaries, its pragmatist and indeterminate reshaping of the *factum* is actually a hyperbolic form of 'secular reason'.[300] Furthermore, he also argues that the 'postmodern fusion of nature and culture' involves a biopolitical collapsing of *physis* into *techne*.[301]

For this reason, while Milbank may establish a genealogical connection between philosophical modernism and postmodernism, I would venture that it is more accurate to see 'Radical Orthodoxy' as reacting to two different constructions of the secular *mythos*. One could argue, therefore, that the secular *mythos* is fragmenting even within 'Radical Orthodoxy'. What distinguishes these two *mythoi* is a matter of theological-genealogical emphasis. Whereas the 'pure reason' of secular modernism is narrated as the theological bastard of Scotic univocity, the pragmatic constructivism of secular postmodernism is narrated as the heretical pastiche of Trinitarian theology.[302] In both instances, the secular is defined by its desacralizing and spatialized logic, which, again ironically, is being deviously secured by a series of theological assumptions.

Suspended by the secular

I would venture that rather than being situated in the 'in-between realm' of divine government, Milbank's natural law resides in a 'suspended middle' between at least these two *mythoi* of the secular. Indications of this position began to surface through the emergence of what are either blatant contradictions, at worst, or the invention of a new series of theological 'both-ands', at best. In reaction against modern secular (epistemological) stability and ontological hylomorphism,

297. Milbank, *Being Reconciled*, x.

298. John Milbank, 'The Programme of Radical Orthodoxy', in *Radical Orthodoxy? – A Catholic Enquiry*, ed. Laurence P. Hemming (Abingdon: Routledge, 2000), 41–2.

299. Milbank, 'Radical Orthodoxy's First Decade', 391.

300. Ibid., 391; Milbank, *The Future of Love*, 156–7.

301. Milbank, *Being Reconciled*, 201.

302. Milbank, *T&ST*, 12.

Milbank proposes a 'theology without substance' and a hylozoistic understanding of 'truth as made'. However, in reaction against postmodern secular instability, he has endeavoured to rescue the *lingua* of 'substance' to denote 'points of stability'. In reaction against the 'modern', post-Suarezian, tendency to normify the natural law as a theory about 'what is to be done', Milbank asserts that it actually provides 'positively little' normative content and that the Church should just remain silent on the specificities of the moral law. However, in reaction against the entropic antinomianism of the postmodern, he declares gay marriage to be a biopolitical aberration and economic capitalism a perilous heresy – for 'decisions that negate the natural law have absolutely no validity whatsoever.'[303]

Perhaps the most striking inconsistency is found in his identification and subsequent opposition to three forms of (proto-)secular violence, namely, the biopolitical violence of (Stoical) natural fate, the modern secular violence of natural (subjective) rights, and the postmodern secular violence of tyrannical indifference.[304] In reaction against these ontologies of violence, Milbank portrays the Church as the 'true polity' of ontological truth and of ontological peace.[305] 'All political theory' and, by extension, all theorizing about the natural law 'is relocated by Christianity as thought about the Church.'[306] For this reason, when finite goods or ends are pursued by the *civitas terrena* without referral to one's supernatural end, they are rendered 'unconditionally bad ends'.[307] Milbank asserts that the only way to place oneself 'outside' of this *polis* of peace is through the use of 'coercive force', an exercise in will-to-power that is 'arbitrary', 'excessive', and constitutive of the 'secular'. This is contrasted with the truth of Christianity which, as I noted above, is secured by the creative force of *caritas* and 'based on persuasion'. But what if people do not find Milbank's rhetorical re-narration of an ontology of peace persuasive? Surprisingly, Milbank argues that it is then appropriate that such individuals should be 'coerced', especially when dealing with 'the young and the deluded'.[308] And what if the state refuses to obey the natural law precepts prescribed by his Church? Surprisingly, Milbank prognosticates that, eventually, 'they might have to be legitimately resisted by more than democratic means.'[309]

303. See the epigraph of this chapter.

304. Milbank, *The Future of Love*, 342.

305. Milbank, *T&ST*, 338.

306. Ibid., 411.

307. Ibid.

308. Milbank, *Being Reconciled*, 38.

309. 'Christians need to remember that democratic decisions that negate the natural law have absolutely no validity whatsoever. The more regimes violate the natural law the more they become tyrannies.

One day they might have to be legitimately resisted by more than democratic means.' John Milbank, 'John Milbank, Twitter', 2018, https://twitter.com/johnmilbank3/status/1000 2739768 10201088?lang=en. Accessed 20 July 2018.

Of course, this obviously begs the question of where exactly is Milbank's Church? Who, besides Milbank, determines whether its political aspirations actually accord and promote divine government and reflect the desire for the beatific vision? Most perplexingly of all, when exactly is it legitimate, according to the natural law, for the Church of ontological peace to authorize the enactment of social and political violence?

After considering how Milbank's approach to natural law has evolved (and continuing to evolve) in reaction to at least two – even if interconnected – *mythoi* of the secular, one also begins to notice why formulating participation as *poesis* is so important to the 'Radical Orthodoxy' project. The final sentence of his programmatic essay against MacKinnon posited that *poesis* may provide the antidote to overcome modernity as well as provide the key to establishing a 'post-modern theology'.[310] Milbank reiterated the same sentiment in the conclusion to the re-published version of this essay in *The Word Made Strange*. However, in this later version, he qualifies the 'antidote' as involving a 'ceaseless re-narrating' of human nature-culture specifically beyond the finite bounds of ('modern Kantian') transcendental idealism.[311] This development points to something critical that is being left 'unsaid' with respect to Milbank's theory of truth. It is his theology of *poesis* that enables him to continually recalibrate his Christian meta-narrative so as to continually 'out-narrate' the ongoing fragmentations of the secular *mythos*. The problem is that, even within Milbank's own meta-narrative, the category of the secular is fragmenting and is becoming too unwieldy a *mythos* to be theologically useful, especially for reconstructing natural law. This notwithstanding, we can recall that Milbank's project is, by its hylozoistic nature, still in the 'making', and, thus, any future contribution will need to negotiate the *aporias* that have surfaced during the course of this analysis.[312]

310. Milbank, *CofR*, 199.

311. John Milbank, *The Word Made Strange* (New York: Blackwell, 1997), 32.

312. Ibid., x.

Part Two

Reconstruction

Chapter 5

DECONSTRUCTING THE SECULAR *MYTHOS*

Section I: An aporetic discourse

What to say?

'I don't know anymore what to say!'[1] Such were the final words of the Athenian Companion in the dialogue of the *Minos*. With this epistemological acquiescence, the ancient discourse into the 'nature of *nomos*' seemingly ends in aporia and silence. After bringing the 'three voices' of Finnis, Porter, and Milbank into an indirect dialogue, one might be inclined to recapitulate and parody the Companion's flummoxed sentiment. For if the preceding chapters have established anything to be 'self-evident' about current debates in natural law, it is how tragically fragmented the discourse has become. Tragic, because despite reasoning within the same Christian/Catholic tradition, the 'three voices' define and delineate natural law in such conflicting terms that their contributions frequently appear to talk past each other.

Prima facie, this intramural inconsonance destabilizes and, thence, undercuts the popular assumption that the discourse can be used, extramurally, as a dialogical framework for public moral reflection. Even more fatally, it raises strong suspicions that the phrase 'natural law' is actually a subjective rhetorical trope that is invoked to masquerade a host of discrete and disparate ideological norms as universal and objective truths.

This chapter hopes to begin to break the silence of the 'unsaid(s)' by illustrating how the (indirect) dialogue between the 'three voices' has helped disclose the forgotten catalytic source of the aporetic 'unsaid(s)' themselves. Once this source has been acknowledged and its influence unmasked, it raises the possibility of investigating alternate starting points with which to envisage how natural law might be constructively reconstructed. For the real value of the evaluative analysis of the 'three voices' is measured by its capacity to enlighten and actualize more promising discoursive horizons for current debates in natural law.

1. Plato, 'Minos', in *Plato: Complete Works*, trans. Malcolm Schofield (Indianapolis: Hackett, 1997), 1317.

It is important to reiterate that the identification of an aporia does not necessarily equate to the identification of an impassable impossibility or, metaphorically speaking, the paralysis of 'non-passage'.[2] Although this interpretation has been popularized by philosophies of deconstruction, it forgets to appropriate the Platonic notion of euporia. For Plato, as for Aristotle, the concepts of aporia and euporia are closely related. In the classical tradition, to raise an aporia means to have arrived at a moment of discoursive perplexity, but not necessarily a moment of discoursive impossibility. In fact, an aporia can opportune moments of new possibility. This is because the experience of perplexity behoves the protagonist(s) to 'state the perplexities well' so that 'distinctions can be made, and important insights reached.'[3] Hence, in the classical tradition, the careful statement of aporetic perplexity always preserved the horizon of euporetic possibility.

If we are to avoid repeating the same aporetic and hegemonic strategies that have stifled the dialogical search for the natural law, then it is crucial now to 'state the perplexities well'. To that end, I will now seek to substantiate the claim that, in light of the preceding analyses of the 'three voices', the fragmentation and ineffectiveness of contemporary natural law discourse is tied to the semantic ambiguity and fragmentation of the concept of the secular.[4] I will underscore this ambiguity and fragmentation by explicating the contradistinctive genealogical *mythoi* that the 'three voices' narrate about the genesis of the secular and its theological significance. I refer to these foundational narratives as 'solipsisms of the secular'. I will then proceed to demonstrate how these *mythoi* generate and regulate the theoretical and normative perplexity that defines current debates in natural law with reference to three principal aporia: (1) alethiological, (2) anthropological, and (3) genealogical.

Section II: 'Solipsisms of the Secular'

United and divided

Finnis, Porter, and Milbank are united by their common appeal to the historical tradition of natural law. Even if only in very elemental terms, the characterizing strengths of their different contributions reflect the development of what might be considered different starting points for dialogical elenchus as found in the *Minos*. Finnis's NNLT reflects and develops Socrates' assertion that the exercise of legal authority is always for the sake of securing what is objectively good. In contemporary discourse, Finnis has been able to shift the debate within jurisprudence onto a deeper consideration of the basic goods and, more broadly, the nature of the common good, thereby offering a powerful corrective and

2. Younis, 'Euporia', 90.

3. Aristotle, *Metaphysics*, Book 3, 995a27-b2. Quoted in, Younis, 'Euporia', 100.

4. This discussion is also conducted with a view to presenting a fresh theo-cultural horizon for further research in Chapter 6.

alternative to the predominance of utilitarian reductionism and other forms of (legal) monism in practical philosophy.

Porter's astute appreciation for the tradition-constitutedness of natural law reasoning reflects Socrates' and the Companion's realization that their search for the definition of law is strongly conditioned by their inheritance of two antithetical *mythoi* about the origins of the most ancient laws of Greece. In contemporary discourse, Porter presents a powerful challenge to the pervasive, yet anachronistic, assumption that the Thomistic-scholastic natural law tradition is a monolithic discourse of 'pure reason' for the derivation of specific moral norms, thereby opening up the possibility that the tradition itself may allow for a plurality of legitimate interpretations and instantiations.[5]

Milbank's genealogical reclamation of the forgotten theological origins of natural law in the political metaphysics of Philo Judaeus is analogical to Socrates' genealogical appeal to the divine laws of Zeus. In contemporary discourse, Milbank has helped lay the cornerstone for restoring natural law to the theological reality of divine government, thereby inviting theologians to reconsider how the recovery of this explicitly theological element of the tradition need not invalidate the discourse but, in fact, grounds its very possibility.

Each of these distinct interventions mediate particular interpretive starting points for navigating a persuasive pathway to reconciling the distinction between *nomos* and *physis*. On this fundamental point, the 'three voices' are united in and through their search for an anthropologically interrelational and interdependent solution to the dilemma of how to delineate the boundaries between nature and culture – that is to say, they share a mutual (even if chastened) aspiration to develop a universal *lingua* of jurisprudence that can give recognition to the *logos* of the 'we' in order to transcend the solipsism of the 'I' of human identity and human flourishing. Interestingly, therefore, the 'three voices' are individually, and yet collectively, committed to exploring how the tradition of natural law can help illuminate our understanding of our own situatedness. They seek to unravel how one's particularity (the uniqueness of one's theo-cultural and moral experiences) relates to, and is structured by, a sense of the universal – the reality of the whole, that is, the world in which we live.

Faithful and unfaithful

But something has been left 'unsaid' here. Something that ultimately divides Finnis, Porter, and Milbank's unifying methodological appeal to the tradition. For when the 'three voices' were brought into sequential conversation, it became swiftly apparent that the way they were retrieving and speaking about the tradition illuminated very different motivating intentions.

5. Theologically speaking, it would be more accurate to say that Porter's sensitivity to the tradition-constitutedness of rationality has helped us to understand why there exists a plurality of different interpretations.

Beginning with Finnis, I noted several instances where he describes the NNLT as a faithful recovery and re-presentation of the authentic tradition of natural law as proposed by Aquinas. Although he left it strategically 'unsaid' in *NLNR*, he would later clarify (albeit in a rather obscure and lone footnote) that his contribution can only be understood aright if one appreciates that he has sought to adopt Aquinas's intended viewpoint. At the same time, Finnis acknowledges that his reading of the Thomistic tradition has been profoundly influenced by Grisez's analytical exegesis. But Grisez, unlike Finnis, has long since resigned from calling his contribution an 'interpretation' of Aquinas. Instead, he and his collaborators have sought to appropriate the 'language' of the 'Thomistic natural law-tradition' only to employ it in a manner that 'differs in various ways' to that of Aquinas.[6]

A similar hermeneutical ambiguity was discerned in Porter's contribution. In several of her major works, her reclamation of the natural law tradition is situated and contextualized by taking critical aim at what she considers to be the 'radical' eschewal of the authentic Thomistic tradition perpetrated by Finnis himself. 'There are too many aspects of Aquinas's moral theory', she argues, 'that his [Finnis'] reading cannot accommodate, aspects that are not merely peripheral or 'merely' theological but seem clearly to be central to Aquinas's account of the moral life.'[7] Hence, Porter views her project as one of 'recovery', asserting that her theory of natural laws '*is* in its essentials that of Aquinas.'[8] In other instances, however, this hermeneutic of recovery is exchanged for a hermeneutic of reformulation, which, in certain pivotal instances, involves 'reading Aquinas against himself'.[9] This obviously gives pause for thought. If Porter, herself, makes no attempt to argue for the exegetical accuracy of her appropriation of scholastic-Thomistic linguistic categories (as she acknowledges), then in what sense or according to what measure can she maintain that her project is in closer continuity with the scholastic-Thomistic tradition than Finnis's NNLT? Moreover, why have her exegetical frustrations with the NNLT remained such a fundamental part of her contextualizing critique?

Of course, Milbank's 'Radical Orthodoxy' has amassed popular notoriety for admonishing the 'mainstream' or 'modern' interpretation(s) of the Thomistic tradition, which typically ties the universal relevance of Aquinas's natural law to its philosophical and ahistorical character. He boldly declares that his *ressourcement* of Aquinas's natural law 'goes clean against' any interpretation that espouses a 'sharp distinction' between philosophy and theology. Although he recognizes that Aquinas does appear to uphold this position in certain passages, nonetheless, he avows that it is an erroneous and even heretical reading. Thus, like Finnis and Porter, Milbank's appeal to the tradition is initially framed by a

6. Finnis, Grisez and Boyle, 'FMU', 99.

7. c.f. Jean Porter, 'A Consideration of John Finnis' *Aquinas*', *The Journal of Religion*, vol. 80, no. 3 (July 2000), 476.

8. Porter, *NasR*, 46. (IAITT).

9. Porter, 'At the Limits of Liberalism', 389.

desire to recover a 'more accurate' account of Aquinas's natural law.[10] Yet, rather confusingly, in order to discern this 'more accurate' reading, one has to adopt 'Sherlock Holmes's last remaining solution', by which he means that often the most implausible or abstruse explanation has to be accepted since all the other straightforward explanations have been rendered impossible.[11] Only superficially, says Milbank, is Aquinas a straightforward thinker. The *arcanum* of his true genius actually lies in reinterpreting his approach through the lens of 'positions he does affirm, often briefly and like a kind of residue.'[12] Employing this 'hermeneutic of Holmes' constitutes the difference between doing an 'exegesis' and performing an 'interpretation'.[13] Aquinas, argues Milbank, 'requires interpretation' – not exegesis.[14]

Although Milbank does not explain in any great detail the definitional difference between 'exegesis' and 'interpretation', he does call attention to a pertinent and perplexing issue. Each of the 'three voices' commence their contributions to natural law by lamenting how something ingenious and insightful within the tradition has been overshadowed by specious and spurious misappropriations of Aquinas's theory of natural law. Each of the 'three voices' then proceed to trace, via a genealogy, the moments of intellectual rupture in order to explain how these misappropriations have proliferated. Each of the 'three voices' then proceed to recover what they believe has been lost. However, even if only tacitly, each of the 'three voices' acknowledge that this recovery involves repressing, or reformulating, or re-narrating the tradition for some other purpose. The aporia, therefore, is that, on the one hand, Finnis, Porter, and Milbank see themselves as faithful exegetes of the 'authentic' Thomistic tradition. But, on the other hand, Finnis, Porter, and Milbank are all interpreting the language of the tradition to promote systems of thought that either go well beyond or even contradict Aquinas's intentions. What 'unsaid', therefore, does this hermeneutical disjunction point us towards?

Language and tradition

Through the analyses in Part One, it became apparent that the appeal to the tradition by the 'three voices' is never just for the sake of recovering a potentially illuminating language; it is also an appeal to and for an authority. One could say that the language itself embodies the authority of the tradition (particularly the language of Aquinas). But the dialogue between the 'three voices' has disclosed the fact that we cannot speak of a 'tradition' without acknowledging another 'unsaid', namely, that the concept of 'tradition' is itself a creation – a point that is reflected in and through the individuated interpretations and genealogies that have now

10. C.f. Milbank, 'The History of Natural Law'.
11. Milbank, *Truth in Aquinas*, 18.
12. Ibid.
13. Ibid., 20.
14. Ibid.

emerged.[15] Therefore, the problematic is not just limited to how the 'three voices' read or speak about the tradition; it also extends to how they construct it and how this construction then inflects the way in which the language of the tradition is defined and deployed.

Of course, this process never occurs in a vacuum.[16] When we begin to explore the possibility of presenting natural law as a dialogical framework, we always have an audience or a particular cultural mindset in mind. We construct (epistemologically) who we are speaking or intending to speak to. One might call this construction an 'inner audience'. In a bid to be found persuasive, we allow the 'inner audience' to reflect back to us a tradition of interpretive horizons (conventions) within which we then begin to contemplate, proleptically, a series of questions being raised and another series of answers being given. In other words, our 'inner audience' bequeaths a series of circumscribing linguistic tropes and categories with which to convey that which we hope to persuasively convey about natural law.

This bequeathal of idiom is crucial not only because it shapes how we determine what can be said and how it should be said, but it also informs what should be left strategically 'unsaid'. (For, undoubtedly, there are aspects of the tradition, especially theological aspects, that cannot be translated into the proscribed idiom, irrespective of how hard one might try.) One might say, then, that, within current debates in natural law, it is the different 'inner audiences' that provide the *real* – even if ultimately illusory – authoritative foundation for how the 'three voices' reconstruct and translate the tradition of natural law for contemporary reflection. Thus, despite their insistence to the contrary, it is worth reflecting upon the extent to which the natural law arguments developed by the 'three voices' (along with many other contemporary natural law theorists) derive their authority from different meta-narratives about the authority of the secular.[17]

At first glance, to speak of 'inner audiences' and the convolution of 'tradition', 'language', and 'authority' might sound rather perplexing. However, what I am addressing is profoundly practical. One of the striking realizations emanating from the analyses undertaken in Part One is that, irrespective of their distinct strategies, each of the 'three voices' is pitching the language of natural law in reaction to their own interpretations and narrations of the secular *mythos*. However, the way in which Finnis, Porter, and Milbank construct the secular – both genealogically and descriptively – is always done in coincidence with, and

15. Porter, *NasR*, 58.

16. To emphasise the point again, like in the *Minos*, Finnis, Porter and Milbank are all interested in natural law because they are questing after a language that goes beyond the sheer conventionalism of the political order. The process itself must at least strive to be relational.

17. To formulate this in terms of a question: Is the common appeal to the authority of the historical tradition within current debates in natural law actually an interpretive mask for the undergirding authority of what are actually different 'inner audiences'?

in reaction to, the construction of their 'inner audience'. (The namelessness of the Athenian Companion in the *Minos* could be considered emblematic of the metamorphic identity of the 'inner audience' within current debates in natural law.) Before turning to outline some of the aporia that this point of departure creates, it is appropriate to first explicate, briefly, how the 'inner audience' mediates and reflects a different account of the secular *mythos* in each of the 'three voices'.

Finnis's 'inner audience'

During the course of my analysis, I referred to Finnis's 'inner audience' as the 'cultured despisers' – liberal-secular students and intellectuals who staunchly adhere to the positivistic principles of modern analytical philosophy and jurisprudence. The principal dispositional trait of Finnis's 'inner audience' is scepticism, especially metaphysical scepticism. Hence, at various junctures in *NLNR*, he enters into various hypothetical arguments with a character he calls the 'sceptic'.[18] In light of the analysis in chapter two, the 'sceptic' could be a pseudonymous foil for his key interlocutor, H. L. A. Hart.[19] In any case, the 'sceptic' is the embodiment of how Finnis constructs the philosophical and cultural temperament of his 'liberal secular' milieu. As one influenced by both Humean empiricism and Kantian rationalism, the 'sceptic' snickers and scorns at the idea of a 'natural law', believing it to be indissociable from an irrational and reductivistic derivation of 'ought' from 'is'. Of course, as a 'secular-liberal', the 'sceptic' is also a sociocultural 'pluralist', which Finnis interprets as a politically charged euphemism for moral relativism and a precipitous recipe for secular nihilism. For if there are no objective moral norms, there can only be the utility and self-assertion of the will, the satisfaction of which often neglects any formal consideration of the basic goods and supersedes any formal consideration of the nature of the common good. Furthermore, for the 'sceptic', all theological and metaphysical forms of reasoning have no legitimate place in 'public discourse'. If a natural law argument is to be found intelligible within the secular sphere, then it must prove itself to be analytically 'freestanding' in the sense of being based upon 'reason alone'.

Although Finnis's construction of the secular may sound unmitigatedly negative (one might even say, given his recourse to the 'art of writing', he fears it), he often approaches and engages the 'sceptic' – his secular 'inner audience' – with a surprising level of positivity. Whilst he certainly deplores the 'secular's' rejection of moral absolutes and its gradual descent into a functional atheism-materialism, he still firmly believes in re-narrating the 'practical meaning of secularism' and of respecting a 'healthy secularity'.[20] Even Aquinas, he says, spoke of the secular as a 'distinction of competencies' and did so 'without negative connotations'.[21]

18. C.f. Finnis, *NLNR*, 72, 73, 75, 127, 378, 412.
19. Or, as I noted in Chapter 2, it could also be a foil for Nietzsche.
20. Finnis, *Moral Absolutes*, 84–5.
21. Finnis, 'On the Practical Meaning of Secularism', 491.

This inspires Finnis to try and persuade the 'cultured despisers' of the timeless intelligibility of the Catholic Church's controversial moral teachings by explicating how the tradition itself can speak to them in their own timeless language of 'practical reason', always respecting, however, the rules of engagement proscribed by the 'secular measure'.

Porter's 'inner audience'

The 'second voice' of Porter believes that Finnis has misjudged his audience by continuing to perpetuate several false assumptions about the secular. In order to tell a 'fuller story' about the natural law, she begins by telling a 'fuller story' about the secular, especially about the intellectual interests and dispositions of her secular interlocutors. In fact, she asserts that the two stories are, in many ways, genealogically intertwined. For this reason, and in an attempt to re-evaluate the 'proper relationship' between Christian and secular ethics, her 'inner audience' is naturally more encompassing than Finnis's – wishing to engage simultaneously theologians, secular jurists, and moral philosophers. However, to speak intelligibly to these different disciplinary scholars does not necessitate the circumscription of one's language within the boundaries of 'mere reason'. She believes the secular academy has moved beyond the scepticism of Ayer and Moore and is now open to reconsidering certain forms of ethical naturalism, natural theology, and even beginning to speak in terms of natural teleologies. This strongly implies that respecting the naturalistic fallacy is no longer an unequivocal dogma within secular discourse, the recognition of which encourages her to retrieve a specifically theological account of human nature and of natural law for jurisprudential reflection. Confusingly, this theological account was shown to focus primarily upon developing the specifically 'philosophical components' of the tradition on the basis that these components are more likely to be found 'rhetorically persuasive'.[22] Nevertheless, she justifies what Finnis described as the 'distinction of competencies' in Aquinas on a theological basis. That basis being a doctrine of creation.

Porter also frequently contextualizes and characterizes the secular as a 'liberal' phenomenon. The term is notoriously ambiguous. It became apparent in Part One that both Finnis and Porter use the term to establish different points of common ground or different dialogical starting points with which to engage their secular 'inner audiences'. As I noted above, Finnis affirms the classically liberal presupposition 'that there is one substantive rationality on which all sufficiently enlightened persons must agree'.[23] Porter asserts that Finnis has again misjudged his secular audience, arguing that the foundationalist assumptions that delimit this form of 'liberalism' have since been questioned and revised by secular philosophers. Consequently, Christian natural law theorists should also forgo

22. Porter, *ROV*, 32.

23. Porter, 'Openness and Constraints', 517.

foundationalist (ahistorical) forms of rhetoric. Instead, Porter appeals to what she considers to be a later form of the earlier liberal tradition. Whilst she certainly affirms the centrality of the 'rational moral individual', her perception of liberalism is foremost defined by 'the practice of the classical liberal virtues of tolerance, openness to change, and the promotion of pluralism.'[24] Interestingly, it is the aspect of liberalism that Finnis (a social conservative) considers most flawed that Porter (a Catholic feminist) wants to 'baptize' on the basis of the pluralism purportedly upheld within scholastic jurisprudence.

Porter performs this 'baptism' genealogically by tracing the origins of much of what presents itself today as 'liberal secular' values to forgotten theological ideas and innovations that emerged from the scholastic-Thomistic natural law tradition. This even extends to the very idea of a 'secular morality' itself, the origins of which she locates both in the scholastics' desacralization of human nature and in their new appreciation for the power of human reason to comprehend the intelligibility that exists within the natural order. Porter thus presents the secular as something theologically instituted (even if Aquinas never spoke of the secular in such terms) rather than something to be philosophically accommodated. Yet, its emergence still represents a 'theological loss' for the sake of a valuable 'theological gain'.[25]

Milbank's 'inner audience'

The 'third voice' of Milbank declares categorically that Finnis and Porter are rendering their own voices 'objectively and demonstrably null and void' by extricating or eschewing the theological from the natural law tradition.[26] One might say that, from Milbank's perspective, their 'inner audiences' are also, genealogically speaking, out of date. Their penchant for maintaining a sharp distinction between philosophy and theology fails to come to terms with how the secular condition is both 'modern' and 'postmodern'. Hence, although Milbank speaks about natural law unabashedly as a theologian, 'Radical Orthodoxy' knows no disciplinary or denominational boundaries. Yet, Milbank has no interest in using natural law to speak to the secular, at least not in the sense of wanting to engage it dialogically or to try and coexist with it sociopolitically. For the secular does not actually exist 'substractively', that is to say, no one actually is 'secular'; everyone is a theologian in disguise. In a similar vein to Porter, Milbank's genealogical deconstruction of the secular also highlights how the desacralizing shift in the Middle Ages, animated by the rediscovery of Aristotelian philosophy, corresponds with the sociocultural collapse of a 'symbolically-realist' and metaphysically participatory world view. But whereas Porter approbates this sociocultural transition in terms of a theological

24. Ibid., 530.

25. A 'loss' and 'gain' which she asserts to be biblically founded to the extent that the integrity and autonomy of the natural order is purportedly underpinned by a sound doctrine of creation.

26. Milbank, *The Future of Love*, 306.

loss for the sake of a valuable theological gain, Milbank admonishes it as merely a 'thinned-out version of the Catholic faith' that is 'certainly not – as so often thought – rooted in the Bible itself.'[27] Broadly speaking, the same desacralizing theology that Porter reconstructs as a positive interpretive basis for engaging secular minds through a natural theology of law is what Milbank deconstructs and negates as an idolatrous mock-theology that is antithetical to Christian orthodoxy, propagative of the 'bastard dualisms' which beget the heresy of 'secular rationalism' and the 'possibility of nihilism'.[28] The only way to overcome this nihilistic metaphysic is to 'out-narrate' it by telling a better, more persuasive, *mythos* – the Christian *mythos*.

The dissonant and conflicting ways that two theologians, Porter and Milbank, evaluate the same genealogical developments in the tradition of natural law illuminates the presence of two dissonant and conflicting 'inner audiences'. For Porter, as for Finnis, the 'inner audience' bequeaths a series of starting points with which to establish common dialogical parameters. In contrast, Milbank's 'inner audience' is constructed as his irreconcilable opposition, against whom he juxtaposes his project of 'Radical Orthodoxy'.[29] Beginning with Donald MacKinnon, his 'inner audience' bequeaths a particular interpretation of Kantian philosophy that establishes the architectonic starting points to announce the 'end of dialogue' and the beginning of a meta-narratological counte-rattack. Milbank tasks himself with trying to out-narrate his 'inner audience' by portraying Kant as the metaphysical villain and not the theological hero. More generally, the secular sociopolitical realm is narrated as a fundamentally liberal philosophical ideology which, among other things, 'refuses to accept anything not rationally proven or demonstrable.'[30]

Although the advent of postmodern secular-liberalism reveals the arbitrariness of this ideology, and so problematizes Finnis's and Porter's constructions of the secular as, epistemologically speaking, a stable entity, it remains equally as much a parasitic inversion and corruption of what Milbank's genealogical story reveals to be intrinsically theological ideas.

The critical difference, therefore, is that Finnis's and Porter's 'inner audiences' provide synoptic frameworks for recovering and enhancing the potential philosophical-theological contiguity between the Thomistic tradition of natural law and secular jurisprudence, whereas, for Milbank, his 'inner audience' provides an initial meta-narrative about the hegemony of Kantian transcendental idealism within the secular academy. The lineaments of which inaugurate points of radical

27. Milbank, *BSO*, 116.

28. Milbank, *T&ST*, 218.

29. Essentially, his 'inner audience' includes anyone who espouses the influential 'both-and' philosophical-theology that MacKinnon's thought epitomised. However, Milbank's 'inner audience' is also less defined since, as I noted in Chapter 4, it adapts to reflect the dynamic evolution of his own construction of the secular *mythos*.

30. John Milbank and Adrian Pabst, *The Politics of Virtue* (London: Rowan & Littlefield, 2016), 45.

juxtaposition that allow him to make Thomistic natural law 'strange' and so, according to his logic, truer.

'Solipsisms of the secular'

Herein lies the conundrum. Finnis, Porter, and Milbank each appeal to the tradition of natural law precisely because they believe it can provide a framework with which to open up new horizons for mutual (human) understanding – to explore, discursively and dialectically, how our individuality relates to and is affirmed by that which is universal. But if, as I have argued, their construction of the tradition is formulated in reaction to contradicting constructions of the secular *mythos*, then the rhetorical purchase and dialogical value of natural law rests entirely upon the accuracy and credibility of their individuated (noetic) articulations of their respective 'inner audiences'. Such an introspective quest, even when ostensibly predicated upon one's extrospective experiences, runs the risk of mistaking *nomos* for *physis*; the particular for the universal; the unsayable for the sayable. Moreover, what if their respective 'inner audiences' are largely, if not entirely, based upon a solipsistic illusion (a theo-cultural mirror for self-reaction) that actually encourages the disremembering of the tradition (the 'unsaid') rather than occasioning its recovery? For what has become apparent is that this disremembering is not simply accidental. It is actually a product of the way in which they construct the secular *mythos*. In other words, the proposed solutions of Finnis, Porter, and Milbank all appear to be closing down or narrowing the natural law tradition in order to put it at the service of certain atrophying narrations of the secular *mythos*. For such reasons, it is appropriate to consider these atrophying constructions as 'solipsisms of the secular'. Although formulated to facilitate dialogue or promote out-narration, ironically, the 'solipsisms of the secular' fracture and prohibit such expectations, folding the discourse back on itself, centripetally, and reducing it to a dismembering polysemy of politically dissonant voices. Ultimately, therefore, the 'solipsisms of the secular' only help to make manifest and to make sense of the unspoken alterity within oneself.

If this preliminary evaluation is sound, then it would be more accurate to say that current debates in natural law *begin* rather than *end* in aporia. In the following sections of this chapter, I will defend this conviction by illustrating how the deconstruction of the 'unsaid(s)' in Part One discloses the superintending and hegemonic force that the *secular* mythos has over current debates in natural law. Section III will draw attention to three principal aporia that have surfaced. I have delineated them as follows: (1) alethiological, (2) anthropological, and (3) genealogical.[31]

31. Of course, there were many other 'perplexities' that arose out of Part One. I have had to limit this discussion to three central issues with the primordial focus being upon the first two since it is here that the power of the 'unsaid(s)' is subtlest.

Section III: Theoretical Aporias

Alethiological perplexity: Philosophy and theology

At the literary inception of jurisprudence in the *Minos*, the definitional inquiry into 'what is law?' both presupposes and discloses an alethiological inquiry into 'what is truth in jurisprudence?' Finnis, Porter, and Milbank align with Socrates' basic ontological conviction insofar as they ground the truth of law beyond the positivistic approbation of things 'loyally accepted'. Additionally, the 'three voices' hope to demonstrate how their approaches to natural law truths regarding human flourishing indicate their shared stance as moral realists. However, the 'three-way' analysis in Part One revealed that their perception of reality's givenness is fractured by certain aporetic 'unsaid(s)' stemming from their construction of the secular *mythos*. This surprising revelation suggests that these 'three (Christian) voices' are corresponding to three different theories of truth, manifested through their diverse utilization and/or suppression of certain forms of philosophical and theological language. To elucidate and explore the specific 'unsaid(s)' that animate this alethiological aporia, I will summarize and evaluate each 'voice' in turn.

Finnis's inverted realism

Whilst undoubtedly a moral realist, Finnis was quick to riposte the 'shaky start' Socrates inaugurated by anchoring the truth of law to a theoretical account of human nature (reality). The 'shakiness' is said to result from the purported emaciation and instrumentalization of practical reason – that is to say, its reduction to an art or craft that simply assists us to achieve the truths (ends) mapped out by theoretical reason.

What he leaves 'unsaid' is that that this 'shakiness' also extends from the irreconcilability of the Socratic trajectory with the metaphysical scepticism that defines his analytical construction of the secular *mythos*.[32] Hence, one of the foremost objections he must overcome is the 'sceptic's' conventional impression that natural law, according to its very semantics, depends upon a correspondence theory of truth – that a judgement possesses (moral) truth by its isomorphic correspondence with certain ontological or metaphysical facts about reality. Finnis renounces this account of truth as an egregious 'illusion' that has been bolstered by egregious 'misreadings' of the classical-Thomistic tradition. In a move that many Thomists consider a 'sell out', he inaugurates a 'new' (though purportedly 'neoclassical') way to establish the truth(s) of natural law that, he claims, appeals only to the autonomous exercise of practical reason.[33] I referred

32. 'Shaky', because, as my analysis has already demonstrated, it is challenged and contradicted by the two other voices' constructions of the secular *mythos*.

33. Finnis at least recognises that his project is 'new' from a contemporary perspective: 'the study of Aquinas' ethics as a systematic and strictly philosophical work of practical reason (at its most general and reflective) is still in its infancy.' John Finnis,

to this Kantian-like emphasis upon the metaphysico-theological autonomy and epistemological priority of practical reason as the 'third critical move'.

Finnis's central conviction is that Aquinas held the first principles of natural law to be 'self-evident', by which he means, unmediated, underived, and unchanging. These principles specify certain ends or basic goods. Basic, because they require no further explication as intelligible, purposeful, and irreducibly good 'reasons for action'. Focusing upon 'reasons for action' allows Finnis to establish a common denominator with how his 'liberal secular' interlocutor, H. L. A. Hart, was also coming to understand 'truth in law'. More fundamentally, the truth of a natural law argument and of practical knowledge is established not by moving from 'is' to 'ought but, rather, from 'ought' to 'is to be'.

Since the principles of natural law are 'self-evident', their truth is indemonstrable. Consequently, the burden is put upon the 'sceptic' to explain why a basic good such as knowledge is not a basic good. Finnis concludes that for the 'sceptic' to try and argue as such would be 'operationally self-refuting'.[34] Thus, he declares that to defy the epistemological coherence of the NNLT is to 'disqualify oneself from the pursuit of knowledge' and to deny the truth of the basic goods (as, for example, postmodern philosophers might be immediately inclined to do) 'is as straightforwardly unreasonable as anything can be.'[35]

Even if Finnis's NNLT refrains from translating theoretical truths about human nature into practical moral norms, there is strong evidence that he is trying to translate what he considers to be the normative truths of the natural law into a system of thought that can correspond with the governing 'truths' of his particular construction of the secular *mythos*. For instance, an illuminating 'unsaid' that I identified in Chapter 2 was his attraction to the Wittgensteinian idea that 'we can draw a boundary – for a special purpose.'[36] Throughout *NLNR* and in his later work on *Aquinas*, Finnis consistently delineates hermeneutical boundaries. Besides the obvious boundary he erects between the truths of theoretical and practical reason, he also draws a particularly sharp boundary between the truths of philosophy and the truths of theology. This distinction is of such 'special' strategic importance to Finnis that he always articulates it in the first paragraphs of each of his major works on natural law. In *NLNR*, for example, he swiftly delineates a boundary around his vocation as a lawyer and around jurisprudence itself by advising his reader to ignore the 'God chapter' if their interest is 'limited to jurisprudence'.[37] Similarly, through his strenuous employment of the hermeneutic of 'economy', he has sought to repress the theological voice of Aquinas almost absolutely – leaving the theological foundations of his thought entirely 'unsaid'.

'Aquinas' Moral, Political, and Legal Philosophy', 2017, https://plato.stanford.edu/entries/aquinas-moral-political/. Accessed on 29 August 2019.

34. Finnis, *NLNR*, 74.

35. Ibid., 69.

36. C.f. Finnis, *Religion & Public Reason*, 104.

37. Finnis, *NLNR*, v.

On reflection, this highlights a further level of unacknowledged tension in Finnis's construction of the secular *mythos*. The apparent irenicism with which he expounds his account of 'self-evidence' in order to meet his secular interlocutors on their 'own terms' is seemingly undercut by the eristical hermeneutical tools he has to utilize in order to justify his 'purely philosophical' reading of natural law in the *Summa Theologiae*. But the fact he believes he is compelled to read the tradition this way actually uncovers the violent or aggressive character of his 'inner audience'.

This gives cause to speculate. Is the truth of Finnis's NNLT grounded in the sophisticated articulation of the 'self-evident' first principles of practical reason? Or, is the language of 'self-evidence' and his threats of 'self-refutation' and 'disqualification' an 'unsaid' rhetorical attempt to invert the pressure (the linguistic onus) against the secular 'sceptic' – persuading him by the force of his philosophical language rather than the force of his theologically neutered arguments?[38] If the latter, then, ironically, is Finnis a legal positivist in disguise?[39]

Porter and the realism of pragmatism

Whilst Porter may have misunderstood the semantics of 'self-evidence' in the NNLT, her sharp declaration that 'there are no such things as "self-evident basic goods"' would, on Finnis's logic, disqualify her from rational discourse.[40] Porter, however, is not concerned. It is her staunch conviction that the truths of natural law do not square solely or exclusively with an understanding of 'nature as reason' (rationalism). She, and I think rightly, believes Finnis is operating within a broadly Kantian framework, which locates the truths of natural law exclusively in the rational apprehension and application of practical principles. Nevertheless, Porter does agree that even a robustly Christian ethic should be able to be found intelligible, possibly even persuasive, by those who reason and reflect in accordance with a set of criteria that is 'external' to the Christian tradition. Following John Courtney Murray, she illuminates what was strategically left 'unsaid' (but found to be hermeneutically indispensable) by Finnis in *NLNR* – that a Catholic intellectual has to understand and then engage with the 'full realism' of the milieu in which they live.

In Porter's case, the 'full realism' of the natural law is actually able to coexist and correspond with the 'full realism' of liberal-secularism. This is why she sees no reason to 'denigrate the goodness of secular culture and society'.[41] In fact, a

38. Douzinas, 'Law and Justice in Postmodernity', 209.

39. This is the conclusion of Costas Douzinas in his assessment of *NLNR*: 'As in all positivism, a sovereign power (the author) commands the subject (the reader) using rewards (self-evidence) and punishments (putting to silence). At the end, the text admits inadvertently that its claims are 'plays on meanings and references'; in other words, rhetoric.' Ibid., 209.

40. Porter, 'Basic Goods and the Human Good in Recent Catholic Moral Theology', 48.

41. Porter, 'At the Limits of Liberalism', 391; Porter, *N&D*, 214.

reconsideration of the 'full realism' of the secular actually promotes rather than inhibits the recovery of the 'full realism' of the scholastic-Thomistic tradition, inclusive of the moral significance it attaches to the pre-rational component of 'nature as nature'. That said, even though Porter overcomes the boundary between theoretical and practical reason, her appreciation for the 'tradition-dependence' of moral truth-claims requires that Aquinas's metaphysical claims also be recalibrated by a 'tradition-guided' understanding of rationality. In practice, this necessitates the permanent disavowal of epistemological foundationalism as well as the refutation of the antithetical approach which considers theological language to be 'self-contained' and 'self-justifying'. The only way for the truth-claims of Aquinas to retain permanent significance is for them to be tested according to their 'liveability' or 'practical workability'. *Contra* Finnis, natural law is not a discourse for the universal justification of specific moral norms, but a discourse animated by the existential persuasiveness and advocacy of certain socially embodied 'ideals of virtue and broad categories of harm.'[42] Porter's account of truth in natural law sees 'no inconsistency between a strong version of metaphysical or epistemic realism, and a secular-pragmatist account of reality.'[43]

There is, however, a 'shakiness' to Porter's voice on the nature of truth in natural law. On the one hand, her pluralist construction of the secular *mythos* encourages her to recover the theological foundations of the scholastic-Thomistic natural law tradition. Yet, on the other hand, she seems to consociate rhetorical persuasion with the bracketing out and repression of the theological lineaments of the scholastic-Thomistic natural law tradition. I argued that this inconsistency discloses an 'unsaid' inconsistency in her construction of, and reaction to, the secular *mythos*. On the one hand, Porter's account of the secular emblemizes the stereotypical postmodern deconstruction of all truth-claims as rhetoric. Hence her prioritization of persuasion over justification. Yet, on the other hand, the boundaries she draws within her theory of natural law imply that the only 'truth' the secular will find persuasive is theologically and metaphysically abstracted – what she calls 'philosophical'. My suspicion is that Porter's prioritization of a doctrine of creation is actually a secular foil for her programmatic neglect of a doctrine of divine government. For, as she says, the attraction of Aquinas's 'sharp distinction' between philosophy and theology is that it allows 'God to be God' and leaves us then 'free to be our limited selves.'[44]

Milbank's hylozoistic realism

Notwithstanding the incommensurable manner in which they formulate the relation between theoretical and practical reason, Finnis and Porter both endorse a theory of truth that allows for the practice of what might broadly be described as

42. Porter, *MOL* 113.
43. Porter, 'Moral Ideals and Human Nature', 69–70.
44. Porter, *MA&CE*, 110.

discoursive 'translation'.[45] In the same way an interpreter might skilfully translate a particular idiom into another language for the sake of abetting meaningful conversation, so Finnis and Porter have sought to translate Aquinas's theologically imbued jurisprudence (its 'windy mysticism') into a theologically abstracted *lingua franca* with which to facilitate dialogue and mutual understanding with their liberal-secular interlocutors. Similarly, the animating premise behind Finnis's and Porter's strategic instantiation of a boundary between philosophy and theology reflects the same fundamental assumption: that in order to be found intelligible, credible, and persuasive within public-political discourse necessitates perforce that Aquinas's (and one's own) underlying metaphysical and theological presuppositions have, to some degree, remain 'unsaid'. But what is also left 'unsaid' is the extent to which Finnis's and Porter's 'translations' still, nonetheless, depend upon the originating insights of Christian revelation and the language it generates in order to be able to formulate their divergent 'philosophical' accounts of human flourishing.[46] One concern is that this process of 'translation', particularly when practised in reaction to the secular *mythoi*, actually encourages the disremembering of what is most integral, efficacious, and true about the natural law tradition. To put this in colloquial terms, are Finnis and Porter trying to have their theological-Thomistic cake and eat it?

What immediately distinguishes Milbank's contribution is his explicit disinterestedness in trying to 'translate' the truth of his discursive *mythos* about natural law on the basis of external criteria or theory of public reason. It is his firm belief that '[t]ruth is not tested in any way'.[47] The public character of truth is preserved by its orientation to, and correspondence with, the 'literary republic' of the Church; the *logos* of which is itself preserved by its own orientation to, and correspondence with, the Gospel. Theologians must, thence, emancipate themselves from the hypostasizing relationship between self-evidence and secular reason and, instead, come to appreciate that 'truth is only available through persuasion.'[48] At first blush, Milbank's prioritization of persuasion over justification marks an interesting point of theoretical kinship with Porter. However, this kinship is undermined by Porter's strategic prioritization of the philosophical over the theological, which suggests that she is still committed to the prioritization of dialectic over narrative, even as a means to persuasion. For this reason, she is still too much of a critical realist for Milbank and, like MacIntyre, insufficiently 'relativistic or historicist' to recover the 'very extreme' theological realism of the Christian meta-narrative.[49]

45. Following Latourian parlance, what I mean here by 'translation' would have a closer definitional affinity with his notion of 'purification'.

46. An implication, for example, of Finnis' recourse to the 'art of writing' is that 'the truth about all *crucial* things is presented exclusively between the lines.' (IA) Strauss, 'Persecution and the Art of Writing', 82.

47. Milbank, Pickstock, *Truth in Aquinas*, 8.

48. Milbank, *T&ST*, 401.

49. Ibid., 327; Milbank, Pickstock, *Truth in Aquinas*, 5.

Milbank narrates instead what he acknowledges to be a 'new reading of Aquinas's understanding of truth' that is 'theological without remainder'.[50] This 'new reading' of Aquinas coincides with the presentation of an alternate 'version of modernity' inspired by Vico's hylozoistic understanding of '*verum est factum*'. In absolute contradistinction to Porter's declaration that neither natural law nor the moral life are a 'locus for transcendence', Milbank insists that, by virtue of the 'transcendenality of the *factum*', our creative participation in the natural law is a 'gateway to transcendence'.[51] But what makes this gateway possible is the event of the Incarnation, the scriptural illumination of which providentially restores our historical-ethical link to divine government, which, as both a prescriptive and descriptive force, obliterates the (artificial) boundaries between faith and reason, philosophy and theology, theoretical reason and practical reason. Boundaries that have, heretofore, been used to stabilize the underlying violence of a secular ontology. As we are 'co-creators' of the natural law, the truth in natural law (which, like 'all truth is matter of faith as well as reason') is both participatory and correspondent.[52] It is participatory because all truth is a dynamic and poetic participation in Christ, who is also the most 'perfect paradigm of *verum-factum*' ('truth as made').[53] Milbank claims that what preserves this dynamic and poetic participation from lapsing into abject relativism is its peaceful and providential correspondence with the 'identity and difference' found in the Trinity.[54]

Putting aside the serious theological difficulty of reconciling the notion of Christ as '*verum-factum*' with the Nicene declaration '*genitum non factum*', there is an inherent alethiological aporia lurking behind Milbank's over-arching emphasis upon making the moral truths of Christianity 'strange'. This aporia is especially pronounced when viewed in light of his other claim that only Christianity 'starkly links particular to universal by conceiving its relationship to transcendence in a rhetorical fashion.'[55] The contradiction lies in the fact that Milbank's project is not entirely immune from the praxis or performance of 'translation'. One might

50. Ibid., xiii, 5.

51. It is also interesting that both Porter and Milbank defend their contradicting understandings of the moral life (in terms of its relationship to the transcendent) on the basis of two contradicting understandings of the doctrine of creation. See: Porter, *N&D*, 100–1. Milbank, *RD1*, 328.

52. Milbank, Pickstock, *Truth in Aquinas*, xiii.

53. Milbank, *RD1*, 108.

54. One could, of course, challenge Milbank's Trinitarian theology here by invoking Anselm's axiom (citied by Aquinas) that states 'that *the Father and Son are in every respect one except in so far as they are distinguished by relative opposition:* and this by reason of the unity of essence.' As Aquinas explains, the relationship is not so much about difference as it is about distinction. In other words, the distinction is relational but there is no difference. Anselm, *De Process*, Sp. S. ii. Quoted in: Thomas Aquinas, *On the Power of God. Third Book*, trans. English Dominican Fathers (London: Burns Oates & Washbourne, 1934), 217.

55. Milbank, *T&ST*, 330.

say that he parodically inverts the process by continually juxtaposing (by which I mean, translating into oppositional terms) his theological *mythos* about the natural law to the secular *mythos* he inherits from MacKinnon, casting doubt over whether 'Radical Orthodoxy' actually deflates the theological by making it 'strange' rather than invigorating the theological voice by raising its hidden presence.

On the one hand, the impenetrability and unintelligibleness of Milbank's hylozoistic rhetoric is said to signify the mysterious idea 'that Christian morality is a thing so strange, that it must be declared immoral or amoral according to all other human norms and codes of morality'.[56] Yet, on the other hand, his 'solution' of telling 'a different story' necessitates that his theological meta-narrative be intelligible if, as he claims, 'a Catholic Christian account of reality might be entertained as the finally most persuasive one.'[57] On the one hand, he celebrates being estranged from, and irrelevant to, discourses of rational justification, but, on the other hand, his focus upon 'rhetoric', 'persuasion', and the purported 'attraction' of his 'words and images' demonstrates a desire to be acknowledged as 'un-strange' (in the sense of resonating with the anthropological universal of the natural desire for God) and, therefore, relevant to discourses of reason. Either way, if 'strangeness' and 'implausibility' are the measures of his *poiesis* of truth, then, for Milbank, the truth of his contribution is inexorable from his continued oppositional narration of MacKinnon's tragic realism and the version of the secular *mythos* it imparts. In simpler terms, the realism of 'Radical Orthodoxy' is dependent upon an ongoing rejection of the secular *mythos*.

This suggests that Milbank is not only the architectonic narrator of a secular *mythos*, but that, in reaction to that *mythos*, he has also become the paragonic founder, mediator, and eschatological embodiment of an exclusive language game. The only way for his particular interpretation of Christian realism to be found intelligible and thus of potential universal appeal is to be inducted into the peculiarity of Milbank's 'comedic' linguistic standpoint, a standpoint which, I have argued, is governed by his contestable reading of Kant that, ironically, still makes Kant pivotal. Only from this perspective does the rhetoric of 'out-narration' become intelligible, and the persuasiveness of its *logos* become 'self-evident' and attractive. Would it not be more accurate, then, to think of out-narration as a rhetorical self-narration – a pathway to an alternate hegemony? What promises to obliterate boundaries and resurrect the theologically unspoken, ultimately only allows for the quasi-eschatological voice of Milbank to surface. Given the fact that he laments the 'premature collapse of the Western colonial empires',[58] is it too far

56. Milbank, 'Can Morality Be Christian?', 45.

57. Milbank, *T&ST*, xi.

58. John Milbank, 'Christianity, the Enlightenment and Islam', 2010, https://www.abc.net.au/religion/ christianity- the-enlightenment-and-islam/10102154. Accessed on 1 November 2018.

an evaluative stretch to think of Milbank's brand of 'Radical Orthodoxy' as being more like a new 'colonising power' than a 'new theology?[59]

Anthropological perplexity: Nature and grace

Investigating how the 'three voices' construct their 'inner audiences' in commensuration with their conflicting constructions of the secular *mythos* gives critical insight into the reasons for the alethiological perplexity that characterizes current debates in natural law. However, it is only by considering how their 'inner audiences' inform the development of their respective (theological) anthropologies that we can also begin to appreciate why each of the 'three voices' is confident that their particular contribution will be found persuasive. On this point, I will give particular attention to the way in which the 'three voices' read the Thomistic tradition on the relationship between nature and grace and the powerful 'unsaid' influence it has upon the way in which they reconstruct the natural law. Through this comparative discussion, it will become clear that the secular *mythos* fragments the way in which the relationship between nature and grace is conceived within current debates in natural law.

Finnis: An 'unsaid' defence of the Duplex-Ordo

No doubt because of the strategic emphasis placed on the inadmissibility of drawing ethical-normative conclusions from a speculative account of human nature, little scholarly consideration has been given to identifying the anthropology that lies behind *NLNR*. In his clarificatory work, *Fundamentals of Ethics*, Finnis does concede that 'a mistaken anthropology will block one's reflective understanding of the way in which one participates in the basic goods', and he even singles out Kant's 'inadequate conception of humanity' as a prime example.[60] The focus upon the anthropological 'unsaid' in Chapter 2 was, in many ways, an attempt to discern how Finnis tries to 'fill out' what he believes was lacking in Kant, namely, an epistemology of the basic goods.[61] To that end, he even enlists the support of the Second Vatican Council, which, he argues, never identified the ultimate end of humankind with the vision of God (nor 'as a participation in holiness and grace'), but rather as 'a participation by a multiplicity of persons in a manifold of goods.'[62] This contention supports the commonplace impression that it was at Vatican II

59. The reference to a 'new theology' is taken from the subtitle of the collection of essays titled, 'Radical Orthodoxy: A New Theology' and the description of Milbank's 'Radical Orthodoxy' as a 'colonising power' is from a reference cited in the following essay: Paul Hedges, 'The Rhetoric and Reception of John Milbank's Radical Orthodoxy: Privileging Prejudice in Theology?', *Open Theology*, vol. 1 (2014), 35.

60. Finnis, *FoE*, 22, 125.

61. Ibid., 125.

62. Finnis, *Philosophy of Law*, 52.

that Catholicism made peace with political liberalism, a rapprochement that was largely pioneered by the likes of John Courtney Murray.

To support his conviction, Finnis references paragraph thirty-nine of *Gaudium et Spes*. Yet, it is difficult to discern how anything described in this passage gives theological approbation to Finnis's position. In contrast, there are very clear points in *Gaudium et Spes* that assert the contrary. For example, that 'the ultimate vocation of man is in fact one, and divine' and that 'all men are called to one and the same goal, namely God Himself', and, most especially, that 'only in the mystery of the incarnate Word does the mystery of man take on light.'[63]

Given that Finnis sees himself as working within the analytical boundaries of the philosophy of law, debating whether or not his NNLT is entirely commensurate with the theological anthropology of the Second Vatican Council is, ostensibly, a moot point. But as was demonstrated through my analysis, there are clear instances where his natural law arguments draw from or overlap with what he otherwise considers to be 'other disciplines' such as philosophy of religion, theological anthropology, and Christian ethics. Take, for example, what I enumerated as the first and second of the 'critical moves' of the NNLT. For the sake of preserving the integrity of human freedom, the first critical move asserts that human fulfilment exists not in a single *ultimus finis* or eschatology but in our individuated participation in a plurality of incommensurable basic goods. This first move undergirds the second move, which asserts that, since human nature is 'not made for 'God', it is appropriate to organize the social and political dimensions of the natural law around a concept of 'pure nature' (which, for Finnis, is basically synonymous with 'pure reason') and the pursuit of the 'true last end' of 'integral human fulfilment'. When taken together with the third critical move, Finnis is able to disentangle, by way of distinction to the point of separation, theology from anthropology, the natural end from the supernatural end, a participation in the basic goods from a participation in holiness and grace, and the natural law from an eschatology of divine government.

These distinctions echo Murray's bold insistence that '[t]he doctrine of natural law has no Roman Catholic presuppositions.'[64] Hence, the dialogical suasion of the NNLT is also built upon the fundamental premise that, as Grisez puts it, 'we must make ourselves intelligible to them'.[65] Nevertheless, the distinctions that the NNLT must maintain in order to establish the 'freestanding' and 'public' character of its epistemology are defended by Finnis as cohering with the 'perennial Catholic doctrine': that, even 'within the heart and mind of the believer', the secular sphere and the supernatural order exist independently ('in parallel') from one another.

63. Second Vatican Council, '*Gaudium et Spes*', 1965, http://www.vatican.va/archive/hist_councils/ii_vatican_ council /documents/vat-ii_const_19651207_gaudium-et-spes_en.html. Accessed on 1 January 2018. (Paragraph numbers: 22 and 23.)

64. Murray, *We Hold These Truths*, 111.

65. Germain Grisez, '*Insight: A Study of Human Understanding* (Book Review)', *The Thomist: A Speculative Quarterly Review*, vol. 21, no. 4 (October 1958), 554.

In other words, human nature is ordered by a *duplex-ordo* ontology.[66] For both believers and unbelievers, for theologians as well as secularists, the 'universal viewpoint' of the natural law is located within an anthropology of the subjective knower (reified from one's subjective desires – including the desire for God – and experiences) and, as such, conversability is tied exclusively to rational intelligibility.

The implicit question I raised in Chapter 2 was whether the anthropological dualism that Finnis obviously defends is, as he claims, being mediated by sound 'Catholic doctrine', or rather, by his discrete construction of the liberal-secular *mythos* or ideology? This touches upon the dialogical issue of whether Finnis's anthropological rationalism and the corresponding praxis of philosophical translation fails to consider the realism of another perennial Catholic doctrine, that of original sin. For if we accept that the epistemology of the NNLT is entirely 'freestanding', then, according to Finnis, it should be possible to establish the intelligibility of something like the Catholic Church's position on artificial contraception. However, the NNLT argument against contraception is quite unorthodox in its reasoning and has been swiftly rejected, albeit for very different reasons, by both supporters and critics of the Catholics Church's teaching.

This is perhaps a quintessential example of where Finnis's vocational predicament comes to the fore. When setting out his analysis of practical rationality and the basic goods, Finnis is careful to obey the rules of analytical jurisprudence, which, comparatively speaking, takes little formal interest in anthropology per se. But when he then tries to employ this analysis to address issues of personal morality in the context of the Church teaching, he smuggles in certain normative conclusions, which arise from, and can only be discerned in light of, the Catholic Church's theological anthropology of marriage. Thus, even if the basic tenets of his argument remain within the bounds of 'secular' or 'pure' reason, he addresses his liberal-secular interlocutors as if the 'universal viewpoint' of reason had already been immanently redeemed – enlightened by theology and illuminated by grace. Hence my suspicion that Finnis is allowing his deeper ('unsaid') theological-anthropological convictions to 'fill in' the normative gaps in his epistemology of 'pure reason' – gaps, which, as I said, would otherwise be indiscernible and unable to be filled in without the aid of the Catholic theological tradition.

Porter: An enlightening excursus

My analysis of Porter's contribution helped shed a disclosive light upon the theological-anthropological 'unsaid' that I identified in Finnis's NNLT. Conversely, identifying the hermeneutical 'unsaid(s)' that define Finnis's protreptic strategy shed a disclosive light on the way in which Porter's re-narration of the secular *mythos* actually brings her into close affinity with her *bête noire*, particularly in terms of her strategic prioritization of the philosophical over the theological in her interpretation of Aquinas. I suspect the anthropological similitude that unites

66. Finnis, *Religion & Public Reason*, 5.

the theological 'unsaid' between these two voices has been overshadowed by the fact that Porter nearly always contextualizes her 'robustly theological' recovery of scholastic jurisprudence in juxtaposition to Finnis's approach of 'pure reason'. Yet, it is precisely in her effort to be different to Finnis, typically by beginning with a metaphysical excursus into human nature, that brings to the surface their theological-anthropological common ground. As Porter acknowledges, it is her theologically informed view of human nature that enables her to draw certain 'needed distinctions' in order to reconcile scholastic natural law with secular jurisprudence, distinctions that bring her project into an uncanny alignment with the first and second of the 'critical moves' of the NNLT.[67] The 'programmatic' link is her intention to engage her liberal-secular interlocutors 'as they actually are', anthropologically, which, on her account, means without reference to an intrinsic supernatural desire for 'grace and glory'.[68]

As a theologian, Porter has no issue in raising awareness of how the 'distinction' between nature and grace affects one's interpretation of the tradition of natural law. In fact, its central importance within her own contribution is accentuated by her decision to conclude the introduction to her seminal work by referring to it as 'theologically indispensable', thereby hinting at its programmatic and strategic importance. What is left 'unsaid' is that, theologically speaking, this 'distinction' is 'indispensable' because it provides the necessary ontology required to mediate an anthropological rapprochement between secular-liberalism and the Catholic natural law tradition. It is on this point that the so-called neoconservative, Finnis, and the so-called liberal-feminist, Porter, are in close, yet unacknowledged, collusion. Finnis and Porter mutually affirm poly-teleological conceptualizations of the natural end as well as integrating a thesis of 'incommensurability' with the tradition of natural law. For Finnis, our rational participation in the basic goods is (prior to choice) incommensurable because each of the basic goods uniquely, yet equally, instantiate an ultimate reason for action. For Porter, since our participation in the moral life takes place within culturally specific and tradition-constituted circumstances, our moral schemas are rationally incommensurable. Prima facie, both of these poly-teleological accounts of the natural law allow scope for a pluralist individualism and a political liberalism. This is because the absence of an explicitly theocentric teleology in grace liberates human nature from an objective hierarchy of goods, a hierarchy that conforms and corresponds with ultimate beatitude. In the words of Joseph Raz, whose legal positivism both Finnis and Porter engage with, 'where there is incommensurability it is the ultimate truth. There is nothing further behind it, nor is it a sign of imperfection.'[69]

However, behind the incommensurability theses of Finnis and Porter, there is, indeed, something further and imperfect, namely, the reifying abstraction

67. Porter, *MOL*, 83.

68. Porter, 'DFG', 68.

69. Joseph Raz, *Morality of Freedom*, (Oxford: OUP, 327), 327. Referenced in: John Gray, 'Agonistic Liberalism', in *Liberalism*, ed. G. W. Smith (London: Routledge, 2002), 9.

of an *imperfecta beatitudo*. I argued that the clue to disinterring the common interpretive origins of this 'unsaid' is found in a relatively obscure footnote in *The Ministers of Law*, wherein Porter declares that she broadly concurs with Murray's endorsement of secular-liberalism on natural law terms. At the centrepiece of Murray's pluralistic political philosophy is a *duplex-ordo* ontology.[70] He writes: 'The dualism of mankind's two hierarchically ordered forms of social life had been Christianity's cardinal contribution to the Western political tradition.'[71] This 'cardinal contribution' of delineating 'distinct [political] orders of reality' is, he argues, governed by 'the relations between nature and grace'.[72] Murray could not be clearer about his belief that there 'is indeed a radical discontinuity between nature and grace.'[73] Despite his insistence that the natural law is unprejudiced by Roman Catholic presuppositions, it is evident that, at a metaphysical level, this is not altogether true.

Of course, one could still argue that Murray's contention remains valid. Henri de Lubac, for instance, rejected this dualistic anthropology and the corresponding theory of a 'pure nature' precisely because it is not authentically Roman Catholic. Rather, it was a neo-scholastic aberration that was born out of 'a feverish enthusiasm for philosophy' in reaction to the proliferation of the Enlightenment's penchant for epistemic universalism.[74] Even though Porter declares that 'there is no such thing as a state of pure nature', she, along with Finnis, are the 'unsaid' exponents of what de Lubac referred to as its 'bitterest fruit' – a methodological or strategic 'pure nature', which involves the solipsistic secularization of theology itself into a philosophical *lingua franca*.[75] Basing his argument upon the Conciliar document, *Dignitatis Humanae*, Murray's extrinsicist anthropology translates into an ecclesiology whereby 'the aim and object of the Church' is not found in 'nostalgic yearnings … to find new forms of sacralising the terrestrial and temporal order in its structures and processes, but the purification of these processes and structures and the sure direction of them to their inherently secular ends.'[76] Murray's desacralizing notion of 'purification' for the sake of augmenting 'inherently secular ends' hearkens to

70. Although the following references are taken from different sources/publications, I am indebted to David Schindler for raising my awareness of Murray's discussion of these issues. C.f. David L. Schindler, 'Religious Freedom, Truth, and America', *Communio* (Winter 1994), 696–741.

71. Murray, *We Hold These Truths*, 75.

72. John Courtney Murray, 'Governmental Repression of Heresy', 1948, https://www.library.georgetown. edu/woodstock/murray/1948c. Accessed 28 November 2019.

73. Murray, *We Hold These Truths*, 177.

74. Henri de Lubac, *Augustinianism and Modern Theology*, 212. Quoted in: Hans Boersma, *Nouvelle Théologie* (Oxford: OUP, 2009), 96.

75. Henri de Lubac, *The Mystery of the Supernatural*, trans. Rosemary Sheed (New York: Crossroad, 1998), xi–xii.

76. John Courtney Murray, *Bridging the Sacred and the Secular*, ed. J. Leon Hooper (Washington, DC: Georgetown University Press, 1994), 193.

the notion of discoursive 'translation' that is practised by Finnis and Porter. I have argued that this practice ends in aporetic perplexity because identifying what these 'secular ends' are is not self-evident since they are tied to a host of fragmenting and conflicting *mythoi* about the secular itself.

The real theological loss (but promoted as a theological gain) is that Porter's anthropology is blocked from the light of Christology, and so natural law is blocked from both deification and divine governance. Paradoxically, despite their mutual disavowal of neo-scholastic reductivism, Finnis and Porter perpetuate what is arguably its 'cardinal' anthropological assumption about the relationship between nature and grace. An assumption, which, particularly in light of the Christological anthropology of the Second Vatican Council, is no longer considered, theologically or dialogically, a persuasive starting point for establishing a public *lingua franca*, especially in and through the tradition of natural law.[77]

Milbank: An unorthodox intrinsicism

Milbank's critical engagement with the post-Kantian flavour of MacKinnon's theology stimulates several of the key questions required to unblock the anthropological 'unsaid(s)' within contributions that seek to preserve the ontological integrity of the 'secular city'. The most pertinent and illuminating of such questions is an existential one. If the natural law is simply the rational power to pursue one's 'true last end' of 'integral human fulfilment', as per Finnis, or the capacity to have 'one's natural aims' fully satisfied by a purely 'natural end' that exists apart from 'grace and glory', as per Porter, then who needs divine revelation or the incarnation?[78]

One could argue that Finnis's and Porter's position simply reiterates the Augustinian distinction between a temporal peace/justice and an eternal peace/justice.[79] This then translates into the more familiar delineation of the distinct operational spheres of church and state. Although this Augustinian inflection would give an air of genealogical orthodoxy to their contributions, Milbank seeks to expose this extrinsic political ontology as an egregious anachronism, arguing that, for Augustine, there is neither a dualism between nature and grace, nor a political disjunction between the operations of church and state.[80] Fundamental to his argument is the anthropological insistence that, for Aquinas as for Augustine, there is within human nature 'a natural drive beyond natural drive'.[81] A natural

77. C.f. Rooney, 'Murray's Balancing Act', 682–9.

78. c.f. Gilson Caitlin Smith, *The Political Dialogue of Nature & Grace* (New York: Bloomsbury, 2015), 33.

79. C.f. Augustine, *The City of God, Books XVII-XXII*, trans. Gerald G. Walsh, Daniel J. Honan (Washington, DC: Catholic University of America Press, 2008), 226.

80. Milbank, *T&ST*, 410.

81. Milbank, *Truth in Aquinas*, 124.

desire for the *ultimus finis* of deification, which is then mediated in and through various modes of divine government.[82]

A valuable dimension of Milbank's 'devious response' is his recognition of the genealogical consociation that exists between the spatialization of the secular and the positing of a new theological anthropology that separates nature from grace. Once this relationship is appreciated, it lends a plausible theological explanation as to why Finnis's morally 'conservative' and Porter's morally 'liberal' accounts of natural law both give theoretical primacy to the self-determining power(s) of the individual. For once a theory of natural law is prophylactically constrained by the boundary instilled by the assimilation of a *duplex-ordo* ontology, it becomes limited to what we might call an epistemological ethics of the sublime, that is to say, an epistemology that sharply recoils from a teleological 'discourse of participated perfections' and gravitates inwards towards a delineated discourse of 'possessive individualism'.[83] Hence, natural law and human nature are defined through the lens of a 'dubious scholastic theology' that preferences a language of 'power' and/or 'capacity' over the language of 'desire'.[84] Milbank's critique of MacKinnon's Kantian inflection also elucidates the possibility that Finnis's and Porter's poly-teleological interpretations of human freedom are the continuants of a Kantian interpretation of human autonomy that is simultaneously understood as 'pure end' (that is to say, 'outside any sequence of process or relation or further [ultimate] teleology') and as 'pure agent' (that is to say, to regard one's will as universal and absolute).[85] Thus, in the same way that Kant exploited the space of 'pure nature' carved out by *duplex-ordo* theologians, so now are certain natural law theorists exploiting the epistemological space of 'pure reason' that Kant carved out for philosophy. On these anthropological issues, especially, Milbank's deconstruction of the secular *mythos* within modern natural law resonates closely with the fundamental *élan* of this book.

Yet, in the same way that the separation of nature from grace can be used strategically to mediate a theological rapprochement between Christian and secular ethics, so, too, can the practical dissolution of the distinction between nature and grace be used strategically to obliterate the boundary between church and state. For all political intents and purposes, Milbank's notion of 'living beyond the law' refuses any duality between nature and grace. Although he admits that this 'general collapse of all that was once regarded natural' will perturb even people of religious faith, his point is to restore the *naturalness* of seeing the transformative power of

82. 'We are in Milbank's debt for his insistence, following de Lubac, on the teleological finality of deification.' Levering, 'A Note on John Milbank and Thomas Aquinas', 534.

83. The tradition of 'possessive individualism is attributed by Milbank to Locke. c.f. Milbank, 'Dignity, not Rights'. However, the phrase itself more likely comes from: C. B. Macpherson, *The Political Theory of Possessive Individualism* (Oxford: OUP, 1964).

84. Milbank, *The Suspended Middle*, 67.

85. John Milbank, 'Maritain's Post-War Compromise', 2019, https://churchlifejournal.nd.edu/articles/maritains-postwar-compromise-of-natural-law/. Accessed on 20 May 2019.

grace as being proper and integral to our *humanum*.[86] To 'live beyond the law', anthropologically speaking, is to dwell upon the porous cusp of the borderlands of nature and grace, a place where the desacralizing discourses of 'pure nature' and 'pure reason' must give way to the sacralizing mystery of the 'suspended middle'.[87] Milbank describes this position as a 'non-ontology'. Confusingly, this does not mean the outright refusal of ontology. Rather, it is the articulation of a 'new ontological discourse'.[88] At the heart of this new discourse is the paradoxical definition of human nature as 'intrinsically raised above itself to the 'super-nature' of divinity.'[89] The pivotal implication being that the radical integration of nature and grace informs the radical integration of nature and culture and, ultimately, the radical integration of church and state.

It is important to recall that the secular-liberal ontology that Milbank wants to out-narrate is built upon a biopolitical logic that engenders an aporetic division between nature and culture. Again, this Latourian inspired conviction sheds light on another aporetic 'unsaid' I identified within Finnis's and Porter's contributions. On the one hand, I demonstrated that both Finnis and Porter allow their metaphysico-theological beliefs about human nature to inform either the normative conclusions, as per Finnis, or the moral foundations, as per Porter, of their natural law. One could say that, in Latourian parlance, both of these approaches require at least an initial ('unsaid') 'hybridisation' of nature and grace, which mediates new jurisprudential paradigms for a Christian rapprochement with the liberal-secular *mythos*. On the other hand, I also demonstrated that, for this rapprochement to be effected, both Finnis and Porter believe they must engage in a process of 'purification' (or, what I referred to above as discoursive 'translation') – nature must be desacralized of grace so as to be able to abstract the philosophical from the theological, and even the Christological from the theological. It could be argued, thence, that nature (*physis*) and culture (*nomos*) are also here split, aporetically, on secular (biopolitical) terms: aporetically, because, on the one hand, it is the anthropological boundary between nature and grace that liberates the cultural sphere to be 'secular', that is to say, purified of the mediating force of a supernatural *telos*, but, on the other hand, this boundary was originally a hybridizing theological hypothesis, which, through continued distillation, was ontologically reified and considered 'natural'.

This aporia notwithstanding, Finnis's definition of culture as all that 'we add, by our choices to nature' reflects this 'secular divide'.[90] And even though Porter

86. Milbank, *Being Reconciled*, 198.

87. According to Milbank, the phrase, 'suspended middle', was Hans von Balthasar's way to surmise de Lubac's gnoseological conviction that philosophy cannot be practiced without transcending into theology and that theology cannot be practiced without recourse to the 'inner structure' endemic to philosophy. Milbank, *The Suspended Middle*, 13 fn. 17.

88. Ibid., 5.

89. Ibid.

90. Finnis, *Religion & Public Reason*, 328.

says she rejects a strict dualism between nature and culture, her analogical elision of culture with 'the individual's personal conception of happiness' reflects her belief that natural law is, itself, a cultural artefact, but an artefact that, through communal reflection, mediates a pragmatic understanding of nature which, like culture, is polyteleological, pluriform, and, one could say, postmodern. In practice, both Finnis and Porter appear to allow their 'inner audiences' to redefine nature so as to permit the cultural-political value of a 'secular groundwork' (an underlying theory of 'pure nature' or 'pure reason') for natural law.

For Milbank, the only route out of this biopolitical aporia is to establish an 'authentically religious' framework for natural law. This route is a one-way street into the politico-ecclesial inhabitation of the 'suspended middle'. Although purportedly left 'unsaid' by de Lubac, Milbank declares the 'suspended middle' to be 'precisely the sphere of culture'.[91] Culture, he says, has to be Christian because, ontologically, it is the natural desire for God that generates the 'diversity and the restlessness' of culture in the first place.[92] At the same time, it is only in the light of the incarnation that the true nature – the true *telos* – of this desire is made manifest. The underlying strategy here is surprisingly simple. If the positing of an extrinsicist anthropology allows for the spatialization of the secular as a sphere of 'pure nature' and 'pure reason', then the positing of a radically intrinsicist anthropology allows for the discrete spatialization of the economy of the Church as the sole mediator of the grace of the natural law. This explains Milbank's avowal that, in light of the incarnation, all political and jurisprudential theory is relocated as 'thought about the church.'[93] In natural law terms, only the Church can determine which manifestations of cultural activity are 'supposed to be' in the sense that they reflect 'our very teleology' – our natural orientation to the beatific vision – and discloses 'what is 'fundamental' for nature.'[94] An incredible power, to say the least.

For this reason, I return to the issue I raised towards the end of Chapter Four. Where exactly is Milbank's Church? Where is the Church that, as the all-encompassing embodiment of the natural law, arbitrates and orientates all human life to the beatific life? Where is the cultural-political sphere of the 'suspended middle'? The fact that Milbank has, himself, raised and engaged with such questions highlights their importance and legitimacy.[95] But, in the context of this work, they also mark the political zenith of how an inquiry into the theological anthropology behind Milbank's natural law discloses what is being left 'unsaid' within the 'Radical Orthodoxy' meta-narrative. The 'authentically religious route' is actually a parodic fabrication of a 'secular groundwork' for natural law.

91. Milbank, *The Suspended Middle*, 14.

92. Ibid., 46.

93. Milbank, *T&ST*, 411.

94. Milbank, 'Culture, Nature, and Mediation'; Milbank, 'Only Theology Saves Metaphysics'.

95. C.f. Milbank, *The Future of Love*, 134.

As an exponent of a 'theology without substance' and by virtue of his hylozoistic integration of nature and grace, Milbank says that he resists envisaging the Church in 'spatial terms'.[96] 'Fortunately the Church is first and foremost … an enacted, serious fiction.'[97] By identifying the Church fundamentally as a 'fiction' he is underscoring his belief that the locality of the Church is inseparable from (in fact, he says it is defined by) the 'Church's own act', which, he says, 'involves critical narratives of the (endless) genesis of the Church'.[98] '[T]o act at all is to re-narrate' and, within the Church, this act is the ceaseless re-narration of a narratological genealogy – an ecclesiocentric, hylozoistic *poiesis* that, once unconstrained by the bounds of Kantian finitude, can continue to enter more deeply and sign more fully the mystery of human redemption.[99] Although he maintains that truth cannot be tested, he does connect narratological 'authenticity' with 'redeeming estrangement'.[100]

Milbank laments that because so much of Christian practice has been reconfigured by the corruption of secular accounts of reality, it has become increasingly difficult to locate authentic Christian practice. On his own logic, it has also become increasingly difficult to locate the Church. But all is not lost. In this uncertainty, Milbank declares that 'the theologian feels almost that the entire *ecclesial* task falls on his *own* head.'[101] Furthermore, 'today it can feel as if it is the theologian *alone* … who must perform this task of redeeming estrangement.'[102] It is the 'theologian *alone* who must perpetuate that original making strange which was the divine assumption of human flesh.'[103]

It is important to draw to the surface the potential implication of what is being argued here. If the Church is synonymous with the practice of *poesis*, and if the practice of *poesis* (the 'entire *ecclesial* task') is the work of the 'theologian *alone*', and if the authenticity of *poiesis* is signed by its 'estrangement', does this not imply that Milbank is, himself, the 'unsaid' embodiment of the Church? And if natural law is 'exactly at one with the establishment of the Church', then is it not the case that the politico-normative conclusions of the natural law must be exactly at one with the establishment of 'Radical Orthodoxy'?[104]

This denotes an archetypical example of how Milbank's desire to demolish secular-liberalism drives his interpretation of natural law into promoting a new space of 'pure power' – a new kind of 'secular'. Moreover, in the same way that Milbank's deconstruction of MacKinnon's 'more excellent way' may have

96. Ibid., 133.
97. Ibid.
98. Ibid., 134.
99. Milbank, *The Word Made Strange*, 32.
100. Ibid., 1.
101. Ibid., 1. (IA).
102. Ibid.
103. Ibid.
104. Milbank, 'Burke's Romantic Restoration of Natural Law'.

helped stimulate the right anthropological questions, it also stimulates a secular *mythos* – an underlying 'secular groundwork' – without which Milbank's radical anthropology cannot be 'made strange'. This is because the 'truth is made' by rehearsing the Christian *mythos* in such a manner that it is perpetually 'made strange' by perpetuating the vehicle of 'estrangement' – the secular *mythos*. *Poesis* thus becomes the paragon of power; the 'suspended middle' become a place of 'pure Milbank'; his ecclesiology becomes its own eschatology.[105]

Genealogical perplexity: Philo and the stoics

Answering the anthropological question, 'who are you speaking to?', was also found to help elucidate the politics behind, and the perplexity that ensues from, the way in which the 'three voices' answer the genealogical question, 'why are you reading the tradition that way?' This is a potentially vast subject. To isolate points of comparison, I focused in Part One upon how the 'three voices' account for the origins of both natural law and the secular *mythos* and then examined how this inflects their assessment of the historical significance of Hugo Grotius's 'impious hypothesis' and the emergence of subjective human rights. The forthcoming discussion is dedicated to highlighting, in more specific terms, the genealogical aporia that has surfaced as a result of this comparison.

Finnis: A 'secular' origin

Given Finnis's stated methodological disinterest in investigating the historical development of natural law, it might seem unreasonable to want to explore how he accounts for the emergence of the very idea itself. Strategically speaking, his declaration that the principles of natural law have no history and, therefore, have no origin, echoes the prevailing hermeneutical sentiment of analytical jurisprudence.[106] Nevertheless, in the course of my analysis, it became apparent that the protreptic edifice of the NNLT is built upon one crucial genealogical assumption that, ironically, was asserted by one of natural law's most 'cultured despisers'. To reiterate, H. L. A. Hart attributed the historical resilience of natural law to its provenance in Greek philosophy, which, on this topic, he deemed to be 'quite secular'.[107]

105. In Chapter 4, I concluded that the series of contradictions I identified within Milbank's contribution to natural law reflects the suspension of his thought between at least two distinct, but interconnected, *mythoi* about the secular, which could be broadly categorised as 'modern' and 'postmodern'.

106. C.f. Salmon, *The First Principles of Jurisprudence*, 5.

107. In this instance, he uses the word 'secular' to denote how a number of natural law's 'elementary truths' can be discerned independently of divine authority and can be disentangled from its underlying metaphysical setting.

Moreover, I argued that Hart's renewal of legal theory as a discourse centred upon 'reasons for action' is what occasioned Finnis's re-presentation of natural law as 'practical reason in action'. By focusing his re-presentation as such, Finnis believed he could simultaneously illuminate the practical character of the secular as a universal discourse centred upon 'integral human fulfilment'. Hence my contention that he re-narrates the secular *mythos* as the 'public reality' of 'practical reason' so that it converges upon the idea that it is virtually synonymous with the timeless 'intelligibility and directiveness' of what Aquinas also called, albeit lamentably, 'natural law'. This would also explain why he is equally disinterested in interrogating the genealogical origins of the secular *mythos*, declaring it to be entirely unprofitable, for example, to estimate whether 'secularism's dominance now is greater in Plato's Athens or lesser than in Stalin's Leningrad'[108] – unprofitable, because it would distract from the underlying genealogical and strategic conviction that the truths inherent to the natural law and to the idea of the secular itself are timeless as mutual expressions of practical reason. To raise the question of the source of the natural law (or perhaps even the source of the secular *mythos*) would be to run the risk of raising the question of the theological-metaphysical 'unsaid'.

However, in the final ('God') chapter, Finnis does make several comparative references to the Stoical-Ciceronian approach to natural law that, perhaps inadvertently, allows this 'unsaid' to surface. His stated reason for this is that, '[s]ince the Stoic speculations (and word-play) on *natura* are an immediate source of the rather unhappy term 'natural law', it is important for us to observe how those speculations are motivated by the same practical questions about the objectivity ... of human goods.'[109] On this point, Finnis acknowledges that, like the NNLT, the Stoics shares the 'same anxiety' that extends from the '"subjectivity" of human effort.'[110] For how do we ground our common obligation to favour and promote the common good? The subjectivity or relativity that emerges here, says Finnis, reflects the 'limitation of "natural reasoning"' and the 'rational instability' that, at the very least, renders 'the whole structure of basic principles and requirements of practical reasonableness' questionable.[111] The Stoics' solution was to cultivate an intuitive, yet quasi-religious, piety towards the natural order as an expression of divine government. Finnis argues that the problem with this approach is that it reduces the practical nature of the good to the pursuit of just one good, specifically, the 'virtue – living-according-to-reason/living-according-to-nature.'[112] Yet, Finnis' own approach falls afoul of the same critique. In the same way that the Stoics relied upon piety to sustain the objectivity of its ethical naturalism, Finnis relies upon the

108. Finnis, 'On the Practical Meaning of Secularism', 493.

109. Finnis, *NLNR*, 374.

110. Ibid., 377.

111. Ibid., 424.

112. Ibid., 377.

cultivation of a respect for a 'healthy secular' (a healthy respect for the integrity of practical reason) so as to be able to leave the source of the natural law in divine government 'unsaid'.[113]

The paradoxical conundrum is that this 'unsaid' is ultimately what Finnis realizes he must say. Even though he knew of Hart's staunch resistance to the inclusion of the 'God chapter' in *NLNR*, his decision to retain it as the lone chapter of a distinct and detached section suggests, implicitly, that he was not able to completely reconcile the genealogical origins of the tradition of natural law with the analytical rules prescribed by his 'inner audience'. For after dismissing the popular 'phantom' that natural law is dependent upon the question of God's existence, and then proceeding to sketch in some detail a 'neoclassical' epistemology that eschews any reliance upon metaphysical and theological judgements, we find in one of the very last paragraphs of *NLNR* a surprising admission: '"God is the basis of obligation."'[114] In the words of Mark Murphy, Finnis 'has committed himself to the position that adherence to the natural law is rationally unstable in the absence of a certain sort of theistic stance.'[115] To which, Finnis later replied, 'I agree.'[116]

The issue, I would argue, is not so much that Finnis mentions God but that he ambushes his reader in a manner that would lead his liberal-secular 'inner audience' to question how 'detached' and 'freestanding' his preceding account of the NNLT actually is. Michael S. Moore, one of the world's leading legal theorists and an atheist, draws this very conclusion. 'Finnis rightly rejects any use for God ... Yet despite this autonomous ethics ... he nonetheless brings in God to save morality form "a certain relativity."'[117] Likewise, the late Nicholas Tonti-Filippini, once a leading bioethicists and a devout Catholic, highlighted the fundamental flaw that the theological 'unsaid' creates: 'A problem with an anthropocentric natural law approach for a Christian is that we can be seen to be fraudulent in not admitting our religious beliefs ... So what is offered to the secular dialogue ... may sound false to secular others and, in fact, is false by our own standards.'[118] For this reason, Tonti-Filippini declared that the NNLT was doomed, genealogically, 'from the outset.'[119]

113. Brian M. McGall, *Building Law on a Solid Foundation* (Notre Dame, IN: Notre Dame University Press, 2018), 457 fn. 118.

114. Finnis, *NLNR*, 407.

115. Murphy, *Finnis on Nature, Reason, God*, 193. Quoted in: Finnis, 'Grounds of Law and Legal Theory', 41.

116. Finnis, 'Grounds of Law and Legal Theory', 41.

117. Michael S. Moore, 'Good without God', in *Natural Law, Liberalism, and Morality*, ed. Robert George (Oxford: OUP, 2011), 251.

118. Nicholas Tonti-Filippini, 'Bioethics, Culture and Collaboration', *Solidarity*, vol. 2, no. 1 (2012), 1.

119. Ibid.

Porter: A strategic stoicism

In what is a salient point of contrast, the starting premise behind Porter's project is that you cannot 'leave history behind'. Furthermore, whereas Finnis declared it to be almost nonsensical to speak of a 'natural law tradition', Porter avows that it is precisely because we can speak of a 'natural law tradition' that we can finally subvert the tendency to dichotomize Christian ethics and secular morality. It is on this basis that I described her genealogical account of the secular *mythos* as being akin to a Hegelian thesis that allows for a 'contemporary synthesis'. Unlike Finnis, who attempts to establish his own Hegelian dialectic upon the 'quite secular' origins of natural law, Porter establishes her synthesis upon the 'robustly theological' origins of 'our common secular morality' in scholastic-Thomistic natural law. But these 'robustly theological' origins turn out to be based upon (as I have already noted) a theology of 'desacralisation'. The paradoxical aporia is that this theology legitimates the atrophication of Christology from theology so as to originate a new philosophy of 'purely earthly legitimation'.[120] For 'philosophy cannot begin except by desacralisation', and desacralization demands the 'secularism of argumentation'.[121] The theo-cultural implication being that the 'fuller story' about the development of the scholastic-Thomistic natural law tradition is being strategically intertwined with Porter's 'fuller story' about the liberal-secular *mythos*. Unsurprisingly, therefore, even though she admits that it is quite likely the scholastics were aware of Philo's theo-political synthesis of *physis* with biblical Torah, she still considers it to be 'of the first importance' to understand scholastic natural law as a recontexualization of fundamentally Stoic principles.[122]

This emphasis is perplexing given her other stated intention of reuniting natural law with its Scriptural foundations. However, the perplexity is mitigated once we appreciate how her attachment to the liberal-secular *mythos* regulates her 'points of entry' for a historical dialogue about the natural law. The aporia is that Philo was the one who was able to do exactly what Porter said she was initially intending to do, namely, to reconcile *nomos* and *physis* within a robustly theological ontology. But because she is ultimately wanting to find a way to uphold a liberal-secular ontology, Porter naturally gravitates towards reading the scholastic natural law tradition through the genealogical lens of the desacralizing immanentism that, rightly or wrongly, is deemed proto-typical of Stoical philosophy.[123] This

120. C.f. Badiou, *The Age of Poets*, 36.

121. Ibid.

122. Porter, *N&D*, 67.

123. Jeanne M. Persuit has argued that it was because of the significant influence of Samuel Pufendorf's extolling of the Stoic conceptualisation of natural law that the Stoics were also accredited with also having the most influence over Aquinas' theory. c.f. Jeanne M. Persuit, 'The Universal and Particular', *The Review of Communication*, vol. 11, no. 1 (January 2011), 54. Other scholars have noted that, like Porter, Pufendorf instrumentalised Stoic thought in order to promote the 'desacralisation of law and politics' as expressed, in particular, in his work *De jure naturae et genitum*. c.f. John M. Headley, *The Europeanization of the World* (Princeton, NJ: Princeton University Press, 2008), 117.

genealogical commitment might lend further explanation as to why there arises an irreconcilable tension between how she tries to reconcile and harmonize the relationship between nature and human history, on the one hand, and how she separates and eschews the relationship between nature and salvation history, on the other. Thus, like the Stoics, who, due to a commitment to natural fate, were never able to fully reconcile *nomos* and *physis*, Porter's Hegelian-like synthesis between Christian *physis* and secular-liberal *nomos* is ultimately undone through the strategic, yet ontologically necessary, perpetuation of a series of 'unsaid' and contradictory antitheses.

Milbank: Exploiting Philo's fusion

Given his theological penchant for 'redeeming estrangement', it was perhaps foreseeable that Milbank would want to challenge the widely held assumption that the Christian (Thomistic) tradition of natural law is basically a recapitulation and reinterpretation of the Stoical dictum: '[L]ive according to nature because this accords with reason.'[124] Whilst Milbank certainly acknowledges a continuum of Stoic influence, he tasks himself with exposing that influence to be 'proto-liberal', 'proto-modern', and 'proto-biopolitical'.[125] A central element of Milbank's genealogy of natural law involves narrating how the incipient vision of the Stoics is sustained and developed through the desacralizing and voluntaristic innovations of medieval – especially Scotic – theology; the varying neo-Stoic permutations of the 'fathers' of modern natural law such as Suárez, Grotius, and Hobbes; and culminating in the Kantian and post-Kantian subjectivization and liberalization of *ius* as a heretical subversion of divine government.

Whether or not this 'broad-brush' excursus is historically accurate has attracted significant scholarly consternation. Though this is not the major issue here. The more cautious responder would note that Milbank's strategic ambition is 'not 'to know' the past", but rather, in the spirit of Vico, to cast 'final judgment upon it.'[126] For the persuasiveness of his contemporary judgements on natural law and the counter-genealogy he wants to narrate are dependent upon knowing and accepting how he narrates his genealogy of desacralizing villains. One might describe this dependency as a 'gnostic apriorism'.[127] The villains provide

124. A. A. Long, *Stoic Studies* (Los Angeles: University of California Press, 1996), 134. Cicero puts it thus: 'True law, however, is right reason corresponding to nature.' *De Republica* III.XXII, 33. Quoted in, Porter, *NasR*, 2.

125. Milbank and Pabst, *The Politics of Virtue*, 90 fn. 43.

126. Milbank, *RD2*, 270.

127. Hence, as with Finnis and Porter, there is an 'unsaid' genealogical collusion between how the origins of the secular *mythos* are narrated and how the origins of the natural law are then located. (I have appropriated the phrase, 'gnostic apriorism', from Carl A. Rash, '*Á-Dieu* to Jacques Derrida', in *Secular Theology*, ed. Clayton Crockett (London: Routledge, 2001), 44.)

the foundational – 'stoic-liberal-nihilist' – counterpoint against which he can 'fabricate', authoritatively, his alternate narratological-genealogical-realism about the natural law.[128] Alethiologically speaking, narrative is the sole 'mode in which the entirety of reality presents itself to us.'[129]

I have already said that Milbank's unconventional judgement that the genealogical origins of natural law are 'mainly located' in Philo's 'politicisation of nature' represents a potentially propitious way to thwart the circumscribing power of the secular *mythos* and recover the theological 'unsaid' of nature's fusion with divine government in Aquinas. The theo-political issue is that, because the ontology of 'Radical Orthodoxy' relies upon the secular *mythos* for the sake of its coherency, Milbank instrumentalizes the 'unsaid' in order to create a new theo-political fusion that fabricates yet another sphere of 'pure power' – the Church of the 'suspended middle', which, as the juridical embodiment of the natural law, has the sole power to narrate the 'way things are'. Milbank's Church thus becomes the only place where the 'gap between nature and history that we call mythology – come together.'[130] But it is also the only place where, in keeping with his hylozoistic *poiesis*, the relationship between nature and history can be continually re-narrated in reaction to the interminable fragmentations and spatializations of the secular *mythos*. Ironically, Milbank's professed genealogical Philonianism actually ends, aporetically, by reinstating a Stoic-like boundary, a boundary that, as the Stoic-like-demiurge of 'Radical Orthodoxy', Milbank can redraw and reconfigure so as to preserve the jurisprudential borderlands of secular 'estrangement'.

The 'impious hypothesis': Innovation or conservation?

The power of the secular *mythos* to fragment how the 'three voices' locate and narrate the genealogical origins of natural law was also found to inflect how the 'three voices' read and interpret several of the watershed moments in the historical development of natural law. As a comparative illustration, I described how each of the 'three voices' approach the genealogical significance of Hugo Grotius's 'impious hypothesis'.[131]

Finnis's evaluation of Grotius's position was actually the most controversial and unconventional. This is surprising given his declared disinterest in outlining the historical vicissitudes of the natural law. Against the standard perception that Grotius's hypothesis, '*etsi Deus non daretur*', helped usher in a new 'secular era' for natural law, Finnis avows that he was actually rehearsing a common scholastic hypothesis 'for the purpose of discussing the roots of obligation'.[132]

128. Milbank, *T&ST*, 331.

129. Ibid., 362.

130. Milbank, *The Word Made Strange*, 250.

131. The decision to focus upon the contradicting and idiosyncratic interpretations of Grotius is meant to act as a paradigmatic example of what is a much more expansive issue.

132. Finnis, *NLNR* 43.

In other words, recognizing autonomous human reason as the authoritative source and foundation of the natural law (rather than God) was a 'pre-modern' conviction and not, as is commonly assumed, a 'modern' aberration.[133] For if Grotius's hypothesis was instigative and promotive of a new secular and secularizing doctrine of natural law, then it would undermine the genealogical basis for his rapprochement of analytical jurisprudence with Thomistic thought via his co-ordinated revision of the secular *mythos* as the timeless reality and public manifestation of practical reason. By challenging his sceptical 'inner audience' to reconsider Grotius's thought as a continuation of, rather than a break from, scholastic thought, he is also obliging them to reconsider whether the foundations of Aquinas's natural law are more secular-analytical-proto-Kantian than has often been assumed.

Porter adopts a similar genealogical strategy but uses it to present an antithetical assessment. She contends that Grotius's famous remark was indeed catalytic and consolidative of a new trajectory in natural law, which, unfortunately, has often been read back (anachronistically) into the scholastic-Thomistic tradition. It is important to stress, however, that she does not challenge the theological legitimacy of the 'impious hypothesis'. To the contrary, Porter views it as a valid theological extrapolation that supports, rather than undermines, the congruency between natural law and specifically theological contentions in public discourse. The unfortunate innovation lies in the tendency to view reason and revelation as two entirely distinct sources of moral knowledge as opposed to seeing reason itself as something to be interpreted theologically, as per the scholastics. This sets in motion the transition towards viewing natural law as a purely philosophical and monolithic framework for establishing absolute moral norms.

When considered in conjunction with Porter's account of the liberal-secular *mythos*, the 'unsaid' reasons for this particular reading of the tradition begin to surface. On this score, there are two points worth emphasizing. First, as a contemporary defender of moral pluralism, it is essential that the scholastic-Thomistic account of natural law is distanced, theoretically and genealogically, from the idea that practical reason can be purified of historico-cultural circumstance. This is because she believes that the 'permanent significance' of scholastic-Thomistic jurisprudence rests upon its reconcilability with a plurality of interpretations of human nature and, thus, a plurality of approaches to the moral life; a move which modern-Grotian inspired incarnations of the natural law as expressions of 'pure reason' would disavow as confused and irrational. Second, the theological efficacy of Porter's baptism of liberal-secularism derives from her prior genealogical conviction that liberal-secular morality (and even the idea of the secular itself as an integral political order of immanent intelligibility)

133. Although, as I noted above, Finnis does, for the sake of ontological-epistemological stability, later admit to a theological basis for the obligation to follow the natural law.

is theologically generated and promoted by the scholastic-Thomistic concept of natural law. This explains her 'tradition-constituted' riposte of the Grotian inspired impulse to establish 'non-theological starting points and arguments' for the sake of secular irenicism.[134] The problem is that Porter's own contribution perpetuates the same aporetic ambiguity she identifies in Grotius precisely because her retrieval of natural law is being governed by the *mythos* of secular irenicism.[135] At first, she writes from a 'theistic standpoint', arguing that scholastic-Thomistic natural law reasoning cannot be understood apart from revelation. Yet, ultimately, she wants to arrive at a 'non-theological' perspective, arguing, like her *bête noire*, that the 'critical point' of scholastic-Thomistic natural law is that it does not depend on revelation.[136]

Finnis's and Porter's interpretations of Grotius harmonize insofar as they both strategically desist from constructing an explicit anti-modernity or anti-secular meta-narrative. In contrast, Milbank's entire theological enterprise is indissociable from his genealogical meta-narrative against the secular *mythos*. Within the 'Radical Orthodoxy' meta-narrative, Grotius is upheld as one of the villainous architects of the violent biopolitical ontology that unites modern natural law with modern secular reason. Furthermore, whereas Finnis and Porter generally respect the philosophical-theological legitimacy of the 'impious hypothesis', Milbank firmly ripostes it as a heretical 'ruse'. The 'ruse' hinges upon the concocted idea that one can legitimately delineate a 'natural' foundation for natural law that exists, dualistically, apart from a participation in divine grace. This 'un-Thomistic' ontology is of particular concern for Milbank. Theologically, it undermines his anthropological *ressourcement* of the *desiderium naturale*. Politically, it propels the separation of the natural law from divine government and, in corollary, the church from the state.

The aporia is that Milbank's ecclesiocentric reaction to the secular *mythos* parodies – albeit in a polarising fashion – Grotius's 'impious hypothesis'. Whilst he might well posit that 'once there was no secular', it is his continual narration of the secular that preserves the *conatus* of 'estrangement' that is intrinsic to the spatialization and delineation of his own jurisprudential borderlands. One might formulate Milbank's 'unsaid hypothesis' of out-narration as follows: What we have been saying (viz. about the natural law) would have a degree of validity even if we should say that which cannot be conceded without undermining the 'Radical Orthodoxy' meta-narrative, that Milbank needs Kant, for the affairs of 'Radical Orthodoxy' cannot be made radical or orthodox without him.[137]

134. Porter, *NasR*, 27.

135. Ibid., 26–7.

136. Porter, *Justice as Virtue*, 57.

137. I'm parodying the translation of Grotius's 'impious hypothesis' as found in: Crowe, *The Changing Profile of Natural Law*, 223, 224 fn. 2.

Human rights: Thomistic or nihilistic?

Aporetic perplexity has also surfaced with respect to how the 'three voices' account for the genealogical origins and contemporary significance of subjective (human) rights. Finnis declares that, even if he never articulated the exact phrase, Aquinas clearly had the concept of subjective *ius*. Porter articulates a similar thesis, arguing that, in many contexts, Aquinas does locate right-claims within the discretion of an individual's will even if he does not exposit a theory of human rights per se. As I also noted, such genealogical claims are of significant, although 'unsaid', political import to both these voices since defending the idea of subjective rights marks a crucial point of linguistic and philosophical rapprochement between Thomistic natural law and their accounts of the liberal-secular *mythos*. That said, there is a vast discrepancy between Finnis and Porter as to what might be included as a normative example of a 'human right'.[138]

Milbank's opposition to MacKinnon's 'theology of right' leads him to narrate a counter perspective on the theo-cultural legitimacy of subjective rights. Following Villey, he declares them to be a modern and secular invention that is precipitous of a 'further nihilistic undoing of our humanity'. Therefore, the idea of natural rights is entirely irreconcilable with the authentic (Thomistic) tradition of natural law.[139] On this point, I discussed how Milbank has taken aim explicitly at Finnis by accusing him of producing a 'novel, modern doctrine' that is 'reducible to a [socially liberal] modern natural rights doctrine'.[140]

It is worth questioning if Milbank's assessment of Finnis is entirely fair or whether it actually illuminates another level of discoursive perplexity. In Chapter Two, I explored the 'unsaid' reasons as to why Finnis's discussion of natural rights oscillates between two different positions. When addressing the 'cultured despisers', he asserts that '[a]lmost everything in this book [*NLNR*] is about human rights.'[141] But when responding to his Thomistic critics, who accuse him of moralizing natural rights to the detriment of natural law, he retorts by saying that *NLNR* 'says nothing about rights until the eighth of its thirteen chapters' and that natural rights takes up 'only a small part' of the book's argument.[142] I argued that these rhetorical shifts reflect adaptations to different 'inner audiences'. When addressing his analytical and metaphysical sceptics, he is keen to signal the marriageability and interchangeability of the metaphysically abstracted notion of natural rights with the 'unhappy [metaphysically loaded]

138. The right for same-sex couples to marry being a prime example. Whilst Finnis and Porter both enumerate a list of 'basics goods' or 'basic *desiderata*', these lists reflect very different normative visions of the moral life and, in consequence, very different lists of human rights.

139. John Milbank, 'The Franciscan Conundrum', *Communio*, vol. 42 (Fall 2015), 491.

140. Milbank, 'A Revisionist Account of Natural Law and Natural Right'.

141. Finnis, *NLNR*, 198.

142. Finnis, 'Grounding Human Rights in Natural Law', 198, 205 fn. 16.

term' of natural law. Conversely, when addressing his fellow Thomists, he is keen to emphasize that his appropriation and approbation of the *lingua* of rights is simply an exercise in the 'art of writing', and his commitment to natural law *qua* natural law is evidenced by his very limited discussion of 'natural rights'. Even in the dedicated chapter on 'Rights', Finnis approaches the topics with caution and modesty. In contrast, he is both candid and confident when speaking about the 'basic goods'. Nevertheless, given the prevailing dominance of rights language, Finnis seems willing to make linguistic concessions, believing that natural rights might be an acceptable way of speaking about the requirements of the goods. As he, himself, says: 'The fact that [the] theology [of natural law] is now *articulated* in terms of rights ... changes its propositional content not at all.'[143]

The same linguistic dilemma that the secular *mythos* creates in Finnis was also found in Milbank. In his programmatic essay against MacKinnon, he forcefully rejects the (Aristotelian) language of 'substance' because he believes it prefigures the Kantian concept of 'thing-in-themselves'. Hence, he proceeds to reconstruct natural law as a hylozoistic 'theology without substance'. In his later work, however, especially when reacting against the postmodern, secular-bio-political fusion of *physis* and *techne*, he seeks to reintroduce a theology of substance as a way to affirm, linguistically, that there do exist certain objective cultural idioms. Similarly, in reaction against the 'modern' – post-Suarezian – tendency to codify the natural law in terms of a series of moral norms, he asserts that the Church should refrain from making specific moral judgements, particularly on matters pertaining to sexual activity. Yet, in opposition to what he perceives as the biopolitical and antinomian tyranny against traditional marriage, he explicates a very specific 'natural law argument' against same-sex marriage. Perhaps, then, it should come as less of a surprise that he has begun to call for 'a new natural law synthesis that would sustain the best gains of natural rights.'[144] In another recent article, he affirms a similar sentiment by asking whether a reconsideration of the EU's Catholic – rather than Kantian – intellectual heritage could contribute towards 'the re-establishment of a natural law horizon, including a reasonable consideration of natural rights?'[145] In the same way Milbank's *poesis* requires the *mythos* of the secular, so, too, it appears he will also require the language of natural rights. The paradox is that Milbank's praxis of out-narration via estrangement always seems to end (eventually) in the parodic assimilation of the very concepts he was endeavouring to displace.

143. Ibid., 218.

144. Milbank, 'The History of Natural Right'.

145. John Milbank, 'Justice and Rights in Europe Today', 2019, https://churchlifejournal.nd.edu /articles/ justice-and-rights-in-europe-today. Accessed on 10 May 2019.

Section IV: A disremembering Agon

A subjective relativism

The purpose of this chapter was to give an innovative diagnosis of the reasons behind the aporetic fragmentation taking place within contemporary natural law discourse by drawing upon the deconstructive analyses of the 'three voices' in Part One. A powerful conclusion arising from this discussion is that the hidden grammar of the 'unsaid(s)' possesses a strategic importance to Finnis, Porter, and Milbank, along with the concomitant tendency to cipher, instrumentalize, or translate the theological voice in natural law for the sake of achieving disparate theo-cultural and political objectives. The aporetic irony is that Finnis, Porter, and Milbank all utilize the suppressing power of the 'unsaid(s)' because they believe it will actually help to redeem their particular theological-normative convictions in public discourse. I have argued that the reverse is true. The dialogical and/or narratological persuasiveness of their convictions is being undermined by that which they leave 'unsaid'. For once the 'unsaid(s)' were 'unfolded and worked out' (to borrow Agamben's phrase); the hegemonic and solipsistic power of the secular *mythos* emerged.[146] Hegemonic, because each of the 'three voices' allows the idea of the secular to govern how they try to reconcile *nomos* with *physis* and how they try to relate the particular to the universal. Solipsistic, because the dissimilitude between how the 'three voices' construct the secular was found to reflect the idiosyncrasies of their own 'inner audience', which largely reflects the subjectivity of their own *Sitz im Leben*.

Confronting this predicament helps to refine the problem I alluded to above. If the tradition of natural law is itself being constructed in reaction to a specific construction of the secular *mythos,* then is it not the case that the secular *mythos* is the *real* authoritative foundation and linguistic arbitrator of the tradition itself? Is this not a self-constituted path to subjective relativism and, thence, the *real* reason why the 'three voices' talk past each other?[147] For even if we think the origins of our deeper metaphysico-political commitments must remain 'unsaid', they continue to manifest themselves by filtering or inflecting the written or spoken word, thereby mediating and structuring the exterior physiognomy of what actually is said.

The aporetic perplexities examined in this chapter support this destabilizing conclusion. In the first instance, I highlighted the different alethiological

146. Giorgio Agamben, 'What Is a Paradigm?', *European Graduate Schools* (25 February 2014). Quoted in: Mikhail Pozdniakov, 'Feelings Sustaining Text: Aphorisms and Inspirations', *Modern Languages and Literatures Annual Graduate Conference*, 2014, https://ir.lib.uwo.ca/cgi/viewcontent.cgi?article=1016 &context=mllgradconference. Accessed on 12 June 2019.

147. Subjective relativism implies that reality and ethics are determined by the private thought processes and existential sentiments of the individual.

boundaries that the 'three voices' inscribe upon the tradition in order to either engage or out-narrate their contemporary 'inner audiences'. Despite the evident differences in how these boundaries are drawn, all of the 'three voices' delineate theories of truth that were found to both diminish or eschew the relationship between natural law and divine government. Recognition of the alethiological perplexity that subverts and fragments how Finnis, Porter, and Milbank try to reconfigure Thomistic realism helped to elucidate the 'unsaid' reasons for the anthropological perplexity that subverts and fragments how they formulate the relationship between nature and grace and nature and reason. In particular, what emboldens each of the 'three voices' to articulate their alethiological convictions is an underlying anthropological conviction about the ontological status of the *desiderium naturale*, which modulates how the 'three voices' understand what it means to speak 'persuasively'.

Yet, once the theo-cultural 'unsaid(s)' were allowed to surface, it became clear that Finnis, Porter, and Milbank were constructing these different anthropologies in a manner that, ultimately and aporetically, parodies the underlying ideologies that they initially set out to deconstruct and denounce.[148] Recognition of this anthropological perplexity helped to elucidate the 'unsaid' reasons for the genealogical perplexity that subverts and fragments how the 'three voices' interpret the relationship between nature and history. I suggested that the conflicting attempts to narrate the tradition-past reflect conflicting attempts to legitimate conflicting interpretations of the tradition-present. In other words, genealogies of natural law (or of the secular *mythos*) are not disinterested production; rather, they are backward creations that are often used to justify a particular theo-cultural or political objective that had already been arrived at through the rehearsal of certain theo-political arguments with a particular 'inner audience'. Thus, if 'reason has a wax nose' in current debates in natural law, so do history and tradition.[149] Although I had to limit this discussion to three illustrative examples – namely, the genealogical origins of natural law, the significance of Grotius's 'impious hypothesis', and the debate over subjective rights – in each case, the narration of history aligned with, bolstered, and illuminated their respective accounts of the secular *mythos*.

148. Several examples could be given to illustrate this point. For instance, Finnis initially sets out to oppose the Suarezian/neo-scholastic anthropological interpretation of Natural Law, yet he ends up parodying its 'cardinal contribution'. Porter sets out to correct a purely philosophical reading of natural law by bring theological reflection to bear upon human nature, yet she ends up eschewing theological reflection for sake of promoting a principally philosophical interpretation of Aquinas. Milbank sets out to riposte the secular, yet he ends up parodying it by creating a new form of secularism.

149. Joseph Ratzinger (now Pope Emeritus Benedict XVI), *On the Way to Jesus Christ* (San Francisco, CA: Ignatius Press, 2005), 35–6.

Tragedians anew

The real tragedy arising from this diagnosis is not that current debates in natural law end in aporia, but that, in a certain sense, they have been founded upon an aporia. This point is reminiscent of the dilemma I identified in the *Minos*. Although the dialogue between Socrates and the Athenian Companion was initiated by a mutual desire to discover the *logos* of law, it is only towards the end of the dialogue that the two interlocutors recognize how their philosophical elenchus was being subverted by a fundamental inattentiveness to a theological-narratological 'unsaid'. In a similar vein, there is a tendency within current scholarship to simply focus upon the different normative conclusions that natural law theorists arrive at. Obviously, as Aquinas, himself, anticipated, it is on the specification of specific moral norms that the fragmentation becomes most explicit.[150] Take the issue of homosexuality, as an example. Finnis's NNLT declares homosexual acts and the notion of same-sex marriage to be egregious attacks upon the basic good of marriage and so are always intrinsically evil. Porter, in contrast, actually expounds a natural law argument in defence of homosexual acts and same-sex marriage. Milbank takes satisfaction in upholding neither a socially conservative nor a socially liberal position, but, rather, in a spirit of estrangement, he opposes same-sex marriage but takes no issue with homosexual acts.

What this chapter has illustrated is that such intramural fragmentation cannot simply be attributed to the extramural fragmentation taking place within the sociocultural fabric of the *polis*. In other words, if we are to traverse a way from aporia to euporia, then we have to deconstruct and expose the 'background stories' that have suppressed the theological voice within the discourse on natural law itself.[151] On this point, the 'solipsisms of the secular' have become the contemporary expression of the 'Attic tragedy' found in the *Minos*. Principally, because they mediate an erroneous and disremembering sense of universality and a false sense of stability that has driven the language of natural law further and further away into theo-cultural obsolescence – into the realm of the 'unsaid'. Hence my supposition that it would be more accurate to say that current debates in natural law *begin* rather than *end* in aporia.

Now that this inaugurating aporia has been exposed and its perplexity stated, it will be the task of the final chapter to investigate, even if only in truncated terms, a euporetic way forward. One luminous possibility is to explore how the surfacing of the theological 'unsaid(s)' themselves might provide the proverbial key to remembering and retrieving an essential soteriological-eschatological horizon for natural law discourse, a horizon made present in and through a moment of 'dialogical *anamnesis*'.

150. C.f. Aquinas, ST I-II q. 94 a. 4.

151. C.f. Stephen Smith, 'Natural Law and Contemporary Moral Thought', *The American Journal of Jurisprudence*, vol. 42 (1) (1997), 326.

Chapter 6

AN ESCHATOLOGICAL AND ANAMNETIC RE-NARRATION OF NATURAL LAW

'Politics is a practice of the imagination.

Sometimes politics is the 'art of the possible', but it is always an art, and engages the imagination just as art does ... Too often the modern Christian theological. imagination has got lost in the stories that sustain modern politics'[1]

Section I: An anamnetic horizon

The anamnesis *of eschatology*

Speaking of natural law as the theory or practice of 'dialogical *anamnesis*' is not entirely original. Though it certainly remains a creative proposition deserving of further research and development. An inchoate attempt to reconsider natural law in similar terms can be found in the then Joseph Ratzinger's thought on conscience. Although Aquinas and medieval scholasticism tied natural law to the notion of *synderesis* (*synteresis*), Ratzinger hoped to 'replace this problematic word with the much more clearly defined Platonic concept of *anamnesis*.'[2] The problem with *synderesis*, he argued, is that, by virtue of its Stoic provenance, its meaning has remained ambiguous within a Christian context. In contrast, the concept of *anamnesis* is both 'linguistically clearer' and 'philosophically deeper and purer'.[3] Most importantly, it 'harmonises with key motifs of biblical thought and the anthropology derived therefrom.'[4] In fact, Ratzinger asserted that *anamnesis* is exactly what St Paul meant by the law inscribed upon the heart (Romans 2:14). Ontologically, the natural law derives from an 'original memory', which is experienced in and through an 'inner ontological tendency' to seek the good and the truth and so move towards the divine.[5] 'This *anamnesis* of the origin', he

1. William T. Cavanaugh, *Theopolitical Imagination* (London: T&T Clark, 2002), 1, 3.
2. Ratzinger, 'Conscience and Truth', 534.
3. Ibid.
4. Ibid.
5. Ibid., 536.

explains, 'is not a conceptually articulated knowing.'[6] Rather, it is 'an inner sense, a capacity to recall, so that the one whom it addresses if he is not turned in on himself, hears its echo from within. He sees: "That's it! That is what my nature points to and seeks."'[7]

One of the aporetic attributes of the secular *mythos* identified in Chapter 5 concerns its ability to dissimulate a centrifugal character. Centrifugal, in the sense that it purports to provide a stable interpersonal foundation (even if, in the case of Milbank, this stable foundation takes the form of a despised counterpoint) with which to retrieve and translate or narrate the tradition persuasively. In reality, the unwieldy character of the secular *mythos* was found to turn the discourse back on itself, centripetally, in reaction to a particular and idiosyncratic 'inner audience'. Hence, the discourse has become solipsistic, fragmented, and unpersuasive in character.[8] It is interesting that the one thing Ratzinger mentions as inhibiting a person's 'capacity to recall' the natural law is being *incurvatus in se*, 'turned in on oneself'. Incidentally, this is how Augustine described the state of original sin.[9] What original sin weakens is both the 'original memory' of the origin of one's being or nature in divine providence and the 'ontological tendency' to seek the good and the true in accordance with that nature through the laws of divine government.

With reference to current debates in natural law, I have argued that the 'solipsisms of the secular' have contributed towards the disremembering of the 'original memory' of the tradition's fundamental theological anthropology. The secular *mythos* is an '*incurvatus in se*'. Although this is a discouraging contention, it is not necessarily a terminal conclusion. Now that the solipsistic character of the secular *mythoi* has been exposed, the task at hand is not to repeat, and so reinterpellate, the same disremembering meta-narrative. One way to fall afoul of this would be to try and reconstruct natural law in reaction to the reactions of the 'three voices' to the secular *mythos*. To react to their reactions would only lead to a new dissimulated foundationalism – another aporia – that is predicated upon the perpetuation of a new variant of the secular *mythos*. Instead, one must now test the fresh dialogical horizon that dawns anew.

What might that euporetic horizon look like? In straightforward terms, there is no reason why natural law needs to be narrated in relation or in reaction to the idea of the secular as if it were the ever-recurring serpent in the garden. In fact, the secular *mythos*, irrespective of how it is constructed, has been shown to be both a theoretical and methodological obstacle to a genuine *ressourcement* of the

6. Ibid.

7. Ibid.

8. It is important to acknowledge that the Catholic Church does not subscribe to a single system of philosophy and thus diversity is to be expected and possibly even hoped for. The problem within current debates in natural law is that the different visions contradict each other to such an extent that scholars would even accuse their fellow theorists of being heretical.

9. C.f. Matt Jenson, *The Gravity of Sin* (London: T&T Clark, 2006), 6–46.

tradition by its suppression or instrumentalization of the theological 'unsaid(s)'. The intention here, however, is not to confront, juxtapose, or out-narrate the secular *mythos* by just invoking theological categories. Nor is the intention to bring in the theological as if it were an artificial superimposition upon a non-theological discourse. The task at hand is to re-narrate in more exact terms how the theological 'unsaid(s)' can contribute to natural law discourse as an already participating force – a force that is both deconstructive and constructive; a force that bears witness to, and makes us aware of, the teleological movement that is already at work in our common desire and dialogical search for justice; a witness to the possibility of 'a nature reformed by grace'. There can be no ontological *duplex-ordo*. For, as Aquinas says in a much 'unsaid' passage, the natural law can only be practiced propitiously 'by the help of Christ's grace.'[10]

Inaugurating the *anamnesis* of this disremembered theological anthropology and explicating its dialogical relationship to natural law is the euporetic horizon I will endeavour to move towards in this final chapter. Ideally, this retrieval would involve a wider reconsideration of how this theological anthropology relates to ethics, how ethics relates to jurisprudence, and how jurisprudence relates to theology. Of course, tracing these interlocking fields is a lifetime's work. For this reason, it is appropriate to see this concluding chapter as heeding an opportunity to identify a constructive gateway for further research as opposed to just providing a concluding summary of the deconstructive analyses already undertaken in this thesis. Nevertheless, it is obviously necessary to limit this constructive gateway to the discussion of one pivotal, yet forgotten, theological 'unsaid' that the secular *mythos* has heretofore suppressed/instrumentalized. Specifically, that the natural desire for justice, which originates and orientates the dialogical and relational character of natural law, requires the theological *anamnesis*/retrieval of, and a participation in, an immanent eschatology. An immanent eschatology is the disclosure of God's self in creation in and through the dynamic manifestation of divine government. I argue that, when viewed from this soteriological perspective, natural law itself becomes an ethic of 'eschatological disclosure' that, whilst of universal import, takes place in and through an immanent experience of dialogical *anamnesis*. Such ideas certainly require further elaboration and clarification.

'Derrida! What is (natural) law?'

A promising, even if preliminary, implication of this horizon is that it allows for a renewal of how the dialogical and relational character of natural law is understood and practiced. Finnis's, Porter's, and Milbank's foundational attachment to the secular *mythos* was found to stifle and foreclose potentially fruitful conversations with both natural law theorists as well as natural law sceptics. As I concluded in the previous chapter, their respective genealogical retrievals of the tradition are being

10. Thomas Aquinas, 'Commentary on the Letter of Saint Paul to the Romans', trans. and ed. J. Mortensen and E. Alarcón (Lander: The Aquinas Institute, 2012), 75.

prejudiced by an underlying reaction to an already conceived theo-cultural and oppositional dualism: sacred/secular, finite/infinite, nature/grace. This common reactionism was found to be explicative of their common dependency upon the category of the 'unsaid'. In consequence, the language of the tradition is 'turned in on itself', aporetically, so that, rather than opening up new possibilities that might advance the discourse, it merely accords with and so confirms the end(s) predetermined by that preconceived opposition.

When we shed the dualistic lens of the secular *mythos*, it open up avenues to re-evaluate the theologico-cultural import and theoretico-epistemological value of contributions erstwhile considered 'anti-natural law'. To illustrate this point, I will engage with the jurisprudential thought of Jacques Derrida. Derrida's deconstructive and antinomian critique of logocentric-metaphysical objectivism has long been deemed antithetical to any system of natural law. In contrast, this chapter will take a more nuanced approach by describing Derrida's contribution, particularly in his essay the *Force of Law*, as a pharmakon (at once a remedy and a poison) to the *anamnesis* of an immanent eschatology in natural law. It is important to stress that Derrida's contribution is not being introduced here as a 'fourth voice'. The reason for including a heuristic summary of his jurisprudential thought is to illustrate how it is in the process of his own search for justice that he unveils the theological dimension of justice, akin to an epiphany of eschatological significance. By outlining this revelation, the aim is to stimulate a renewed appreciation for the theological aspects of jurisprudence within contemporary natural law discourse.

Section II: A 'work of mourning'

The unsaid 'unsaid'

This section will begin by considering the principal hermeneutic employed in this book: the deconstruction of the theo-cultural 'unsaid(s)' that secretly sustain the fragmenting spell of the secular *mythos* in current debates in natural law. Since this hermeneutic has guided us to now recognize the aporetic end(s) that haunt the discourse, we are, in a certain sense, obliged to reflect back upon the wider theological and dialogical significance of the hermeneutic itself.[11] This point echoes and observes a further contention of Agamben: 'Only a thought that does not hide its own unsaid, but incessantly takes it up and develops it anew, can possibly lay

11. It is important to acknowledge the 'unsaid' that is at work in this book. Time and space do not permit a detailed exploration of this point though I do hope to do so in the near future in a further publication. One aspect that will need to be considered is the underdeveloped political ecclesiology at work in this work, which would reveal in more exacting terms why discordancy is such a problem within contemporary debates in natural law. Further thought would also need to be given as to the implications of the argument against the secular *mythos* for the Catholic Church today, especially given Finnis' continued influence upon natural law.

claim to originality.'[12] One way to 'lay claim to originality' is to acknowledge and highlight the valuable influence that the deconstructive impulse can have upon the discourse of natural law, especially in raising the theological 'unsaid(s)' and interrogating their political significance. One might say, then, that Derrida has been the unnamed companion throughout this thesis.[13] Recognizing this 'haunting presence' raises a twofold, but interrelated, question that I will address in Sections III and IV. First, to what extent can the deconstructive impulse itself be linked to the natural law tradition? Second, if, as Derrida asserts, 'deconstruction is justice', is there anything beyond a constructive deconstruction of the mechanisms of suppression that have turned a 'work of memory' (a dialogical *anamnesis*) into a 'work of mourning' (a solipsistic *hypomnesis*)?

Reason and refinement

Desire serves as the catalyst for dialogue, and dialogue, in turn, paved the way for jurisprudence. In 'Plato's' *Minos*, Socrates' desire to grasp the essence of law ontologically – 'what is law' – is inherently intertwined with a desire to know and affirm what 'law is intent on'. Ultimately, this natural desire propels a search that culminates in the remembrance that the justice of the law can only be secured by acknowledging its theological grounding in divine government (Zeus).[14] Returning to this universal (original) desire for justice as a starting point for natural law could provide a powerful alternative to the secular *mythos*. For when natural law is firmly re-associated with the notion of desire, especially the universal desire for justice, the dialogical character of the discourse is also re-orientated towards discerning what we might call an authentic (that is to say, non-solipsistic) 'rhetoric of the self'. As I have said on several occasions, the rhetoric of the 'I' yearns to be recognized in and through our relationships with others – the 'rhetoric of the we'. This raises an important issue. Given that the desire for justice is always expressed in and through language and so reflects an anthropological-relational quality, to what extent does this language need to be theological? Can one afford to leave the theological 'unsaid'?[15]

12. Giorgio Agamben, *Signatura rerum* 8. Quoted in and translated by Nicholas Heron, 'The Ungovernable', *Angelaki: Journal of the Theoretical Humanities*, vol. 16, no. 2 (June 2011), 159.

13. Although I introduced this thesis with specific reference to Agamben's thought on the 'un-said(s)', Kevin Attell has argued that, even when punctuated by way of an unconscious or conscious critique, 'Agamben views [Derridean] deconstruction as perhaps the most significant body of philosophical thought in the post-war period', and 'the work against which he must continuously measure his own.' Kevin Attell, *Giorgio Agamben: Beyond the Threshold of Deconstruction* (New York: Fordham University Press, 2015), 3–4.

14. Ibid., 61.

15. Even if justice can be shown to be a universal concept, it does not necessarily mean that it is a univocal term. Like the word 'tradition', justice is equally determined by the vagaries of history, culture and circumstance. Nevertheless, perhaps when viewed from a

A fresh conclusion arising out of this work is that certain methodological tenets of the deconstructive impulse should be welcomed into current debates in natural law. Deconstruction is not deleterious of natural law, as some have assumed, nor is it a 'quasi-nihilistic abdication before the ethic-political-juridical question of justice'.[16] Rather, in Derrida's own words, 'deconstruction is, in itself, a positive response to an alterity, which necessarily calls, summons, and motivates'.[17] In this instance, deconstruction can be employed constructively to help interrogate the alterity of the theological 'unsaid(s)', which operate latently – in one form or another – behind all jurisprudential speech. Once the theological 'unsaid(s)' are no longer instrumentalized or displaced from jurisprudential discourse, they themselves perform a creative function by re-ordering and, thence, re-narrating the meaning and significance of our common search for the (moral) law and for justice.

How is this the case? One preliminary way to express this would be to borrow Ratzinger's phrase 'purify and exalt'. Raising the theological 'unsaid(s)' helps to 'purify and exalt' jurisprudential language by purifying and exalting reason, 'thereby enabling it to broaden its horizons to enter into a field of research as unfathomably expansive as [the] mystery [of law] itself'.[18] For, as I have already noted, reason tends to have a "wax nose"'. It can be moulded and shaped in order to hide, disguise, or instrumentalize the theo-cultural 'unsaid(s)' that always animate our thinking.[19] However, I would suggest that it is theologically sharper to speak of the 'refinement' (as opposed to the 'purification') of reason. The difference in terminology is subtle but significant. The word 'purification' still tends to imply that we can possess a superior epistemological perspective which is untainted by or filtered from all the conditions – historical and existential – that condition human thinking. Refinement resists the idea that we can arrive at some realm of pure thought. Instead, it encourages the conscious recognition of how thought itself, particularly within current debates in natural law, has been and

theological perspective, it is still possible to see a universal desire for justice as underlining the many different forms of justice that distinguish human endeavours. Again, to explore this matter appropriately would necessitate considerable time and space.

16. Jacques Derrida, 'Force of Law: The "Mystical Foundation of Authority"', in *Acts of Religion*, ed. Gil Anidjar (Milton Park: Routledge, 2010), 247. C.f. Merold Westphal, 'Derrida as Natural Law Theorist', in *Overcoming Onto-Theology* (Fordham: Fordham University Press, 2001), 219–20.

17. Jacques Derrida, 'Deconstruction and the Other', in *Debates in Continental Philosophy*, ed. Richard Kearney (Fordham: Fordham University Press, 2004), 149.

18. Benedict XVI, 'The Relationship of Faith and Reason', in *A Reason Open to God*, ed. Steven Brown (Washington, DC: Catholic University of America, 2013), 35.

19. Ratzinger, *On the Way to Jesus Christ*, 37. This was the problem I identified with John Courtney Murray's ecclesiology. Murray spoke of 'purification' as a process of linguistic and structural revision, whereby the Church focuses its socio-cultural efforts on augmenting 'inherently secular ends'.

still is conditioned and, thus, to some degree, remains contingent. This does not mean that natural law is without a foundation. Nor does it negate the belief that the natural law is grounded via critical (dialogical) reason. But, in light of the deconstructive analyses in Part One, it has become clear that this critical reason must be critically honest about its own (theological) 'unsaid(s)' in order for natural law to grasp the *eros* of its own ontology – its 'original memory' and the true *telos* of its 'ontological tendency'. For this reason, it is perhaps possible to consider the impulse of deconstruction to be an already intrinsic, even if neglected, part of the lost theological tradition of natural law.

The negation of solipsistic hegemonies

Theological language is, by its very nature, deconstructive. At least in the sense that it is self-subversive and, thus, self-disclosive, and, thence, in a certain sense, self-refining.[20] In fact, it must be so if it is to speak truly about that which is beyond speech. The true refinement of language, especially jurisprudential language, takes place before the inexhaustible disclosure of the Word, in Christ, since all words thence become self-conscious of their finite nature and their limitation. Far from paralysing the discourse in a state of aporetic silence, recognizing the theological horizon of the Word becomes the impetus for its creativity. In this context, one might say, that the discourse of natural law travels alongside an 'eschatological underdetermination'.[21] Here, Rowan Williams's eschatological emphasis could be insightfully developed, as Brett Gray explains:

> For Williams, Christian apophaticism is governed by an intuition of unending progress. Revelation is to him, by nature, generatively propulsive; it fractures 'existing frames of reference' and 'extends debate' … There is 'always more to say' … and 'this 'more' is always more compelling and wonderful' … It could be called a 'catholic' act, wherein a stolid and defensive territorialisation of the self is refused by seeking a good that cannot be had without the other … It is rather 'dependent for its definition and realisation on dialogue extended in time' … In relation to Christ, all things – the catholic whole of reality – slip their moorings as objects and are drawn into a divine orbit. The world becomes endlessly iconic, but not less creaturely. Its endlessness it not its own, but had only in relation to the divine life into which it endlessly journeys, and of which it becomes endlessly significant.[22]

20. Once the theological 'unsaid(s)' are understood as being of service to the discourse, it also becomes possible to interpret the dialogical character of natural law as itself a theological movement towards a continuing (constructive) deconstruction of what is being said. The trajectory itself reflects the self-subversive character of theological language by not only calling attention to and confronting the 'unsaid(s)', but by asking whether the 'unsaid(s)' can be said and, if so, whether it is actually what needs to be said.

21. Brett Gray, *Jesus in the Theology of Rowan Williams* (London: Bloomsbury, 2016), 150.

22. Ibid., 153.

Unlike the secular *mythos*, which either suppresses theological language on the misleading supposition that it stifles dialogue or, in the case of Milbank, gnostifies theological language in order to declare the 'end of dialogue', the theological 'unsaid(s)' are what keep the dialogue open, preventing us from becoming the hegemonic master/mistress of the discourse. In this sense, they perform an immanent critique of the discourse.

What is being argued here is more modest than it might sound. A fundamental reason why we hold fast to the discourse of natural law is because it creates a creative space for human beings to manifest, dialogically, 'the truth of what they are'.[23] For justice is a discourse of 'attentive truth telling', which begins in response 'to the reality of another' – not in reaction to a constructed 'inner audience'.[24] The gift of revelation sublimates and intensifies this alethiological and anthropological manifestation by awakening reason to its epistemological limitations. To reiterate, this theological recognition in no way disables reason; in fact, it enables it precisely because it allows reason to come to know the nature and structure of its own desire. At the same time, it mediates a renewed level of confidence in reason – a confidence that the search for justice is purposeful and the desire for justice is realizable both within the political and the eschatological orders.

An embraced impotence

Another way to put this is to say that the *anamnesis* of theology and the surfacing of the theological 'unsaid(s)' are the negation of all solipsistic hegemonies. This is an important conclusion. Fundamentally, natural law is a discourse about the desire to be in, and the right ordering of, relationships. This is essential to both the human person and to human society. If the natural law tradition exists to make manifest certain universal truths about human nature by fostering a vocabulary with which to reason adequately about our most important desires, then it is antithetical to the disclosive character of the discourse to transmogrify it into a tradition of concealment – a discourse of strategic 'unsaid(s)'. In order to be an authentically relational discourse, natural law theory must practise, and therefore encourage, a trans-cultural freedom to 'speak without fear of punishment.'[25] For a discourse of concealment is inevitably a discourse that 'sets out to foreclose the possibility of a genuine response.'[26]

This point illuminates a further reason why the constructive deconstruction of the theological 'unsaid(s)' is integral to understanding current debates in natural law. Put simply, the deconstructive impulse not only excavates what has

23. Ibid., 34–5.

24. Ibid.

25. Aristotle Papanikolaou, *The Mythical as Political: Democracy and Non-Radical Orthodoxy* (Notre Dame, IN: Notre Dame University Press, 2012), 56.

26. Rowan Williams, 'Theological Integrity', *Cross Currents*, vol. 45, no. 3 (Fall 1995), 312.

been left 'unsaid', but it also helps to explain why the discourse/dialogue cannot succeed without the 'unsaid(s)'. In the case of the 'three voices', it could be said that the spirit of Derridean deconstruction exposes the retrieval of the natural law tradition by the 'three voices' to be a 'work of mourning', that is to say, a work that is in a state of interminable and inconsolable loss, which, ultimately, thwarts genuine relationality.[27] Aporetically, it is the deconstructive exposure of the buried theo-cultural 'unsaid(s)' that are the very possibility of natural law's vitality/generativity. However, it is precisely this vitality/generativity that the secular *mythos* suppresses. (Or, in the case of Milbank, the vitality/generativity is exploited to construct an alternate – parodically violent – political *mythos*.) This is the trauma that propels the 'work of mourning',[28] which, to appropriate once more from Agamben's thought, is an 'unsaid' decision to 'embrace [relational and dialogical] impotence'![29]

Section III: A 'work of memory'

Re-narrating Derrida

In the last section, I discussed *how* deconstruction can help open up the dialogical and relational horizons of the discourse. This section will investigate *why* deconstruction is helpful by exploring the possibility that it has an 'unsaid' relationship with the disremembered tradition of natural law. The only scholar to have even begun to seriously consider such a possibility is Merold Westphal. Although he later acknowledged that his decision to call Derrida a 'natural law theorist' was 'playful and provocative',[30] he still maintains his earlier avowal that 'Derrida's theory of natural law represents a serious contribution to the ongoing conversation.'[31] Since then, no one has really tried to investigate whether Derrida's thought might be fruitfully engaged with for the sake of future reclamations or reconstructions of natural law. This section hopes to build upon and strengthen Westphal's controversial claim by demonstrating how Derrida's defence of deconstruction in the *Force of Law* is disclosive of an 'unsaid' appeal to a theory of natural law, an appeal that, even if oblique, can contribute towards the dialogical *anamnesis* (the 'work of memory') of 'who

27. Jacques Derrida, *The Work of Mourning*, ed. Paul-Anne Brault and Michael Naas (Chicago: University of Chicago Press, 2001), 94–5, 143.

28. 'Mourning always follows a trauma …' Jacques Derrida, *Specters of Marx*, trans. Peggy Kamuf (New York: Routledge, 1994), 121.

29. Agamben, *The Coming of Community*, 35. Quoted in: Karen J. Engle, 'Putting Mourning to Work', *Theory, Culture & Society*, vol. 24, no. 1 (January 2007), 63, 80 fn. 3.

30. Merold Westphal, 'Reply to Jack Caputo', *Journal of the Society of Christian Philosophers*, vol. 22, no. 3 (2005), 298.

31. Westphal, 'Derrida as Natural Law Theorist', 228.

we are' – a theological anthropology – and to the refinement of jurisprudential discourse. I will centre this discussion around one pertinent aspect of Derrida's thought, specifically, his emphasis upon the role of 'interpretive memory' in jurisprudence.

Deconstruction on trial

Like Westphal, I intend to take Derrida's essay *Force of Law* as the principle literary justification for considering him as a natural law theorist. *Force of Law* was originally delivered as a speech at a conference titled, 'Deconstruction and the Possibility of Justice', held at Cardozo Law School in 1989. Derrida was suspicious of this chosen theme and with good reason. The conference was held in the wake of the 'de Man affair', a moment of grave 'crisis' for deconstruction.[32] Whilst deconstruction had long been accused of promoting radical scepticism and philosophical relativism, critics of Derrida now had grounds to question whether it secretly colludes with and promotes a fascist ideology. The conference, thus, occasioned the trial of deconstruction, and the *Force of Law* became Derrida's case for the defence.[33]

An alternate way to formulate the conference title and, accordingly, the charge would be to ask, 'Is deconstruction capable of arriving at political or moral judgments?' If so, can deconstruction provide a coherent account of both the search and the possibility of justice?

Or, does it ultimately have to resign itself to articulating a philosophy of arbitrariness and anarchy? Derrida actually seems to welcome this interrogation, declaring that it was both 'foreseeable and desirable' that the study of deconstruction 'should culminate in the problematic of right, of law [*loi*] and justice.'[34] But the fact that he described this as a culmination in his thinking, which, therefore, denotes a limit in his thinking, suggests that he had also arrived at a moment whence he felt obliged to reflect back upon his thinking and, in the process, remember and disclose his own 'unsaid'. Thus, in the words of John P. McCormick, *Force of Law* becomes the moment when Derrida 'lets his guard down'.[35]

32. Paul de Man was the Sterling Professor of Humanities at Yale. Besides being a personal friend of Derrida, he was considered the leading practitioner and interpreter of deconstruction. Posthumously, it was discovered that he had written over one hundred articles for a 'Pro-Nazi' tabloid in his native Belgium, *Le Soir*. C.f. James Atlas, 'The Case of Paul de Man', 1988, https://www.nytimes.com/1988/08/28/magazine/the-case-of-paul-de-man.html. Accessed on 1 December 2018.

33. John P. McCormick, 'Derrida on Law; Or, Poststructuralism gets Serious', *Political Theory*, vol. 29, no. 3 (June 2001), 396.

34. Derrida, 'Force of Law', 235.

35. McCormick, 'Derrida on Law', 396.

Inverting the charge

Derrida begins his defence by inverting the charges made against deconstruction by performing a deconstruction of the paradoxical authority (the *Gewalt*), which is at once a violent and yet legitimating force that grounds and ungrounds the logic of the legal system itself.[36] This foundational authority or force is an aporia, which, when identified, is also experienced phenomenologically. Phenomenological, in the sense that the experience of this aporia is, simultaneously, an epistemological awakening to the aporia that structures the experience of that which we are unable to experience, in this instance, 'a just call for justice.'[37] This hearkens to the problematic of decisionism and the problematic of foundationalism.[38] All law has a historical institution in time (a genesis) and results from and reflects a process of cognitive calculation. Justice, however, cannot be reduced to just a process of the law. 'Law is the element of calculation', says Derrida, 'but justice is incalculable.'[39] In fact, he goes on to declare that justice is 'infinite' and 'irreducible' because it is 'owed to the other, owed to the other before any contract, because it has *come*, it is a *coming*, the coming of the other as always other singularity.'[40] Although it is an 'infinite task' that remains 'to-come', justice cannot wait.[41] This central, yet consistently paradoxical, distinction signs the 'madness' inherent within legal decisionism and raises the question of the authority of the law.[42]

Is law always, thence, a supremely political construction and execution? Strategically, this is a very important point. When legal discourse remembers that which it has forgotten, namely, the aporetic origin of its authority, it also encounters the aporia of its own epistemological and linguistic limitations. Jurisprudential discourse thus reaches a threshold and becomes conscious of an erstwhile silent 'foundational secret'.[43] The 'foundational secret' is the dilemma of the 'founding act', that is to say, the justificatory and instituting moment of law, which is always calculated, conventional, self-authorizing, and, as such, is always an act of ontological violence inasmuch as it forcefully assumes the extra-linguistic and extra-legal legitimacy of its own genesis.[44] For this reason, 'deconstructive questioning' is, as Derrida asserts, 'through and through a questioning of [the foundations of] law and justice' – interrogating and disclosing how 'convention

36. Ibid., 234.

37. Ibid., 244.

38. 'Decisionism emphasizes the ultimately ungrounded nature of human choice such that all action is rendered irredeemably arbitrary and divorced from reason.' McCormick, 'Derrida on Law', 396–7.

39. Derrida, 'The Force of Law', 244.

40. Ibid., 254. (IAITT).

41. Ibid., 255.

42. Ibid., 236, 248.

43. Ibid., 243. C.f. Peter Gehring, 'The Jurisprudence of the "Force of Law"', in *Derrida and Legal Philosophy*, ed. Peter Goodrich (Basingstoke: Palgrave and Macmillan, 2008), 58.

44. Derrida, 'Force of Law', 243.

often masquerades as nature'; how injustice masquerades itself linguistically and logocentrically as justice; how positive law masquerades as natural law; how religious convictions masquerade as a 'secular' authority; how that which is 'said' can masquerade and conceal that which is left 'unsaid'.[45]

'Mad' for memory and 'mad' for justice

The crucial implication of this strategy is that Derrida refuses to definitionally conflate that which is law with that which is just. Hence, he argues for something 'beyond' the codifying reductivism of legal positivism. For to collapse justice into law is to construct yet another disremembering *mythos*. This is why he avows right from the beginning of *The Force of Law* that he wanted 'to reserve the possibility of a justice, indeed of a law [*loi*] that not only exceeds or contradicts law but also, perhaps, has no relation to law, or maintains such a strange relation to it that it may just as well demand law as exclude it'.[46] It is because Derrida defers to a 'higher law or norm to which all actual moral and legal codes are answerable' that Westphal believes he is justified in calling Derrida a 'natural law theorist'.[47]

Although Westphal's explication is certainly insightful, it is limited by its focus upon the political dimension of Derrida's 'natural law posture', which concerns its critique of the structural and linguistic violence that constitutes both law and legal theory. As a consequence, he overlooks the anthropological grounding of his deferral to a 'higher law', which, I would argue, is where the *Force of Law* holds genuine promise. The anthropological dimension of Derrida's thought surfaces when one begins to examine how exactly the structural immanence of deconstruction is schematized with respect to evaluating law's relationship to justice. For deconstruction, he asserts, is in some way the movement or operation that is already at work within, and inherent to, the discourse on law itself.[48] At the heart of this operation or movement is 'the *task* of historical and interpretive memory', which can critically engage with the fundamental substrate of all thinking about law.[49] In this sense, every act of 'interpretive memory' is a dialogue with the 'unsaid(s)'. For 'every dialogue becomes halting and fruitless if it confines itself obdurately to nothing but what is directly said'.[50]

45. Westphal, 'Derrida as Natural Law Theorist', 225.

46. Derrida, 'Force of Law', 233.

47. Westphal, 'Derrida as Natural Law Theorist', 224.

48. Derrida, 'Force of Law', 264. Derrida uses Walter Benjamin's 'Critique of Violence' as an 'exemplary' case-study or foil for what is occurring in every text 'before the law'. C.f. Attell, Giorgio Agamben, 137.

49. Ibid., 248; Adam Gearey, 'Thinking, Poetics, Law', in *Derrida and Legal Philosophy*, ed. Peter Goodrich *et al* (Basingstoke: Palgrave and Macmillan, 2008), 201. (IAITT).

50. Martin Heidegger, *What is Called Thinking*, 178. Quoted in: Gearey, 'Thinking, Poetics, Law', 208.

Deconstruction is animated by a 'sense of responsibility without limits' that takes place 'before memory.'[51] This involves a constant process of recollection, specifically, a recollection of the history and the origins of the law in a bid to remember the contingency and conventionality of the interpretive force that delineates the quasi-transcendental limits of concepts like justice, law, and right.[52] One might say, then, that deconstruction tries to inscribe justice upon the law by encouraging the remembrance of what the law has disremembered. In fact, Derrida posited that the 'antonym of 'forgetting' is not 'remembering' but *justice*?'[53] He would go on to affirm in a lone footnote that this was indeed his thinking behind the *Force of Law*:

> I have, for my part, notably in *Force de loi* and *Specters of Marx*, tried to situate justice, the justice which exceeds but also requires the law, in the direction of the act of memory, of resistance to forgetting, whether this be of the injunction in general or of its place of assignation: other people, living or dead.[54]

This 'resistance to forgetting' is also a forestalling of apodictic closure, a desire to keep the jurisprudential dialogue going. For deconstruction 'desires to keep things open' and to be open to 'constant reinvention.'[55] In this instance, 'to reinvent ancient traditions in new contexts,'[56] but in a manner that supports and reflects the ecstatic nature of the desire and the demand for justice.[57] Deconstruction is 'mad about', and originates from, 'this desire for justice.'[58] Thus, it becomes the metaphysical site upon which the true nature of our desire(s) can emerge and, subsequently, be refined and strengthened 'before memory'.

A law of 'being'

It is this anthropological consociation and interrelation of desire with memory that possibly explains *why* Derrida's contribution is potentially fruitful for future research. Principally, because it brings him into curious alignment with the idea of natural law as a 'work of memory', a theory of dialogical *anamnesis*. At the very

51. Derrida, 'Force of Law', 248.

52. Ibid., 246.

53. Jacque Derrida, *Archive Fever: A Freudian Impression*, trans. Eric Prenowitz (Chicago: University of Chicago, 1996), 77. (IAITT).

54. Ibid., 76 fn. 14.

55. Caputo, *Deconstruction in a Nutshell*, 159. Quoted in: Ronald T. Michener, *Engaging Deconstructive Theology* (Abingdon: Routledge, 2016), 71.

56. Ibid., 71.

57. For Derrida, to yield to the idea that 'this is justice' is, in a certain sense, to have neutralised one's interest in, and desire for, justice – we become insensitive to the call of alterity such that the search is ended. C.f. Derrida, 'Force of Law', 244.

58. Ibid., 254.

least, and even on allegedly 'post-modern' terms, Derrida's contribution dissociates the search for justice from addressing the disremembering *mythos* (the *Gewalt*) of the 'secular' and moves it in the 'direction of the act of memory', specifically, the memory of human nature.[59] Speaking from an explicitly jurisprudential perspective, several legal scholars have drawn a similar conclusion:

> It was through juxtaposing justice and law … that Derrida questioned and implicitly challenged the complacency and the poor scholarship of the legal academy. He reminded us of *who we are* and that is often a painful and awkward recollection.[60]

Derrida asserts that the 'essence of memory manoeuvres between Being and the law.'[61] This reference to 'Being' (which is possibly a salute to Heidegger) once again denotes and reiterates an appeal to an idea or principle of linguistic refinement that exists beyond the conventionalism of law, 'a law of being – a law prior to law'.[62] If deconstruction can be viewed 'as an engagement with a law of Being', then it is also possible to view deconstruction anthropologically since it 'returns to a "foundation", even if the dig never hits bottom.'[63] On this point, the task of 'interpretive memory' could be considered an expression of natural law theory precisely because it involves the critical identification of, and engagement with, the 'dis/junctures of law and "Being"' that haunt the foundations of jurisprudence.[64] By destabilizing the established and dominating metaphysico-anthropocentric axioms of the legal/natural law tradition, one begins to remember that there might be a less violent and, consequently, a more just way to articulate, decide, and practice the law. This restorative insight coheres with a central conclusion of this thesis. Current debates in natural law are spellbound by an attachment to the determinacy of the secular *mythos*, such that natural law has become a solipsistic and disremembering discourse of subjective relativism and, ironically, an 'ally of legal positivism and ethical relativism'.[65]

59. In fact, Derrida denounced the secular *mythos*, stating: 'I do not think that there is anything secular in our time.' Jacques Derrida, 'On Forgiveness', in *Questioning God*, ed. John D. Caputo, Mark Dooley and Michael Scanlon (Bloomington: Indiana University Press, 2001), 6.

60. Peter Goodrich, FlorianHoffman, Michel Rosenfeld, Cornelia Vismann, 'Introduction: A Philosophy of Legal Enigmas', in *Derrida and Legal Philosophy*, ed. Peter Goodrich et al. (New York: Palgrave Macmillan, 2008), 13. (IAITT).

61. Derrida, *Memoires for Paul de Man*, 11. Quoted in: Gerhard Richter, *Afterness* (New York: Columbia University Press, 2011), 190.

62. Gearey, 'Thinking, Poetics, Law', 204.

63. Ibid., 209.

64. Ibid., 201.

65. Westphal, 'Derrida as Natural Law Theorist', 224.

Section IV: An eschatological horizon

An 'ultimatology'

The previous two sections have sought to expound *how* and *why* the act or impulse of deconstruction can expose current debates in natural law to be equivalent to a 'work of mourning' – a work that is about what is lost and effectively irrecoverable. I have also sought to develop the claim that Derrida is a natural law theorist by explicating how the movement of deconstruction relies upon an 'idea of justice' that is 'beyond the law'. Of course, this is not a theory of natural law in its stereotypical form. Nevertheless, an 'authentic' custodian or interpreter of the tradition can also be the one who 'respects its logic to the point of turning, on occasions against those who pretend to be its depositaries.'[66] The purpose of this 'turning', however, is to give sight to 'the very thing that, in the heritage, has never before been seen'; to remember that which has been disremembered.[67]

Interestingly, these quintessentially Derridean sentiments resonate with an understanding of theology as itself 'an act of 'remembering', and remembering better', which John McDade says is at the heart of the theological project of *ressourcement*.[68] (One might qualify this by saying that 'remembering better' is a precursor to retrieval/*ressourcement*.) Perhaps, therefore, it is unsurprising that Derrida came to acknowledge (even if he was only speaking hypothetically) in *Force of Law* that deconstruction would be 'more at home' in theological discourse as well as in law schools.[69] Another pertinent reason for this is that Derrida defers to the 'critical memory of justice' as a 'mystical' horizon which transcends and lies beyond the articulable limits that certain foundational and regulative *mythoi* have long instantiated and enforced.[70]

It is important to reiterate that this disclosure took place in a moment of crisis for deconstruction. Similarly, particularly in the aftermath of Nazistic positivism, there was a shy reawakening amongst legal philosophes to the idea that, even when left 'unsaid', jurisprudence is always in search of an 'ultimatology': 'In every legal system, there must be an ultimate criterion for the legitimacy of law. Thus, in a real sense a god must exist in every legal system. The god will take the form of a spiritual entity or the state.'[71] The word 'ultimatology' was originally coined as a 'less

66. Jacques Derrida, 'Admiration of Nelson Mandela, or The Laws of Reflection', *Law and Literature*, vol. 26, no. 1 (2014), 12.

67. Ibid.

68. John McDade, '"*Ressourcement*" in Retrospect', in *Ressourcement*, ed. Gabriel Flynn and Paul D. Murray (Oxford: OUP, 2011), 508.

69. Derrida, *Force of Law*, 236.

70. C.f. Matthias Fritsch, *Promise of Memory* (New York: State University of New York Press, 2012), 107.

71. Charles Rice, 'The Problem of Unjust Laws', *Scholarly Works*, Paper 75 (1981), 278–9.

invidious term' for theology or, more exactly, an eschatology.[72] What it sought to articulate was how the turn to jurisprudence, specifically amongst lawyers, reflects an 'instinctive' epistemological aspiration to search for a philosophical 'ultimate' or 'event'.[73] For Derrida, the interrogative force of 'interpretive memory' uncovers this 'opening to the future' precisely by deconstructing the aporetic instability upon which the law is grounded and, thence, immanently ungrounded. Hence, the reason why Derrida speaks of the 'mystical foundation' of law is because the memory of this underlying event of injustice strengthens the desire for the 'advent of justice'.[74] In ostensibly robust 'theological' terms, he claims that 'justice always has an eschatological dimension', even, he says, 'for the non-believer'.[75]

By attending to the relationship between the dialogical-jurisprudential and the theological-eschatological, Derrida has, at least thematically, restored sight to the possibility of understanding the eschatological dimension as being intrinsic – rather than extrinsic – to the anthropology of (natural) law. But, although the deconstructive impulse might serve to reawaken the memory and refine the language of this theological-eschatological horizon, it will be the subject of this concluding section to elucidate why it ultimately poisons this memory and cannibalizes its theological-eschatological language by turning the discourse back into a 'windy mysticism' and another aporetic 'work of mourning'.

Another 'windy mysticism'?

With the deconstruction of the disremembered *Gewalt* that is at the structural heart of law, Derrida concludes that '[d]iscourse here meets its limits – in itself.'[76] This limit or 'ultimatology' is again referred to as 'mystical', which is said to be denotative of the suspension of language and the advent of silence. Derrida clarifies that this appeal to the language of the 'mystical' should also be interpreted in a 'rather Wittgensteinian' sense: 'There is here a silence walled up in the violent structure of the founding act.'[77] Yet, when we arrive at the linguistic threshold of that which lies mystically 'beyond the law', deconstruction confronts the ineluctable undecidability of that which is undeconstructible, which, at once, illuminates and yet conceals the promise of justice.[78] For Derrida, the 'walled up' silence signs the absence of narrative; the absence of a *mythos*; and, therefore, the

72. Edward F. Barrett, 'A Lawyer Looks at Jurisprudence', *The American Journal of Jurisprudence*, vol. 23 (1978), 8.

73. Ibid., 3.

74. Jacques Derrida, 'Faith and Knowledge', in *Jacques Derrida; Acts of Religion*, ed. Gil Anidjar (Abingdon: Routledge, 2010), 56.

75. Jacques Derrida and Maurizio Ferraris, *A Taste for the Secret*, trans. Giacomo Donis (Cambridge: CUP, 2001), 20.

76. Derrida, *Force of Law*, 242.

77. Ibid.

78. Ibid., 272–3.

purported absence of linguistic violence. Linguistic, because what the process of 'interpretive memory' addresses is how the performative force of law is invariably propelled by a 'legitimate fiction'.[79] In other words, although the ideality of law is esteemed as being supra-contextual and ahistorical, the actualization of the law is always tied to a particular *mythos* that accounts for its inaugurating force and interpretive violence. The issue is that, theoretically, 'law as such should never give rise to any story.'[80] In order to maintain 'its categorical authority, the law must be without history, genesis, or any possible derivation.'.[81] Thus, whilst jurisprudential myths desire to cross the threshold into the horizon of 'the law of the laws' in search of stability, the advent of justice forever remains a 'non-event'; 'an event of nothing'; a 'non-passage'; another 'windy mysticism'.[82] It turns out, therefore that the only possibility for deconstruction once it reaches this 'mystical' limit or 'ultimatology' is to remember to pray – 'Come'.[83]

The outworking of deconstruction

'To pray', in deconstructive terms, is 'to say "Yes, Yes" ' or 'come' to justice.[84] However, what exactly is 'justice' according to Derrida? Is it just another 'legitimate fiction' that is being equivocated, linguistically, with the idea of the 'mystical'? Derrida 'touches' upon such matters in his explication of the paradox we encounter when we arrive at the 'mystical' limit of the law, beyond which lies, aporetically, the fulfilment of our desire for justice:

> One 'touches' here without touching on this extraordinary paradox: the inaccessible transcendence of the law [*loi*], before which and prior to which 'man' stands fast, only appears infinitely transcendent and thus theological to the extent that, nearest to him, it depends only on him, on the performative act by which he institutes it: the law [*loi*] is transcendent, violent and nonviolent, because it depends only on who is before it (and so prior to it), on who produces it, founds it, authorizes it in an absolute performative whose presence always escapes him. The law [*loi*] is transcendent and theological, and so always to come, always promised, because it is immanent, finite, and thus already past.[85]

There is an obvious tension within this passage. On the one hand, the law is affirmed as 'infinitely transcendent and thus theological' but with the carefully

79. Ibid., 240.
80. Ibid., 183.
81. Ibid.
82. Ibid., 198.
83. Ibid., 270.
84. John Caputo, *The Prayers and Tears of Jacques Derrida* (Bloomington: Indiana University Press, 1997), 298.
85. Derrida, *Force of Law*, 270.

placed caveat that it 'only appears' as if this is the case because of the performative act by which the 'being' institutes it. Yet, on the other hand, the caveat is then immediately dispensed with and the law is affirmed that it *is* 'transcendent and theological'. A similar caveat is made with respect to what we might call the essence of justice and deconstruction. On the one hand, Derrida refers to 'justice in itself', 'deconstruction itself', and avows that 'deconstruction is justice'.[86] On the other hand, this intimation to a noumenal-like existence and to a potentially ontological kinship between justice and deconstruction is undermined by subsequent stipulations such as 'if such a thing [deconstruction] existed' or 'if such a thing [justice] exist.'[87]

It is little surprise that erstwhile supporters of Derrida expressed concern at his discourse on justice. For instance, writing in the early wake of the publication of the *Force of Law*, Caputo said that unless Derrida had 'lost his senses', he 'cannot mean that justice in itself, were there such a thing, is a kind of Platonic *agathon* … a subsistent absolute against which all sensible, particular actions and transactions should be measured.'[88] Nor does he accept that Derrida could have meant 'that the undeconstructible of justice represents an Idea in the Kantian sense', namely, as a 'regulative ideal which monitors the empirical search for justice.'[89] However, not every scholar agrees. On Douglas Litowitz's reading, 'Derrida's conception of justice is largely problematic because, ironically, it carries metaphysical and epistemic claims which Derrida has elsewhere rejected.'[90] *Contra* Caputo, Litowitz asserts that Derrida 'borrows quite heavily from Plato and Kant, and thereby retains much of the 'logocentric' metaphysics of presence which he has found objectionable in these and other thinkers.'[91] The implication being that Derrida's turn to a transcendent[-al] and 'mystical' understanding of justice contradicts his riposte of speculative metaphysics.

Despite the evident opposition of opinion, Caputo and Litowitz frame their respective evaluations of Derrida's account of justice according to the same fundamental either/or. Either his ostensible employment of Platonic/Kantian/Christian linguistic categories denotes a pensive metaphysical acquiescence to the idea of being-in itself or to the form of justice in itself and thus hints at a discontinuity in his thinking. Or, Derrida's espousal of an 'undeconstructible' justice is in fact a strategic *mythos* that denotes a hyperbolic, 'not true', reproduction of his long-held anti-metaphysical, yet ethico-political, discourse on respecting the singularity, the difference, of the other.

86. Ibid., 243.

87. Ibid.

88. John Caputo. 'Hyperbolic Justice', *Research in Phenomenology*, vol. 21 (1991), 11.

89. Ibid.

90. Douglas Litowitz, 'Derrida on Law and Justice', *Canadian Journal of Law and Jurisprudence*, vol. 8, no. 2 (July 1995), 325.

91. Ibid.

I would propose a third interpretation: that Derrida's invocation of a 'transcendent and theological' horizon in the *Force of Law* signifies neither a continuation nor a transition away from his deconstructive philosophy; rather, it represents the logical outworking of the unspoken *logos* of deconstruction itself. An explicative parallel might be drawn between how Derrida's experience of the aporia of justice inspires him to address and include the 'mystical' in the *Force of Law* and how Kant's experience of the aporia of radical evil inspires him to use and include the biblical scriptures in the *Religion*.[92] Derrida even asks, '[w]here is one to go after recognizing this ineluctable undecidability?'[93] For it seems 'there is no way out, and so there is no hope.'[94] This admission is itself instructive. What both Kant and Derrida are trying to salvage is a narrative of hope when their respective discourses arrive at their linguistic limits; at their respective mystical moments of *différance*. Kant constructs his narrative of hope on the boundary of mere reason in response to predominantly soteriological concerns, whereas Derrida admits that the refining force of deconstruction depends upon the promise of justice – a natural law theory – which, he believes, 'always has an eschatological dimension.'[95] He even reiterates this point again in (quasi–)transcendental or (quasi–)ontological terms revealing that he had come to appreciate the fact that '[j]ustice *is* eschatological and messianic.'[96] The force of deconstruction which is justice, which moves towards justice, and which anticipates justice is propelled by nothing less than that which is 'above reason', namely, 'God: another, a wholly other "mystical foundation of authority"' (even if Derrida's intermittent caveats cast down upon whether such categories even exist).[97] On this matter, Graham Ward's observation is correct. Derrida's philosophical economy 'seems to deny the theological categories of revelation and the eschaton, on the one hand, and yet require them, on the other.'[98]

Deferral is injustice

Something further might be said to clarify Ward's insight. The central issue involves exploring in what sense or in what way does Derrida actually 'require' theological language, particularly the language of 'messianism' and 'eschatology'. A revealing

92. A few years prior to writing the *Religion*, Kant stated that it is permissible to 'employ a sacred document as my map' in order to 'fill gaps' and speculate about the ineffable 'on the wings of imagination.' Immanuel Kant, 'Conjectures on the Beginning of Human History', in *Political Writings*, ed. H. S. Reiss, trans. H. B. Nisbet (Cambridge: CUP, 1970), 222.

93. Derrida, *Force of Law*, 285.

94. Ibid.

95. Derrida and Ferraris, *A Taste for the Secret*, 20.

96. Ibid.

97. Derrida, *Force of Law*, 285, 243.

98. Graham Ward, *Barth, Derrida and the Language of Theology* (Cambridge: CUP, 1995), 216.

and related consideration is to note that, although Derrida frequently refers to the 'idea of justice', or the 'call for justice', and speaks of justice as an 'experience', an 'event', and a 'possibility', it is not clear whether he ever attempts to define 'justice'. On one occasion he does refer to Levinas, whose definition of justice, he says, 'is very minimal but which I [Derrida] love' – namely, 'that justice is the relation to the other. That is all.'[99] But is this 'minimalism' sufficient? Is that really all that can be said?

Similarly, Derrida never specifies what ultimately determines or defines the 'mystical'. In fact, he says that it is the 'experience of aporia' at the linguistic threshold of the origins of law 'that is not unrelated to what we just called the *mystical*.'[100] This is an illuminating admission, which gives reason for caution. Although we might have been tempted to interpret his recourse to the 'mystical' as possessing genuinely theological meaning and import (a relation to the transcendent), it is actually a linguistic euphemism for a Derridean aporia – a 'non-path'.[101] From this perspective, Derrida acknowledges that 'justice would be the experience of what we are unable to experience. We shall soon encounter more than one aporia that we shall not be able to pass.'[102] It seems, then, that there is a linguistic legerdemain operating behind and within Derrida's deconstructive impulse. If justice is, 'ultimatologically', the aporetic experience of an unfulfillable desire, then is it really justice? What actually is being 'remembered' by the movement of deconstruction if all we ever encounter is one Derridean aporia (a 'non-path') after another? Is the 'mystical' just a euphemism for another 'fiction'? Furthermore, if justice entails an infinite deferral and is never realized, does it not become an even greater injustice? As the old legal adage goes: 'Justice delayed [or deferred] is justice denied.' All we are left with then is the memory of a series of historical injustices. Could this be, 'ultimatologically' speaking, what Derrida is wanting to point towards?

An 'ultra-Kantian'

Obviously, this has an important implication for understanding what Derrida actually meant by the intrinsically 'eschatological dimension' of deconstruction. In another text, Ward identifies 'a frank espousal of a messianic eschatology as an aspect of deconstruction itself' in Derrida's later work,[103] although this is 'a messianism without a messiah, without content, without religion.'[104] This notwithstanding, Derrida does raise the question: 'Can one conceive an atheological heritage of

99. Jacques Derrida, *Deconstruction in a Nutshell*, ed. John Caputo (New York: Fordham University Press, 1997), 17.

100. Derrida, *Force of Law*, 244. (IAITT).

101. Ibid., 244.

102. Ibid.

103. Graham Ward, 'On Time and Salvation', in *Facing the Other*, ed. Seán Hand (Abingdon: Routledge, 1996), 154.

104. Ibid.

the messianic?'[105] It is possible that Derrida is using the theological 'unsaid(s)' (possibly even drawing discretely upon his own Judaic heritage) strategically. This provides him with a vocabulary with which to defend deconstruction's relationship to justice and to articulate a necessary theory of natural law. But he always remains silent about what this vocabulary actually means, a silence that denotes a fundamental absence, and so perpetuates a 'windy mysticism.'

For instance, the eschatological promise that propels the deconstructive force of, and the desire for, justice is reduced to the interminably destabilizing experience of *différance*, which he describes as the 'unnameable movement of *difference-itself*.'[106] *Différance* thus becomes a close synonym for the undecidable character and non-event of eschatological justice. The programmatic exposition of this predicament is made manifest in Derrida's reading of the popular parable *Before the Law* by Franz Kafka. The boundary gate which separates us from the Law (and thus from justice) is identified by Derrida as the threshold of *différance*.[107] As Ward aptly put it, *différance* functions as 'a language condition.'[108] Hence, it is the doorkeeper's linguistic discourse of prohibition, rather than any physical barrier (for the gate is left wide open), which marks the limit and defers entry into direct relation with the Law.[109] But this linguistic deferral is interminable because the country man is never told 'no' only 'not yet', but indefinitely so.[110] This interminable experience of being in a state of expectation, and the aporetic condition of the Law appearing both simultaneously accessible and yet interminably inaccessible, grounds the immanent teleological desire for a justice to come. However, the eschatological dimension of the desire, by virtue of the fact that it is animated by a phenomenology of endless *différance*, is ultimately 'the stuff of mythic desire'.[111] That is to say, it is permanently frustrated and has no genuine anthropological grounding even if the outworking of deconstruction elusively points towards it. This implies that the horizon of justice and the desire for justice performs a sheerly regulative function – akin to a Kantian '*als* ob' – which allows one to reconcile the exercise of *phronesis* with a historical teleology of infinite progress.[112]

Ultimately, the experience of *différance* is the experience of a desire to grasp the impossible – a gate that we strive to traverse but will finally be shut. Consequently, the natural desire for justice that was thought to link deconstruction to the tradition of natural law is in fact spun from an ethico-political fiction of the '*als ob*',

105. Ibid.; Derrida, *Specters of Marx*, 211.

106. Jacques Derrida, *Of Grammatology*, trans. Gayatri Chakravorty Spivak (Baltimore, MD: John Hopkins University Press, 2016), 101.

107. Jacques Derrida, 'Before the Law', in Gifts of Literature, ed. Derek Attridge (London: Routledge, 1992), 203.

108. Ward, *Barth, Derrida and the Language of Theology*, 226 fn.20.

109. Derrida, 'Before the Law', 203.

110. Ibid., 204.

111. Caputo, 'Hyperbolic Justice', 6.

112. Ibid., 190.

but an ethico-practical fiction that violently cannibalizes the theological language it needs for this destabilizing 'fiction' to have any stabilizing ethico-political force or power.

Derrida, thus, described himself as an 'ultra-Kantian'. 'I am Kantian', he writes, 'I am more than Kantian.'[113] Although he never explained exactly what he meant by this, it seems at different junctures that Derrida goes ever so slightly 'beyond' the boundary he delineates in a more overt way than Kant ever did. This slight edging across the threshold into the theological-noumenal of the Law that is undeconstructible is all that is required. For instance, in Kafka's parable, we are simply told that the countryman would stoop down in order 'to peer through the gateway into the interior' of the beyond.[114] No indication is given in the text as to what the countryman saw or did not see. Yet, in Derrida's interpretation, he makes the epistemological-ontological claim that the interior spaces 'appear empty' – 'nothing really presents itself in this appearance'.[115] The eschatological emptiness of the Law and of justice is also revealed to be both immanent and yet ultimate. At the same time, the nothingness of the 'beyond', which *différance* governs and regulates, must remain a (literary) secret.

The outworking of the performative logic of deconstruction is also the unfolding of *différance*. Derrida once referred to this as a 'strategy without finality'.[116] Deconstruction is thereby secretly propelled by a deeply tragic *mythos* – that there will only ever be injustice. If Kafka's parable of the origins of the Law is the story of the prohibition of *différance*, and is, therefore, a prohibitive story, then the performance of deconstruction is the story of nothing, and is, therefore, what we might call a 'nothing story'.[117] Significantly, the remedic notion of 'interpretive memory' thus becomes an ongoing interpretation of this *mythos* of the unknown that Derrida claims to know, a *mythos* that is equally as foundational and as poisonous as the secular *mythos* because it points to nothing and so

113. Derrida, 'On Forgiveness', 66. This admission reflects a change from his position as stated in the *Force of Law* wherein he states that:

> One of the reasons I'm keeping such a distance from all these horizons – from the Kantian regulative idea or from the messianic advent, for example – is that they are, precisely, horizons. As its Greek name suggests, a horizon is both the opening and the limit that defines an infinite progress or a period of waiting. But justice, however unpresentable it may be, doesn't wait.' (Derrida, 'Force of Law', 255)

114. Kafka, 'Before the Law', 183.

115. Derrida, 'Before the Law', 203, 191. Hence his avowal the origin of *différance* can never be presented or penetrated for *différance* 'is not.' Jacques Derrida, '*Différance* (from the Margins of Philosophy, trans. Alan Bass)', in *The Theory of Difference*, ed. Douglas L. Donkel (Albany: State University of New York Press, 2001), 295.

116. Jacques Derrida, *Margins of Philosophy*, trans. Alan Boss (Chicago: University of Chicago Press, 1982), 7. Derrida, 'Force of Law', 56.

117. Derrida, 'Before the Law', 200.

remains trapped within the aporia of its own nothingness. For this reason, the experience of *anamnesis* always 'breaks off … too soon' and, like justice, must always remain something 'to come.'[118] Paradoxically, the remedic subversiveness of deconstruction is subverted by the poison of its own subversive narratological secret. For this reason, Derridean deferral is another 'work of mourning'.

It is important to add that Derrida insinuated that he was aware of the problematics within his 'strategy without finality'. When asked whether his references to a transcendental horizon concealed an interpretive decision about the boundary between the unknown and the known (which I would extend to his understanding of the way teleology relates to eschatology), he confessed that he was 'struggling with things which remain problematic and unclear' and that, essentially, he had 'no response.'[119] 'Having worked … within the heritage' and 'of transforming the heritage', he admitted that he had begun to enter into the process of 'understanding a little more' – 'and going, I do not know where. I really do not know where.'[120]

Section V: Conclusion

Going to Christ

Like Derrida, current debates in natural law manifest a destabilizing uncertainty as to where to go next. Nonetheless, a contribution of this work has been to discern where the discourse should not go – or, more precisely, where it should not persist. Through the deconstructive analysis of the 'three voices', I explained why the natural law tradition will fragment and, on this count, fail if it is repeatedly constructed in reaction to the secular *mythos*. This became particularly apparent in Chapter 5, wherein I discussed how this reactionism ends in a series of aporia: alethiological, anthropological, and genealogical. Detaching natural law from the secular *mythos* in both academic and political debates will pose challenges, especially given that many natural law theorists continue to ground the dialogical value of natural law almost exclusively upon its 'secular' character. However, I have also shown that if we are prepared to interrogate the secular *mythos* and expose its unwieldy and contingent character, then we are also able to begin to escape from its solipsistic and disremembering power; a power that has turned the discourse in on itself, '*incurvatus in se*', by suppressing the theological 'unsaid(s)'.

As an illustration, I have endeavoured to demonstrate how a 'dialogue with Derrida' (a supposed 'enemy' of the natural law) can possibly contribute towards the restoration of natural law as a 'work of memory'. Building upon Westphal's provocative description of Derrida as a 'natural law theorist', I have intimated how Derrida's anthropological synergy between the desire for justice with the

118. Derrida, *The Work of Mourning*, 67.
119. Derrida, 'On Forgiveness', 66.
120. Ibid.

movement of 'interpretive memory' can also help to recover and revivify the value of the theological 'unsaid(s)'. For instance, I noted how Derrida's defence of deconstruction outworks itself into the explicit appropriation of speculative and theological categories, culminating in his avowal that 'deconstruction is justice' and in his admission that 'justice always has an eschatological dimension'. The principal value of deconstruction is precisely that it allows such robustly theological insights to emerge.

Unfortunately, and 'ultimatologically', Derrida's theory of natural law is as anthropocentric as the secular *mythos* he, ostensibly, rejects. For in the same way that the retrieval of the tradition by the 'three voices' points towards the subjective authority of an 'inner audience', Derrida's infinite deferral of justice points towards the subjective authority of a narratological fiction, a 'nothing story' guised by the assimilation and cannibalization of the language of the theological 'unsaid(s)'. For this reason, a Derridean deferral is just another manifestation of a 'secular solipsism'. As Heidegger said: 'As we are drawing towards what withdraws, we ourselves are pointers pointing towards it … [H]e points towards what withdraws. *As* he is pointing that way, man *is* the point.'[121] Either way, a 'secular'-inspired retrieval or a Derridean-inspired deferral are both 'works of mourning' since both trajectories make the theological *content* 'unsaid'.

What this realization points towards and affirms is that the contemporary reconstruction of natural law requires an anthropology that unifies (human) nature with a *genuinely* theological, yet immanent, eschatology. At the very least, it points to the fact that the discourse can no longer leave the eschatological dimension 'unsaid'. It has to be addressed. But as Steven T. Ostovich explains: 'Eschatology depends on memory and hope for understanding; memory and hope in turn demand a communal context.'[122] To some extent, this sentence draws together several of the creative threads that have been touched upon in this chapter. These threads are not without a Thomistic foundation. In his *Commentary on the Letter of Saint Paul to the Romans*, Aquinas equates those 'who show' the natural law as if they were 'a law to themselves' with an external law that is customarily promulgated 'in writing on account of memory's weakness.'[123] For the natural law is also written, but written, 'not *with ink, but* first and chiefly *with the Spirit of the living God* (2 Cor 3:3).'[124] At least implicitly, Aquinas would seem to be implying that the natural law is inscribed upon the heart because, 'on account of memory's weakness', we can desire falsely, love falsely, and act evilly.[125] Eugene Rogers also draws a similar conclusion. In his pioneering research on reading Aquinas's

121. Heidegger, *What Is Called Thinking*, 9–10. Quoted in: Gearey, 'Thinking, Poetics, Law', 205. (IAITT).

122. Steven Ostovich, 'Pauline Eschatology', in *Time: Limits and Constraints*, ed. Jo Alyson Parker, Paul A. Harris, Christian Steineck (Leiden: Brill, 2010), 325.

123. Aquinas, 'Commentary on the Letter of Saint Paul to the Romans', 75. (IAITT).

124. Ibid.

125. Ibid., 76.

treatment of natural law in the *Summa Theologiae* through his *Commentary on Romans*, Rogers asserts that, even though 'Aquinas believes there is such a thing as natural law', nevertheless, 'he is completely comfortable admitting that we don't, in fact, know what it is.'[126] At least, we don't know what it is (or, cannot *remember* what it is) by 'pure reason' or 'reason alone'.

Confronting this epistemological predicament returns us to the anthropological horizon upon which this chapter – and, in a certain sense, this book – commenced with. Socrates' desire to know the reality of the law and Ratzinger's desire to recover the 'original memory' of the natural law are both, 'ultimatologically', a desire to uncover the mysterious origin of the natural desire for justice, a desire that originates in us, as Aquinas says, '*by nature*'.[127] When '*by nature*' is constructed in reaction to the secular *mythos* or when deconstructed as just a 'mystical' foundation (a 'windy mysticism'), it tends to be reified into an epistemological-ontological threshold. The interesting thing is that, within current debates in natural law, this threshold has been strategically instrumentalized in order to delineate and instantiate an autonomy from the theological. In the case of Milbank, he inverts the threshold in order to delineate and instantiate a point of meta-narratological 'estrangement'. On this matter, the 'three voices' harmonize discretely with the poisonous inflection that I identified in the pharmakonic voice of Derrida. For in the same way that the secular *mythos* bequeaths an – illegitimate and erroneous – point of rational, narratological, or linguistic stability (upon or against which the autonomy of the discourse is then secured), Derridean deconstruction also arrives at a linguistic limit that, as Michael Alternburger puts it, 'indicates the illusion of a stability structurally powerful enough to ground transcendent systems of meaning.'[128]

Aquinas, himself, warned against this inclination to establish an anthropocentric point of stability or limit for discerning the natural law. 'For it seems', he said, 'to favour the Pelagians, who taught that man could [discern and] observe all the precepts of the law by his own natural power.'[129] In other words, the power of natural reason tends to be overaccentuated or gnosticized in order to bypass the anthropological predicament I described above. The fact is, however, that we never truly bypass this predicament. Rather, we just gradually disremember it by suppressing, instrumentalizing, or evacuating the theological and leaving it 'unsaid'. Paradoxically, it is the very surfacing of the theological 'unsaid(s)' which discloses the apophatic and soteriological character of natural law. In what is a seldom discussed passage in his *Commentary on Romans*, Aquinas states explicitly that '*by nature*' is always to be understood theocentrically as 'nature reformed

126. Rogers, *Aquinas and the Supreme Court*, 26.

127. Aquinas, 'Commentary on the Letter of Saint Paul to the Romans', 75. (IAITT).

128. Michael Altenburger, 'Derrida, Politics, and the Little Way', 2018, https://churchlifejournal.nd.edu/articles/ derrida-politics-and-the-little-way/. Accessed on 1 March 2019.

129. Aquinas, 'Commentary on the Letter of Saint Paul to the Romans', 75.

by grace' – 'Christ's grace.'[130] Theologically speaking, thence, the identification of reason's 'limit' is actually the 'condition for constructive creativity because it is a shared limit of embodied human existence.'[131] Soteriologically, it is an affirmation that we cannot grasp the natural law by our own efforts of reason, law, or any other agency for that matter. As I have argued, it will always prove to be unrealizable and unattainable, disintegrating into the disremembering irrationalities of the secular *mythoi* or the anti-foundationalism of a Derridean deferral, all of which are disguised 'mourning's'.

Natural law begins when we are able to acknowledge (apophatically) that, although we desire to know the law and to know justice, we do not (yet) know what they are. This is what it means to speak of an authentic 'rhetoric of the self'. Yet, this mysterious desire to know the law and to know justice is, as I have said, what inaugurates the dialogical character of the discourse. In this context, dialogue is not about 'translating', or 'out-narrating', or 'fictionalising'. Instead, dialogue – the search – is itself a form of participation in God, which, ultimately, is a 'work of memory' and a work of refinement.[132] Aquinas avowed that 'we do such works in virtue of an infused habit of justice', a grace that is restored through the event of 'divine justice' the 'cause of justice' – Christ's cross.[133]

Although the ontological desire for justice is a law written upon the heart (*physis*), it requires the *ressourcement* of the epistemological *nomos* of theological language (which, because of its self-subverting character, is itself intrinsically centripetal and dialogical in character) to be recalled effectively, efficaciously, and immanently. One could say that the 'original memory' and 'ontological tendency' of natural law is where the purported hierarchization of speech over writing or writing over speech is overcome. Furthermore, within this context, discoursal silence connotes neither an aporetic absence nor a nihilistic emptiness but an irreducible fullness that points to that which lies beyond speech precisely because it cannot be contained within speech. Unlike Derrida, mysticism for theology is not the same as unknowability. It is the capacity for inexhaustible meaning. This is why I suggested that the tradition of natural law is 'eschatologically underdetermined', which is congruent with the notion that what makes a 'tradition' a 'tradition' is its revelatory and unconcealing nature.[134] Therefore, could it be that one way in which grace manifests itself in natural law is by keeping the discourse open? The Church's mission, thence, becomes part of that discourse by continually raising the possibility that the discourse is not complete in itself.

130. Ibid.

131. Altenburger, 'Derrida, Politics, and the Little Way'.

132. I have tried to demonstrate in this chapter how the recovery of the 'unsaid' can take place through a dialogical encounter between erstwhile opponents. Just as in the *Minos*.

133. Aquinas, 'Commentary on the Letter of Saint Paul to the Romans', 74.

134. I'm drawing here upon Rowan William's insight quoted above.

To speak of natural law, anthropologically, as a theory of dialogical *anamnesis*, is to contend that language – the theological 'unsaid(s)' – should be put at the service of memory for memory refines the *eros* of our desire(s). Similarly, the 'divine madness' that Plato spoke of being at work in *anamnesis* is that it 'reveals to us what it means to be functionally human.'[135] This is not a gnosticism. It is not that the natural law is some 'great secret' or 'mysterious method'. It is, by nature, 'orientated to understanding what is – "what is" being something other than "what is thought to be"'.[136] Yet, this *anamnesis* takes place within and depends upon a 'communal context'. Human relationships are not utopian myths. They are an intrinsic part of our nature and what it means to be fully human. The point of natural law is that it allows justice to surface in the ordinary relationships of people (outside of individuated interpretations of the law), without which there can be no society. Justice surfaces here because it is precisely in and through dialogue that one can begin to make sense of one's own deep need and desire for justice. This is why the dialogue is important. It is, one might say, the critical process by which we are constructing what it means to be human, which, again, creates a creative space for the intellectual and cultural plurality of the discourse. But as humanity enters into a deeper dialogical reflection about what the just life is, the discourse must inevitably retrieve and remember the *imago Dei*.

A distinctive aspect of Judaeo-Christian theological discourse is the understanding that God's ordering of creation is itself soteriological. It is ordered to God who is the Truth and our *Summum Bonum*. When we allow God – the theological 'unsaid(s)' – to come into the dialogue and hence into memory, not as a threat or as some coercive sovereignty but as an abiding soteriological promise, the immanence of the supernatural order ensures us that our hope in, and our search for, justice is not in vain. Otherwise, it stands, 'ultimatologically', under the banner of futility. This soteriological conviction situates the 'communal context' of natural law – socially, ecologically, and theologically. Only in this context can the full agency of the human person, which is at the core of the natural law, be appreciated and, therefore, the full significance of natural law itself be disclosed.[137] This immanent eschatological hope is what the *telos* inscribed upon our nature points us towards. It is the realization of that 'original memory'; that 'ontological tendency'; that natural desire for justice! The eschatological dimension of natural law thus becomes both the retrieval – the *anamnesis* – of this 'unsaid' and the dialogical recognition of the immanent transcendality in our relationships that structure them towards a future hope – eschatological justice. 'For the object of hope is a future good, arduous but not impossible to obtain.'[138]

135. Charles Griswold, *Self-Knowledge in Plato's Phaedrus* (New Haven, CT: Yale University Press, 1986), 113.

136. Ibid.

137. In a future 'reconstructive' work, I intend to elaborate further on the use of memory and mourning as ethical-phenomenological categories and not just epistemological categories.

138. ST II-II q. 17 a.7.

BIBLIOGRAPHY

John Finnis

Finnis, John. 'Aquinas Lecture 1985: Practical Reasoning, Human Goods and the End of Man'. *New Blackfriars*, Vol. 66, No. 784 (October 1985): 438–51.

Finnis, John. *Aquinas. Moral, Political, and Legal Theory*. Oxford: Oxford University Press, 2004.

Finnis, John. 'Equality and Difference'. *The American Journal of Jurisprudence*, Vol. 56, No. 1 (2011): 17–44.

Finnis, John. *Fundamentals of Ethics*. Oxford: Clarendon Press, 1983.

Finnis, John. 'Grounding Human Rights in Natural Law'. *The American Journal of Jurisprudence*, Vol. 60, No. 2 (2015): 199–225.

Finnis, John. 'Grounds of Law and Legal Theory: A Response'. *Legal Theory*, Vol. 13 (2007): 315–44.

Finnis, John. 'H. L. A. Hart: A Twentieth-Century Oxford Political Philosopher'. *The American Journal of Jurisprudence*, Vol. 54 (2009): 161–85.

Finnis, John. *Human Rights & Common Good, Collected Essays Volume III*. Oxford: Oxford University Press, 2011.

Finnis, John. *Moral Absolutes*. Washington, DC: Catholic University of America, 1991.

Finnis, John. 'Natural Law and Legal Reasoning'. *Cleveland State Law Review*, Vol. 38, No. 1 (1990): 1–13.

Finnis, John. *Natural Law and Natural Rights. Second Edition*. Oxford: Oxford University Press, 2011.

Finnis, John. 'Natural Law and the Ethics of Discourse'. *Ratio Juris*, Vol. 12, No. 4 (December 1999): 53–73.

Finnis, John. 'Natural Law Theory: Its Past and Its Present'. *The American Journal of Jurisprudence*, Vol. 57 (2012): 81–101.

Finnis, John. 'On Hart's Way: Law as Reason and as Fact'. *The American Journal of Jurisprudence*, Vol. 52, No. 1 (2007): 25–53.

Finnis, John. 'On the Practical Meaning of Secularism'. *Notre Dame Law Review*, Vol. 73, No. 3 (1998): 491–516.

Finnis, John. *Philosophy of Law: Collected Essays Volume IV*. Oxford: Oxford University Press, 2011.

Finnis, John. *Reason in Action. Collected Essays Volume I*. Oxford: Oxford University Press, 2011.

Finnis, John. 'Reflections and Responses'. In *Reason, Morality, and Law*. Edited by John Keown and Robert P. George. Oxford: Oxford University Press, 2013: 459–584.

Finnis, John. *Religion and Public Reason. Collected Essays Volume V*. Oxford: Oxford University Press, 2011.

Finnis, John. 'Religion in Politics'. *On Dit*, Vol. 28, No. 4 (14 April 1960): 6.

Finnis, John. 'The "Natural Law Tradition"'. *Journal of Legal Education*, Vol. 36, No. 492 (1986): 492–5.

Finnis, John. 'Unjust Laws in a Democratic Society: Philosophical and Theological Reflections'. *Notre Dame Law Review*, Vol. 71, No. 4 (1996): 595–604.

Finnis, John. 'What Is the Philosophy of Law'. *The American Journal of Jurisprudence*, Vol. 59, No. 2 (2014): 133–42.

Finnis, John and Grisez, Germain. 'The Basic Principles of Natural Law: A Reply to Ralph McInerny'. *The American Journal of Jurisprudence*, Vol. 26, No. 1 (1981): 21–31.

Finnis, John, Grisez, Germain, and Boyle, Joseph. 'Direct and Indirect: A Reply to Critics of Our Action Theory'. *The Thomist*, Vol. 65 (2001): 1–44.

Finnis, John, Grisez, Germain, and Boyle, Joseph. *Nuclear Deterrence, Morality and Realism*. New York: Clarendon Press, 1987.

Finnis, John, Grisez, Germain, and Boyle, Joseph. 'Practical Principles, Moral Truth and Ultimate Ends'. *The American Journal of Jurisprudence*, Vol. 32, No. 32 (1987): 99–151.

Finnis, John, Boyle, Joseph, and Grisez, Germain. 'A Sounder Theory of Morality'. In *The Historical Development of Fundamental Moral Theology in the United States*. Edited by Charles E. Curran and Richard A. McCormick. New York: Paulist Press, 1999: 200–18.

John Milbank

Milbank, John. 'A Closer Walk on the Wild Sides'. In *Varieties of Secularism: In A Secular Age*. Edited by Michael Warner, Jonathan Vanantwerpen, Craig Calhoun. Cambridge, MA: Harvard University Press, 2010: 54–82.

Milbank, John. 'A Conversation: José Casanova, Michael Jon Kessler, John Milbank, and Mark Lilla'. In *Political Theology for a Plural Age*. Edited by Michael Jon Kessler. Oxford: Oxford University Press, 2013: 13–40.

Milbank, John. 'A Critique of the Theology of Right'. In *The Word Made Strange*. New York: Blackwell, 1997: 161–96.

Milbank, John. 'Against Human Rights: Liberty in the Western Tradition'. *Oxford Journal of Law and Religion*, Vol. 1, No. 1 (2012): 203–34.

Milbank, John. 'Against Human Rights: Liberty in the Western Tradition'. In *The Meaning of Rights*. Edited by Costas Douzinas and Conor Gearty. Cambridge: Cambridge University Press, 2014: 39–70.[1]

Milbank, John. *Being Reconciled: Ontology & Pardon*. London: Routledge, 2003.

Milbank, John. *Beyond Secular Order: The Representation of Being and the Representation of the People*. Chichester: Wiley Blackwell, 2013.

Milbank, John. 'Can Morality Be Christian?' *Society for the Study of Christian Ethics*, Vol. 8, No. 1 (April 1995): 45–59.

Milbank, John. 'Culture and Justice'. *Theory, Culture & Society*, Vol. 27, No. 6 (2010): 107–24.

Milbank, John. 'Intensities'. *Modern Theology*, Vol. 15, No. 4 (October 1999): 445–97.

Milbank, John. 'Knowledge: The Theological Critique of Philosophy in Hamann and Jacobi'. In *Radical Orthodoxy: A New Theology*. Edited by John Milbank, Catherine Pickstock and Graham Ward. London: Routledge, 1999: 21–37.

Milbank, John. 'Paul Against Biopolitics'. *Theory, Culture & Society*, Vol. 25, Nos. 7–8 (2008): 15–172.

1. Both 2012/2014 versions were consulted as there were some changes/additions made to the 2014 version.

Milbank, John. 'Materialism and Transcendence'. In *Theology and the Political: The New Debate*. Edited by Creston Davis, John Milbank and Slavoj Zizek. Durham, NC: Duke University Press, 2005: 153–82.
Milbank, John. 'Postmodern Critical Augustinianism: A Short Summa in Forty-Two Responses to Unasked Questions'. In *The Radical Orthodoxy Reader*. Edited by John Milbank and Simon Oliver: London: Routledge, 2009: 49–61.
Milbank, John. 'Radical Orthodoxy's First Decade'. In *The Radical Orthodoxy Reader*. Edited by John Milbank and Simon Oliver. London: Routledge, 2009: 367–404.
Milbank, John. 'Sophiology and Theurgy: The New Theological Horizon'. In *Encounter Between Eastern Orthodoxy and Radical Orthodoxy*. Edited by Christoph Schneider and Adrian Pabst. Farnham: Ashgate, 2009: 45–85.
Milbank, John. 'Theology and Philosophy in Vico's Account of Human Creativity'. *History of European Ideas*, Vol. 2, No. 4 (1981): 299–314.
Milbank, John. *Theology & Social Theory: Beyond Secular Reason*. Malden, MA: Blackwell, 2006.
Milbank, John. 'The Double Glory, or Paradox Versus Dialectics: On Not Quite Agreeing with Slavoz Žižek'. In *The Monstrosity of Christ: Paradox or Dialectic?* Edited by Creston Davis Cambridge, MA: MIT Press, 2009: 110–233.
Milbank, John. 'The End of Dialogue'. In *Christian Uniqueness Reconsidered. The Myth of a Pluralistic Theology of Religions*. Edited by Gavin D' Costa. New York: Orbis Books, 1990: 393–426.
Milbank, John. 'The Franciscan Conundrum'. *Communio*, 42 (Fall 2015): 465–92.
Milbank, John. *The Future of Love: Essays in Political Theology*. Eugene, OR: Cascade Books, 2009.
Milbank, John. 'The Last of the Last: Theology, Authority and Democracy'. *Revista Portuguesa de Filosofia*, T. 58, Fasc. 2, Politica & Sociedade: Ensaios Filosoficos (April–June, 2002): 271–98.
Milbank, John. 'The Programme of Radical Orthodoxy'. In *Radical Orthodoxy? – A Catholic Enquiry*. Edited by Laurence P. Hemming. Abingdon: Routledge, 2000: 33–45.
Milbank, John. *The Religious Dimension in the Thought of Giambattista Vico (1668–1774). Part 1: The Early Metaphysics*. New York: Edwin Mellen Press, 1991.
Milbank, John. *The Religious Dimension in the Thought of Giambattista Vico (1668–1774). Part 2: Language, Law and History*. New York: Edwin Mellen Press, 1992.
Milbank, John. 'The Sublime in Kierkegaard'. In *Post Secular Philosophy. Between Philosophy and Theology*. Edited by Philip Blond. London: Routledge, 1998, 131–56.
Milbank, John. *The Suspended Middle: Henri de Lubac and the Renewed Split in Modern Catholic Theology. (Second Edition)*. Grand Rapids, MI: W. B. Eerdmans, 2005.
Milbank, John. 'The Thomistic Telescope: Truth and Identity'. *American Catholic Philosophical Quarterly*, Vol. 80, No. 2 (2006): 193–216.
Milbank, John. 'Theology Without Substance: Christianity, Signs, Origins'. *Journal of Literature & Theology*, Vol. 2, No. 1 (March 1988): 1–17.
Milbank, John. *The Word Made Strange: Theology, Language, Culture*. New York: Blackwell, 1997.
Milbank, John. 'Truth and Vision'. In *The Radical Orthodoxy Reader*. Edited by John Milbank and Simon Oliver. London: Routledge, 2009: 69–115.
Milbank, John and Pabst, Adrian. 'The Meta-Crisis of Secular Capitalism'. *International Review of Economics*, Vol. 62, No. 3 (2015): 197–212.

Milbank, John and Pabst, Adrian. *The Politics of Virtue*. London: Rowan & Littlefield, 2016.
Milbank, John and Pickstock, Catherine. *Truth in Aquinas*. London: Routledge Press 2001.
Milbank, John, Pickstock, Catherine and Ward, Graham. 'Introduction. Suspending the Material: The Turn of Radical Orthodoxy'. In *Radical Orthodoxy*. Edited by John Milbank, Catherine Pickstock and Graham Ward. Abingdon: Routledge, 1999: 1–20.
Milbank, John and Oliver, Simon 'Radical Orthodoxy: A Conversation'. In *The Radical Orthodoxy Reader*. Edited by John Milbank and Simon Oliver. London: Routledge, 2009: 28–48.

Jean Porter

Porter, Jean. 'A Consideration of John Finnis' *Aquinas*'. *The Journal of Religion*, Vol. 80, No. 3 (July 2000): 476–84.
Porter, Jean. 'A Response to Martin Rhonheimer'. *Studies in Christian Ethics*, Vol. 19, No. 3 (2006): 379–95.
Porter, Jean. 'At the Limits of Liberalism: Thomas Aquinas and the Prospects for a Catholic Feminism'. In *Thomas Aquinas*. Edited by John Inglis. Aldershot: Ashgate, 2006: 389–404.
Porter, Jean. 'A Tradition of Civility: The Natural Law as a Tradition of Moral Inquiry.' *Scottish Journal of Theology*, Vol. 56, No. 1 (2003): 27–48.
Porter, Jean. 'Basic Goods and the Human Good in Recent Catholic Moral Theology'. *The Thomist*, Vol. 57, No. 1 (January 1993): 27–49.
Porter, Jean. 'Chastity as a Virtue.' *Scottish Journal of Theology*, Vol. 58, No. 3 (2005): 285–301.
Porter, Jean. 'Christian Ethics and the Concept of Morality: A Historical Inquiry'. *Journal of the Society of Christian Ethics*, Vol. 26, No. 2 (September 2006): 3–21.
Porter, Jean. 'Comments on Nicholas Wolterstorff's Justice: *Rights and Wrongs*'. *Studies in Christian Ethics*, Vol. 23, No. 2 (2010): 192–6.
Porter, Jean. 'Contested Categories: Reason, Nature, and the Natural Order in Medieval Accounts of the Natural Law'. *The Journal of Religious Ethics*, Vol. 24, No. 2 (October 1996): 207–32.
Porter, Jean. 'Contraceptive Use and the Authority of the Church. A Case Study on Natural Law and Moral Discernment'. In *Just and True Love: Feminism at the Frontiers of Theological Ethics: Essays in Honour of Margaret Farley*. Edited by Maura A. Ryan and Brian F. Linnane, S.J. Notre Dame, IN: University of Notre Dame Press, 2008: 369–405.
Porter, Jean. 'Desire for God: Ground of the Moral Life in Aquinas'. *Theological Studies*, Vol. 47 (1986): 48–68.
Porter, Jean. '"Direct" and "Indirect" in Grisez's Moral Theory'. *Theological Studies*, Vol. 57 (1996): 611–32.
Porter, Jean. 'Disposition of the Will.' *Philosophia*, Vol. 41 (2013): 289–300.
Porter, Jean. 'Divine Commands, Natural Law, and the Authority of God'. *Journal of the Society of Christian Ethics*, Vol. 34, No. 1 (2013): 3–20.
Porter, Jean. 'Does the Natural Law Provide a Universally Valid Morality?' In *Intractable Disputes about the Natural Law*. Edited by Lawrence S. Cunningham. Notre Dame, IN: Notre Dame University Press, 2009: 53–95.

Porter, Jean. 'From Natural Law to Human Rights: Or, Why Rights Talk Matters'. *Journal of Law and Religion*, Vol. 14, No. 1 (1999–2000): 446–60.

Porter, Jean. 'In the Wake of a Doctrine: A Reassessment of the Doctrine of the Natural Law as Developed in *We Hold These Truths*'. In *John Courtney Murray & the Growth of Tradition*. Edited by J. Leon Hooper and Todd David Whitmore. Kansas City: Sheed & Ward, 1996: 24–40.

Porter, Jean. *Justice as Virtue*. Grand Rapids, MI: W. B. Eerdmans, 2016.

Porter, Jean. 'Justice, Equality, and Natural Rights Claims: A Reconsideration of Aquinas's Conception of Right'. *Journal of Law and Religion*, Vol. 30, No. 3 (October 2015): 446–59.

Porter, Jean. 'Mere History: The Place of Historical Studies in Theological Ethics'. *The Journal of Religious Ethics*, Vol. 25, No. 3, 25th Anniversary Supplement (1997): 103–26.

Porter, Jean. *Ministers of the Law. A Natural Law Theory of Legal Authority*. Grand Rapids, MI: W. B. Eerdmans, 2010.

Porter, Jean. 'Moral Ideals and Human Nature'. In *Universalism VS. Relativism*. Edited by Don Browning. Plymouth: Rowman & Littlefield, 2006: 59–78.

Porter, Jean. 'Moral Rules and Moral Actions: A Comparison of Aquinas and Modern Moral Theology'. *The Journal of Religious Ethics*, Vol. 17, No. 1 (April 1989): 123–49.

Porter, Jean. *Natural & Divine Law. Reclaiming the Tradition for Christian Ethics*. Grand Rapids, MI: W. B. Eerdmans, 1999.

Porter, Jean. 'Natural Law, Legal Authority, and the Independence of Law: New Prospects for a Jurisprudence of the Natural Law'. In *Searching for a Universal Ethic. Multidisciplinary, Ecumenical, and Interfaith Responses to the Catholic Natural Law Tradition*. Edited by John Berkman and William C. Mattison III. Grand Rapids, MI: W.B. Eerdmans, 2014: 146–55.

Porter, Jean. *Nature as Reason. A Thomistic Theory of Natural Law*. Grand Rapids, MI: W. B. Eerdmans, 2005.

Porter, Jean. 'Openness and Constraint: Moral Reflection as Tradition-Guided Inquiry in Alasdair MacIntyre's Recent Works.' *The Journal of Religion*, Vol. 73, No. 4 (October 1993): 514–36.

Porter, Jean. 'Reason, Nature and the End of Human Life: A Consideration of John Finnis's Aquinas'. *The Journal of Religion*, Vol. 80, No. 3 (July 2000): 476–84.

Porter, Jean. 'Review: Three Rival Versions of Moral Enquiry: Encyclopaedia, Genealogy, and Tradition by Alasdair MacIntyre'. *The Journal of Religion*, Vol. 72, No. 1 (January 1992): 133–5.

Porter, Jean. 'The Natural Law and the Normative Significance of Nature'. *Studies in Christian Ethics*, Vol. 26, No. 2 (2013): 166–73.

Porter, Jean. 'The Natural Law and Innovative Forms of Marriage: A Reconsideration'. *Journal of the Society of Christian Ethics*, Vol. 30, No. 2 (Fall/Winter 2010): 79–97.

Porter, Jean. *The Recovery of Virtue. The Relevance of Aquinas for Christian Ethics*. London: SPCK, 1994.

Porter, Jean. 'The Search for a Global Ethic'. *Theological Studies*, Vol. 62 (2001): 105–21.

Porter, Jean. 'The Subversion of Virtue: Acquired and Infused Virtues in the "Summa Theologiae"'. *The Annual of the Society of Christian Ethics*, Vol. 12 (1992): 19–41.

Porter, Jean. 'The Unity of the Virtues and the Ambiguity of Goodness: A Reappraisal of Aquinas's Theory of the Virtues'. *Journal of Religious Ethics*, Vol. 21, No. 1 (Spring 1993): 13–163.

Porter, Jean. 'Tradition in the Recent Work of Alasdair MacIntyre'. In *Alasdair MacIntyre*. Edited by Mark C. Murphy. Cambridge: Cambridge University Press, 2003: 38–69.
Porter, Jean. 'Virtue'. In *The Oxford Handbook of Theological Ethics*. Oxford: Oxford University Press, 2007: 202–19.

Cristina Traina[2]

Trains, Cristina. '(Book Reviews) Biggar, Nigel. *Behaving in Public: How to do Christian Ethics*. Grand Rapids, Michigan: Wm. B. Eerdmans, 2011'. *The Journal of Religion*, Vol. 93, No. 1 (January 2013): 107–8.
Trains, Cristina. *Feminist Ethics and Natural Law*. Washington, DC: Georgetown University Press, 1999.
Trains, Cristina. 'Maternal Experience and the Boundaries of Christian Sexual Ethics'. *Signs*, Vol. 25, No. 2 (Winter 2000): 369–405.
Trains, Cristina. 'Patriarchal Religion, Sexuality, and Gender: A Critique of New Natural Law by Nicholas Bamforth, David A. J. Richards (Book Review)'. *Journal of Law and Religion*, Vol. 25, No. 1 (2009–10): 311–16.
Trains, Cristina. 'Oh, Susanna: The New Absolutism and Natural Law'. *Journal of the American Academy of Religion*, Vol. 65, No. 2 (Summer 1997): 371–401.
Trains, Cristina. 'The Johnson Case and the Practice of Theology: An Interim Report'. *Horizons*, Vol. 38, No. 2 (2011): 286–92.

Other Sources

Adair-Toteff, Christopher. 'Ernst Troeltsch and the Philosophical History of Natural Law'. *British Journal for the History of Philosophy*, Vol. 13, No. 4 (2005): 733–44.
Adams, Nicholas. *Habermas and Theology*. Cambridge: Cambridge University Press, 2006.
Agamben, Giorgio. *The Kingdom and the Glory. For A Theological Genealogy of Economy and Government*. Translated by Lorenzo Chiesa, Matteo Mandarini. Stanford, CA: Stanford University Press, 2011.
Algra, Keimpe. 'Stoic Theology'. In *The Cambridge Companion to the Stoics*. Edited by Brad Inwood. Cambridge: Cambridge University Press, 2003: 153–78.
Anderson, Owen. *The Natural Moral Law*. Cambridge: Cambridge University Press, 2012.
Aquinas, Thomas. *Commentary on the Letter to the Romans*. Edited by J. Mortensen and E. Alarcón. Translated by F. R. Larcher. Lander: The Aquinas Institute, 2012.
Aquinas, Thomas. *De Malo*. Translated by Jean T. Oesterle. Notre Dame, IN: Notre Dame University Press, 1995.
Aquinas, Thomas. *Faith, Reason and Theology. Questions I-IV of his Commentary on the De Trinitate of* Boethius. Translated by Armand Mauer. Ontario: Pontifical Institute of Mediaeval Studies, 1987.
Aquinas, Thomas. *On the Power of God. Third Book*. Translated by English Dominican Fathers. London: Burns Oates & Washbourne, 1934.

2. To keep within the word count, the chapter on Cristina Traina's contribution to current debates in natural law had to be removed from the final version of the thesis.

Aquinas, Thomas. *Summa Theologica*. Translated by Fathers of the English Dominican Province. Notre Dame IN: Ave Maria Press, 1948.
Aquinas, Thomas. *The Treatise on the Divine Nature*. Translated by Brian Shanle. Indianapolis: Hackett, 2006.
Aquinas, Thomas. *Truth*. Vol. 1. Questions I-IX. Translated by Robert W. Mulligan. Indianapolis: Hackett, 1994.
Aristotle. *The Nicomachean Ethics*. Translated by C. D. C. Reeve. Indianapolis: Hackett, 2014.
Asad, Talal. *Formations of the Secular. Christianity, Islam, Modernity*. Stanford, CA: Stanford Press, 2003.
Ashley, Benedict M. 'What is the End of the Human Person?' In *Moral Truth and Tradition*. Edited by Luke Gormally, Dublin: Four Corners Press, 1994: 68–96.
Attell, Kevin. *Giorgio Agamben: Beyond the Threshold of Deconstruction*. New York: Fordham University Press, 2015.
Auerbach, Carl A. 'On Professor H. L. A. Hart's Definition and Theory in Jurisprudence'. *Journal of Legal Education*, Vol. 9, No. 1 (1956): 39–51.
Augustine. *Confessions*. Dublin: Richview Press, 1946.
Augustine. *On Order (De Ordine)*. South Bend, IN: St Augustine's Press, 2007.
Augustine. *The City of God, Books VIII-XVI*. Translated by Gerald G. Walsh and Grace Monahan. Washington, DC: CUA, 2008.
Badiou, Alain. *The Age of Poets*. London: Verso, 2014.
Baker, Gideon. *Politicising Ethics in International Relations*. Oxford: Routledge, 2011.
Bamforth, Nicholas and Richards, David A. J. *Patriarchal Religion, Sexuality and Gender: A Critique of New Natural Law*. Cambridge: CUP, 2009.
Barnett, Christopher B. *Kierkegaard, Pietism, and Holiness*. New York: Routledge, 2016.
Barrett, Edward F. 'A Lawyer Looks at Natural Law Jurisprudence'. *The American Journal of Jurisprudence*, Vol. 23, No. 1 (1978): 1–20.
Barth, Karl, *Church Dogmatics* 1/1. Translated by G. W. Bromiley and T. F. Torrance. Edinburgh: T&T Clark, 1975.
Bauerschmidt, Frederick. *Thomas Aquinas. Faith, Reason, and Following Christ*. Oxford: Oxford University Press, 2013.
Baum, Gregory. 'For and Against John Milbank'. In *Essays in Critical Theology*. Kansas City: Sheed and Ward, 1994: 52–76.
Baym, Nina. 'The Agony of Feminism: Why Feminist Theory Is Necessary after All'. In *The Emperor Redressed: Critiquing Critical Theory*. Edited by Dwight Eddins. Tuscaloosa: University of Alabama Press, 1995: 101–17.
Beardsworth, Richard. *Derrida and the Political*. London: Routledge, 1996.
Benedict XVI. 'The Relationship of Faith and Reason: Faith, Reason, and the University'. In *A Reason Open to God*. Edited by Steven Brown. Washington, DC: Catholic University of America, 2013: 7–44.
Bengston, Josef. *Explorations in Post-Secular Metaphysics*. New York: Palgrave MacMillan, 2015.
Benson, Bruce Ellis. 'Introduction'. In *Words of Life: New Theological Turns in French Phenomenology*. Edited by Bruce Ellis Benson and Norman Wirzba. New York: Fordham Press, 2010: 1–12.
Bix, Brian. 'Ideals, Practices, and Concepts in Legal Theory'. In *Neutrality and Theory of Law*. Edited by Jordi Ferrer Beltrán, José Juan Moreso, Diego M. Papayannis. Girona: Springer, 2012: 32–48.

Bockmuehl, Markus. *Jewish Law in Gentile Churches: Halakhah and the Beginning of Christian Public Ethics*. Edinburgh: T&T Clark, 2000.

Boersma, Hans. 'Being Reconciled: Atonement as the Ecclesio-Christological Practice of Forgiveness in John Milbank'. In *Introducing Radical Orthodoxy: Mapping a Post-Secular Theology*. Edited by James K. A. Smith and James H. Olthuis. Grand Rapids, MI: Baker Academic, 2005: 183–204.

Boersma, Hans. *Nouvelle Théologie*. Oxford: Oxford University Press, 2009.

Bowyer, Andrew. *To Perceive Tragedy without the Loss of Hope: Donald MacKinnon's Moral Realism*, 2016. Accessed through ProQuest Dissertations Publishing.

Boyd, Craig. *A Shared Morality: A Narrative Defence of Natural Law Ethics*. Grand Rapids, MI: Brazos Press, 2007.

Boyle, Joseph. 'Natural Law and the Ethics of Tradition'. In *Natural Law Theory: Contemporary Essays*. Edited by Robert P. George. Oxford: Clarendon, 1992: 3–30.

Bradley, Gerard. George, Robert. 'The New Natural Law Theory: A Reply to Jean Porter'. *The American Journal of Jurisprudence*, Vol. 39 (1994): 303–15.

Braybrooke, David. *Natural Law Modernized*. Toronto: Toronto Press, 2003.

Briggs, Robert. 'Just Traditions? Deconstruction, Critical Legal Studies, and Analytic Jurisprudence'. *Social Semiotics*, Vol. 11, No. 3 (2001): 257–74.

Bushlack, Thomas J. *Politics for a Pilgrim Church: A Thomistic Theory of Civic Virtue*. Grand Rapids, MI: W. B. Eerdmans, 2015.

Cady, Linell Elizabeth. 'Identity, Feminist Theory, and Theology'. In *Horizons in Feminist Theology: Identity, Tradition, and Norms*. Edited by Rebecca S. Chopp and Sheila Greeve Davaney. Minneapolis: Fortress Press, 1997: 17–32.

Cahill, Lisa Sowle. 'Gender and Christian Ethics'. In *The Cambridge Companion to Christian Ethics (Second Edition)*. Edited by Robin Gill. Cambridge: Cambridge University Press, 2012: 103–16.

Cameron, Averil. *Christianity and the Rhetoric of Empire. The Development of Christian Discourse*. Los Angeles: University of California Press, 1994.

Caputo, John. *Demythologising Heidegger*. Bloomington: Indiana University Press, 1993.

Caputo, John. 'Hyperbolic Justice: Deconstruction. Myth, and Politics'. *Research in Phenomenology*, Vol. 21 (1991): 3–20.

Caputo, John. 'Methodological Postmodernism on Merold Westphal's Overcoming Onto-Theology'. *Faith & Philosophy*, Vol. 22, No. 3 (July 2005): 284–96.

Caputo, John. *The Prayers and Tears of Jacques Derrida*. Bloomington: Indiana University Press, 1997.

Caputo, John. *The Weakness of God: A Theology of the Event*. Bloomington: Indiana University Press, 2006.

Carter, Jenni. 'Mobilising Literacy Policy Through Resources'. In *Language and Literacies as Mobile and Placed Resources*'. Edited by Sue Nichols and Collette Snowden. Abingdon: Routledge, 2017: 124–37.

Carty, Anthony. *Philosophy of Law. Second Edition*. Edinburgh: Edinburgh University Press, 2017.

Cassatella, Andrea. 'Jacques Derrida on the Secular as Theologico-Political'. *Philosophy and Social Criticism*, Vol. 42, No. 10 (July 2015): 1–23.

Cavanaugh, William T. *Theopolitical Imagination: Christian Practices of Space and Time*. London: T&T Clark, 2002.

Charles, Daryl J. *Retrieving the Natural Law. A Return to Moral First Things*. Cambridge: Wm. B. Eerdmans, 2008.
Coakely, Sarah. *God, Sexuality and the Self: An Essay 'On the Trinity'*. Cambridge: Cambridge University Press, 2013.
Cochran, Molly. 'The Ethics of the English School'. In *The Oxford Handbook of International Relations*. Edited by Christian Reuss-Smit and Duncan Snidal. Oxford: Oxford University Press, 2008: 286–97.
Connor, Timothy G. *The Kenotic Trajectory of the Church in Donald MacKinnon's Theology*. London: T&T Clark, 2011.
Conybeare, Fred C. 'On the Armenian Version of Plato's Laws and Minos'. *The American Journal of Philology*, Vol. 45, No. 2 (1924): 105–40.
Corrington, Robert S. 'Natural Law and Emancipation: Toward a Theonomous Democracy'. In *Law and Semiotics, Volume 1*. Edited by Robert Kevelson. New York: Plenum Press, 1987: 159–80.
Cowan, Thomas A. 'Law Without Force'. *California Law Review*, Vol. 58, No. 3 (1971): 683–694.
Crowe, Jonathan. 'Natural Law Beyond Finnis'. *Jurisprudence*, Vol. 2, No. 2 (2011): 293–308.
Crowe, Michael Bertram. *The Changing Profile of the Natural Law*. The Hague: Martinus Nihjoff, 1977.
Cupitt, Don. 'Kant and the Negative Theology'. In *The Philosophical Frontiers of Christian Theology: Essays Presented to D. M. MacKinnon*. Edited by Brian Hebblethwaite and Stewart Sutherland. Cambridge: Cambridge University Press, 1982: 55–67.
Curran, Charles. *Catholic Moral Theology in the United States: A History*. Washington, DC: Georgetown University Press, 2008.
D'Andrea, Thomas. *Tradition, Rationality and Virtue. The Thought of Alasdair MacIntyre*. Aldershot: Ashgate, 2006.
Danielson, Peter. 'Reviews of Books: *Natural Law and Natural Rights* John Finnis…' *The University of Toronto Law Journal*, Vol. 30, No. 4 (Autumn 1980): 441–7.
Davies, Paul. *God and the New Physics*. New York: Simon and Schuster, 1983.
Davis, Michael. 'Plato's *Minos*: The Soul of the Law'. *The Review of Politics*, Vol. 78 (2016): 343–63.
Davitt, Thomas E. 'St. Thomas Aquinas and the Natural Law'. In *Origins of the Natural Law Tradition*. Edited by Arthur L. Harding. Dallas: Southern Methodist University Press, 1954: 26–47.
Dawson, Christopher. *Progress & Religion*. London: Sheed & Ward, 1945.
Deanne-Drummond, Celia. 'Aquinas, Wisdom Ethics and the New Genetics'. In *Re-Ordering Nature. Theology, Society and the New Genetics*. Edited by Celia Deane-Drummond, Bronislaw Szerszyski, Robin Grove-White. London: T&T Clark, 2003: 293–311.
De Lubac, Henri. *Augustinianism and Modern Theology*. Translated by Lancelot Sheppard. London: Geoffrey Chapman, 1969.
De Lubac, Henri. 'Duplex Hominis Beatitudo'. *Communio*, Vol. 35 No. 4 (Winter 2008): 599–612.
De Lubac, Henri. *The Mystery of the Supernatural*. Translated by Rosemary Sheed. New York: Crossroad Herder, 2008.
Derrida, Jacques. *Acts of Literature*. Edited by Derek Attridge. London: Routledge, 1992: 181–229.

Derrida, Jacques. 'Admiration of Nelson Mandela, or the Laws of Reflection'. *Law and Literature*, Vol. 26, No. 1 (2014): 9–30.

Derrida, Jacques. *Archive Fever: A Freudian Impression*. Translated by Eric Prenowitz. Chicago: University of Chicago, 1996.

Derrida, Jacques. 'Deconstruction and the Other: Interview with Richard Kearney'. In *Debates in Continental Philosophy*. Edited by Richard Kearney. Fordham: Fordham University Press, 2004: 139–56.

Derrida, Jacques. *Deconstruction in a Nutshell: A Conversation with Jacques Derrida*. Edited by Jack Caputo. New York: Fordham University Press, 1997.

Derrida, Jacques. '*Différance* (From the Margins of Philosophy. Translated by Alan Bass)'. In *The Theory of Difference*. Edited by Douglas L. Donkel. Albany: State University of New York Press, 2001: 279–304.

Derrida, Jacques. 'Faith and Knowledge: The Two Sources of "Religion" at the Limits of Reason Alone'. In *Jacques Derrida; Acts of Religion*. Edited by Gil Anidjar. Abingdon: Routledge, 2010: 40–101.

Derrida, Jacques. 'Force of Law: The "Mystical Foundation of Authority"'. In *Jacques Derrida: Acts of Religion*. Edited by Gil Anidjar. Abingdon: Routledge, 2010: 228–98.

Derrida, Jacques. *Limited Inc*. Evanston, IL: Northwestern University Press, 1988.

Derrida, Jacques. *Margins of* Philosophy. Translated by Alan Boss. Chicago: University of Chicago Press, 1982.

Derrida, Jacques. *Of Grammatology*. Translated by Gayatri Chakravorty Spivak. Baltimore, MD: John Hopkins University Press, 2016.

Derrida, Jacques. 'On Forgiveness: A Roundtable Discussion with Jacques Derrida'. In *Questioning God*. Edited by John D. Caputo, Mark Dooley and Michael Scanlon. Bloomington: Indiana University Press, 2001: 52–72.

Derrida, Jacques. *Specters of Marx*. Translated by Peggy Kamuf. London: Routledge, 2006.

Derrida, Jacques. *The Work of Mourning*. Edited by Paul-Anne Brault and Michael Naas. Chicago: University of Chicago Press, 2001.

Derrida, Jacques and Ferraris, Maurizio. *A Taste for the Secret*. Translated by Giacomo Donis. Cambridge: Cambridge University Press, 2001.

Desmond, William. 'Neither Servility nor Sovereignty: Between Metaphysics and Politics'. In *Theology and the Political: The New Debate*. Edited by Creston Davis, John Milbank, and Slavoj Zizek. Durham, NC: Duke University Press, 2005: 153–82.

Devanny, Christopher. 'Truth, Tragedy and Compassion: Some reflections on the theology of Donald MacKinnon'. *New Blackfriars*, Vol. 78, No. 911 (January 1997): 33–42.

Di Blasi, Fulvio. 'Ultimate End, Human Freedom, and Beatitude'. *The American Journal of Jurisprudence*, Vol. 46 (2001): 113–35.

Di Censo, James *Kant, Religion, and Politics*. Cambridge: Cambridge University Press, 2011.

Donnelly, Bebhinn. *A Natural Law Approach to Normativity*. London: Routledge, 2007.

Douzinas, Costas. 'Law and Justice in Postmodernity'. In *The Cambridge Companion to Postmodernism*. Edited by Steven Connor. Cambridge: Cambridge University Press, 2004: 196–223.

Duke, George. 'Finnis on the Authority of Law and the Common Good.' *Legal Theory*, Vol. 9, No. 1 (March 2013): 44–62.

Duke, George. 'The Aristotelian *Spoudaios* as Ethical Exemplar in Finnis's Natural Law Theory'. *The American Journal of Jurisprudence*, Vol. 58, No. 2 (2013): 183–204.

Durantaye, Leland de la. *Giorgio Agamben: A Critical Introduction*. Stanford, CA: Stanford University Press, 2009.
Emon, Anver M., Levering, Matthew and Novak, David. *Natural Law: A Jewish, Christian, and Islamic Trialogue*. Oxford: Oxford University Press, 2014.
Engle Karen J., 'Putting Mourning to Work'. *Theory, Culture & Society*, Vol. 24, No. 1 (January 2007): 61–88.
Fink, Hans. 'The Conception of Ethics and the Ethical in K. E. Løgstrup's *The Ethical Demand*. In *Concern for the Other*. Edited by Svend Anderson, Kees van Kooten Niekerk. Notre Dame, IN: University of Notre Dame Press, 2007: 9–28.
Flannery, Kevin. 'Rule of Law and the Virtue of Justice: The Socrates of Plato's *Crito* and a Pair of Later Moral Issues.' *Proceedings of the American Catholic Philosophical Association*, Vol. 90 (2017): 1–19.
Floyd, Jonathan. Stears, March. 'Introduction'. In *Political Philosophy Versus History? Contextualism and Real Politics in Contemporary Political Thought*. Edited by Jonathan Floyd and Marc Stears. Cambridge: Cambridge University Press, 2011: 1–9.
Foran, Lisa. 'The Untranslatable to Come: From Saying to Unsayable'. In *Heidegger, Levinas, Derrida: The Question of Difference*. Edited by Lisa Foran, Rozemund Uljée. Switzerland: Springer, 2016, 59–74.
Fortin, Ernst L. *Human Rights, Virtue, and the Common Good*. Edited by J. Brian Benestad. London: Rowman & Littlefield, 1996.
Fortin, Ernst L. 'Review: The New Rights Theory and the Natural Law'. *The Review of Politics*, Vol. 44, No. 4 (October 1982): 590–612.
Frei, Christopher. 'Faith and Feeling in Lonergan'. *Australian E-Journal of Theology* (August 2014): 139–154.
Fritsch, Matthias. *Promise of* Memory. New York: State University of New York Press, 2012.
Fuller, Lon. *The Meaning of Law*. New Haven, CT: Yale University Press, 1963.
Gadamer, Hans-Georg. 'Man and Language'. In *Philosophical Hermeneutics*. Translated by David E. Linge. Los Angeles: University of California Press, 1976: 59–68.
Garcia, Kenneth N. '"Reversing the Secular Drift": John Courtney Murray and the Telos of Catholic Higher Education'. *Theological Studies*, Vol. 73 (2012): 890–908.
Gardner, H. Grose, C. Macdonald and N. Watts. Cambridge, MA: Harvard University Press, 2014.
Gearey, Adam. 'Thinking, Poetics, Law'. In *Derrida and Legal Philosophy*. Edited by Peter Goodrich, Florian Hoffman, Michel Rosenfeld and Cornelia Visman. Basingstoke: Palgrave and Macmillan, 2008: 201–26.
Gehring, Peter. 'The Jurisprudence of the "Force of Law"'. In *Derrida and Legal Philosophy*. Edited by Peter Goodrich, Florian Hoffman, Michel Rosenfeld and Cornelia Visman. Basingstoke: Palgrave and Macmillan, 2008: 55–70.
George, Robert. 'The Achievement of John Finnis'. In *Reason, Morality, and Law*. Edited by John Keown and Robert P. George. Oxford: OUP, 2013: 2–9.
Gergen, Mary. 'Social Constructionist Theory'. In *Encyclopaedia of Women and Gender (L-Z, Volume 2)*. Edited by Judith Worell. San Diego: Academic Press, 2002: 1043–58.
Geroulanos, Stefanos. 'Theoscopy: Transparency, Omnipotence, and Modernity'. In *Political Theologies: Public Religions in a Post-Secular World*. Edited by Hent de Vries and Lawrence E. Sullivan. Fordham: Fordham University Press, 2006: 633–51.
Gilson, Caitlin Smith. *The Political Dialogue of Nature and Grace. Towards a Phenomenology of Chaste Anarchism*. New York: Bloomsbury, 2015.

Glendinning, Simon. '*Derrida and the Philosophy of Law and Justice*'. *Law Critique*, 27 (2016): 187–203.
Goetschel, Willi. *Constituting Critique: Kant's Writing as Critical Praxis*. Translated by Eric Schwab. Durham, NC: Duke University Press, 1994.
Goodhart, Howard L. and Goodenough, Erwin R. *The Politics of Philo Judaeus. Practice and Theory*. New Haven, CT: Yale University Press, 1938.
Goodrich, Peter. '*Un Cygne Noir*'. In *Derrida and Legal Philosophy*. Edited by Peter Goodrich, Florian Hoffman, Michel Rosenfeld and Cornelia Vismann. New York: Palgrave Macmillan, 2008: 227–37.
Goodrich, Peter, Hoffman, Florian, Rosenfeld, Michel and Vismann, Corenelia. 'Introduction: A Philosophy of Legal Enigmas'. In *Derrida and Legal Philosophy*. Edited by Peter Goodrich, Florian Hoffman, Michel Rosenfeld and Cornelia Vismann. New York: Palgrave Macmillan, 2008: 1–18.
Goodson, Jacob Lynn. 'Theology After Epistemology: Milbank Between Rorty and Taylor on Truth'. In *Contemporary Pragmatism, Volume 1*. Edited by John R. Shook, Paulo Ghiraldelli. Amsterdam: Rodopi, 2004: 155–69.
Gordis, Robert. 'Natural Law and Religion'. In *Natural Law and Modern Society*. Edited by John Cogley. New York: World, 1961: 240–76.
Goyette, John. Latkovic, Mark.Myers, Richard. 'Introduction'. In *St. Thomas Aquinas and the Natural Law Tradition: Contemporary Perspectives*. Edited by John Goyette, Mark S. Latkovic and Richard S. Myers. Washington, DC: Catholic University of America, 2004: ix–xxiii.
Gray, Brett. *Jesus in the Theology of Rowan Williams*. London: T&T Clark, 2016.
Gray, John. 'Agonistic Liberalism'. In *Liberalism*. Edited by G. W. Smith. London: Routledge, 2002: 3–26.
Greenawalt, Kent. 'Natural Law and Public Reasons'. *Villanova Law Review*, Vol. 47, No. 3 (2002): 531–52.
Grisez, Germain. '*Insight*: *A Study of Human Understanding* (Book Review)'. *The Thomist: A Speculative Quarterly Review*, Vol. 21, No. 4 (October 1958): 554–60.
Grisez, Germain. 'Natural Law and the Transcendent Source of Human Fulfilment'. In *Reason, Morality, and Law*. Edited by John Keown and Robert P. George. Oxford: Oxford University Press, 2013: 443–56.
Grisez, Germain. 'The First Principle of Practical Reason. A Commentary on the *Summa Theologiae*, I-II, Question 94, Article 2.' *Natural Law Forum*, Vol. 168 (1965): 168–201.
Grisez, Germain. *The Way of the Lord Jesus. Volume 1*. Chicago: Franciscan Press, 1997.
Griffin, Leslie C. 'A Response to Michael J. Perry'. *CTSA Proceedings*, Vol. 55 (2000): 83–5.
Griffin, Leslie C. 'Good Catholics Should Be Rawlsian Liberals'. *Southern California Interdisciplinary Law Journal*, Vol. 5, No. 297 (1997): 297–373.
Griswold, Charles. *Self-Knowledge in Plato's Phaedrus*. New Haven, CT: Yale University Press, 1986.
Grotius, Hugo. *De Jure Belli ac Pacis*. Translated by Francis W. Kelsey. Oxford: Clarendon Press, 1925.
Haddorff, David. 'Barth and Democracy'. In *Commanding Grace: Studies in Karl Barth's Ethics*. Edited by Daniel L. Migliore. Grand Rapids, MI: W. B. Eerdmans, 2010: 96–121.
Handler, Joel F. *Law and the Search for Community*. Philadelphia: University of Pennsylvania Press, 1990.
Hanna, Robert. *Kant, Science and Human Nature*. Oxford: Oxford University Press, 2006.
Hanna, Robert. 'Kant, Truth and Human Nature'. *British Journal for the History of Philosophy*, 8, 2 (2000): 225–50.

Hare, John. 'A Kantian Response to Jean Porter'. *Studies in Christian Ethics*, Vol. 26, No. 2 (2013): 174–5.
Hart, H. L. A. 'Analytical Jurisprudence in Mid-Twentieth Century: A Reply to Professor Bodenheimer'. *University of Pennsylvania Law Review*, Vol. 105 (1957): 953–75.
Hart, H. L. A. *Definition and Theory in Jurisprudence*. Oxford: Oxford University Press, 1983.
Hart, H. L. A. 'Jhering's Heaven of Concepts and Modern Analytical Jurisprudence'. In *Essays in Jurisprudence and Philosophy*. Oxford: Oxford University Press, 1983: 265–77.
Hart, H. L. A. 'Positivism and the Separation of Law and Morals'. *Harvard Law Review*, Vol. 71, No. 4 (February 1958): 593–629.
Hart, H. L. A. 'Problems of the Philosophy of Law'. In *Essays in Jurisprudence and Philosophy*. Edited by H. L. A Hart. Oxford: Oxford University Press, 1983: 89–119.
Hart, H. L. A. *The Concept of Law. Third Edition*. Oxford: Oxford University Press, 2012.
Hauerwas, Stanley. 'Natural Law, Tragedy, and Theological Ethics'. *The American Journal of Jurisprudence*, Vol. 20, No. 1 (1975): 1–19.
Hauerwas, Stanley and Pinches, Charles. *Christians among the Virtues. Theological Conversations with Ancient and Modern Ethics*. Notre Dame, IN: University of Notre Dame Press, 1997.
Hayman, Gavin. *The Predicament of Postmodern Theology: Radical Orthodoxy or Nihilist Textualism*. Louisville, KY: Westminster John Knox Press, 2001.
Haynes, Daniel. 'The Metaphysics of Christian Ethics: Radical Orthodoxy and Theosis'. *Heythrop Journal*, Vol. LII (2011): 659–71.
Headley, John M. *The Europeanization of the World*. Princeton, NJ: Princeton University Press, 2008.
Hedges, Paul. 'The Rhetoric and Reception of John Milbank's Radical Orthodoxy: Privileging Prejudice in Theology?' *Open Theology*, Vol. 1 (2014): 24–44.
Heidegger, Martin. *What is Called Thinking*. New York: Harper and Row, 1968.
Henderson, Jeffrey. 'Introduction to the *Minos*'. In *Plato XII*. Translated by W. R. M. Lamb. Edited by Jeffrey Henderson. Cambridge, MA: Harvard University Press, 1955: 387.
Heron, Nicholas. 'The Ungovernable'. *Angelaki: Journal of the Theoretical Humanities*, Vol. 16, No. 2 (June 2011): 159–74.
Hibbs, Thomas S. *Virtue's Splendour: Wisdom, Prudence, and the Human Good*. New York: Fordham University Press, 2001.
Hittinger, Russell. *A Critique of the New Natural Law Theory*. Notre Dame, IN: University of Notre Dame Press, 1987.
Hittinger, Russell. 'Natural Law and Catholic Moral Theology'. In *A Preserving Grace: Protestants, Catholics, and Natural Law*. Edited by Michael Cromartie. Grand Rapids, MI: Ethics and Public Policy Centre-Eerdmans, 1997: 1–30.
Hobbes, Thomas. *Leviathan*. Oxford: Oxford University Press, 1998.
Hodge, Joanna. 'Derrida on Time'. Abingdon: Routledge, 2007.
Hoffman, Thomas Sören. *Georg Wilhelm Friedrich Hegel – A* Propaedeutic. Translated by David Healan. Leiden: Brill, 2015.
Hogan, Trevor. 'With and Beyond Barth? John Milbank's Postmodern Christian Socialism as an Alternative Modernity.' In *Karl Barth: A Future for Postmodern Theology?* Edited by Geoff Thompson and Christian Mostert. Hindmarsh: The Australian Theological Forum, 2000: 253–75.
Holsinger, Bruce. *The Premodern Condition: Medievalism and the Making of Theory*. Chicago: University of Chicago Press, 2005.

Hooper, J. Leon 'General Introduction'. In *Religious Liberty: Catholic Struggles with Pluralism. By John Courtney Murray*. Edited by J. Leon Hooper S.J. Louisville, KY: Westminster/ John Knox, 1993: 7–48.

Horsley, Richard A. 'The Law of Nature in Philo and Cicero'. *The Harvard Theological Review*, Vol. 71, No. 1/2 (January–April 1978): 35–59.

Hume, David. *A Treatise of Human Nature*. Edited by D. F. Norton and M. J. Norton. Oxford: Oxford University Press, 2014.

Inglis, John. 'Aquinas's Replication of the Acquired Moral Virtues: Rethinking the Standard Philosophical Interpretation of Moral Virtue in Aquinas'. *Journal of Religious Ethics*, Vol. 27, No. 1 (Spring 1999): 3–27.

Insole, Christopher J. 'Against Radical Orthodoxy: The Dangers of Overcoming Political Liberalism'. *Modern Theology*, Vol. 20, No. 2 (April 2004): 213–41.

Insole, Christopher J. 'A Metaphysical Kant: A Theological Lingua Franca?'. *Studies in Christian Ethics*, Vol. 25, No. 2 (2012): 206–14.

Insole, Christopher J. *Kant and the Creation of Freedom: A Theological Problem*. Oxford: Oxford University Press, 2013.

Insole, Christopher J. *The Intolerable God: Kant's Theological Journey*. Grand Rapids, MI: Wm. B. Eerdmans, 2016.

Insole, Christopher J. *The Realist Hope: A Critique of Anti-Realist Approaches to Contemporary Philosophical Theological*. Aldershot: Ashgate, 2006.

Jacobs, Jonathan A. 'Introduction'. In *Reason, Religion, and Natural Law: From Plato to Spinoza*. Edited by Jonathan A. Jacobs. Oxford: Oxford University Press, 2012: 3–20.

Jaggar, Alison M. *Feminist Politics and Human Nature (Philosophy and Society)*. Oxford: Rowman and Littlefield, 1983.

Jensen, Steven J. *Knowing the Natural Law. From Precepts and Inclinations to Deriving Oughts*. Washington, DC: Catholic University of America, 2015.

Jenson, Matt. *The Gravity of Sin: Augustine, Luther and Barth on 'homo incurvatus in se'*. London: T&T Clark, 2006.

Jones, Meirav. 'Philo Judaeus and Hugo Grotius's Modern Natural Law'. *Journal of the History of Ideas*, Vol. 74, No. 3 (July 2013): 339–59.

Judaeus, Philo. *The Contemplative Life, the Giants, and Selections*. Translated by David Winston. London: SPCK, 1981.

Judaeus, Philo. *Fragments of Philo Judaeus*. Edited by J. R. Harris. Cambridge: Cambridge University Press, 1886.

Judaeus, Philo. *The Works of Philo Judaeus* (Volumes 1–4). Translated by C. D. Yonge. London: Henry G. Bohn, 1854.

Kaniz, Howard. *Natural Law: An Introduction and Re-Examination*. Chicago: Open Court, 2004.

Kant, Immanuel. 'Conjectures on the Beginning of Human History'. In *Political Writings*. Edited by H. S. Reiss. Translated by H. B. Nisbet. Cambridge: Cambridge University Press, 1970: 221–34.

Kant, Immanuel. *Critique of Judgment*, Walker. Translated by James Creed Meredith. Edited by Nicholas Walker. Oxford: Oxford University Press, 2008.

Kant, Immanuel. *Critique of Pure Reason*. Translated and edited by Paul Guyer and Allen W. Wood. Cambridge: Cambridge University Press, 1998.

Kant, Immanuel. 'Jäsche Logic'. In *Lectures on Logic*. Translated by J. Michael Young. Cambridge: Cambridge University Press, 1992.

Kant, Immanuel. *The Metaphysics of Morals*. In *The Cambridge Edition of the Works of Immanuel Kant: Practical Philosophy*. Translated and edited by Mary J. Gregory. Cambridge: Cambridge University Press, 1996: 341–592.
Kelsen, Hans. 'Is and Ought in Kant's Philosophy'. In *General Theory of Norms*. Translated by Michael Hartney. Oxford: Clarendon Press, 1991: 79–83.
Kelsen, Hans. *Pure Theory of Law. Legality and Legitimacy*. Oxford: Oxford University Press, 2007.
Kerr, Fergus. 'Book Review: Ecstatic Morality and Sexual Politics: A Catholic and *Antitotalitarian* Theory of the Body by G. J. McAleer'. *New Blackfriars*, Vol. 88, No. 1016 (July 2007): 497–8.
Kerr, Fergus. 'Comment: Remembering Donald MacKinnon'. *New Blackfriars*, Vol. 85, No. 997 (May 2004): 265–9.
Kirste, Stephan. 'Natural Law in Germany in the 20th Century'. In *A Treatise of Leal Philosophy and General Jurisprudence, Volume 12*. Edited by Enrico Pattaro and Corrado Roversi. Netherlands: Springer, 2016: 91–110.
Koester, Helmut. 'The Concept of Natural Law in Greek Thought'. In *Religions in Antiquity*. Edited by Jacob Neusner (Ledien: Brill, 1968): 523–41.
Kramer, Matthew H. Grant, Claire. 'Introduction'. In *The Legacy of H. L. A. Hart: Legal, Political and Moral Philosophy*. Edited by Matthew Kramer. Oxford: Oxford University Press, 2008: viii–xviii.
Kucer, Peter Samuel. *Truth & Politics: A Theological Comparison of Joseph Ratzinger and John Milbank*. Minneapolis, MN: Fortress Press, 2014.
Lacey, Nicola. *A Life of H. L. A. Hart*. Oxford: Oxford University Press, 2006.
Lacroix, Justine and Pranchére, Jean-Yves. *Human Rights on Trial*. Translated by Gabrielle Mas. Cambridge: Cambridge University Press, 2016: 25–58.
Larsen, Sean. 'The Politics of Desire: Two Readings of Henri de Lubac on Nature and Grace'. *Modern Theology*, Vol. 29, No. 3 (July 2013): 279–310.
Latour, Bruno. *We Have Never Been Modern*, trans. Catherine Porter. Cambridge, MA: Harvard University Press, 1993.
Lawrence, Frederick G. 'Finnis on Lonergan: A Reflection'. *Villanova Law Review*, Vol. 57, No. 5 (2012): 849–72.
Lawrence, Frederick G. 'John Courtney Murray and the Ambiguities of Liberalism'. In *John Courtney Murray & the Growth of Tradition*. Edited by J. Leon Hooper and Todd David Whitmore. Kanas City: Sheed & Ward, 1996: 41–59.
Lee, Patrick. 'The New Natural Law Theory'. In *The Cambridge Companion to Natural Law Ethics*. Edited by Tom Angier. Cambridge: Cambridge University Press, 2019: 73–91.
Legarre, Santiago. 'HLA Hart and the Making of the NNLT'. *Jurisprudence*, 8:1 (2017): 82–98.
Leiter, Brian. 'The End of Empire: Dworkin and Jurisprudence in the 21st Century'. *Rutgers Law Journal*, 36 (2004–5): 165–81.
Levering, Matthew. 'A Note on John Milbank and Thomas Aquinas'. *New Blackfriars*, Vol. 95, No. 1059 (2014): 525–34.
Levering, Matthew. 'Christian and Natural Law'. In *Natural Law: A Jewish, Christian, and Islamic Trialogue*. By Anver M. Emon, Matthew Levering and David Novak. Oxford: Oxford University Press, 2014: 66–110.
Levinas, Emmanuel and Kearney, Richard. 'Dialogue with Emmanuel Levinas'. In *Face to Face with Levinas*. Edited by Richard Cohen. Albany: State University of New York Press, 1986: 13–34.

Lewis, V. Bradley. 'Plato's "Minos": The Political and Philosophical Context of the Problem of Natural Right'. *The Review of Metaphysics*, Vol. 60 (September 2006): 17–53.

Liederbach, Mark. 'Natural Law and the Problem of Postmodern Epistemology'. *Liberty University Law Review*, Vol. 2, No. 3 (Spring 2008): 781–96.

Lilla, Mark. *The Shipwrecked Mind: On Political Reaction*. New York: NYRB, 2016.

Lisska, Anthony J. *Aquinas's Theory of Natural Law. An Analytic Reconstruction*. Oxford: Clarendon Press, 1996.

Lisska, Anthony J. 'Natural Law and the Roman Catholic Tradition: The Importance of Philosophical Realism'. *American Journal of Economics and Sociology*, Vol. 71, No. 4 (October, 2012): 745–86.

Lisska, Anthony J. 'On the Revival of Natural Law: Several Books from the Last Half-Decade'. *American Catholic Philosophical Quarterly*, Vol. 81, No. 4 (2007): 613–38.

Litowitz, Douglas. 'Derrida on Law and Justice: Borrowing (Illicitly?) From Plato and Kant'. *Canadian Journal of Law and Jurisprudence*, Vol. 8, No. 2 (July 1995): 325–446.

Logue, John. 'The Revenge of John Selden: The Draft Convention on the Law of the Sea in the Light of Hugo Grotius' *Mare Liberium*'. *Grotiana*, Vol. 3, No. 1: 27–56.

Lonergan, Bernard. *Collected Works of Bernard Lonergan: A Third Collection*. Edited by Robert M. Doran and John D. Dadosky. Toronto: University of Toronto Press, 1985.

Lonergan, Bernard. *Collected Works of Bernard Lonergan: Collection*. Edited by Frederick E. Crowe and Robert M. Doran. Toronto: University of Toronto Press, 1988.

Lonergan, Bernard. *Early Works on Theological Method. Volume 1*. Edited by Robert M. Doran and John D. Dadosky. Toronto: University of Toronto Press, 210.

Lonergan, Bernard. 'Insight: Truth and Interpretation'. In *The Lonergan Reader*. Edited by Mark D. Morelli and Elizabeth Morelli. Toronto: University of Toronto Press, 1997: 263–74.

Lonergan, Bernard. *Method in Theology*. Edited by Robert M. Doran and John D. Dadosky. Toronto: University of Toronto Press, 2017.

Lonergan, Bernard. 'Method in Theology: Dialectic'. In *The Lonergan Reader*. Edited by Mark D. Morelli and Elizabeth Morelli. Toronto: University of Toronto Press, 1997: 518–30.

Lonergan, Bernard. 'Natural Right and Historical Mindedness'. *Proceedings of the American Catholic Philosophical Association*, Vol. 51 (1977): 132–43.

Long, A. A. *Stoic Studies*. Los Angeles: University of California Press, 1996.

Long, A. Steven. *Natura Pura: On the Recovery of Nature in the Doctrine of Grace*. New York: Fordham University Press, 2010.

Long, D. Stephen. *Divine Economy: Theology and the Market*. London: Routledge, 2000.

Long, D. Stephen. *Speaking of God: Theology, Language, and Truth*. Grand Rapids, MI: W. B. Eerdmans, 2009.

Lücke, Horst Klaus. 'John Finnis and the University of Adelaide: The Christian Faith Half a Century Ago'. *University of Queensland Law Journal*, Vol. 35, No. 2 (2016): 193–249.

Lujipen, W. *Phenomenology of the Natural Law*. Pittsburgh: Duquesne University Press, 1967.

Lutz, Mark J. *Divine Law and Political Philosophy in Plato's Laws*. DeKalb, IL: Northern Illinois University Press, 2012.

Lutz, Mark J. 'The Minos and the Socratic Examination of Law'. *American Journal of Political Science*, Vol. 54, No. 4 (October 2010): 988–1002.

MacCormick, Neil. 'Natural Law and the Separation of Law and Morals'. In *The Autonomy of Law: Essays on Legal Positivism*. Edited by Robert P. George. Oxford: Clarendon Press, 1996: 105–33.

MacIntyre, Alasdair. *After Virtue. Third Edition*. Notre Dame, IN: University of Notre Dame Press, 2007.
MacIntyre, Alasdair. *Three Rival Versions of Moral Inquiry: Encyclopaedia, Genealogy, and Tradition*. Notre Dame, IN: University of Notre Dame Press, 1990.
Maciejewski, Jeffrey J. 'Reason as a Nexus of Natural Law and Rhetoric'. *Journal of Business Ethics*, Vol. 59 No. 3 (2005): 247–257.
MacKinnon, Donald. 'Aspects of Kant's Influence on British Theology'. In *Kant and His Influence*. Edited by George MacDonald Ross. London: Continuum, 1990: 348–66.
MacKinnon, Donald. *Borderlands of Theology and Other Essays*. Edited by George W. Roberts and Donovan E. Smucker. London: Lutterworth Press, 1968.
MacKinnon, Donald. 'Can Two Walk Together? By Ian Henderson' (Book Review). *Scottish Journal of Theology*, Vol. 3 (March 1950): 94–6.
MacKinnon, Donald. 'Ethical Intuitionism'. In *Contemporary British Philosophy: Third Series*. Edited by H. D. Lewis. London: George Allen & Unwin Ltd, 1956: 313–33.
MacKinnon, Donald. 'Kant's Philosophy of Religion'. In *Themes in Theology*, Edinburgh: T&T Clark, 1987: 20–39.
MacKinnon, Donald. 'Moral Freedom' (1969). In *Philosophy and the Burden of Theological Honesty: A Donald MacKinnon Reader*. Edited by John McDowell. London: T&T Clark, 2011: 83–98.
MacKinnon, Donald. 'Natural Law'. In *Diplomatic Investigations*. Edited by Herbert Butterfield and Martin Wright. London: George Allen & Unwin, 1966: 74–88.
MacKinnon, Donald. 'Natural Law'. In *Philosophy and the Burden of Theological Honesty: A Donald MacKinnon Reader*. London: T&T Clark, 2011: 115–30.
MacKinnon, Donald. 'Revelation and Social Justice' (1941). In *Philosophy and the Burden of Theological Honesty: A Donald MacKinnon Reader*. Edited by John McDowell. London: T&T Clark, 2011: 137–60.
MacKinnon, Donald. 'Theology as a Discipline of a Modern University' (1972). In *Philosophy and the Burden of Theological Honesty*. Edited by John McDowell London: T&T Clark, 2011: 64–74.
MacKinnon, Donald. *The Problem of Metaphysics*. Cambridge: Cambridge University Press, 1974.
Macpherson, C. B. *The Political Theory of Possessive Individualism: Hobbes to Locke*. Oxford: Oxford University Press, 1964.
Magna, Joseph. 'Radical Orthodoxy: A Catholic Enquiry' (Book Review). *Scottish Journal of Theology*, Vol. 54, No. 3 (2001): 427–9.
Manko, R. Zomerski, W. Kauczor, W. 'Conference Report: 1st International Workshop on Law and Ideolody (Wroclaw, 29–30 May 2014)'. *Wroclaw Review of Law, Administration and Economics*, Vol. 3, No. 2 (January 2015): 84–7.
Mansueto, Anthony. *Knowing God [Volume Four]: Doing Justice*. Eugene, OR: Pickwick, 2011.
Markham, Ian. *Truth and the Reality of God: An Essay in Natural Theology*. Edinburgh: T&T Clark, 1998.
Marsh, James L. 'William Desmond's Overcoming of the Overcoming of Metaphysics'. In *Between System and Poetics. William Desmond and Philosophy after Dialectic*. Edited by Thomas A. F. Kelly. Aldershot: Ashgate Publishing Limited, 2007: 95–106.
Martínez, Mario Silar, and José M. Torralba. Newcastle: Cambridge Scholars, 2008.
Marx, Karl. *The Portable Karl Marx. Selected, Translated in part, and with an Introduction by Eugene Kamenka*. Edited by Eugene Kamenka. London: Penguin Books 1983.

Matthews, Graham. *Ethics and Desire in the Wake of Postmodernism: Contemporary Satire*. London: Continuum, 2012.
Mattison III, William C. 'The Changing Face of Natural Law: The Necessity of Belief for Natural Law Norm Specification'. *Journal of the Society of Christian Ethics*, Vol. 27, No. 1 (2007): 251–77.
McAleer, Graham James. *Ecstatic Morality and Sexual Politics*. New York: Fordham University Press, 2005.
McCormick, John P. 'Derrida on Law; Or, Poststructuralism gets Serious'. *Political Theory*, Vol. 29, No. 3 (June 2001): 395–423.
McCormick, Richard A. 'Ambiguity in Moral Choice'. In *Doing Evil to Achieve Good*. Edited by Richard McCormick and Paul Ramsey. Chicago: Loyola University Press, 1978: 7–53.
McCusker, Claire. 'Between Natural Law and Legal Positivism: Plato's Minos and the Nature of Law'. *Yale Journal of Law & the Humanities*. Vol. 22, No. 1 (2013): 1–22.
McDade, John. ''*Ressourcement*' in Retrospect'. In *Ressourcement: A Movement for Renewal in Twentieth Century Catholic Theology*. Edited by Gabriel Flynn and Paul D. Murray. Oxford: Oxford University Press, 2011: 508–22.
McGall, Brian M. *Building Law on a Solid Foundation*. Notre Dame, IN: Notre Dame University Press, 2018.
McInerny, Ralph. *Praeambula Fidei: Thomism and the God of the Philosophers*. Washington, DC: Catholic University of America, 2006.
Meijer, P. A. *Stoic Theology. Proofs for the Existence of the Cosmic God and of the Traditional Gods*. Delft: Eburon, 2007.
Mensch, Elizabeth. Freeman, Alan. *The Politics of Virtue: Is Abortion Debateable*? London: Duke University Press, 1995.
Meyer, William J. *Metaphysics and the Future of Theology: The Voice of Theology in Public Life*. Eugene, OR: Wipf and Stock, 2010.
Michalson Jr., Gordon E. 'Re-Reading the Post-Kantian Tradition with Milbank'. *Journal of Religious Ethics*, Vol. 32, No. 2 (Summer, 2004): 357–83.
Michener, Ronald T. *Engaging Deconstructive Theology*. Abingdon: Routledge, 2016.
Miller, Fred D. 'The Rule of Reason in Plato's Laws'. In *Reason, Religion, and Natural Law: From Plato to Spinoza*. Edited by Jonathan A. Jacobs. Oxford: Oxford University Press, 2012: 31–56.
Money, Robert A. *The Bible, Natural Theology, and Natural Law: Conflict or Compromise*? Millerstown, PA: Xulon Press, 2010.
Moon, Joshua. *Jeremiah's New Covenant: An Augustinian Reading*. Winona Lake, IN: Eisenbrauns, 2011.
Moonen, Christopher. 'Is An Actual God Intelligible?' In *Theology and the Quest for Truth*. Edited by Mathijs Lamberigts, Lieven Boeve and Terrence Merrigan. Leuven: Leuven University Press, 2006: 228–40.
Moore, Michael S. 'Good without God'. In *Natural Law, Liberalism, and Morality*. Edited by Robert George Oxford: Oxford University Press, 2011: 221–61.
Morrison, Roy D. 'Tillich, Einstein, and Kant: Method, Epistemology, and the Personal God'. In *Theonomy and Autonomy: Studies in Paul Tillich's Engagement with Modern Culture*. Edited by John Carey. Macon GA: Mercer University Press, 1984: 35–66.
Moses, Greg. 'A Response to Lonergan and Finnis'. In *Australian Lonergan Workshop*. Edited by William J. Danaher. Maryland: University Press of America, 1993: 211–22.

Mulcahy, Bernard. *Aquinas's Notion of Pure Nature and the Christian Integralism of Henri de Lubac*. New York: Peter Lang, 2011.
Murphy, Mark C. 'Finnis on Nature, Reason, and God'. *Legal Theory*, Vol. 13 (2007): 187–209.
Murphy, Tim. 'St. Thomas Aquinas and the Natural Law Tradition'. In *Western Jurisprudence*. Edited by Tim Murphy. Dublin: Thomson Round Hall, 2004: 94–125.
Murray, John Courtney. *Bridging the Sacred and the Secular: Selected Writings of John Courtney Murray*. Edited by J. Leon Hooper. Washington, DC: Georgetown University Press, 1994.
Murray, John Courtney. 'Reversing the Secularist Drift'. *Thought*, 24 (1949): 36–46.
Murray, John Courtney. *We Hold These Truths*. Oxford: Rowman & Littlefield, 2005.
Newman, John Henry. *History of My Religious Opinions*. London: Longman, Green, 1865.
Newman, John Henry. *The Arians of the Fourth Century*. London: Longman, Green, 1908.
Offen, Karen. 'Reclaiming the European Enlightenment for feminism'. In *Perspectives on Feminist Political Thought in European History: From the Middle Ages to the Present*. Edited by Tjitske Akkerman and Siep Stuurman. London: Routledge, 1998: 85–103.
Oliver, Simon. 'Introduction to Part II'. In *The Radical Orthodoxy Reader*. Edited by John Milbank and Simon Oliver. London: Routledge, 2009: 65–8.
Ophi, Adi. 'The Ideal Speech Situation: Neo-Kantian Ethics in Habermas and Apel'. *Kant's Practical Philosophy Reconsidered: Papers Presented at the Seventh Jerusalem Philosophical Encounter, December 1986*. Edited by Yirmiyahu Yovel. Dordrecht: Kluwer Academic, 1986: 213–34.
Ormerod, Neil. 'Lonergan and Finnis on the Human Good'. In *Australian Lonergan Workshop*. Edited by William J. Danaher. Maryland: University Press of America, 1993: 199–210.
Orrego, Cristóbal. 'Hart's last legal positivism: morality might be objective; legality certainly is not'. In *Law, Morality, and Legal Positivism: Proceeding of the 21st World Congress of the International Association for Philosophy of Law and Social Philosophy (IVR); Lund, Sweden, 12–18 August 2004*. Edited by Kenneth Einar Himma. Stuttgart: Franz Steiner Verlag, 2004: 73–80.
Ostovich, Steven. 'Pauline Eschatology'. In *Time: Limits and Constraints*. Edited by Jo Alyson Parker, Paul A. Harris, Christian Steineck. Leiden: Brill, 2010: 305–27.
Pabst, Adrian. "A habitual disposition to the good': on reason, virtue and realism'. *Global Discourse*, Vol. 5, No. 2 (2015): 261–79.
Papanikolaou, Aristotle. *The Mythical as Political: Democracy and Non-Radical Orthodoxy*. Notre Dame, IN: Notre Dame University Press, 2012.
Patterson, Dennis. *A Companion to Philosophy of Law and Legal Theory*. London: Blackwell, 1999.
Perreau-Saussine, Amanda. *Natural Law with Gloves On: A Critical Exposition of John Finnis's Natural Law Theory*. PhD Thesis, Faculty of Law, University of Cambridge, 2002.
Persuit, Jeanne M. 'The Universal and Particular: Stephen Toulmin's Rhetorical Theory and the Natural Law Tradition'. *The Review of Communication*, Vol. 11, No. 1 (January 2011): 51–65.
Philips, Mark Salber. 'Introduction: What is Tradition when it is not 'Invented'?' In *Questions of Tradition*. Edited by Mark Salber Philips, Mark Philips and Gordon J. Schochet. Toronto: University of Toronto, 2004: 3–30.

Philpott, Daniel. Anderson, Ryan T. 'Introduction: The Review of Politics and the Story of American Catholic Liberalism'. In *A Liberalism Safe for Catholicism*. Notre Dame, IN: Notre Dame University Press, 2017: 1–36.

Pickstock, Catherine. 'Duns Scotus: His Historical and Contemporary Significance'. In *The Radical Orthodoxy Reader*. Edited by John Milbank and Simon Oliver. London: Routledge, 2009: 116–46.

Pickstock, Catherine. 'Radical Orthodoxy and the Mediations of Time'. In *Radical Orthodoxy: A Catholic Inquiry*. Edited by Laurence P. Hemming. Abingdon: Routledge, 2000: 63–74.

Pieper, Josef. *Living the Truth*. San Francisco, CA: Ignatius Press, 1989.

Pieper, Josef. 'The Art of Making the Right Decisions'. In *Josef Pieper: An Anthology*. San Francisco, CA: Ignatius Press, 1989: 51–3.

Pierce, Christine. *Immovable Laws, Irresistible Rights: Natural Law, Moral Rights, and Feminist Ethics*. Kansas: University Press of Kansas, 2000.

Pinckaers, Servais. *The Pinckaers Reader, Renewing Thomistic Moral Theology*. Washington, DC: Catholic University of America, 2005.

Plant, Raymond. *Politics, Theology and History*. Cambridge: Cambridge University Press, 2001.

Plato. *Laws 1 and 2*. Translated by Susan Sauvé Meyer. Oxford: Oxford University Press, 2015.

Plato. 'Minos'. In *Plato: Complete Works*. Translated by Malcolm Schofield. Indianapolis: Hackett, 1997: 1307–17.

Plato. 'Minos'. In *Plato XII*. Translated by W. R. M. Lamb. Edited by Jeffrey Henderson. Cambridge, MA: Harvard University Press, 1955: 385–422.

Platsas, Antonios E. 'At the Crossroads of Law and Ideology: The Ideology of Law as a Reflection on Social Ontology'. *Wroclaw Review of Law, Administration, & Economics*, Vol. 7, No. 2 (2018): 1–13.

Pompa, Leon. *Vico: A Study of the 'New Science' (Second Edition)*. Cambridge: Cambridge University Press, 1990.

Pope, Stephen J. *The Evolution of Altruism and the Ordering of Love*. Washington, DC: Georgetown University Press, 1994.

Porpora, Douglas V. 'Do Realists Run Regressions'. In *After Postmodernism: An Introduction to Critical Realism*. Edited by José López and Garry Potter. London: Athlone Press, 2001: 260–7.

Rash, Carl A. '*Á-Dieu* to Jacques Derrida'. In *Secular Theology*. Edited by Clayton Crockett. London: Routledge, 2001: 37–50.

Rashkover, Randi. *Revelation and Theopolitics: Barth, Rosenzweig and the Politics of Praise*. London: T&T Clark, 2005.

Ratzinger, Joseph (now Pope Emeritus Benedict XVI). 'Conscience and Truth'. *Communio*, Vol. 37 (Fall 2010): 529–38.

Ratzinger, Joseph. *On the Way to Jesus Christ*. San Francisco: Ignatius, 2005.

Raunio, Antti. 'Divine and Natural Law in Luther and Melanchthon'. In *Lutheran Reformation and the Law*. Edited by Virpi Mäkinen. Leiden: Brill, 2006: 21–62.

Raz, Joseph. 'About Morality and the Nature of Law'. *The American Journal of Jurisprudence*, Vol. 48, No. 1 (2003): 1–15.

Raz, Joseph. *The Authority of Law*. Oxford: Oxford University Press, 2009.

Rech, Walter. 'History and Normativity: Vico's 'Natural Law of Nations." *Journal of the History of International Law*, Vol. 17 (2015): 147–69.

Rhonheimer, Martin. 'Review of Jean Porter's *Nature as Reason*'. In *The Perspective of the Acting Person: Essays in the Renewal of Thomistic Moral Philosophy*. Edited by William F. Murphy Jr. Washington, DC: Catholic University of American Press, 2008: 283–306.
Rhonheimer, Martin. 'Review Article: Nature as Reason'. *Studies in Christian Ethics*, Vol. 19, No. 3 (2006): 357–78.
Rice, Charles. 'The Problem of Unjust Laws'. *Scholarly Works*, Paper 75 (1981): 278–85.
Richter, Gerhard. *Afterness: Figures of Following in Modern Thought and Aesthetics*. New York: Columbia University Press, 2011.
Riordan, Patrick. 'Natural Law Revivals: A Review of Recent Literature'. *Heythrop Journal*, Vol. 51, No. 2 (2010): 314–23.
Rogers, Eugene. *Aquinas and the Supreme Court. Race, Gender, and the Failure of Natural Law in Thomas's Biblical Commentary*. Chichester: Wiley-Blackwell, 2013.
Rogers, Eugene. 'The Narrative of Natural Law in Aquinas's Commentary on Romans'. *Theological Studies*, Vol. 59 (1998): 254–76.
Rogers, Eugene. *Thomas Aquinas and Karl Barth*. Notre Dame, IN: University of Notre Dame Press, 1995.
Rooney, James Dominic. 'Murray's Balancing Act: The Harmony of Nature and Grace'. *Journal of Church and State*, Vol. 58, No. 4 (May 2015): 1–24.
Rorty, Richard. *Philosophy and the Mirror of Nature*. Princeton, NJ: Princeton University Press, 2009.
Rowland, Tracey. *Catholic Theology*. London: Bloomsbury, 2017.
Rowland, Tracey. 'Natural Law: From Neo-Thomism to Nuptial Mysticism'. *Communio*, Vol. 35 (Fall 2008): 374–96.
Rowland, Tracey. 'The Case Against the Marriage of Natural Law & Natural Rights'. In *The Cambridge Handbook of Natural Law and Human Rights*. Edited by Tom Angier and Iain T. Benson. Cambridge: Cambridge University Press, 2023: 74–87.
Ryle, Gilbert. 'Heidegger's 'Sein und Zeit''. In *Critical Essays. Volume 1*. London: Routledge, 2009: 205–22.
Saccenti, Riccardo. *Debating Medieval Natural Law: A Survey*. Notre Dame, IN: University of Notre Dame Press, 2016.
Salmon, John. *The First Principles of Jurisprudence*. London: Steven & Hayes, 1893.
Sandmel, Samuel. *Philo of Alexandria: An Introduction*. Oxford: Oxford University Press, 1979.
Schindler, David L. 'Religious Freedom, Truth, and America'. *Communio*, Vol. 21 (Winter 1994): 696–741.
Schlesinger, Sybil. 'Working Definitions: A Critique of H. L. A. Hart's Use of Wittgenstein in *The Concept of Law*'. *ARSP*, Vol. 83, No. 1 (1997): 103–24.
Schleiermacher, Friedrich. 'Minos'. In *Schleiermacher's Introductions to the Dialogues*. Translated by William Dobson. London: John William Parker, 1836: 163–4.
Schleiermacher, Friedrich. *On Religion: Speeches to Its Cultured Despisers*. Cambridge: Cambridge University Press, 1996.
Schlueter, Nathan. 'A Conservative Conversation Worth Having: Alasdair MacIntyre and John Finnis on Morality, Politics and the Common Good'. *Perspectives on Political Science*, Vol. 44, No. 2 (2015): 102–8.
Schneewind, J. B. 'Hugo Grotius: Introduction'. In *Moral Philosophy from Montaigne to Kant*. Edited by J. B. Schneewind. Cambridge: Cambridge University Press, 2003: 88–9.
Schumacher, Michele M. *A Trinitarian Anthropology: Adrienne Von Speyr & Hans Urs Von Balthasar in Dialogue with Thomas Aquinas*. Washington, DC: Catholic University of America Press, 2014.

Sheldrake, Philip. 'Spirituality and its Critical Methodology'. In *Exploring Christian Spirituality: Essays in Honour of Sandra M. Schneiders*. Edited by Bruce Lescher and Elizabeth Liebert. New York: Paulist Press, 2006: 15–34.

Simpson, A. W. Brian. *Reflections on 'The Concept of Law'*. Oxford: Oxford University Press, 2011.

Sinnerbrink, Robert. 'Deconstructive Justice and the 'Critique of Violence': On Derrida and Benjamin'. *Social Semiotics*, Vol. 16. No. 3 (September 2006): 485–97.

Smith, Stephen D. 'Book Review, *Ministers of the Law*'. *Ethics*, Vol. 122 (10/2011): 203–7.

Smith, Stephen. 'Natural Law and Contemporary Moral Thought: A Guide from the Perplexed'. *The American Journal of Jurisprudence*, Vol. 42, No. 1 (1997): 299–330.

Sokoloff, William. 'Between Justice and Legality: Derrida on Decision'. *Political Research Quarterly*, Vol. 58, No. 2 (June 2005), 341–52.

Sophocles. *Antigone*. Translated by David Mulroy. Madison: University of Wisconsin Press, 2013.

Staley, Kevin M. 'New Natural Law, Old Natural Law, or the Same Natural Law'. *The American Journal of Jurisprudence*, Vol. 38, No. 1 (1993): 109–33.

Strauss, Leo. *Liberalism: Ancient & Modern*. Chicago: University of Chicago Press, 1995.

Strauss, Leo. 'Persecution and the Art of Writing' (1941). *Social Research*, Vol. 82, No. 1 (Spring 2015), 79–97.

Strauss, Leo. *Studies in Platonic Political* Philosophy. Chicago: University of Chicago Press, 1983.

Svavarsdóttir, Sigrún. 'Objective Values: Does Metaethics Rest on a Mistake?' In *Objectivity in Law and Morals*. Edited by Brian Leiter. Cambridge: Cambridge University Press, 2001: 144–93.

Syse, Henrik. *Natural Law, Religion, and Rights*. Indiana: St. Augustine's Press, 2006.

Tan, Seow Hon. 'Validity and Obligation in Natural Law Theory: Does Finnis Come to Close to Positivism?' *Regent University Law Review*, Vol. 15, No. 195 (2003): 195–221.

Taylor, Charles. 'A Catholic Modernity?' In *Catholic Modernity? Charles Taylor's Marianist Responses by William M. Shea, Rosemary Luling Haughton, George Marsden and Jean Bethke Elshtain*. Edited by James L. Heft. Oxford: Oxford University Press, 1999: 13–38.

Taylor, Charles. *A Secular Age*. Cambridge, MA: Belknap Press of Harvard University Press, 2007.

Taylor, Charles. *Human Agency and Language. Philosophical Papers 1*. Cambridge: Cambridge University Press, 1986.

Taylor, Charles. 'Modern Social Imaginaries'. *Public Culture*, Vol. 14, No. 1: 91–124.

Taylor, Charles. 'Religious Mobilizations'. *Public Culture*, Vol. 18, No. 2 (2006): 281–300.

Taylor, Charles. *Sources of the Self. The Making of the Modern Identity*. Cambridge: Cambridge University Press, 2012.

Taylor, Victor E. 'General Commentary'. In *Postmodernism: Critical Comments. Volume 1*. Edited by Victor E. Taylor and Charles E. Winquist. London: Routledge, 1998: x–xx.

Thompson, Alan. *Culture in a Post-Secular Context: Theological Possibilities in Milbank, Barth, and Bediako*. Eugene, OR: Wipf and Stock, 2014.

Thomason, Steven. 'Philosophy and Law: An Interpretation of Plato's "Minos"'. *The Journal for Ancient Greek Political Thought*, Vol. 3, No. 5: 53–75.

Tierney, Brian. 'Natural Law and Natural Rights'. In *Christianity and Law. An Introduction*. Edited by John Witte, Jr. and Frank S. Alexander. Cambridge: Cambridge University Press, 2008: 89–104.

Tollefsen, Christopher. 'First-and Third-Person Standpoints in the New Natural Law Theory'. In *Subjectivity: Ancient and Modern*. Edited by R. J. Snell and Steven F. McGuire. Lanham, MD: Lexington Books, 2016: 95–124.

Tonti-Fillipini, Nicholas. 'Bioethics, Culture, and Collaboration'. *Solidarity: Journal of Catholic Social Thought and Secular Ethics*. Vol. 2, No. 1 (2012): 1–27.

Tosas, Mar Rosás. 'Derrida's way out of the dead end of contemporary messianism'. *Journal for Cultural Research*, Vol. 18, No. 4 (2014): 350–69.

Troeltsch, Ernst. *The Social Teaching of the Christian Churches, Vol. 1*. Translated by Olive Wyon. London: George Allen & Unwin, 1956.

Tuck, Richard. 'Review: Natural Law & Natural Rights'. *The Philosophical Quarterly*, Vol. 31, No. 124 (July 1981): 282–4.

Vanhoozer, Kevin. 'Once more into the Borderlands'. In *Transcending Boundaries in Philosophy and Theology*. Edited by Kevin Vanhoozer and Martin Warner. Aldershot: Ashgate, 2007: 31–54.

Vanhoozer, Kevin. *The Drama of Doctrine: A Canonical-Linguistic Approach to Christian Theology*. Louisville, KY: Westminster John Knox Press, 2005.

Veatch, Henry. Rautenberg, Joseph. 'Does the Grisez-Finnis-Boyle Moral Philosophy Rest on a Mistake?' *The Review of Metaphysics*, Vol. 44, No. 4 (June 1991): 807–30.

Vicini, Andrea. 'The Search for a Universal Ethic'. *Concilium. International Review of Theology* (2010/3): 111–17.

Vico, Giambattista. *Principi Di Una Scienza Nuova*. Translated by Leon Pompa. Cambridge: Cambridge University Press, 2002.

Voegelin, Eric. *Anamnesis*. Translated and edited by Gerhard Niemeyer. London: University of Notre Dame, 1978.

Wachterhouser, Brice. 'Getting it Right: Relativism, Realism and Truth'. In *The Cambridge Companion to Gadamer*. Edited by Robert J. Dostal. Cambridge: Cambridge University Press, 2002: 52–78.

Waldron, Jeremy. 'Kant's Legal Positivism'. *Harvard Law Review*, Vol. 109, No. 7 (May 1996): 1535–66.

Wallenstein, Sven-Olov. 'Introduction: Foucault, Biopolitic and Governmentality'. In *Foucault, Biopolitic, and Governmentality*. Edited by Jacob Nilsson and Sven-Olov Wallenstein. Huddinge: Södertörn University Publications, 2013: 7–34.

Waller, Giles. 'Freedom, Fate and Sin in Donald MacKinnon's use of Tragedy'. In *Christian Theology and* Tragedy. Edited by Kevin Taylor and Giles Waller. Surrey: Ashgate, 1988: 101–18.

Wallin, Alex E. 'John Finnis's Natural Law Theory and a Critique of the Incommensurable Nature of the Basic Goods.' *Campbell Law Review*, Vol. 59 (2012): 59–81.

Ward, Graham. *Barth, Derrida and the Language of Theology*. Cambridge: Cambridge University Press, 1995.

Ward, Graham. 'Cultural Hermeneutics and Christian Apologetics'. In *Imaginative Apologetics: Theology, Philosophy and the Catholic Tradition*. Edited by Andrew Davison. London: SCM, 2011: 115–25.

Ward, Graham. 'John Milbank's Divina Commedia'. *New Blackfriars*, Vol. 73, No. 861 (June 1992): 311–18.

Ward, Graham. 'On Time and Salvation'. In *Facing the Other*. Edited by Seán Hand. Abingdon: Routledge, 1996: 153–71.

Weed, Elizabeth. 'Introduction: Terms of Reference'. In *Coming to Terms (RLE Feminist Theory): Feminism, Theory, Politics, Vol. 3*. Edited by Elizabeth Weed. London: Routledge, 1989: ix–xxxi.

Westermann, Pauline. *The Disintegration of Natural Law: Aquinas to Finnis*. Leiden: Brill, 1998.

Westphal, Kenneth R. *How Hume and Kant Reconstruct Natural Law. Justifying Strict Objectivity Without Debating Moral Realism*. Oxford: Oxford University Press, 2016.

Westphal, Merold. 'Derrida as Natural Law Theorist'. In *Overcoming Onto-Theology: Towards a Postmodern Christian Faith*. Fordham: Fordham University Press, 2001: 219–28.

Westphal, Merold. 'Reply to Jack Caputo'. *Journal of the Society of Christian Philosophers*, Vol. 22, No. 3 (2005): 297–300.

Wilkin, Robert N. 'Cicero and the Law of Nature'. In *Origins of the Natural Law Tradition*. Edited by Arthur L. Harding. Dallas: Southern Methodist University Press, 1954: 1–25.

Williams, Rowan. 'Theological Integrity'. *Cross Currents*, Vol. 45, No. 3 (Fall 1995): 312–25.

Wittgenstein, Ludwig. *Philosophical Investigations*. Translated by G. E. M. Anscombe. Oxford: Blackwell, 1968.

Wittgenstein, Ludwig. *Tractatus Logico-Philosophicus*. Translated by D. F. Pears, B. F. McGuiness. London: Routledge, 2006.

Wolfson, Harry Austryn. *Philo: Foundations of Religious Philosophy in Judaism, Christianity, and Islam. Volume I*. Cambridge, MA: Harvard University Press, 1947.

Younis, Raymond Aaron. '*Euporia*: On the Limits, Horizons and Possibilities of Critique (Or: On Reconstruction)'. In *Reconstructing Social Theory, History, and Practice*. Edited by Harry F. Dahms, Eric R. Lybeck. Bingley: Emerald Group, 2017: 89–107.

Zaborowski, Holger. *Robert Spaemann's Philosophy of the Human Person. Nature, Freedom, and the Critique of Modernity*. Oxford: Oxford University Press, 2010.

Electronic Sources

Altenburger, Michael, 'Derrida, Politics, and the Little Way', 2018, https://churchlifejournal.nd.edu/articles/ derrida-politics-and-the-little-way/. Accessed on 1 March 2019.

Atlas, James, 'The Case of Paul de Man', 1988, https://www.nytimes.com/1988/08/28/magazine/the-case-of-paul-de-man.html. Accessed on 1 December 2018.

Finnis, John, 'Aquinas' Moral, Political, and Legal Philosophy', 2017, https://plato.stanford.edu/entries/aquinas-moral-political/. Accessed on 29 August 2019.

Finnis, John, 'Natural Law Theories', 2007, https://plato.stanford.edu/entries/natural-law-theories. Accessed on 10 March 2018.

Finnis, John, 'New Classical Natural Law: Critics, God, and the Human Function', 2016, https://www.youtube.com/watch?v=gB5z2BSTdyo. Accessed on 10 December 2017.

Finnis, John, 'Secularism, Morality, and Politics', 2003, https://www.ewtn.com/library/ISSUES/SECULAR.HTM. Accessed on 1 May 2018.

Finnis, John and Germain Grisez, 'About John Finnis', Publication Date Unknown, http://www.twotlj.org/Finnis.html. Accessed on 1 January 2019.

Grisez, Germain, 'My Collaboration with John Finnis', Publication Date Unknown, http://www.twotlj.org/Finnis.html. Accessed on 2 February 2019.

Hanna, Robert, 'Kant's Theory of Judgment' (2013), http://plato.stanford. edu/entries/kant-judgment/. Accessed on 29 January 2016.
International Theological Commission, 'In Search of a Universal Ethics', 2009, http://www.vatican.va/roman_curia/ congregations/ cfaith/cti_documents /rc_con_cfaith_doc_20090520_legge-naturale_en.html. Accessed on 1 May 2019.
Milbank, John, 'A Revisionist Account of Natural Law and Natural Right', 2018, https://churchlifejournal.nd.edu/articles/a-revisionist-account-of-natural-law-and-natu ral-right. Accessed on 1 February 2019.
Milbank, John, 'Burke's Romantic Restoration of Natural Law', 2019, https://churchlife journal. nd.edu /articles/burkes-romantic-restoration-of-natural-law. Accessed on 1 March 2019.
Milbank, John, 'Christianity, the Enlightenment and Islam', 2010, https://www.abc.net.au/religion/christianity- the-enlightenment-and-islam/10102154. Accessed on 1 November 2018.
Milbank, John, 'Culture, nature, and mediation', 2010, https://tif.ssrc.org/2010/12/01/culture-nature-mediation/. Accessed on 25 October 2017.
Milbank, John, 'Dignity, Not Rights: Against Liberal Autonomy', 2016, https://www.abc.net.au/religion/dignity-not-rights-against-liberal-autonomy/10097418. Accessed on 10 December 2018.
Milbank, John, 'Gay Marriage and the Future of Human Sexuality', 2012, https://www.abc.net.au/religion/gay-marriage-and-the-future-of-human-sexuality/10100726. Accessed on 12 March 2018.
Milbank, John, 'John Milbank Interview', 2019, https://www.gold.ac.uk/faithsunit/curr ent -projects/reimaginingreligion/landmark-interviews/john-milbank/. Accessed on 1 August 2019.
Milbank, John, 'John Milbank, Twitter', 2018, https://twitter.com/johnmilbank3/status /1000273976810201088?lang=en. Accessed 20 July 2018.
Milbank, John, 'Maritain's Post-War Compromise of Natural Law', 2019, https://churchlife journal.nd.edu/articles/maritains-postwar-compromise-of-natural-law/. Accessed on 20 May 2019.
Milbank, John, 'Only Theology Saves Metaphysics', 2007, http://theologyphilosophy centre.co.uk/papers/Milbank_OnlyTheologySavesMetaphysics.doc. Accessed on 1 May 2019.
Milbank, John, 'Radical Orthodoxy and Protestantism Today', 2017, http://www.Scielo .org.za/scielo.php? script=sci_arttext&pid=S1015-87582017000200004. Accessed on 11 September 2019.
Milbank, John, 'Stanton Lecture 1: The Return of Metaphysics in the 21st Century', 2011, https://www.abc.net.au/religion/stanton-lecture-1-the-return-of-metaphys ics-in-the-21st-century/10101748. Accessed on 1 May 2019.
Milbank, John, 'Stanton Lecture 2: Immanence and Life', 2011, https://www.abc.net.au/religion/stanton-lecture-2-immanence-and-life/10101740. Accessed on 1 May 2019.
Milbank, John, 'Stanton Lecture 3: Immanence and Number', 2011, http://theologyphilo sophycentre.co.uk/ papers/Milbank_StantonLecture3.pdf. Accessed on 1 May 2019.
Milbank, John,'Stanton Lecture 4: Transcendence Without Participation', 2011, http://theologyphilosophycentre.co.uk/papers/Milbank_StantonLecture4.pdf. Accessed on 6 April 2017.

Milbank, John, 'Stanton Lecture 5: Participated Transcendence Reconceived', 2011, http://theologyphilosophycentre.co.uk /papers/Milbank_StantonLecture5.pdf. Accessed on 1 May 2019.

Milbank, John, 'Stanton Lecture 8: The Surprise of the Imagined', 2011, http://theol ogyphilosophycentre. co.uk/papers/Milbank_StantonLecture8.pdf. Accessed on 10 May 2019.

Milbank, John, 'The Ethics of the Soul', 1999, https://www.firstthings.com/article/1999/03/004-the-ethics-of-self-sacrifice. Accessed on 15 December 2018.

Milbank, John, 'The History of Natural Law', 2018, https://churchlifejournal.nd.edu/articles/the-history-of-natural-law/. Accessed on 1 February 2019.

Milbank, John, 'The History of Natural Right', 2019, https://churchlifejournal.nd.edu/artic les/the-history-of-natural-right/. Accessed on 1 February 2019.

Milbank, John, 'The Impossibility of Gay Marriage', 2013, https://www.abc.net.au/religion/the-impossibility-of-gay-marriage-and-the-threat-of-biopolitical/10099888. Accessed on 10 December 2017.

Murray, John Courtney, 'Governmental Repression of Heresy', 1948, https://www.library.georgetown. edu/woodstock/murray/1948c. Accessed 28 November 2019.

Murray, John Courtney, 'Reversing the Secular Drift', 1949, https://www.library.georgetown.edu/woodstock/murray/1949. Accessed on the 21 May 2019.

Murray, John Courtney, 'The Deeper Significance of Religious Freedom', 1966, https://www.library.georgetown.edu/woodstock/murray/1966e. Accessed on 1 May 2018.

Norton, Sam Charles, 'Radical Orthodoxy: The Official Twenty-Four Theses' (July 2007). http://elizaphanian.blogspot.co.uk/2007/07/radical-orthodoxy-official-twenty-four.html Accessed on 25 October 2017.

Oxford Conversations: John Finnis, 'New Classical Natural Law: Critics, God, and the Human Function', 2016, https://www.youtube.com/watch?v=gB5z2BSTdyo. Accessed on 10 December 2017.

Pope John Paul II, '*Veritatis Splendor*', 1993, http://www.vatican.va/holy_father/ john_ paul_ii /encyclicals/documents/ hf_jp-ii_enc_06081993 _veritatis-splendor_en.html. Accessed on 1 March 2018.

Pozdniakov, Mikhail, 'Feelings Sustaining Text: Aphorisms and Inspirations', *Modern Languages and Literatures Annual Graduate Conference*, 2014, https://ir.lib.uwo.ca/cgi/viewcontent.cgi?article=1016 &context=mllgradconference. Accessed on 12 June 2019.

Second Vatican Council, '*Gaudium et Spes*', 1965, http://www.vatican.va/archive/ hist_ councils / ii_vatican_council /documents/vat-ii_const_19651207_gaudium-et-spes_ en.html. Accessed on 1 January 2018.

The Holy See, 'Catechism of the Catholic Church', 1993, https://www.vatican.va/ archive/ ENG0015/_ INDEX.HTM. Accessed 21 May 2019.

Name Index

SUBJECT INDEX

www.ingramcontent.com/pod-product-compliance
Ingram Content Group UK Ltd.
Pitfield, Milton Keynes, MK11 3LW, UK
UKHW021543041026
15470UKWH00019B/844

9 780567 716972